Richard Hakluyt, Edward John Payne

Voyages of the Elizabethan Seamen to America

Thirteen Original Narratives from th Collection of Hakluyt

Richard Hakluyt, Edward John Payne

Voyages of the Elizabethan Seamen to America
Thirteen Original Narratives from th Collection of Hakluyt

ISBN/EAN: 9783337217594

Printed in Europe, USA, Canada, Australia, Japan

Cover: Foto ©Thomas Meinert / pixelio.de

More available books at **www.hansebooks.com**

VOYAGES

OF THE

ELIZABETHAN SEAMEN

TO

AMERICA.

THIRTEEN ORIGINAL NARRATIVES FROM THE COLLECTION OF

HAKLUYT,

SELECTED AND EDITED, WITH HISTORICAL NOTICES,

BY

E. J. PAYNE, M.A.,

AUTHOR OF "A HISTORY OF EUROPEAN COLONIES."

LONDON:
THOS. DE LA RUE & CO.
110, BUNHILL ROW.

1880.

PRINTED BY
THOMAS DE LA RUE AND CO., BUNHILL ROW,
LONDON.

CONTENTS.

No.		Begun in	Page
1.	Hawkins' First Voyage	(1562)	7
2.	,, Second Voyage	(1564)	9
3.	,, Third Voyage	(1567)	52
4.	Frobisher's First Voyage	(1576)	64
5.	,, Second Voyage	(1577)	70
6.	,, Third Voyage	(1578)	97
7.	Drake's Famous Voyage	(1577)	145
8.	Gilbert's Voyage	(1583)	175
9.	Amadas and Barlow's Voyage	(1584)	211
10.	Drake's Second Great Voyage	(1585)	226
11.	Cavendish's First Voyage	(1586)	258
12.	,, Last Voyage	(1591)	303
13.	Raleigh's Voyage to Guiana	(1595)	332

INTRODUCTION.

It was not until the great period of maritime discoveries which lasts from the middle of the fourteenth century to the middle of the seventeenth (1350–1650) was already well advanced, and the chief problems of geography had been solved, that Englishmen began to take part in the movement. The map of the world, as we have it at this day, had been constructed by adventurers of other nations. Until the thirteenth century, no advance in geographical knowledge had been made since the classical age. The philosophers of Oxford and Paris, and the merchants of the Hanse Towns and the Italian maritime republics, knew no more of geography than had been known to the Alexandrian philosophers and merchants a thousand years before. Even as late as the time of Columbus, the standard authority on geography continued to be Ptolemy; and it is on record that the two favourite authors of the discoverer of America were the famous geographer of Alexandria and the mendacious English traveller, Sir John Mandeville.

The chief seat of the arts and sciences, in the Middle Ages, was Italy; and to Italian energy and sagacity the vast extension of man's knowledge of the globe which he inhabits is mainly due. In the golden age of the Papacy and of the Italian maritime republics, Italian monks and merchants penetrated the heart of Asia. Italian seamen passed the Pillars of

Hercules, braved the unknown dangers of the stormy Atlantic, explored the desolate shores of Barbary, rediscovered the Fortunate Isles of the Ancients, and increased the Ptolemaic map of the world by the addition of the Madeiras and the Azores. The remote regions to which they thus penetrated were beyond the scope of Italian political or mercantile interests. They thus fell into the hands of the reigning powers of the Spanish peninsula; and the exploration of the Atlantic was continued under the direction and at the expense of the monarchs of Portugal and Castile. Until recently it was believed that the gradual exploration of the coast of Africa, which ultimately led to the passing of the Cape of Good Hope and the establishment of a connection by sea between Lisbon and India, was exclusively the work of Portuguese seamen. But the researches of antiquaries have now made it abundantly clear that the expeditions of the Spanish and Portuguese monarchs were for the most part made under Italian captains, with Italian crews, and in vessels built by Italian shipwrights. Italian mathematicians constructed the charts and instruments by which they sailed, and Italian bankers furnished the funds with which they were equipped. It was the same in England: the Italian merchants of London and the Italian seamen of Bristol were the links between the great movement of maritime exploration and an insular people which at the eleventh hour began to take part in it. The Genoese were well known in Bristol, though it was a Venetian who first conducted English sailors to the shores of America. The skill and science of Italy had penetrated everywhere; and, in union with the spirit of territorial conquest and commercial enterprise in other lands, they had wrought out the exploration of the coasts of Africa, the crossing of the Atlantic before the trade winds, and the discovery of the New World of

America, long before the spirit of maritime enterprise was aroused in England, France, and Holland. Columbus did but add the finishing stroke to a work on which his countrymen had been incessantly employed for two centuries; and when this stroke was made, the part of Italy was completed. Science had done its work; and then began the struggle of commercial enterprise and political ambition for a share in its substantial results. It is at this stage of the history of maritime exploration that England steps in.

It needs no deep research to account for the forwardness of Italy, and the backwardness of England, in the great maritime movement of modern history. It is sufficient to observe that England was far removed from the latitudes where the process of discovery was being matured, and that English seamen had not yet begun to make very long voyages. In the time of Columbus, English seamen were familiar with all the shores of Western Europe, from Spain to Norway. They traded to Iceland; but they had scarcely penetrated the Mediterranean, nor had they rounded the North Cape and reached the White Sea, as they did a few years later. English commerce was chiefly carried on by means of the English Channel and thé German Ocean; and the maritime enterprise which English seamen naturally emulated was not that of the Italian republics, but of the Hanse Towns. Hence, except in a few isolated instances, the great discoveries to which the navigation of the southern latitudes of the Atlantic had conducted had at first little effect on English enterprise. It was not until the vast extent of the New World, its enormous wealth in the precious metals, and its unlimited capacity for further development had become universally notorious,—until the Spanish monarchy, from feeble and obscure beginnings, had swollen by the possession of America into a political monster that threatened to absorb Christendom, and until England was being forced into a struggle with it which promised to be a struggle for life and death,—that Englishmen began seriously to consider the mighty changes in national relations which the greatest geographical discoveries the world ever saw had once for all effected. It was in the reign of Elizabeth that this revolution in thought took place; and the reign of Elizabeth produced a race of men who were capable of converting this revolution in thought into a revolution in fact. The wicked and tyrannous power which English Protestants hated and dreaded was the spoilt child of the Papacy, and the Papacy had endowed it with the New World. Catholic England had acquiesced in the title thus acquired. Protestant England prepared to dispute it; and the narratives in the present volume show how the dispute was begun and carried on, though the reader must travel beyond the present volume, and turn to the history of American colonization in the succeeding reigns, to see how it was terminated.

The narratives contained in this volume thus fill up a remarkable gap in history. In tracing the continuous history of the relations between the Old World and the New, the exact connection which unites the history of Spanish America to the history of English America is found to be extremely obscure. The incidents of the Discovery of America, of the gradual exploration of its coasts, and of the Spanish conquest of Mexico and Peru, are well known; and so are the incidents of English colonization in New England, Virginia, and the Windward Islands. But a gulf of half a century, more or less, divides the period of English colonization from the period of Spanish conquest. How is this gulf to be bridged over, and where is the light which shall illuminate this dark half-century, and explain the transition from the old America,— an America enslaved, mediæval, Spanish, and Catholic,—

to the new America, an America free, modern, English, and Protestant? Fixing narrower limits to the inquiry, we may ask, How is it that in the beginning of its history we find America wholly Spanish and Portuguese, and at the end of a century find that it has become European? How is it that in the sixteenth century we find Europe tranquilly acquiescing in the Spanish occupation of America, and entertaining no suspicion whatever as to its ultimate destiny, while in the seventeenth we find all the powers of Western Europe engaged in a struggle for its possession? And how is it that in this struggle we find England taking the lead from the beginning, in course of time absorbing all foreign elements, and ultimately bringing about the great change which has made America, in all its length and breadth, a continent of free states, framed more or less on an English model, and all having their principal commercial and social connection with England, and that connection an increasing one?

Of these interesting historical questions the narratives of the Elizabethan seamen furnish the solution. They tell the story of a mighty reaction against the claim of a single Catholic power, based on a title derived from the Pope, to the exclusive possession of the New World; and this reaction followed closely upon, and was intimately connected with, that great reaction against the general claims of the Papacy in Europe which goes by the name of the Reformation. In both movements England took a leading part; and, in order to understand the history of English America, it is necessary to go back to the beginning of each. It is a mistake to regard the Puritan emigrants of New England and the commercial adventurers who cultivated the tobacco plant in Virginia, as the founders of English America. These great enterprises were the last of a long series. When Jamestown and Plymouth were founded, English vessels had frequented the Atlantic shores of the New World for half a century. In early times, the trade of Spanish America had been free to the English. When the false and selfish colonial policy of Spain excluded them from it, the beginnings of the struggle made their appearance. The English pursued their trade, in spite of all the ordinances of the Spanish councils. The force and determination of the English traders overbore the official resistance which they encountered, and the cessation of legitimate trade thus gave birth to smuggling. The profits of smuggling necessarily exceed the profits of lawful commerce; and, as it became more and more lucrative, it was engaged in more widely. From smuggling there is but one step to piracy, and from piracy but one step to territorial conquest; and it was by these successive steps that English enterprise advanced, in its slow encroachment on the inheritance the daring of a few Spaniards had won for their Crown in the New World.

It has been truly said that all history rests on an economical basis; and the great extension of English enterprise which the Atlantic voyages represent could certainly not have taken place unless it had been supported by a corresponding increase in the wealth of England. It is well known that such an increase took place in the reign of Elizabeth. The fertility of England's soil, the comparatively large number, the thrift, and the industry of the inhabitants of its towns, had always made of England a capital-making country; and the stoppage of the continual drain of money to Rome, the dispersion of one-third of the land, previously belonging to monasteries, among the mass of the people, the cessation of wars, and the great reduction in numbers of the unproductive classes which these causes involved, had by this time increased its gross capital yet more. All the trades of England increased, and many of them were connected with the shipping trade, and contributed to the increase of that also. London and other towns increased vastly in extent, a movement which statesmen in vain tried to check by Act of Parliament. Of the increase of personal wealth at this period the face of the land still affords ample evidence. The great country houses, the magnificent tombs to be found in churches, the costly furniture and pictures with which Englishmen now began to surround themselves, still remain to testify to it; and this increase of personal wealth accounts in some measure for the readiness of Englishmen to engage in remote and romantic enterprises.

But other causes than increase of internal wealth and activity contributed to the great change which was being wrought out. Without some powerful external stimulus these steps would not have been taken. Jealousy of Spanish wealth and power, and resentment of Spanish religious tyranny, supplied such a stimulus. The death of Mary, in 1558, set the match to the train. Henceforth no respect was shown to the rights and claims of the Spanish Crown, and the English seamen regarded the New World as their own. The growth of English maritime power had by this time reached a critical stage. It had fully kept pace with the growing maritime power of the other nations of Western Europe. From early times down to the age of the Plantagenets, England had been little more than a peninsula of France; and the constant necessity of traversing the English Channel or "Narrow Sea" had produced a numerous race of hardy seamen in the south and west of England. The addition of England to the dominions of Anjou, the conquest of Ireland, and the growth of trade with the Low Countries and the Baltic, led to a widening of the scope of English seamanship; and Chaucer represents his shipman as knowing the coast from Gothland to Finisterre, and every creek in Brittany and Spain. When the plan of Columbus had been rejected by Genoa, Venice, and Portugal, he sent his brother to London to propose that the westward voyage should be undertaken by the English King; and the age of the Tudors saw a great increase in the shipping of England, as well as a great extension of the field over which it sailed. English vessels now traded in great numbers to the Levant; and in the reign of Mary they first reached the northern ports of Russia. Following the track of the Italians, Spaniards, and Portuguese, they coasted the shores of Africa and reached Guinea. This coast was on the highway to the New World; and English ships were now embarked on the course which had led Columbus and his followers thither. The zone of the trade-winds thus gained, the time was not far distant when English vessels would ply to-and-fro between America and Europe.

The beginning of the reign of Elizabeth thus saw several powerful causes united to force English enterprise irresistibly on the path of its destiny. To accomplish this end, an economical cause, dependent on the increase of wealth, a commercial cause, dependent on the steady widening of the field of navigation, and a political cause, dependent on the impending breach with Spain, blended their forces. But another, of not less importance, was at work also; and this may be described as an intellectual cause. It is difficult to over-estimate the change which half-a-century had wrought in the habits and objects of English thought. In every direction the area over which it ranged was widened; and, as ever happens, its strength and sagacity increased with the increase in the field of its operations. To understand the change which less than a century produced, Shakspere must be compared with Skelton, and Bacon with "The Golden Legend."

This change was greatly assisted by the total transformation which astronomy and geography had undergone. The old theory of the physical sciences faded away like a dream, and many other things began to fade with it. On the other hand, there was a deepening of man's faith in himself, and in the physical wonders which were yet to be revealed to him by the due use of the intellectual instrument with which the Creator had equipped him. Bacon did but express a general feeling when he augured for his times the fulfilment of the prophecy that many should pass to and fro, and that knowledge should be increased.

And yet, with the single exception of Raleigh, it cannot be said that the Elizabethan seamen were affected in their own persons by this intellectual movement. They were rather its unconscious instruments; and their enterprises may all be accounted for by the law that forces capital into remunerative channels. With Raleigh it was otherwise. He had studied the growing sciences at Oxford; and it is possible that he had there heard Hakluyt himself lecture on the new cosmography. Raleigh had, to the best of his ability, mastered the history of the New World. The story of the Spanish conquests stimulated his imagination, as the wondrous natural history of the New World stimulated the imagination of Bacon. Raleigh's dream was to make the New World the inheritance of the Englishman. Bacon aspired more highly, and sought to make man absolute master over that realm of nature which was now being revealed in all its extent. Neither lived to see their dream realized; but time has done, and is still doing, much to realize both.

Though the shore of the American continent had been reached by an English crew before Columbus himself reached it in 1498, the English had long abandoned it to the two powers of the Peninsula; and in the attempt to gain a footing on it, as in so many other things, they were following the example of the French. When Hawkins undertook his first voyage, in 1562, the voyages of the English to the American coast which had been occasionally made in the time of the Henries, were out of mind. Spain had found the New World a great treasury of the precious metals. Leaving the Brazilian shore to Portugal, as being within the meridian of demarcation agreed on between the two Crowns by the treaty made in 1495, Spain had claimed to exclude the rest of Europe from the whole of the trans-Atlantic continent; and in this exclusion the rest of Europe had acquiesced. France alone had hitherto set up an adverse claim. In 1521, Francis of France, jealous of Charles V., his successful rival for the Imperial Crown, had provoked war with him; and one of his first acts was to despatch the Genoese seaman Verazzano to take possession of the coast of North America. In this war, in which the Spanish pretensions were first disputed, Henry VIII. had taken the side of Spain; and it was brought to an end in 1525 by the defeat of Pavia, and the capture of the French King. Of this episode no traces remained in the New World beyond the empty name of New France, applied by the enemies of Spain to the whole continent of North America. But the hardy seamen of Brittany and Gascony had, in the course of this war, already begun to infest the West Indian shores for the double purpose of smuggling and piracy. The way once discovered, it was never forgotten; and it was from their French neighbours that the English seamen learnt the way to the West Indies, and the profit that the voyage thither yielded. France thus became the pioneer of England in smuggling and piracy, as she afterwards became the pioneer of England in colonization.

The struggle of France against the rising power of Spain

continued until the accession of Elizabeth. Throughout this struggle, save during the short reign of Edward VI., the English Crown, swayed partly by a traditional enmity to its near neighbour, and partly by sympathy with the old religion, had sided with Spain; and the loss of Calais to the French was the last penalty it paid for this policy. The death of Mary changed the face of affairs. It gave a presumptive head to the growing Protestant faction throughout Europe, in the person of the English sovereign. For the struggle in Europe was no longer a mere struggle against the political predominance, but against the intense religious bigotry of the new power which overshadowed it; and it was the avowed policy of Philip to re-establish the old religion throughout Europe. Many years elapsed before the breach actually took place. But it was long foreseen, and long before it happened events were adapting themselves to it. When the fire had once burst forth, it quickly spread to America; and for two centuries and more thenceforth, whenever the flame of war was lighted in the Old World, it was destined similarly to envelope the New. It was out of the question to attack Philip in the Spanish peninsula. Its Italian possessions had been the place where the Spanish Crown had usually been attacked by the French; but the policy of attacking Spain in Italy had proved unfruitful. The exploits of the Protestant smugglers and pirates of England and France pointed the way to one more effectual. It was from the West Indies that Philip derived the wealth that enabled him to pay armies and corrupt politicians; and these exploits proved that it was possible to cut short his supplies. To harass him in America, to seize his huge ships with their loads of gold and silver, was at once to cripple him and supply his enemy with the sinews of war. The politicians of England looked forward to the time when they could do this openly. The shifting policy of Elizabeth prevented this during the earlier period of her reign. But from its very beginning the English smugglers and pirates were busy in the West Indies, and the politicians of England winked at their deeds. The interlopers soon discovered that the Spaniards were totally incapable of keeping them out of the American seas. This fact had long been known to the French, and it now became known to the English. The continued piracies of the French on the treasure fleets had led to their being protected by a small convoy of war ships. Spain was incapable of doing more. To maintain the command of the huge American shore was quite out of her power. She could barely hold the ports; and the ports were as yet unfortified. It needed nothing but a small armed force for the English pirate to make himself master of the capital towns of the New World.

The breach with England let loose upon Spanish America a swarm of the most experienced pirates in the world, and the greatest among them was the famous West-countryman who was the first among Englishmen to "put a girdle round about the earth." Shakspere is not more conspicuously the first of English poets, and Bacon the first of English philosophers, than Drake is the first of English pirates. His first attacks on the Spaniards were made by way of lawful reprisal for his private wrongs. He had a share in the last venture of Hawkins; and the perfidy of the Spanish Viceroy in the port of St. John had caused him severe pecuniary loss. The claim founded upon this was vigorously prosecuted by Drake in the only way in which its prosecution was possible. After some years of experience in his adopted calling of plundering the Spaniards, Drake resolved on an expedition of a novel and extremely daring character. He was by this time too well known on the Atlantic coast. On this side of

America the Spanish ports and fleets were jealously guarded; on the Pacific side, the source of the supply of gold and silver, it was quite otherwise. The Spaniards never dreamed that the corsairs of England and France would dare to pass the Straits of Magellan and attack them on the very shores of Peru, and they had on this side neither soldiers, nor ships of war, nor fortifications. The huge vessels which brought gold from Valdivia, and silver from Arica, to the port of Panama, to be then carried over the isthmus and shipped to Europe, were merely manned by a small mixed crew, and the work of navigation was even entrusted to negro slaves. The ports had no garrisons. It was Drake's plan to pass the Straits of Magellan secretly, appear suddenly on the coast of Peru, plunder ships and ports, and sail before the trade-winds across the Pacific, thus reaching home with his plunder by circumnavigating the globe. This feat had been rarely performed since the squadron of Magellan, above half-a-century before, had first proved its possibility; and no English vessel had hitherto navigated the Pacific Ocean. No English vessel had hitherto been to the east of the Cape of Good Hope, or seen the rich and wonderful East, which the Portuguese had reached three-quarters of a century before, and of the trade of which they were now in possession.

Drake's plan of plundering the Pacific coast, and navigating the Pacific and the Indian seas, had been several years ripening. When it was put into execution, another project had been brought forward for putting England in communication with the Pacific Ocean and India. This was Frobisher's project for making the North-West Passage. Frobisher's project had passed the stage of mere discussion. An attempt had been made to execute it. After fifteen years of fruitless endeavour, its author had succeeded in procuring a couple of barques of twenty and twenty-five tons, with which he proposed to sail to the north, leaving Greenland on the right, to pass round the continent of America, and then reach the Indies by sailing to the south-west. The year before Drake started on his "Famous Voyage," Frobisher had made the ice-bound coasts which lay opposite to Greenland, on the further side of the great straits which separate that dreary region from the American shores. He had discovered, as he thought, a strait leading thence to the Pacific. Along this strait he had sailed for sixty leagues; and he returned home with the intelligence that he had undoubtedly discovered the passage on the north corresponding to that which had been discovered by Magellan in the south. As Magellan had done, he called this passage by his own name, and denominated it Frobisher's Strait.

This had taken place in 1576; and in 1577 Frobisher started on his second voyage with one of the Queen's large ships. He returned in the same year without having reached the Pacific. But little doubt was felt as to his ultimate success; and if he were successful, he would have been the first Englishman to navigate the Pacific and reach the Indies by way of the west. Drake was determined to secure this distinction for himself; and accordingly, while Frobisher was returning from this second voyage, Drake was making his preparations for executing his cherished project of passing the Straits of Magellan. Frobisher was for making the North-West passage which, as was believed, had been discovered, but not passed. Drake was for making the South-West passage, by a route which was known to exist, but which was full of dangers and difficulties, the extent of which was unknown. One thing was common to both plans: this was the hope of plunder. Frobisher had brought back, on his first voyage, from the icy shores of Davis's Straits, some lumps of a black stone, which was pronounced by certain goldsmiths to contain gold. On his second voyage he brought back great quantities of this worthless rubbish, which was immediately on his return safely secured in Bristol Castle; and in the ensuing year he was to return and bring back yet more, lest other adventurers should seek to avail themselves of his fortunate discovery. The treasure of which Drake was in search was of a more certain sort. It consisted of gold and silver, of no doubtful quality; and it lay ready to his hand in the ships and storehouses of the Spanish Government.

It was in November, 1577, that Drake sailed from Plymouth on his "Famous Voyage," giving out that he was bound for Alexandria; and in November, 1580, he reached England, after making the circuit of the globe. From this date English enterprise takes its widest scope; for the "Famous Voyage" first introduced English sailors to the Pacific and the Indian Oceans. Drake merely circumnavigated the globe for the purpose of carrying his booty home more securely. No part of his voyage involved any difficult feat of seamanship. He soon discovered the falsehood of the traditional description of the Strait as a long and intricate passage, through dreary and inhospitable shores, where the weather was always bleak and tempestuous, and where the danger of shipwreck was continual. The passage of the Strait is, in fact, perfectly safe and easy for small vessels, and Drake effected it in fifteen days. Nor was the westward voyage over the Pacific fraught with any great difficulty. It was not like the return voyage from the Moluccas to Acapulco, which it had taken the Spaniards half-a-century to learn how to make. Like the celebrated voyage of Columbus, it was in reality a very simple matter, demanding nothing but perseverance in a straight course, with a fair wind provided by an invariable natural law. The latitude of the Moluccas, which Drake knew accurately, once reached, he was back in the Old World, and had only to follow the return course of the Portuguese pilots round the Cape of Good Hope.

The successful piracies of Drake and his fellows suggested the idea of territorial conquest. The English Crown had always been possessed of territory beyond seas. It had once held nearly the whole seaboard of France: it still held Ireland and the Channel Islands, and Calais had only recently been lost. The exploits of the last fifteen years amply proved two things. They proved that the power of England at sea had not diminished, but increased. They also proved that the Crown of Spain was utterly unable to protect its vast acquisitions in the New World. The consequence was obvious. So far as America was held by the fleets of Spain, it lay at the mercy of the English; for the English were supreme on the Atlantic. But here the power of the enemies of Spain ceased. The adventurers who plundered the Spanish ports were too wise to attempt permanent occupation. Such an attempt would have presented insurmountable difficulties. On land the Spaniards were as formidable in America as in Europe ; and to displace them in their colonial governments would have demanded regular military armaments, such as England was incapable of furnishing. No one who knows the story of the military helplessness of England when Philip dispatched the Great Armada to reduce it, can wonder that no attempt was ever made to bring Spanish colonies under the permanent sway of England. One thing remained. The English might seize those parts of America which were yet unoccupied by the Spaniards. The sturdy agricultural population of England was increasing beyond the demand for agricultural labour. The desire for territorial possessions was increasing among the poorer gentry. The landless adventurers of Spain and Portugal had obtained grants, formed colonies, reduced the natives to subjection and Christianity. English adventurers, it was argued, might do the like where Spain had left the ground unoccupied; and the idea of territorial conquest thus gave birth to the idea of colonization.

As English pirates had trodden in the footsteps of the French pirates, so English colonists now trod in the footsteps of French colonists. Piracy had suggested colonization to the French a few years before; and under the auspices of Coligny attempts had been successively made to found French Protestant colonies on the coasts of Brazil and Florida. When Elizabeth came to the English Throne, the settlement of Fort Coligny at Rio de Janeiro was yet in existence. Two years afterwards it was destroyed by the Portuguese; and the French statesman then turned his attention to Florida. Fort Caroline was founded by Laudonnière in the same year in which Hawkins made his first voyage to the West Indies. But the French adventurers who followed Laudonnière found their new occupation less profitable than that in which they had been bred; and their leader had no sooner left them than they forsook the cultivation of the soil and the conversion of the Indians for the easier and more lucrative pursuit of piracy. The colony of Fort Caroline was in great straits when Hawkins relieved it on his return home from his second voyage; and it was soon afterwards destroyed by the Spaniards.

The failure of the French to occupy America had been due, not to the energy of Spain, but to want of proper materials and organization on their own part. The same thing happened to the English; and it took our ancestors thirty years to learn the art of colonization. The success of the founders of

Virginia and New England is due to the experience which was gradually stored up by the failures of Gilbert and Raleigh. Both Gilbert and Raleigh seem to have satisfied themselves that the French had struck out the right path. The former intended to make the St. Lawrence the base of his colonial undertakings, thus imitating the failure of Roberval. The latter imitated Coligny in placing his colony to the southward, selecting, however, a spot more remote than Fort Caroline from the centre of the Spanish Indies, and with a climate better adapted to English labourers. New England was founded by pursuing the path of Gilbert, and Virginia by pursuing that of Raleigh. But success was only made possible by repeated failures; and in the midst of these failures another path seemed to open itself for the planting of the English power in America. Sir Walter Raleigh suddenly conceived the plan of following in the footsteps of Cortes, and conquering for England the fabled empire of Guiana.

Raleigh's attempt to discover and conquer the fabled empire of Guiana may seem at first to stand alone in English colonial history. It takes, however, a perfectly natural place in that history. The false belief in a third great aboriginal empire, rivalling in wealth and extent those famous empires which had been won for Spain by Cortes and Pizarro, was exactly adapted to catch the imagination of the Elizabethan adventurer at the moment when piracy was developing into conquest and colonization. Spain had left it untouched, and apparently left it for that nation which had proved how incapable Spain was of extending its conquests. Nor was Raleigh culpably imposed upon by a gross fabrication, such as men of more sense and less enthusiasm would have rejected. He was following up an enterprise which had actively occupied the Spaniards during half a century, and which had absorbed far more lives and money than were involved in his own venture; and the scanty results of his expedition of 1595, the narrative of which concludes the present volume, abated not a whit of his hopes. To the end of his life he believed in Guiana; and the belief was equally current among the adventurous spirits of England after his death.

The enterprises of Raleigh, with which that of his half-brother Gilbert must be classed, are the true beginnings of Anglo-American history. Those who went before him had merely prepared the way. Hawkins had led English seamen across the Atlantic, and opened the American seas. Drake had proved the inability of Spain to keep them off. Conquest of the Spanish settlements being out of the question, Hakluyt had urged the English, in imitation of French example, to plant colonies in those parts of America which the Spaniards had not occupied. Gilbert had attempted to make a beginning in this undertaking. But Raleigh was the first to put his hand to the plough in right earnest, and to persevere undaunted by failure. Uniformly unfortunate as were his schemes for conquest and colonization, it was through his failures that success at length became possible; and his name is better entitled than any other to rank in history as the founder of the Anglo-American nation.

Such is the general historical outline which the narratives contained in the present volume enable the reader to fill up. Little needs to be said of the narratives themselves. They reflect, with the closeness and fidelity which only belongs to contemporary records, the aspect presented to English eyes by the great field of new enterprise which was opened beyond the sea to Englishmen of Elizabeth's reign: and they also show with what patience and energy this field was explored. Those who wrote them were, for the most part, men who had themselves taken an active part in the work, and who were scholarly enough to use the pure and expressive English of Shakspere's day with ease and effect. Without claiming for them any high literary rank, it may be said that they are, from a merely literary point of view, good specimens of English narrative written when the language was in its prime. Most of them are here for the first time, it is believed, extracted from the black-letter obscurity of Hakluyt's collection, and arranged in chronological order.

VOYAGES
OF THE
ELIZABETHAN SEAMEN.

HAWKINS.

The history of English America begins with the three slave-trading voyages of John Hawkins, made in the years 1562, 1564, and 1567. Nothing that Englishmen had done in connection with America, previously to those voyages, had any result worth recording. England had known the New World nearly seventy years, for John Cabot had reached it shortly after its discovery by Columbus; and, as the tidings of the discovery spread, many English adventurers had crossed the Atlantic to the American coast. But as years passed, and the excitement of novelty subsided, the English voyages to America had become fewer and fewer, and at length ceased altogether. It is easy to account for this. There was no opening for conquest or plunder, for the Tudors were at peace with the Spanish sovereigns: and there could be no territorial occupation, for the Papal title of Spain and Portugal to the whole of the new continent could not be disputed by Catholic England. No trade worth having existed with the natives: and Spain and Portugal kept the trade with their own settlers in their own hands. Meanwhile English commerce found profitable openings elsewhere.

In 1521, Francis I. began the great struggle against the European domination of Spain: and the French began to plunder and smuggle in Spanish America. The English in time imitated them. But a legitimate connection also subsisted. Emigrants of other nations had always been allowed to proceed in Spanish and Portuguese vessels to the Spanish and Portuguese settlements. Most of these were Italian or French. But Englishmen and Scotchmen were found among them; and long before there was formed any definite idea of English colonization in the New World, there existed in more than one town of importance a little colony of British, Catholics by religion, and half Spaniards or Portuguese by manners. Letters passed between them and their friends at home; in time they returned in person; and through this channel a distinct idea of the New World reached England long before the face of England was changed by the accession of Elizabeth. Besides this, the Portuguese had begun to avail themselves of the help of English mariners, as in former times they had availed themselves of the help of Italian mariners; and early in the reign of Henry the Eighth a connection existed between England and the Portuguese plantations in Brazil, by way of the Guinea coast. Hakluyt was assured that old William Hawkins, of Plymouth, father of the more famous seaman whose voyages follow, had made the Brazilian voyage, by way of Guinea, in 1530 and 1532. No mention is made of slaves in Hakluyt's account of old William Hawkins; but it is extremely probable that the voyages of the father, if they ever took place, were slavery ventures, like the voyages of the son.

As the plantations in America grew and multiplied, the demand for negroes rapidly increased. The Spaniards had no African settlements; but the Portuguese had many, and, with the aid of French and English adventurers, they procured from these settlements slaves enough to supply both themselves and the Spaniards. But the Brazilian plantations grew so fast, about the middle of the century, that they absorbed the entire supply, and the Spanish colonists knew not where to look for negroes. This penury of slaves in the Spanish Indies became known to the English and French captains who frequented the Guinea coast; and John Hawkins, who had been engaged from boyhood in the trade with Spain and the Canaries, resolved in 1562 to take a cargo of negro slaves to Hispaniola. The little squadron with which he executed this project was the first English squadron which navigated the West Indian seas. This voyage opened those seas to the English.

England had not yet broken with Spain, and the law excluding English vessels from trading with the Spanish colonists was not strictly enforced. The trade was profitable, and Hawkins found no difficulty in disposing of his cargo to great advantage. A meagre note (pp. 7, 8) from the pen of Hakluyt, contains all that is known of the first American voyage of Hawkins. In its details it must have closely resembled the second voyage. In the first voyage, however, Hawkins had no occasion to carry his wares further than three ports on the northern side of Hispaniola. These ports, far away from San Domingo, the capital, were already well-known to the French smugglers. He did not venture into the Caribbean sea; and, having loaded his ships with their return cargo, he made the best of his way back. In his second voyage, as will be seen, he entered the Caribbean Sea, still keeping, however, at a safe distance from San Domingo, and sold his slaves on the mainland.

This voyage was on a much larger scale, and the Earls of Pembroke and Leicester swelled the number of the adventurers who supported him. On the other hand new difficulties confronted him. The news of his previous expedition had reached Philip, and had resulted in complaints to Elizabeth, and in an order strictly prohibiting the Spanish colonists in the New World from trading with him. The common statement that Hawkins "forced the defenceless Spanish colonists to take his negroes at prices fixed by him" (J. G. Kohl, *History of the Discovery of Maine*, p. 443,) is incorrect. Hawkins, indeed, broke down, by threats or force, the opposition of the Spanish military officials; but the colonists, as the narrative shows, were ready enough to buy when this had been done.

The second voyage of Hawkins differed from the first, in that it was prolonged so as to become an important voyage of discovery. Having sold his slaves in the continental ports, and loaded his vessels with hides and other goods bought with the produce, Hawkins determined to strike out a new path and sail home with the Gulf-stream, which would carry him northwards past the shores of Florida. Sparke's narrative, which follows, proves that at every point in these expeditions the Englishman was following in the track of the French. He had French pilots and seamen on board, and there is little doubt that one at least of these had already been with Laudonnière in Florida. The French seamen guided him to Laudonnière's settlement, where his arrival was most opportune. They then pointed him the way by the coast of North America, then universally known in the mass as New France, to Newfoundland, and thence, with the prevailing westerly winds, to Europe. This was the pioneer voyage made by Englishmen along coasts afterwards famous in history through English colonization. It corresponded to that of Verazzano, forty years earlier, which had opened the way to French colonization in Florida and Canada.

The extremely interesting narrative which is here given

(p. 9), is from the pen of John Sparke, one of Hawkins' gentlemen companions. It contains the first information concerning America and its natives, which was published in England by an English eye-witness, and ranks in all respects among the most interesting pieces in Hakluyt's collection. The style is singularly free, simple, and graceful, and contrasts markedly with the condensed narrative which follows it.

The second voyage of Hawkins won him wealth and reputation. In 1565 he obtained his well-known grant of arms, with the crest of "a demi-moor, bound and captive." The breach was widening between England and Spain, and his successes opened a tempting prospect to English adventurers. The inferiority of Spain at sea was more than suspected; and the fears of the Spaniards were by this time thoroughly aroused. The Spanish Ambassador met Hawkins at Court, and invited him to dinner. Hawkins accepted, and at dinner told the representative of Philip that he proposed to repeat his voyage in the next May (1566). Accidents delayed the equipment of the fleet until October. Meanwhile the remonstrances of Philip had their effect; and, just as Hawkins was on the point of starting, a letter arrived at Plymouth from Cecil, forbidding him, in the Queen's name, to traffic in breach of the laws of Spain, and requiring from him a bond in £500 to this effect before his vessels started. Hawkins executed the bond, and despatched the ships, himself remaining at home. No narrative of the expedition has survived; but it is certain that the ships returned richly freighted, and that large profits were made. In another year's time the aspect of things had changed yet more. Elizabeth had given open countenance to the insurrection in the Netherlands: and Hawkins was now able to execute his plans without restraint. He founded a permanent fortified factory on the Guinea coast, where negroes might be collected all the year round. Thence he sailed for the West Indies a third time. Young Francis Drake sailed with him in command of the Judith, a small vessel of fifty tons. It is curious that in the narrative of Hawkins the name of Drake is not mentioned. When the Minion and the Judith escaped from the jaws of destruction in the port of San Juan, Drake sailed straight for England. Possibly Hawkins regarded this as an act of desertion; but it is difficult to see what better course Drake could have taken. He could render Hawkins no help, and might have been a cause of embarrassment.

Of the crushing blow which Hawkins in this expedition received from the Spanish fleet, it can only be said that his own astounding audacity exposed him to it; and that the only wonder is that either he or Drake escaped to tell the tale. The maxim that no faith was to be kept with heretics amply justified the Spanish commander. Unable to find food for the crowded passengers on board the Minion, Hawkins put half of them ashore. Two of the wretched survivors of this party, named Job Hartop and Miles Philips, lived to write the adventures which afterwards befell them. Both narratives are in Hakluyt's collection. That of Philips is particularly worth attention in connection with the brief narrative from the pen of Hawkins, which is here printed. The misfortunes of this last voyage naturally discouraged its projector; and it is many years before he reappears in Anglo-American history. His share in the reorganization of Elizabeth's navy, and in repelling the Great Armada, has been too often described to need here more than a passing allusion.

HAWKINS.—FIRST VOYAGE.

The FIRST VOYAGE *of the Right Worshipful and Valiant Knight* SIR JOHN HAWKINS, *sometime Treasurer of Her Majesty's Navy Royal, made to the* WEST INDIES, 1562.

MASTER JOHN HAWKINS having made divers voyages to the Isles of the Canaries, and there by his good and upright dealing being grown in love and favour with the people, informed himself amongst them, by diligent inquisition, of the state of the West India, whereof he had received some knowledge by the instructions of his father, but increased the same by the advertisements and reports of that people. And being amongst other particulars assured that negroes were very good merchandise in Hispaniola, and that store of negroes might easily be had upon the coast of Guinea, resolved with himself to make trial thereof, and communicated that device with his worshipful friends of London: namely, with Sir Lionell Ducket, Sir Thomas Lodge, Mr. Gunson his father-in-law, Sir William Winter, Mr. Bromfield, and others. All which persons liked so well of his intention, that they became liberal contributors and adventurers in the action. For which purpose there were three good ships immediately provided: the one called the Salomon, of the burden of 120 tons, wherein Mr. Hawkins himself went as General: the second the Swallow, of 100 tons, wherein went for Captain Mr. Thomas Hampton: and the third the Jonas, a barque of 40 tons, wherein the Master supplied the Captain's room: in which small fleet Mr. Hawkins took with him not above 100 men, for fear of sickness and other inconveniences, whereunto men in long voyages are commonly subject.

With this company he put off and departed from the coast of England in the month of October, 1562, and in his course touched first at Teneriffe, where he received friendly entertainment. From thence he passed to Sierra Leone, upon the coast of Guinea, which place by the people of the country is called Tagarin, where he stayed some good time, and got into his possession, partly by the sword and partly by other means, to the number of 300 negroes at the least, besides other merchandise which that country yieldeth. With this prey he sailed over the ocean sea unto the island of Hispaniola, and arrived first at the port of Isabella: and there he had reasonable utterance of his English commodities, as also of some part of his negroes, trusting the Spaniards no further than that by his own strength he was able still to master them. From the port of Isabella he went to Puerto de Plata, where he made like sales, standing always upon his guard: from thence also he sailed to Monte Christi, another port on the north side of Hispaniola, and the last place of his touching, where he had peaceable traffic, and made vent of the whole number of his negroes: for which he received in those three places, by way of exchange, such a quantity of merchandise that he did not only lade his own three ships with hides, ginger, sugars, and some quantity of pearls, but he freighted also two other hulks with hides and other like commodities, which he sent into Spain. And thus, leaving the island, he returned and disembogued, passing out by the islands of the Caicos, without further entering into the Bay of Mexico, in this his first voyage to the West India. And so, with prosperous success and much gain to himself and the aforesaid adventurers, he came home, and arrived in the month of September, 1563.

HAWKINS.—SECOND VOYAGE.

NARRATIVE BY JOHN SPARKE.

The VOYAGE *made by* MR. JOHN HAWKINS, *afterwards Knight, Captain of the* JESUS *of Lubeck, one of Her Majesty's ships, and General of the* SALOMON, *and other two barques going in his company to the coast of* GUINEA *and the* INDIES OF NOVA HISPANIOLA, *begun in* A.D. 1564.

MASTER JOHN HAWKINS, with the Jesus of Lubeck, a ship of 700, and the Salomon, a ship of 140, the Tiger, a barque of 50, and the Swallow, of 30 tons, being all well furnished with men to the number of one hundred threescore and ten, as also with ordnance and victuals requisite for such a voyage, departed out of Plymouth on the 18th day of October, in the year of our Lord 1564, with a prosperous wind; at which departing, in cutting the foresail, a marvellous misfortune happened to one of the officers in the ship, who by the pulley of the sheet was slain out of hand, being a sorrowful beginning to them all. And after their setting out ten leagues to sea, he met the same day with the Minion, a ship of the Queen's Majesty's, whereof was captain David Carlet, and also her consort, the John Baptist, of London, being bound to Guinea also, who hailed one another, after the custom of the sea, with certain pieces of ordnance for joy of their meeting; which done, the Minion departed from him to seek her other consort, the Merlin, of London, which was astern out of sight, leaving in Mr. Hawkins' company the John Baptist, her other consort.

Thus sailing forwards on their way with a prosperous wind until the 21st of the same month; at that time a great storm arose, the wind being at north-east about nine o'clock in the night, and continued so twenty-three hours together, in which storm Mr.

Hawkins lost the company of the John Baptist aforesaid, and of his pinnace called the Swallow, his other three ships being sore beaten with a storm. On the 23rd day, the Swallow, to his no small rejoicing, came to him again in the night, ten leagues to the northward of Cape Finisterre, he having put roomer, not being able to double the Cape, in that there rose a contrary wind at southwest. On the 25th, the wind continuing contrary, he put into a place in Galicia called Ferrol, where he remained five days, and appointed all the masters of his ships an order for the keeping of good company in this manner:—The small ships to be always ahead and aweather of the Jesus, and to speak twice a-day with the Jesus at least. If in the day the ensign be over the poop of the Jesus, or in the night two lights, then shall all the ships speak with her. If there be three lights aboard the Jesus, then doth she cast about. If the weather be extreme, that the small ships cannot keep company with the Jesus, then all to keep company with the Salomon, and forthwith to repair to the Island of Teneriffe, to the northward of the road of Sirroes. If any happen to any misfortune, then to show two lights, and to shoot off a piece of ordnance. If any lose company and come in sight again, to make three yaws and strike the mizen three times. Serve God daily, love one another, preserve your victuals, beware of fire, and keep good company.

On the 26th day the Minion came in also where he was, for the rejoicing whereof he gave them certain pieces of ordnance, after the courtesy of the sea, for their welcome. But the Minion's men had no mirth, because of their consort the Merlin, whom, at their departure from Master Hawkins upon the coast of England, they went to seek, and, having met with her, kept company two days together; and at last, by misfortune of fire (through the negligence of one of their gunners), the powder in the gunner's room was set on fire, which, with the first blast, struck out her poop, and therewithal lost three men, besides many sore burned (which escaped by the brigantine being at her stern), and immediately, to the great loss of the owners, and most horrible sight to the beholders, she sank before their eyes.

On the 20th day of the month Mr. Hawkins, with his consorts and company of the Minion, having now both the brigantines at her stern, weighed anchor, and set sail on their voyage, having a prosperous wind thereunto.

On the 4th of November they had sight of the Island of

Madeira, and, on the 6th, of Teneriffe, which they thought to
have been the Canary, in that they supposed themselves to have
been to the eastward of Teneriffe, and were not. But the Minion,
being three or four leagues ahead of us, kept on her course to
Teneriffe, having better sight thereof than the other had, and by
that means they parted company. For Mr. Hawkins and his
company went more to the west, upon which course having sailed
awhile, he espied another island, which he thought to be Teneriffe;
and not being able, by means of the fog upon the hills, to discern
the same, nor yet to fetch it by night, went roomer until the
morning, being the 7th of November, which as yet he could not
discern, but sailed along the coast the space of two hours to
perceive some certain mark of Teneriffe, and found no likelihood
thereof at all, accounting that to be, as indeed it was, the Isle of
Palms: and so sailing forwards, espied another island called
Gomera, and also Teneriffe, to the which he made, and sailing
all night, came in the morning the next day to the port of Adecia,
where he found his pinnace which had departed from him on the
6th of the month, being in the weather of him; and, espying the
pike of Teneriffe all a-high, bare thither. At his arrival, somewhat before he came to anchor, he hoisted out his ship's pinnace,
rowing ashore, intending to have sent one with a letter to Peter
de Ponte, one of the Governors of the island, who dwelt a league
from the shore. But, as he pretended to have landed, suddenly
there appeared upon the two points of the road, men levelling of
bases and arquebuses at them, with divers others, to the number
of fourscore, with halberds, pikes, swords, and targets, which
happened so contrary to his expectation that it did greatly amaze
him; and the more because he was now in their danger, not
knowing well how to avoid it without some mischief. Wherefore
he determined to call to them for the better appeasing of the
matter, declaring his name, and professing himself to be an
especial friend to Peter de Ponte, and that he had sundry things
for him which he greatly desired. And in the meantime, while he
was thus talking with them, whereby he made them to hold their
hands, he willed the mariners to row away, so that at last he got
out of their danger. And then asking for Peter de Ponte, one of
his sons, being Señor Nicolas de Ponte, came forth, whom he
perceiving, desired to put his men aside, and he himself would
leap ashore and commune with him, which they did. So that
after communication had between them of sundry things, and of the

fear they both had, Master Hawkins desired to have certain necessaries provided for him. In the mean space, while these things were providing, he trimmed the mainmast of the Jesus, which in the storm aforesaid was sprung. Here he sojourned seven days, refreshing himself and his men. In which time Peter de Ponte, dwelling at Santa Cruz, a city twenty leagues off, came to him, and gave him as gentle entertainment as if he had been his own brother. To speak somewhat of these islands, being called in old time Insulæ Fortunatæ, by means of the flourishing thereof, the fruitfulness of them doth surely far exceed all other that I have heard of; for they make wine better than any in Spain, they have grapes of such bigness that they may be compared to damsons, and in taste inferior to none. For sugar, suckets, raisins of the sun, and many other fruits, abundance. For rosin ànd raw silk there is great store. They want neither corn, pullets, cattle, nor yet wild fowl. They have many camels also, which, being young, are eaten of the people for victuals, and, being old, they are used for the carriage of necessaries; whose property is that he is taught to kneel at the taking of his load and unlading again; of understanding very good, but of shape very deformed, with a little belly, long misshapen legs, and feet very broad of flesh, without a hoof, all whole, saving the great toe, a back bearing up like a molehill, a large and thin neck, with a little head, with a bunch of hard flesh, which nature hath given him in his breast, to lean upon. This beast liveth hardly, and is contented with straw and stubble, but of force strong, being well able to carry five hundred-weight. In one of these islands, called Fierro, there is, by the report of the inhabitants, a certain tree that raineth continually, by the dropping whereof the inhabitants and cattle are satisfied with water, for other water have they none in all the island. And it raineth in such abundance that it were incredible unto a man to believe such a virtue to be in a tree; but it is known to be a divine matter and a thing ordained of God, at whose power therein we ought not to marvel, seeing He did by His providence, as we read in the Scriptures, when the children of Israel were going into the promised land, feed them with manna from heaven for the space of forty years. Of the trees aforesaid we saw in Guinea many, being of great height, dropping continually; but not so abundantly as the other, because the leaves are narrower, and are like the leaves of a pear-tree.

About these islands are certain flitting islands, which have been oftentimes seen, and when men approached near them, they vanished. As the like hath been of these islands now known by the report of the inhabitants, which were not found of long time one after the other; and therefore it should seem he is not yet born to whom God hath appointed the finding of them. In this island of Teneriffe there is a hill called The Pike, because it is piked, which is in height, by their reports, twenty leagues, having, both winter and summer, abundance of snow on the top of it. This Pike may be seen on a clear day fifty leagues off; but it showeth as though it were a black cloud a great height in the element. I have heard of none to be compared with this in height; but in the Indies I have seen many, and in my judgment not inferior to the Pike, and so the Spaniards write.

On the 15th of November, at night, we departed from Teneriffe, and on the 20th of the same we had sight of ten caravels that were fishing at sea, with whom we would have spoken, but they, fearing us, fled into a place of Barbary, called Cape de las Barbas.

On the 20th the ship's pinnace, with two men in her, sailing by the ship, was overthrown by the oversight of them that went in her, the wind being so great that, before they were espied, and the ship had cast about for them, she was driven half a league to leeward of the pinnace, and had lost sight of her, so that there was small hope of recovery had not God's help and the captain's diligence been, who, having well marked which way the pinnace was by the sun, appointed twenty-four of the lustiest rowers in the great boat to row to the windward, and so recovered, contrary to all men's expectations, both the pinnace and the men sitting upon the keel of her.

On the 25th he came to Cape Blanco, which is upon the coast of Africa, and a place where the Portuguese do ride, that fish there in the month of November especially, and is a very good place of fishing for pargoes, mullet, and dog-fish. In this place the Portuguese have no hold for their defence, but have rescue of the barbarians, whom they entertain as their soldiers, for the time of their being there and for their fishing upon that coast of Africa, paying a certain tribute to the King of the Moors. The people of that part of Africa are tawny, having long hair, without any apparel. Their weapons in wars are bows and arrows.

On the 26th we departed from St. Avis Bay, within Cape Blanco, where we refreshed ourselves with fish and other necessaries; and on the 29th we came to Cape Verde, which lieth in fourteen degrees and a-half. These people are all black, and are called negroes, without any apparel, * * * of stature goodly men, and well liking by reason of their food, which passeth all other Guineans for kine, goats, pullen, rice, fruits, and fish. Here we took fishes with heads like conies, and teeth nothing varying, of a jolly thickness, but not past a foot long, and is not to be eaten without flaying or cutting off his head. To speak somewhat of the sundry sorts of these Guineans: the people of Cape Verde are called Leophares, and counted the goodliest men of all other, saving the Congoes, which do inhabit on this side the Cape de Buena Esperança. These Leophares have wars against the Jeloffes, which are borderers by them. Their weapons are bows and arrows, targets, and short daggers, darts also, but varying from other negroes'; for whereas the others use a long dart to fight with in their hands, they carry five or six small ones apiece, which they cast with. Thèse men also are more civil than any other, because of their daily traffic with the Frenchmen, and are of nature very gentle and loving; for while we were there we took in a Frenchman, who was one of the nineteen that, going to Brazil, in a barque of Dieppe, of 60 tons, and being a-seaboard of Cape Verde, 200 leagues, the planks of their barque with a sea brake out upon them so suddenly, that much ado they had to save themselves in their boats. But, by God's providence, the wind being westerly, which is rarely seen there, they got to the shore, to the Isle Brava, and in great penury got to Cape Verde, where they remained six weeks, and had meat and drink of the same people. The said Frenchman having forsaken his fellows, which were three leagues off from the shore, and, wandering with the negroes to and fro, fortuned to come to the water's side; and, communing with certain of his countrymen which were in our ship, by their persuasions came away with us. But his entertainment amongst them was such that he desired it not; but, through the importunate request of his countrymen, consented at last. Here we stayed but one night and part of the day; for on the 7th of December we came away, in that pretending to have taken negroes there perforce, the Minion's men gave them there to understand of our coming, and our pretence, wherefore they did avoid the snares we had laid for them.

On the 8th of December we anchored by a small island called Alcatrarsa,* wherein at our going ashore we found nothing but sea-birds, as we call them gannets, but by the Portugals called alcatrarses, who for that cause gave the said island the same name. Herein half of our boats were laden with young and old fowl, who, not being used to the sight of men, flew so about us that we struck them down with poles. In this place the two ships riding, the two barques, with their boats, went into an island of the Sapies called La Formio, to see if they could take any of them, and there landed to the number of eighty in armour, and, espying certain, made to them; but they fled in such order into the woods, that it booted them not to follow. So, going on their way forward till they came to a river which they could not pass over, they espied on the other side two men, who with their bows and arrows shot terribly at them. Whereupon we discharged certain arquebuses at them again; but the ignorant people weighed it not, because they knew not the danger thereof; but used a marvellous crying in their fight, with leaping and turning their tails that it was most strange to see, and gave us great pleasure to behold them. At the last, one being hurt with an arquebus upon the thigh, looked upon his wound and wist not how it came, because he could not see the pellet. Here Master Hawkins perceiving no good to be done amongst them, because we could not find their towns, and also not knowing how to go into Rio Grande for want of a pilot, which was the very occasion of our coming thither; and finding so many shoals, feared with our great ships to go in, and therefore departed on our pretended way to the Idols.

On the 10th of December we had a north-east wind, with rain and storm, which weather continuing two days together, was the occasion that the Salomon and Tiger lost our company. For whereas the Jesus and pinnace anchored at one of the islands called Sambula † on the 12th day, the Salomon and Tiger came not thither till the 14th. In this island we stayed certain days, going every day on shore to take the inhabitants, with burning and spoiling their towns, who before were Sapies, and were conquered by the Samboses, inhabitants beyond Sierra Leone. These Samboses had inhabited there three years before our coming

---

* The Alcatraz is the Man-of-war Bird, a species of cormorant.
† Probably the island now called Sherborough Island.

thither, and in so short space have so planted the ground that they had great plenty of mill, rice, roots, pompions, pullen, goats, of small fry dried; every house full of the country fruit planted by God's providence, as palm-trees, fruits like dates, and sundry other, in no place in all that country so abundantly, whereby they lived more deliciously than others. These inhabitants have divers of the Sapies which they took in the wars as their slaves, whom only they kept to till the ground, in that they neither have the knowledge thereof, nor yet will work themselves, of whom we took many in that place, but of the Samboses none at all, for they fled into the main. All the Samboses have white teeth as we have, far unlike to the Sapies which do inhabit about Rio Grande; for their teeth are all filed, which they do for a bravery, to set out themselves, and do jag their flesh, both legs, arms, and bodies, as workmanlike as a jerkinmaker with us pinketh a jerkin. These Sapies are more civil than the Samboses; for whereas the Samboses live most by the spoil of their enemies, both in taking their victuals and eating them also, the Sapies do not eat man's flesh, unless in the war they be driven by necessity thereunto, which they have not used, but by the example of the Samboses, but live only on fruits and cattle, whereof they have great store. This plenty is the occasion that the Sapies desire not war, except they be thereunto provoked by the invasions of the Samboses, whereas the Samboses for want of food are enforced thereunto, and therefore are not wont only to take them that they kill, but also keep those that they take until such time as they want meat, and then they kill them. There is also another occasion that provoketh the Samboses to war against the Sapies, which is for covetousness of their riches. For whereas the Sapies have an order to bury their dead in certain places appointed for that purpose with their gold about them, the Samboses dig up the ground to have the same treasure. For the Samboses have not the like store of gold that the Sapies have. In this island of Sambula we found about fifty boats called almadies, or canoes, which are made of one piece of wood, digged out like a trough, but of a good proportion, being about eight yards long and one in breadth, having a beakhead and stern very proportionably made, and on the outside artificially carved, and painted red and blue. They are able to carry twenty or thirty men; but about the coast they are able to carry threescore and upward. In these canoes they row standing upright, with an oar somewhat longer than a man, the end whereof is made about the breadth and length of a man's hand of the largest sort. They row very swift, and in some of them four rowers and one to steer make as much way as a pair of oars in the Thames of London.

Their towns are prettily divided with a main street at the entering in, that goeth through their town, and another overthwart street, which maketh their towns crossways. Their houses are built in a rank very orderly in the face of the street, and they are made round, like a dove-cot, with stakes set full of palmito* leaves, instead of a wall. They are not much more than a fathom large, and two of height, and thatched with palmito leaves very close, and some with reeds, and over the roof thereof, for the better garnishing of the same, there is a round bundle of reeds, prettily contrived like a louver. In the inner part they make a loft of sticks, whereupon they lay all their provision of victuals. A place they reserve at the entrance for the kitchen, and the place they lie in is divided with certain mats artificially made with the rind of palmito trees. Their bedsteads are of small staves laid along, and raised a foot from the ground, upon which is laid a mat, and another upon them when they list; for other covering they have none. In the middle of the town there is a house larger and higher than the others, but in form alike, adjoining unto the which there is a place made of four good stanchions of wood, and a round roof over it, the ground also raised round with clay a foot high, upon the which floor were strawed many fine mats. This is the Consultation-house, the like whereof is in all towns, as the Portugals affirm: in which place, when they sit in council, the king or captain sitteth in the midst, and the elders upon the floor by him (for they give reverence to their elders), and the common sort sit round about them. There they sit to examine matters of theft, which if a man be taken with, to steal but a Portugal's cloth from another, he is sold to the Portugals for a slave. They consult, also, and take order what time they shall go to war; and, as it is certainly reported by the Portugals, they take order in gathering of the fruits in the season of the year, and also of palmito wine, which is gathered by a hole cut in the top of a tree, and a gourd set for the receiving thereof, which falleth in by drops, and yieldeth fresh wine again within a month, and this

---

* The Areca or Cabbage Palm, a native both of Africa and America.

divided part and portion-like to every man by the judgment of the captain and elders, every man holdeth himself contented. And this surely I judge to be a very good order; for otherwise, whereas scarcity of palmito is, every man would have the same, which might breed great strife. But of such things as every man doth plant for himself, the sower thereof reapeth it to his own use, so that nothing is common but that which is unset by man's hands. In their houses there is more common passage of lizards like evats, and others greater, of black and blue colour, of near a foot long, besides their tails, than there is with us of mice in great houses. The Sapies and Samboses also use in their wars bows, and arrows made of reeds, with heads of iron poisoned with the juice of a cucumber, whereof I had many in my hands. In their battles they have target-men, with broad wicker targets, and darts with heads of iron at both ends, the one in form of a two-edged sword, a foot and a-half long, and at the other end, the iron long of the same length made to counterpoise it, that in casting it might fly level, rather than for any other purpose as I can judge. And when they espy the enemy, the captain, to cheer his men, crieth "Hungry," and they answer "Heygre," and with that every man placeth himself in order. For about every target-man three bowmen will cover themselves, and shoot as they see advantage. And when they give the onset, they make such terrible cries that they may be heard two miles off. For their belief, I can hear of none that they have, but in such as they themselves imagine to see in their dreams, and so worship the pictures, whereof we saw some like unto devils. In this island aforesaid we sojourned until the 21st of December, where, having taken certain negroes and as much of their fruits, rice, and mill as we could well carry away (whereof there was such store that we might have laden one of our barques therewith), we departed. And at our departure, divers of our men being desirous to go on shore to fetch pompions, which, having proved, they found to be very good, certain of the Tiger's men went also. Amongst the which there was a carpenter, a young man, who, with his fellows, having fetched many and carried them down to their boats, as they were ready to depart, desired his fellow to tarry while he might go up to fetch a few which he had laid by for himself. Who, being more licorous than circumspect, went up without weapon, and, as he went up alone, possibly being marked of the negroes that were upon the trees, espying him what he did, perceiving him to be alone, and without weapon, dogged him. And

finding him occupied in binding his pompions together, came
behind him, overthrowing him, and straight cut his throat, as he
afterwards was found by his fellows, who came to the place for
him, and there found him naked.

On the 22nd the Captain went into the river called Callowsa,
with the two barques, and the John's pinnace, and the Salomon's
boat, leaving at anchor in the river's mouth the two ships, the
river being twenty leagues in, where the Portuguese rode. He
came thither on the 25th, and dispatched his business, and so
returned with two caravels laden with negroes.

On the 27th the Captain was advertised by the Portugals of a
town of the negroes called Bymba, being in the way as they
returned, where was not only a great quantity of gold, but also
that there were not above forty men and a hundred women and
children in the town, so that if he would give the adventure upon
the same, he might get a hundred slaves. With the which tidings
he being glad, because the Portugals should not think him to be
of so base a courage, but that he durst give them that, and greater
attempts; and being thereunto also the more provoked with the
prosperous success he had in other islands adjacent, where he had
put them all to flight and taken in one boat twenty together,
determined to stay before the town three or four hours, to see
what he could do; and thereupon prepared his men in armour
and weapon together, to the number of forty men well appointed,
having as their guides certain Portugals in a boat, who brought
some of them to their death. We landing boat after boat, and
divers of our men scattering themselves, contrary to the Captain's
will, by one or two in a company, for the hope that they had to
find gold in their houses, ransacking the same, in the meantime
the negroes came upon them, and hurt many (being thus scattered),
whereas if five or six had been together they had been able (as
their companions did) to give the overthrow to forty of them; and,
being driven down to take their boats, were followed so hardly by
a rout of negroes, who by that took courage to pursue them to
their boats, that not only some of them, but others standing on
shore, not looking for any such matter, by means that the negroes
did flee at the first, and our company remained in the town,
were suddenly so set upon that some with great hurt recovered
their boats; othersome, not able to recover the same, took the
water, and perished by means of the ooze. While this was doing,
the Captain, who, with a dozen men, went through the town,

returned, finding 200 negroes at the water's side, shooting at those in the boats, and cutting them in pieces which were drowned in the water, at whose coming they ran all away. So he entered his boats, and, before he could put off from the shore, they returned again, and shot very fiercely and hurt divers of them. Thus we returned back somewhat discomforted, although the Captain in a singular wise manner carried himself, with countenance very cheerful outwardly, as though he did little weigh the death of his men, nor yet the great hurt of the rest, although his heart inwardly was broken in pieces for it; done to this end, that the Portugals, being with him, should not presume to resist against him, nor take occasion to put him to further displeasure or hindrance for the death of our men: having gotten by our going ten negroes and lost seven of our best men, whereof Mr. Field, Captain of the Salomon, was one, and we had twenty-seven of our men hurt. In the same hour while this was doing there happened at the same instant a marvellous miracle to them in the ships, who rode ten leagues to seaward, by many sharks, or tiburons, who came about the ships; among which one was taken by the Jesus and four by the Salomon, and one, very sore hurt, escaped. And so it fell out of our men, whereof one of the Jesus' men and four of the Salomon's were killed, and the fifth, having twenty wounds, was rescued, and escaped with much ado.

On the 28th they came to their ships, the Jesus and the Salomon, and on the 30th departed from thence to Taggarin.

On the 1st of January the two barques and both the boats forsook the ships and went into a river called the Casserroes, and on the 6th having despatched their business, the two barques returned and came to Taggarin, where the two ships were at anchor. Not two days after the coming of the two ships thither, they put their water-cask ashore, and filled it with water, to season the same, thinking to have filled it with fresh water afterwards; and while their men were some on shore and some in their boats, the negroes set upon them in the boats and hurt divers of them, and came to the casks and cut off the hoops of twelve butts, which lost us four or five days' time, besides great want we had of the same. Sojourning at Taggarin, the Swallow went up the river about her traffic, where they saw great towns of the negroes, and canoes that had threescore men in apiece. There they understood by the Portugals of a great battle between them of Sierra Leone side and them of Taggarin. They of Sierra Leone had had prepared three hundred canoes to invade the other. The time was appointed not past six days after our departure from thence, which we would have seen, to the intent we might have taken some of them, had it not been for the death and sickness of our men, which came by the contagiousness of the place, which made us to make haste away.

On the 18th of January, at night, we departed from Taggarin, being bound for the West Indies, before which departure certain of the Salomon's men went on shore to fill water in the night. And as they came on shore with their boat, being ready to leap on land, one of them espied a negro in a white coat, standing upon a rock, being ready to have received them when they came on shore, having in sight also eight or nine of his fellows, some in one place leaping out and some in another, but they hid themselves straight again. Whereupon our men, doubting they had been a great company, and sought to have taken them at more advantage, as God would, departed to their ships, not thinking there had been such a mischief pretended toward them as then was indeed. Which the next day we understood of a Portugal that came down to us, who had trafficked with the negroes, by whom he understood that the King of Sierra Leone had made all the power he could to take some of us, partly from the desire he had to see what kind of people we were that had spoiled his people at the Idols, whereof he had news before our coming, and, as I judge also, upon other occasions provoked by the Tangomangos; but sure we were that the army was come down, by means that in the evening we saw such a monstrous fire, made by the watering place, that before was not seen, which fire is the only mark for the Tangomangos to know where their army is always. If these men had come down in the evening, they had done us great displeasure, for that we were on shore filling water; but God, who worketh all things for the best, would not have it so, and by Him we escaped without danger. His name be praised for it.

On the 29th of this same month we departed with all our ships from Sierra Leone towards the West Indies, and for the space of eighteen days we were becalmed, having now and then contrary winds and some tornados amongst the same calm, which happened to us very ill, being but reasonably watered for so great a company of negroes and ourselves, which pinched us all, and that which was worst, put us in such fear that many never thought to have reached to the Indies without great death of negroes and of themselves; but the Almighty God, who never suffereth His elect to perish, sent us, on the 16th of February, the ordinary Breeze,* which is the north-east wind, which never left us till we came to an island of the cannibals called Dominica, where we arrived on the 9th of March, upon a Saturday. And because it was the most desolate place in all the island we could see no cannibals, but some of their houses where they dwelled, and, as it should seem, forsook the place for want of fresh water; for we could find none there but rain-water and such as fell from the hills and remained as a puddle in the dale, whereof we filled for our negroes. The cannibals of that island, and also others adjacent, are the most desperate warriors that are in the Indies by the Spaniards' report, who are never able to conquer them; and they are molested by them not a little when they are driven to water there in any of those islands. Of very late, not two months past, in the said island, a caravel, being driven to water, was in the night set upon by the inhabitants, who cut their cable in the halser, whereby they were driven ashore, and so taken by them and eaten. The Green Dragon of Newhaven, whereof was captain one Bontemps, in March also, came to one of those islands called Granada, and, being driven to water, could not do the same for the cannibals, who fought with him very desperately two days. For our part also, if we had not lighted upon the desertest place in all that island, we could not have missed, but should have been greatly troubled by them, by all the Spaniards' reports, who make them devils in respect of men.

On the 10th day at night we departed from thence, and on the 15th had sight of nine islands called the Testigos; and on the 16th of an island called Margarita, where we were entertained by the Alcalde, and had both beeves and sheep given to us for the refreshing of our men. But the Governor of the island would neither come to speak with our Captain, neither yet give him any licence to traffic; and, to displease us the more, whereas we had hired a pilot to have gone with us, they would not only not suffer him to go with us, but also sent word by a caravel out of hand to Santo Domingo to the Viceroy, who doth represent the King's person, of our arrival in those parts, which had like to have turned us to great displeasure by the means that the same Viceroy

---

* Spanish "Brisa," the ordinary name for the Trade-Winds.

did send word to Cape De la Vela, and to other places along the coast, commanding them that, by virtue of his authority and by the obedience that they owe to their Prince, no man should traffic with us, but should resist us with all the force they could. In this island, notwithstanding that we were not within four leagues of the town, yet were they so afraid, that not only the Governor himself, but also all the inhabitants, forsook their town, assembling all the Indians to them, and fled into the mountains, as we were partly certified, and also saw the experience ourselves, by some of the Indians coming to see us, who, by three Spaniards on horseback passing hard by us, went unto the Indians, having every one of them their bows and arrows, procuring them away who before were conversant with us.

Here, perceiving no traffic to be had with them, nor yet water for the refreshing of our men, we were driven to depart on the 20th day, and on the 22nd we came to a place in the main called Cumana, whither the Captain going in his pinnace, spake with certain Spaniards, of whom he demanded traffic; but they made him answer they were but soldiers newly come thither, and were not able to buy one negro. Whereupon he asked for a watering place, and they pointed him a place two leagues off called Santa Fé, where we found marvellously goodly watering, and commodious for the taking in thereof; for that the fresh water came into the sea, and so our ships had aboard the shore twenty fathom water. Near about this place inhabited certain Indians, who the next day after we came thither came down to us, presenting mill and cakes of bread, which they had made of a kind of corn called maize, in bigness of a pease, the ear whereof is much like to a teasel, but a span in length, having thereon a number of grains. Also they brought down to us hens, potatoes, and pines, which we bought for beads, pewter whistles, glasses, knives, and other trifles.

These potatoes be the most delicate roots that may be eaten, and do far exceed our parsnips or carrots. Their pines be of the bigness of two fists, the outside whereof is of the making of a pine-apple, but it is soft like the rind of a cucumber, and the inside eateth like an apple; but it is more delicious than any sweet apple sugared. These Indians being of colour tawny like an olive, having every one of them, both men and women, hair all black, and no other colour, the women wearing the same hanging down to their shoulders, and the men rounded, and without beards, neither men nor women suffering any hair to grow on any part of their body, but daily pull it off as it groweth.

* * * * * *

These people be very small feeders; for travelling they carry but two small bottles of gourds, wherein they put in one the juice of sorrel, whereof they have great store, and in the other flour of their maize, which, being moist, they eat, taking sometimes of the other. These men carry every man his bow and arrows, whereof some arrows are poisoned for wars, which they keep in a cane together, which cane is of the bigness of a man's arm, other some with broad heads of iron, wherewith they strike fish in the water; the experience whereof we saw not once or twice, but daily for the time we tarried there; for they are so good archers that the Spaniards for fear thereof arm themselves and their horses with quilted canvas of two inches thick, and leave no place of their body open to their enemies, saving their eyes, which they may not hide, and yet oftentimes are they hit in that so small a scantling. Their poison is of such force that a man being stricken therewith dieth within four-and-twenty hours, as the Spaniards do affirm; and, in my judgment, it is like there can be no stronger poison as they make it, using thereunto apples which are very fair and red of colour, but are a strong poison, with the which, together with venomous bats, vipers, adders, and other serpents, they make a medley, and therewith anoint the same.

* * * * * *

The beds which they have are made of Gossopine cotton, and wrought artificially of divers colours, which they carry about with them when they travel, and making the same fast to two trees, lie therein, they and their women. The people be surely gentle and tractable, and such as desire to live peaceably, or else had it been impossible for the Spaniards to have conquered them as they did, and the more to live now peaceably, they being so many in number and the Spaniards so few.

From hence we departed on the 28th, and the next day we passed between the mainland and the island called Tortuga, a very low island, in the year of our Lord God one thousand five hundred and sixty-five aforesaid, and sailed along the coast until the 1st of April, at which time the Captain sailed along in the Jesus' pinnace to discern the coast, and saw many Caribs on shore, and some, also, in their canoes, which made tokens unto him of friendship, and shewed him gold, meaning thereby that they would traffic for wares. Whereupon he stayed to see the manners of them; and so for two or three trifles they gave such things as they had about them, and departed. But the Caribs were very importunate to have them come on shore, which, if it had not been for want of wares to traffic with them, he would not have denied them, because the Indians which we saw before were very gentle people, and such as do no man hurt. But, as God would have it, he wanted that thing, which if he had had would have been his confusion. For these were no such kind of people as we took them to be, but more devilish a thousand parts, and are eaters and devourers of any man they can catch, as it was afterwards declared unto us at Burboroata, by a caravel coming out of Spain with certain soldiers, and a captain-general sent by the King for those eastward parts of the Indians, who, sailing along in his pinnace, as our Captain did to descry the coast, was by the Caribs called ashore with sundry tokens made to him of friendship, and gold shewed as though they desired traffic, with the which the Spaniard being moved, suspecting no deceit at all, went ashore amongst them. Who was no sooner ashore but, with four or five more, was taken; the rest of his company being invaded by them, saved themselves by flight; but they that were taken paid their ransom with their lives, and were presently eaten. And this is their practice, to toll with their gold the ignorant to their snares. They are bloodsuckers both of Spaniards, Indians, and all that light in their laps, not sparing their own countrymen if they can conveniently come by them. Their policy in fight with the Spaniards is marvellous; for they choose for their refuge the mountains and woods, where the Spaniards with their horses cannot follow them. And if they fortune to be met in the plain, where one horseman may overrun 100 of them, they have a device of late practised by them to pitch stakes of wood in the ground and also small iron pikes to mischief their horses, wherein they show themselves politic warriors. They have more abundance of gold than all the Spaniards have, and live upon the mountains; where the mines are in such number, that the Spaniards have much ado to get any of them from them; and yet sometimes by assembling a great number of them, which happeneth once in two years, they get a piece from them, which afterwards they keep sure enough.

Thus having escaped the danger of them, we kept our course along the coast, and we came the 3rd of April to a town called Burboroata,* where his ships came to an anchor, and he himself went ashore to speak with the Spaniards, to whom he declared himself to be an Englishman, and come thither to trade with them by way of merchandise, and therefore required licence for the same. Unto whom they made answer, that they were forbidden by the king to traffic with any foreign nation, upon penalty to forfeit their goods; therefore they desired him not to molest them any further, but to depart as he came, for other comfort he might not look for at their hands, because they were subjects and might not go beyond the law. But he replied that his necessity was such, as he might not do so; for being in one of the Queen's Armadas of England, and having many soldiers in them, he had need both of some refreshing for them, and of victuals, and of money also, without which he could not depart; and with much other talk persuaded them not to fear any dishonest part on his behalf towards them, for neither would he commit any such thing to the dishonour of his prince, nor yet for his honest reputation and estimation, unless he were too rigorously dealt with, which he hoped not to find at their hands, in that it should as well redound to their profit as his own; and also he thought they might do it without danger, because their princes were in amity one with another; and for our parts we had free traffic in Spain and Flanders, which are his dominions; and, therefore, he knew no reason why he should not have the like in all his dominions. To the which the Spaniards made answer that it lay not in them to give any licence, for that they had a governor to whom the government of those parts was committed, but if they

---

* Burburata, or Barbarotta, now in the territory of Venezuela.

would stay ten days, they would send to their governor, who was threescore leagues off, and would return answer, within the space appointed of his mind.

In the meantime they were content he should bring his ships into harbour, and there they would deliver him any victuals he would require. Whereupon the fourth day we went in, where being one day, and receiving all things according to promise, the captain advised himself that to remain thěre ten days idle, spending victuals and men's wages, and perhaps in the end receive no good answer from the governor, it were mere folly; and therefore determined to make request to have licence for the sale of certain lean and sick negroes which he had in his ship like to die upon his hands if he kept them ten days, having little or no refreshing for them, whereas other men having them they would be recovered well enough. And this request he was forced to make, because he had not otherwise wherewith to pay for victuals and for necessaries which he should take. Which request being put in writing and presented, the officers and town-dwellers assembled together, and finding his request so reasonable, granted him licence for thirty negroes, which afterwards they caused the officers to view, to the intent that they should grant to nothing but that were very reasonable, for fear of answering thereunto afterwards. This being passed, our captain, according to their licence, thought to have made sale, but the day passed and none came to buy, who before made show that they had great need of them, and therefore wist not what to surmise of them; whether they went about to prolong the time of the governor's answer, because they would keep themselves blameless, or for any other policy, he knew not, and for that purpose sent them word, marvelling what the matter was, that none came to buy them. They answered because they had granted licence only to the poor to buy those negroes of small price, and their money was not so ready as other men's of more wealth. More than that, as soon as ever they saw the ships, they conveyed away their money by their wives, that went into the mountains for fear, and were not yet returned, and yet asked two days to seek their wives and fetch their money. Notwithstanding, the next day divers of them came to cheapen, but could not agree of price, because they thought the price too high. Whereupon the captain, perceiving they went about to bring down the price, and meant to buy, and would not confess if he had licence, that he might sell at any reasonable rate, as they were worth in other places, did send for the principals of the town, and made a show he would depart, declaring himself to be very sorry that he had so much troubled them, and also that he had sent for the governor to come down, seeing now that his pretence was to depart; whereat they marvelled much, and asked him what cause moved him thereunto, seeing by their working it was in possibility to have his licence.

To the which he replied that it was not only a licence that he sought, but profit, which he perceived was not there to be had, and therefore would seek further; and withal showed them his writings what he paid for his negroes, declaring also the great charge he was at in his shipping and men's wages, and, therefore, to countervail his charges, he must sell his negroes for a greater price than they offered. So they, doubting his departure, put him in comfort to sell better there than in any other place. And if it fell out that he had no licence, that he should not lose his labour in tarrying, for they would buy without licence. Whereupon, the captain being put in comfort, promised them to stay, so that he might make sale of his lean negroes, which they granted unto. And the next day he did sell to some of them. Who having bought and paid for them, thinking to have had a discharge of the Customer for the custom of the negroes, being the king's duty, they gave it away to to the poor for God's sake, and did refuse to give the discharge in writing; and the poor, not trusting their words, for fear lest hereafter it might be demanded of them, did refrain from buying any more; so that nothing else was done until the governor's coming down, which was the fourteenth day, and then the captain made petition, declaring that he was come thither in a ship of the Queen's Majesty's of England, being bound to Guinea, and thither driven by wind and weather, so that being come thither, he had need of sundry necessaries for the reparation of the said navy, and also great need of money for the payment of his soldiers, unto whom he had promised payment; and therefore, although he would, yet would not they depart without it, and for that purpose he requested licence for the sale of certain of his negroes, declaring that although they were forbidden to traffic with strangers, yet as there was a great amity between their princes, and that the thing pertained to our queen's highness, he thought he might do their prince great service, and that it would be well taken at his hands to do it in this cause. The which allegations, with divers others put in request, were presented to the governor, who, sitting in council for that matter, granted his request for licence. But yet there fell out another thing, which was the abating of the king's customs, being upon every slave thirty ducats, which would not be granted unto.

Whereupon the captain perceiving that they would neither come near his price he looked for by a great deal, nor yet would abate the king's custom of that they offered, so that either he must be a great loser by his wares, or else compel the officers to abate the same king's custom, which was too unreasonable, for to a higher price he could not bring the buyers, therefore, on the 16th of April, he prepared one hundred men well armed with bows, arrows, arquebuses, and pikes, with which he marched to the townwards: and being perceived by the governor, he straight with all expedition sent messengers to know his request, desiring him to march no further forward until he had answer again, which incontinent he should have. So our captain, declaring how unreasonable a thing the king's custom was, requested to have the same abated, and to pay seven and a half per cent., which is the ordinary custom for wares through his dominions there, and unto this if they would not grant he would displease them. And this word being carried to the governor, answer was returned that all things should be to his content; and thereupon he determined to depart, but the soldiers and mariners, finding so little credit in their promises, demanded gages for the performance of the premisses or else they would not depart. And thus they being constrained to send gages, we departed, beginning our traffic, and ending the same without disturbance.

Thus having made traffic in the harborough until the 28th, our captain with his ships intended to go out of the road, and purposed to make show of his departure; because now the common sort having employed their money, the rich men were come to town, who made no show that they were come to buy, so that they went about to bring down the price, and by this policy the captain knew they would be made the more eager, for fear lest we departed, and they should go without any at all.

On the 29th, we being at anchor without the road, a French ship called the Green Dragon, of Newhaven, whereof one Bontemps was captain, came in, who saluted us after the manner of the sea, with certain pieces of ordnance, and we re-saluted him with the like again. With whom having communication, he declared that he had been at the Mine in Guinea, and was beaten off by the Portugals' galleys, and enforced to come thither to make sale of such wares as he had; and further, that the like was happened unto the

Minion; besides the Captain Davie Carlet and a merchant with a dozen mariners betrayed by the negroes at their first arrival thither, and remaining prisoners with the Portugals; and besides other misadventures of the loss of their men, happened through the great lack of fresh water, with great doubts of bringing home the ships; which was most sorrowful for us to understand.

Thus having ended our traffic here, on the 4th of May we departed, leaving the Frenchman behind us; the night before which the Caribs, whereof I have made mention before, being to the number of two hundred, came in their canoes to Burboroata, intending by night to have burned the town, and taken the Spaniards, who being more vigilant because of our being there, than was their custom, perceiving them coming, raised the town, who in a moment were on horseback (by means their custom is for all doubts to keep their horses ready saddled), in the night set upon them and took one; but the rest making shift for themselves, escaped away. But this one, because he was their guide, and was the occasion that divers times they had made invasion upon them, had for his travail a stake thrust through his fundament, and so out at his neck.

On the 1st of May aforesaid, we came to an island called Curaçao, where we had thought to have anchored, but could not find ground, and having let fall an anchor with two cables, were fain to weigh it again; and on the 7th, sailing along the coast to seek a harbour, and finding none, we came to an anchor where we rode open in the sea. In this place we had traffic for hides, and found great refreshing, both of beef, mutton, and lambs, whereof there was such plenty, that saving the skins, we had the flesh given us for nothing; the plenty thereof was so abundant, that the worst in the ship thought scorn not only of mutton, but also of sodden lamb, which they disdained to eat unroasted.

The increase of cattle in this island is marvellous, which from a dozen of each sort brought thither by the governor, in twenty-five years, he had a hundred thousand at the least, and of other cattle was able to kill, without spoil of the increase, fifteen hundred yearly, which he killeth for the skins, and of the flesh saveth only the tongues, the rest he leaveth to the fowl to devour. And this I am able to affirm, not only upon the governor's own report, who was the first that brought the increase thither, which so remaineth unto this day, but also by that I saw myself in one field, where a hundred oxen lay one by another all whole, saving the skin and tongue taken away. And it is not so marvellous a thing why they do thus cast away the flesh in all the islands of the West Indies, seeing the land is great and more than they are able to inhabit, the people few, and having delicate fruits and meats enough besides to feed upon, which they rather desire, and the increase which passeth man's reason to believe, when they come to a great number: for in Santo Domingo, an island called by the finders thereof Hispaniola, there is so great a quantity of cattle, and such increase thereof, that notwithstanding the daily killing of them for their hides, it is not possible to assuage the number of them; but they are devoured by wild dogs, whose number is such by suffering them first to range the woods and mountains, that they eat and destroy 60,000 a year, and yet small lack found of them. And no marvel, for the said island is almost as big as all England, and being the first place that was found of all the Indies, and long time inhabited before the rest, it ought, therefore, of reason to be most populous: and to this hour, the Viceroy and Council Royal abideth there, as the chief place in all the Indies, to prescribe orders to the rest for the King's behalf; yet have they but one city and thirteen villages in all the same island, whereby the spoil of them in respect of the increase is nothing.

On the 15th of the foresaid month, we departed from Curaçao, being not a little to the rejoicing of our Captain and us that we had there ended our traffic; but notwithstanding our sweet meat, we had sour sauce, for by reason of our riding so open at sea, what with blasts, whereby, our anchors being aground, three at once came home, and also with contrary winds blowing, whereby, for fear of the shore, we were fain to haul off to have anchor-hold, sometimes a whole day and a night we turned up and down; and this happened not once, but half a dozen times in the space of our being there.

On the 16th we passed by an island called Aruba, and on the 17th, at night, we anchored six hours at the west end of Cabo de la Vela, and in the morning, being the 18th, weighed again, keeping our course, in the which time the captain, sailing by the shore in the pinnace, came to the Rancheria, a place where the Spaniards use to fish for pearls, and there spoke with a Spaniard, who told him how far off he was from Rio de la Hacha, which because he would not overshoot, he anchored that night again, and on the 19th came thither; where having talk with the king's treasurer of the Indies resident there, he declared his quiet traffic in Burboroata, and showed a certificate of the same, made by the governor thereof, and therefore he desired to have the like there also; but the treasurer made answer that they were forbidden by the viceroy and council of Saint Domingo, who having intelligence of our being on the coast, did send express commission to resist us, with all the force they could, insomuch that they durst not traffic with us in no case, alleging that if they did, they should lose all that they did traffic for, besides their bodies at the magistrate's commandment. Our captain replied that he was in an armada of the Queen's Majesty's of England, and sent about other her affairs, but driven besides his pretended voyage, was enforced by contrary winds to come into those parts, where he hoped to find such friendship as he should do in Spain; to the contrary whereof he knew no reason, in that there was amity betwixt their princes. But seeing they would, contrary to all reason, go about to withstand his traffic, he would it should not be said by him, that, having the force he hath, to be driven from his traffic perforce; but he would rather put it in adventure to try whether he or they should have the better, and therefore willed them to determine, either to give him licence to trade, or else to stand to their own harms. So upon this it was determined he should have licence to trade, but they would give him such a price as was the one half less than he had sold for before; and thus they sent word they would do, and none otherwise, and if it liked him not, he might do what he would, for they were determined not to deal otherwise with him. Whereupon the captain, weighing their unconscionable request, wrote to them a letter, that they dealt too rigorously with him, to go about to cut his throat in the price of his commodities, which were so reasonably rated as they could not by a great deal have the like at any other man's hands. But seeing they had sent him this to his supper, he would in the morning bring them as good a breakfast. And therefore in the morning, being the 21st of May, he shot off a whole culverin to summon the town, and preparing one hundred men in armour, went ashore, having in his great boat two falcons of brass, and in the other boats double bases in their noses, which being perceived by the townsmen, they incontinent in battle array, with their drum and ensign displayed, marched from the town to the sands, with footmen to the number of a hundred and fifty, making great brags with their cries, and waving us ashore, whereby they made a semblance to have fought with us indeed. But our captain, perceiving them to brag, commanded the two falcons to be discharged at them, which put them in no small fear to see (as they afterward declared) such great pieces in a boat. At every shot they fell flat to the ground; and as we approached near unto them, they broke their array, and dispersed themselves so much for fear of the ordnance, that at last they all went away with their ensign. The horsemen, also, being about thirty, made as brave a show as might be, coursing up and down with their horses, their brave white leather targets in the one hand, and their javelins in the other, as though they would have received us at our landing. But when we landed, they gave ground, and consulted what they should do. For little they thought we should have landed so boldly; and, therefore, as the captain was putting his men in array, and marched forward to have encountered with them, they sent a messenger on horseback, with a flag of truce to the captain, who declared that the treasurer marvelled what he meant to do, to come ashore in that order, in consideration that they had granted to every reasonable request that he did demand. But the captain, not well contented with this messenger, marched forwards. The messenger prayed him to stay his men, and said if he would come apart from his men, the treasurer would come and speak with him, whereunto he did agree to commune together. The captain only with his armour, without weapon, and the treasurer on horseback with his javelin, was afraid to come near him for fear of his armour, which he said was worse than his weapon, and so keeping aloof communing together, granted in fine to all his requests. Which being declared by the captain to the company, they desired to have pledges for the performance of all things, doubting that otherwise, when they had made themselves stronger, they would have been at defiance with us; and seeing that now they might have what they would request, they judged it to be more wisdom to be in assurance, than to be forced to make any more labours about it. So upon this, gages were sent, and we made our traffic quietly with them. In the meantime while we stayed here, we watered a good breadth off from the shore, where, by the strength of the fresh water running into the sea, the salt water was made fresh. In this river we saw many crocodiles of various sizes, but some as large as a boat, with four feet, a long broad mouth, and a long tail, and whose skin is so hard that a sword will not pierce it. His nature is to live out of the water, as a frog doth, but he is a great devourer, and spareth neither fish, which is his common food, nor beasts, nor men, if he take them, as proof thereof was known by a Negro, who, as he was filling water in the river, was by one of them carried clean away and never seen after.

His nature is ever when he would have his prey, to cry and sob like a Christian body, to provoke them to come to him, and then he snatcheth at them, and thereupon came this proverb, that is applied unto women when they weep, *lachrymæ crocodili*, the meaning whereof is, that as the crocodile when he crieth goeth then about most to deceive, so doth a woman most commonly when she weeps. Of these the master of the Jesus watched one, and by the bank's side struck him with the pike of a bill in the side, and after three or four times turning in sight, he sunk down, and was not afterwards seen. In the time of our being in the rivers of Guinea, we saw many of a monstrous bigness, amongst which the captain, being in one of the barks coming down the same, shot a falcon at one, which very narrowly he missed, and with affear he plunged into the water, making a stream like the way of a boat.

Now while we were here, whether it were of a fear that the Spaniards doubted we would have done them some harm before we departed, or for any treason that they intended towards us, I am not able to say ; but then came thither a captain from some of the other towns, with a dozen soldiers upon a time when our captain and the treasurer cleared all things between them, and were in a communication of a debt of the governor of Burboroata, which was to be paid by the said treasurer, who would not answer the same by any means. Whereupon certain words of displeasure passed betwixt the captain and him, and parting the one from the other, the treasurer possibly doubting that our captain would perforce have sought the same, did immediately command his men to arms, both horsemen and footmen : but because the captain was in the river on the back-side of the town with his other boats, and all his men unarmed and without weapons, it was to be judged he meant him little good, having that advantage of him, that coming upon the sudden, he might have mischiefed many of his men : but the captain, having understanding thereof, not trusting to their gentleness, if they might have the advantage, departed aboard his ships, and at night returned again, and demanded amongst other talk, what they meant by assembling their men in that order, and they answered, that their captain being come to town did muster his men according to his accustomed manner. But it is to be judged to be a cloak, in that coming for that purpose he might have done it sooner, but the truth is, they were not of force until then, whereby to enterprise any matter against us, by means of pikes and arquebuses, whereof they have want, and were now furnished by our captain, and also three falcons, which having got in other places, they had secretly conveyed thither, which made them the bolder, and also for that they saw now a convenient place to do such a feat, and time also serving thereunto, by the means that our men were not only unarmed and unprovided, as at no time before the like, but also were occupied in hewing of wood, and least thinking of any harm: these were occasions to provoke them thereunto. And I suppose they went about to bring it to effect, in that I with another gentleman being in the town, thinking of no harm towards us, and seeing men assembling in armour to the treasurer's house, whereof I marvelled, and revoking to mind the former talk between the captain and him, and the unreadiness of our men, of whom advantage might have been taken, departed out of the town immediately to give knowledge thereof, but before we came to our men by a flight-shot, two horsemen riding a-gallop were come near us, being sent, as we did guess, to stay us lest we should carry news to our captain. But seeing us so near our men they stayed their horses, coming together, and suffering us to pass, belike because we were so near, that if they had gone about the same, they would have been espied by some of our men which then immediately would have departed, whereby they should have been frustrate of their pretence: and so the two horsemen rode about the bushes to espy what we did, and seeing us gone, to the intent they might shadow their coming down in post, whereof suspicion might be had, feigned a simple excuse in asking whether he could sell any wine, but that seemed so simple to the captain, that standing in doubt of their courtesy, he returned in the morning with his three boats, appointed with bases in their noses, and his men with weapons accordingly, whereas before he carried none: and thus dissembling all injuries conceived of both parts, the captain went ashore, leaving pledges in the boats for himself, and cleared all things between the treasurer and him, saving for the governor's debt, which the one by no means would answer, and the other, because it was not his due debt, would not molest him for it, but was content to remit it until another time, and therefore departed, causing the two barques which rode near the shore to weigh and go under sail, which was done because that our captain demanding a testimonial of his good behaviour there, could not have the same until he were under sail ready to depart: and therefore at night he went for the same again, and received it at the treasurer's hand, of whom very courteously he took his leave and departed, shooting off the bases of his boat for his farewell, and the townsmen also shot off four falcons and thirty arquebuses, and this was the first time that he knew of the conveyance of their falcons.

On the 31st of May we departed, keeping our course to Hispaniola, and on the 4th of June we had sight of an island, which we made to be Jamaica, marvelling that by the vehement course of the seas we should be driven so far to leeward; for setting our course to the west end of Hispaniola, we fell in with the middle of Jamaica, notwithstanding that to all men's sight it shewed a headland, but they were all deceived by the clouds that lay upon the land two days together, in such sort that we thought it to be the headland of the said island. And a Spaniard being in the ship, who was a merchant, and inhabitant in Jamaica, having occasion to go to Guinea, and being by treason taken by the negroes, and afterwards bought by the Tangomangos, was by our captain brought from thence, and had his passage to go into his country, who perceiving the land, made as though he knew every place thereof, and pointed to certain places which he named to be such a place, and such a man's ground, and that behind such a point was the harbour, but in the end he pointed so from one point to another that we were a lee-board of all places, and found ourselves at the west end of Jamaica before we were aware of it, and being once to leeward, there was no getting up again, so that by trusting of the Spaniard's knowledge, our captain sought not to speak with any of the inhabitants, which if he had not made himself sure of, he would have done as his custom was in other places: but this man was a plague not only to our captain, who made him lose by overshooting the place £2,000 by hides, which he might have got, but also to himself, who being three years out of his country, and in great misery in Guinea, both among the negroes and Tangomangos, and in hope to come to his wife and friends, as he made sure account, in that at his going into the pinnace, when he went to shore he put on his new clothes, and for joy flung away his old, could not afterwards find any habitation, neither there nor in all Cuba, which we sailed all along, but it fell out ever by one occasion or other that we were put beside the same, so that he was fain to be brought into England, and it happened to him as it did to a duke of Samaria, when the Israelites were besieged, and were in great misery with hunger, and being told by the Prophet Elizæus, that a bushel of flour should be sold for a shekel, would not believe him, but thought it unpossible ; and for that cause Elizæus prophesied he should see the same done, but he should not eat thereof: so this man being absent three years, and not ever thinking to have seen his own country, did see the same, went upon it, and yet was it not his fortune to come to it, or to any habitation, whereby to remain with his friends according to his desire.

Thus having sailed along the coast two days, we departed on the 7th of June, being made to believe by the Spaniard that it was not Jamaica, but rather Hispaniola. Of which opinion the captain also was, because that which he made Jamaica seemed to be but a piece of the land, and thereby took it rather to be Hispaniola, by the lying of the coast; and also for that being ignorant of the force of the current, he could not believe he was so far driven to leeward, and therefore setting his course to Jamaica, and after certain days not finding the same, perceived then certainly that the island which he was at before was Jamaica, and that the clouds did deceive him, whereof he marvelled not a little. And this mistaking of the place came to as ill a pass as the overshooting of Jamaica : for by this did he also overpass a place in Cuba, called Santa Cruz, where, as he was informed, was great store of hides to be had. And thus being disappointed of two of his ports, where he thought to have raised great profit by his traffic, and also to have found great refreshing of victuals and water for his men, he was now disappointed greatly. And such want he had of fresh water, that he was forced to seek the shore to obtain the same, which he had sight of after certain days overpassed with storms and contrary winds, but yet not of the main of Cuba, but of certain islands in number two hundred, whereof the most part were desolate of inhabitants. By the which islands the captain passing in his pinnace, could find no fresh water until he came to an island bigger than all the rest, called the Isle of Pinas, where we anchored with our ships on the 16th of June, and found water, which although it were neither so toothsome as running water, by the means it is standing, and but the water of rain, and also being near the sea, was brackish, yet did we not refuse it, but were more glad thereof, as the time then required, than we should have been another time with fine conduit water. Thus being reasonably watered we were desirous to depart, because the place was not very convenient for such ships of charge as they were, because there were many shoals to leeward, which also lay open to the sea for any wind that should blow : and therefore the captain made the more haste away, which was not unneedful : for little sooner were their anchors weighed and foresail set, but there arose such a storm, that they had not much to spare for doubling out of the shoals: for one of the barques not being fully ready as the rest, was fain for haste to cut the cable in the hawse, and lose both anchor and cable to save herself.

Thus on the 17th of June we departed, and on the 20th we fell with the west end of Cuba, called Cape St. Antony, where for the space of three days we doubled along, till we came beyond the shoals, which are twenty leagues beyond St. Antony. And the ordinary breeze taking us, which is the north-east wind, put us on the 24th from the shore, and therefore we went to the north-west to fetch wind, and also to the coast of Florida to have the help of the current, which was judged to have set to the eastward: so on the 29th we found ourselves in twenty-seven degrees, and in the soundings of Florida, where we kept ourselves the space of four days, sailing along the coast as near as we could, in ten or twelve fathom water, having all the while no sight of land.

On the 5th of July we had sight of certain islands of sand, called the Tortugas (which is low land) where the captain went in with his pinnace, and found such a number of birds, that in half-an-hour he laded her with them; and if they had been ten boats more they might have done the like. These islands bear the name of Tortoises, because of the number of them which there do breed, whose nature is to live both in the water and upon land also, but breed only upon the shore, in making a great pit wherein they lay eggs, to the number of three or four hundred, and covering them with sand, they are hatched by the heat of the sun; and by this means cometh the great increase. Of these we took very great ones, which have both back and belly all of bone, of the thickness of an inch: the fish whereof we proved, eating much like veal; and finding a number of eggs in them, tasted also of them, but they did eat very sweetly. Here we anchored six hours, and then a fair gale of wind springing, we weighed anchor, and made sail towards Cuba, whither we came on the sixth day, and weathered as far as the Table, being a hill so called, because of the form thereof; here we lay off and on all night, to keep that we had gotten to windward, intending to have watered in the morning, if we could have done it, or else if the wind had come larger, to have plied to windward to Havana, which is a harbour whereunto all the fleet of the Spaniards, come, and do there tarry to have one the company of another. This hill we thinking to have been the Table, made account (as it was indeed) that Havana was but eight leagues to windward, but by the persuasion of a Frenchman, who made the captain believe he knew the Table very well, and had been at Havana, said that it was not the Table, and that the Table was much higher, and nearer to the sea-side, and that there was no plain ground to the eastward, nor hills to the westward, but all was contrary, and that behind the hills to the westward was Havana. To which persuasion credit being given by some, and they not of the worst, the captain was persuaded to go to leeward, and so sailed along on the seventh and eighth days, finding no habitation, nor no other Table; and then perceiving his folly to give ear to such praters, was not a little sorry, both because he did consider what time he should spend ere he could get so far to windward again, which would have been, with the weathering which we had, ten or twelve days' work, and what it would have been longer he knew not, and (that which was worst) he had not above a day's water, and therefore knew not what shift to make: but in fine, because the want was such, that his men could not live with it, he determined to seek water, and to go farther to leeward, to a place (as it is set in the card) called Rio de los Puercos, which he was in doubt of, both whether it were inhabited, and whether there were water or not, and whether for the shoals he might have such access with his ships, that he might conveniently take in the same. And while we were in these troubles, and kept our way to the place aforesaid, Almighty God our guide (who would not suffer us to run into any further danger, which we had been like to have incurred, if we had ranged the coast of Florida along as we did before, which is so dangerous, by reports, that no ship escapeth which cometh thither, as the Spaniards have very well proved the same) sent us on the eighth day at night a fair westerly wind, whereupon the captain and company consulted, determining not to refuse God's gift, but every man was contented to pinch his own belly, whatsoever had happened; and taking the said wind, on the 9th day of July got to the Table, and sailing the same night, unawares overshot Havana; at which place we thought to have watered: but the next day, not knowing that we had overshot the same, sailed along the coast seeking it, and the eleventh day in the morning, by certain known marks, we understood that we had overshot it twenty leagues; in which coast ranging we found no convenient watering place, whereby there was no remedy but to disembogue, and to water upon the coast of Florida; for, to go further to the eastward we could not for the shoals, which are very dangerous; and because the current shooteth to the north-east, we doubted by the force thereof to be set upon them, and therefore durst not approach them; so making but reasonable way the day aforesaid and all the night, the twelfth day in the morning we fell in with the islands upon the cape of Florida, which we could scant double, by the means that fearing the shoals to the eastwards, and doubting the current coming out of the west, which was not of that force that we made account of, for we felt little or none till we fell with the cape, and then felt such a current that, bearing all sails against the same, yet were driven back again a great pace; the experience whereof we had by the Jesus pinnace, and the Salomon's boat, which were sent the same day in the afternoon, whiles the ships were becalmed, to see if they could find any water upon the islands aforesaid, who spent a great part of the day in rowing thither, being further off than they deemed it to be; and in the meantime a fair gale of wind springing at sea, the ships departed, making a sign to them to come away, who, although they saw them depart, because they were so near the shore, would not lose all the labour they had taken, but determined to keep their way, and see if there were any water to be had, making no account but to find the ships well enough; but they spent so much time in filling the water which they had found, that the night was come before they could make an end. And having lost the sight of the ships, they rowed what they could, but were wholly ignorant which way they should seek them again; as indeed there was a more doubt than they knew of; for when they departed the ships were in no current, and sailing but a mile further, they found one so strong, that bearing all sails it could not prevail against the same, but were driven back; whereupon the captain sent the Salomon with the other two barques to bear near the shore all night, because the current was less there a great deal, and to bear light, with shooting off a piece now and then, to the intent the boats might better know how to come to them.

The Jesus also bare a light in her top-gallant, and shot off a piece also now and then, but the night passed, and the morning was come, being the thirteenth day, and no news could be heard of them; but the ships and barques ceased not to look still for them, yet they thought it was all in vain, by the means they heard not of them all the night past; and therefore determined to tarry no longer, seeking for them till noon, and if they heard no news, then they would depart to the Jesus, who perforce (by the vehemency of the current) was carried almost out of sight; but as God would have it, now time being come, and they having tacked about in the pinnace's top, had sight of them and took them up: they in the boats, being to the number of one-and-twenty, having sight of the ships, and seeing them tacking about, whereas before at the first sight of them they did greatly rejoice, were now in a greater perplexity than ever they were; for by this they thought themselves utterly forsaken, whereas before they were in some hope to have found them. Truly God wrought marvellously for them, for they themselves having no victuals but water, and being sore oppressed with hunger, were not of opinion to bestow any further time in seeking the ships than that present noon-time; so that if they had not at that instant espied them, they had gone to the shore to have made provision for victuals, and with such things as they could have gotten, either to have gone for that part of Florida where the Frenchmen were planted (which would have been very hard for them to have done, because they wanted victuals to bring them thither, being a hundred and twenty leagues off), or else to have remained among the Floridians, at whose hands they were put in comfort by a Frenchman, who was with them, that had remained in Florida at the first finding thereof, a whole year together, to receive victuals sufficient and gentle entertainment, if need were for a year or two, until which time God might have provided for them. But how contrary this would have fallen out to their expectations, it is hard to judge, seeing those people of the coast of Florida are of more savage and fierce nature, and more valiant than any of the rest; which the Spaniards well proved, who being five hundred men who intended there to land, returned few or none of them, but were enforced to forsake the same; and of their cruelty mention is made in the book of Decades, of a friar, who, taking upon him to persuade the people to subjection, was by them taken, and his skin cruelly pulled over his ears, and his flesh eaten.

In these Islands they being ashore found a dead man, dried in a manner whole, with other heads and bodies of men; so that these sorts of men are eaters of the flesh of men, as well as the cannibals. But to return to our purpose.

The fourteenth day the ship and barques came to the Jesus, bringing them news of the recovery of the men, which was not a little to the rejoicing of the captain and the whole company; and so then altogether they kept on their way along the coast of Florida, and the fifteenth day came to an anchor, and so from six-and-twenty degrees to thirty degrees and a-half, where the Frenchmen abode, ranging all the coast along, seeking for fresh water, anchoring every night because we would overshoot no place of fresh water, and in the day time the captain in the ship's pinnace sailed along the shore, went into every creek, speaking with divers of the Floridians, because he would understand where the Frenchmen inhabited; and not finding them in eight-and-twenty degrees, as it was declared unto him, marvelled thereat, and never left sailing along the coast till he found them, who inhabited in a river, by them called the river of May, and standing in thirty degrees and better. In ranging this coast along, the captain found it to be all an island, and therefore it is all low land, and very scant of fresh water; but the country was marvellously sweet, with both marish and meadow ground, and goodly woods among. There they found sorrel to grow as abundantly as grass, and where their houses were, great store of maize and mill, and grapes of great bigness, but of taste much like our English grapes. Also deer great plenty, which came upon the sands before them. Their houses are not many together, for in one house a hundred of them do lodge; they being made much like a great barn, and in strength not inferior to ours, for they have stanchions and rafters of whole trees, and are covered with palmetto leaves, having no place divided, but one small room for their king and queen. In the midst of this house is a hearth, where they make great fires all night, and they sleep upon certain pieces of wood hewn in for the bowing of their backs, and another place made high for their heads, which they put one by another all along the walls on both sides. In their houses they remain only in the nights, and in the day they desire the fields, where they dress their meat and make provision for victuals, which they provide only for a meal from hand to mouth. There is one thing to be marvelled at, for the making of their fire, and not only they, but also the negroes do the same, which is made only by two sticks, rubbing them one against another; and this they may do in any place they come, where they find sticks sufficient for the purpose. In their apparel the men only use deer skins, which skins are painted, some yellow and red, some black and russet, and every man according to his own fancy. They do not omit to paint their bodies also with curious knots, or antique work, as every man in his own fancy deviseth, which painting, to make it continue the better, they use with a thorn to prick their flesh, and dent in the same, whereby the painting may have better hold. In their wars they use a slighter colour of painting their faces, thereby to make themselves show the more fierce; which after their war is ended they wash away again. In their wars they use bows and arrows, whereof their bows are made of a kind of yew, but blacker than ours, and for the most part passing the strength of the negroes or Indians, for it is not greatly inferior to ours. Their arrows are also of a great length, but yet of reeds, like other Indians, but varying in two points, both in length and also for nocks and feathers, which the others lack, whereby they shoot very steady; the heads of the same are vipers' teeth, bones of fishes, flint stones, piked points of knives, which they having gotten of the Frenchmen, broke the same, and put the points of them in their arrow-heads; some of them have their heads of silver; other some that have want of these put in a kind of hard wood, notched, which pierceth as far as any of the rest. In their fight, being in the woods, they use a marvellous policy for their own safeguard, which is by clasping a tree in their arms, and yet shooting notwithstanding. This policy they used with the Frenchmen in their fight, whereby it appeareth that they are people of some policy; and although they are called by the Spaniards *Gente triste*, that is to say "Bad people," meaning thereby that they are not men of capacity; yet have the Frenchmen found them so witty in their answers that, by the captain's own report, a counsellor with us could not give a more profound reason.

The women also for their apparel use painted skins, but most of them gowns of moss, somewhat longer than our moss, which they sew together artificially, and make the same surplice-wise, wearing their hair down to their shoulders, like the Indians. In this river of May aforesaid the Captain, entering with his pinnace, found a French ship of fourscore ton, and two pinnaces of fifteen ton apiece by her, and speaking with the keepers thereof, they told him of a fort two leagues up, which they had būilt, in which their captain Monsieur Laudonnière was, with certain soldiers therein. To whom our Captain sending to understand of a watering place, where he might conveniently take it in, and to have licence for the same, he straight, because there was no convenient place but up the river five leagues, where the water was fresh, did send him a pilot for the more expedition thereof, to bring in one of his barques, which, going in with other boats provided for the same purpose, anchored before the fort, into the which our Captain went, where he was by the General, with other captains and soldiers, very gently entertained, who declared unto him the time of their being there, which was fourteen months, with the extremity they were driven to for want of victuals, having brought very little with them; in which place they, being two hundred men at their first coming, had in short space eaten all the maize they could buy of the inhabitants about them, and therefore were driven certain of them to serve a king of the Floridians against other his enemies for mill and other victuals, which having gotten, could not serve them, being so many, so long a time; but want came upon them in such sort that they were fain to gather acorns, which, being stamped small and often washed to take away the bitterness of them, they did use for bread, eating withal at sundry times roots, whereof they found many good and wholesome, and such as serve rather for medicines than for meats alone. But this hardness not contenting some of them, who would not take the pains so much as to fish in the river before their doors, but would have all things put in their mouths, they did rebel against the captain, taking away first his armour, and afterwards imprisoning him: and so, to the number of fourscore of them, departed with a barque and a pinnace, spoiling their store of victuals, and taking away a great part thereof with them, and so went to the islands of Hispaniola and Jamaica a-roving, where they spoiled and pilled the Spaniards; and having taken two caravels laden with wine and cassava, which is a bread made of roots, and much other victuals and treasure, had not the grace to depart therewith, but were of such haughty stomachs that they thought their force to be such that no man durst meddle with them, and so kept harbour in Jamaica, going daily ashore at their pleasure. But God, who would not suffer such evil-doers unpunished, did indurate their hearts in such sort that they lingered the time so long that a ship and galliasse being made out of St. Domingo, came thither into the harbour and took twenty of them, whereof the most part were hanged and the rest carried into Spain, and some (to the number of five-and-twenty) escaped in the pinnace and came to Florida, where, at their landing, they were put into prison; and incontinent four of the chiefest being condemned, at the request of the soldiers did pass the arquebusers, and then were hanged upon a gibbet. This lack of threescore men was a great discourage and weakening to the rest, for they were the best soldiers that they had; for they had now made the inhabitants weary of them by their daily craving of maize, having no wares left to content them withal, and therefore were enforced to rob them, and to take away their victual perforce, which was the occasion that the Floridians (not well contented therewith) did take certain of their company in the woods, and slew them; whereby there grew great wars betwixt them and the Frenchmen: and therefore they, being but a few in number, durst not venture abroad, but at such time as they were enforced thereunto for want of food to do the same; and going, twenty arquebusers in a company, were set upon by eighteen kings, having seven or eight hundred men, which with one of their bows slew one of their men, and hurt a dozen, and drove them all down to their boats; whose policy in fight was to be marvelled at; for having shot at divers of their bodies which were armed, and perceiving that their arrows did not prevail against the same, they shot at their faces and legs, which were the places that the Frenchmen were hurt in. Thus the Frenchmen returned, being in ill case by the hurt of their men, having not above forty soldiers left unhurt, whereby they might ill make any more invasions upon the Floridians, and keep their fort withal, which they must have been driven unto had not God sent us thither for their succour; for they had not above ten days' victuals left before we came. In which perplexity our Captain seeing them, spared them out of his ship twenty barrels of meal and four pipes of beans, with divers other victuals and necessaries which he might conveniently spare; and to help them the better homewards, whither they were bound before our coming, at their request we spared them one of our barques of fifty ton. Notwithstanding the great want that the Frenchman had, the ground doth yield victuals sufficient if they would have taken pains to get the same; but they, being soldiers, desired to live by the sweat of other men's brows; for while they had peace with the Floridians they had fish sufficient by weirs which they made to catch the same; but when they grew to wars the Floridians took away the same again, and then would not the Frenchmen take the pains to make any more. The ground yieldeth naturally grapes in great store, for in the time that the Frenchmen were there they made twenty hogsheads of wine. Also it yieldeth roots passing good, deer marvellous store, with divers other beasts and fowl serviceable to the use of man. These be things wherewith a man may live, having corn or maize wherewith to make bread; for maize maketh good savoury bread and cakes as fine as flour. Also it maketh good meal, beaten and sodden with water, and eateth like pap wherewith we feed children. It maketh also good beverage, sodden in water, and nourishable, which the Frenchmen did use to drink of in the morning, and it assuaged their thirst so that they had no need to drink all the day after. And this maize was the greatest lack they had, because they had no labourers to sow the same, and therefore to them that should inhabit the land it were requisite to have labourers to till and sow the ground; for they, having victuals of their own, whereby they neither rob nor spoil the inhabitants, may live not only quietly with them, who naturally are more desirous of peace than of wars, but also shall have abundance of victuals proffered to them for nothing; for it is with them as it is with one of us, when we see another man ever taking away from us, although we have enough besides, yet then we think all too little for ourselves. For surely we have heard the Frenchmen report, and I know it by the Indians, that a very little contenteth them; for the Indians, with the head of maize roasted, will travel a whole day; and when they are at the Spaniards' finding, they give them nothing but sodden herbs and maize: and in this order I saw threescore of them feed, who were laden with wares, and came fifty leagues off. The Floridians when they travel have a kind of herb dried, who, with a cane and an earthen cup in the end, with fire, and the dried herbs put together, do suck through the cane the smoke thereof, which smoke satisfieth their hunger, and therewith they live four or five days without meat or drink, and this all the Frenchmen used for this purpose; yet do they hold opinion withal that it causeth water and steam to void from their stomachs. The commodities of this land are more than are yet known to any man; for besides the land itself, whereof there is more than any king Christian is able to inhabit, it flourisheth with meadow, pasture-ground, with woods of cedar and cypress, and other sorts, as better cannot be in the world. They have for apothecary herbs, trees, roots, and gums great store, as storax liquida, turpentine, gum, myrrh, and frankincense, with many others whereof I know not the names. Colours, both red, black, yellow, and russet, very perfect, wherewith they so paint their bodies and deer-skins which they wear about them, that with water it neither fadeth away nor altereth colour. Gold and silver they want not; for at the Frenchmen's first coming thither they had the same offered them for little or nothing; for they received for a hatchet two pound weight of gold, because they knew not the estimation thereof. But the soldiers being greedy of the same, did take it from them, giving them nothing for it, the which they perceiving, that both the Frenchmen did greatly esteem it, and also did rigorously deal with them, at last would not have it be known they had any more, neither durst they wear the same for fear of being taken away. So that, saving at their first coming, they could get none of them. And how they came by this gold and silver the Frenchmen know not as yet, but by guess, who, having travelled to the south-west of the cape, having found the same dangerous by means of sundry banks, as we also have found the same, and there finding masts which were wrecks of Spaniards coming from Mexico, judged that they had gotten treasure by them. For it is most true that divers wrecks have been made of Spaniards having much treasure. For the Frenchmen having travelled to the capeward a hundred and fifty miles, did find two Spaniards with the Floridians, whom they brought afterward to their fort, whereof one was in a caravel coming from the Indies, which was cast away fourteen years ago, and the other twelve years, of whose fellows some escaped, othersome were slain by the inhabitants. It seemeth they had estimation of their gold and silver, for it is wrought flat and graven, which they wear about their necks; and others made round like a pancake, with a hole in the midst, to bolster up their breasts withal, because they think it a deformity to have great breasts. As for mines, either of gold or silver, the Frenchmen can hear of none they have upon the island, but of copper, whereof as yet also they have not made the proof, because they were but few men. But it it is not unlike but that in the main, where are high hills, may be gold and silver as well as in Mexico, because it is all one main. The Frenchmen obtained pearls of them of great bigness, but they were black, by means of roasting of them; for they do not fish for them as the Spaniards do, but for their meat. For the Spaniards use to keep daily a-fishing some two or three hundred Indians, some of them that be of choice a thousand. And their order is to go in canoes, or rather great pinnaces, with thirty men in a-piece, whereof the one-half or most part be divers, the rest do open the same for the pearls. For it is not suffered that they should use dragging; for that would bring them out of estimation, and mar the beds of them. The oysters which have the smallest sorts of pearls are found in seven or eight fathom water; but the greatest, in eleven or twelve fathom.

The Floridians have pieces of unicorns' horns, which they wear about their necks, whereof the Frenchmen obtained many pieces. Of those unicorns they have many; for that they do affirm it to be a beast with one horn, which, coming to the river to drink, putteth the same into the water before he drinketh. Of this unicorn's horn there are of our company that, having gotten the same of the Frenchmen, brought home thereof to show. It is therefore to be presupposed that there are more commodities as well as that, which, for want of time and people sufficient to inhabit the same, cannot yet come to light; but I trust God will reveal the same before it be long, to the great profit of them that shall take it in hand. Of beasts in this country besides deer, foxes, hares, polecats, coneys, ounces, and leopards, I am not able certainly to say; but it is thought that there are lions and tigers as well as unicorns—lions especially, if it be true that is said of the enmity between them and the unicorns; for there is no beast but hath his enemy, as the coney the polecat, a sheep the wolf, the elephant the rhinoceros, and so of other beasts the like, insomuch that whereas the one is the other cannot be missing. And seeing I have made mention of the beasts of this country, it shall not be from my purpose to speak also of the venomous beasts, as crocodiles, whereof there is great abundance, adders of great bigness, whereof our men killed some of a yard and a half long. Also I heard a miracle of one of these adders, upon the which a falcon seizing, the said adder did clasp her tail about her, which the French captain seeing, came to the rescue of the falcon, and took her, slaying the adder; and this falcon being wild, he did reclaim her, and kept her for the space of two months, at which time for very want of meat he was fain to cast her off. On these adders the Frenchmen did feed, to no little admiration of us, and affirmed the same to be a delicate meat. And the captain of the Frenchmen saw also a serpent with three heads and four feet, of the bigness of a great spaniel, which for want of an arquebus he durst not attempt to slay. Of fish, also, they have in the river pike, roach, salmon, trout, and divers other small fishes, and of great fish, some of the length of a man and longer, being of bigness accordingly, having a snout much like a sword of a yard long. There be also of sea-fishes, which we saw coming along the coast, flying, which are of the bigness of a smelt, the biggest sort whereof have four wings, but the others have but two. Of these we saw coming out of Guinea a hundred in a company, which, being chased by the gilt-heads, otherwise called the bonitos, do, to avoid them the better, take their flight out of the water; but yet are they not able to fly far, because of the drying of their wings, which serve them not to fly but when they are moist, and therefore when they can fly no further, they fall into the water, and having wet their wings, take a new flight again. These bonitos be of bigness like a carp, and in colour like a mackerel; but it is the swiftest fish in swimming that is, and followeth her prey very fiercely, not only in the water, but also out of the water; for as the flying-fish taketh her flight, so doth this bonito leap after them, and taketh them sometimes above the water. There were some of those bonitos which, being galled by a fizgig,* did follow our ship coming out of Guinea 500 leagues. There is a sea-fowl, also, that chaseth this flying-fish as well as the bonito; for as the flying-fish taketh her flight, so doth this fowl pursue to take her, which to behold is a greater pleasure than hawking; for both the flights are as pleasant, and also more often than a hundred times; for the fowl can fly no way but one or other lighteth in her paws, the number of them are so abundant. There is an innumerable young fry of these flying fishes, which commonly keep about the ship, and are not so big as butterflies, and yet by flying do avoid the unsatiableness of the bonito. Of the bigger sort of these fishes we took many, which both night and day flew into the sails of our ship, and there was not one of them which was not worth a bonito; for being put upon a hook drabbling in the water, the bonito would leap thereat, and so was taken. Also we took many with a white cloth made fast to a hook, which being tied so short in the water that it might leap out and in, the greedy bonito, thinking it to be a flying fish, leapeth thereat, and so is deceived. We took also dolphins, which are of very goodly colour and proportion to behold, and no less delicate in taste. Fowls also there be many, both upon land and upon sea; but concerning them on the land I am not able to name

---

* Spanish, Fisga, a small trident with barbed points, fixed on a staff ten or twelve feet long, attached by a long cord to the ship's side. It is still in use for catching the dolphin and bonito.

them, because my abode was there so short. But for the fowl of the fresh rivers these two I noted to be the chief—whereof the flamingo is one, having all red feathers and long red legs like a heron, a neck according to the bill, red, whereof the upper neb hangeth an inch over the nether; and an egript, which is all white as the swan, with legs like to a heronshaw, and of bigness accordingly; but it hath in her tail feathers of so fine a plume, that it passeth the ostrich's feather. Of the sea-fowl above all other not common in England, I noted the pelican, which is feigned to be the lovingest bird that is, which, rather than her young should want, will spare her heart's blood out of her belly; but for all this lovingness she is very deformed to behold, for she is of colour russet. Notwithstanding, in Guinea I have seen them as white as a swan, having legs like the same and a body like a heron, with a long neck and a thick long beak, from the nether jaw whereof down to the breast passeth a skin of such a bigness as is able to receive a fish as big as one's thigh, and this her big throat and long bill doth make her seem so ugly.

Here I have declared the estate of Florida and the commodities therein to this day known, which although it may seem unto some, by the means that the plenty of gold and silver is not so abundant as in other places, that the cost bestowed upon the same will not be able to quit the charges, yet am I of the opinion that, by that which I have seen in other islands of the Indians, where such increase of cattle hath been, that of twelve head of beasts in five-and-twenty years did in the hides of them raise a thousand pounds profit yearly, that the increase of cattle only would raise profit sufficient for the same. For we may consider, if so small a portion did raise so much gains in such short time, what would a greater do in many years? And surely I may this affirm, that the ground of the Indians for the breed of catttle is not in any point to be compared to this of Florida, which all the year long is so green as any time in the summer with us; which surely is not to be marvelled at, seeing the country standeth in so watery a climate; for once a day, without fail, they have a shower of rain, which, by means of the country itself, which is dry and more fervent hot than ours, doth make all things to flourish therein. And because there is not the thing we all seek for, being rather desirous of present gains, I do therefore affirm the attempt thereof to be more requisite for a prince, who is of power able to go through with the same, rather than for any subject.

From thence we departed on the 28th of July upon our voyage homewards, having there all things as might be most convenient for our purpose; and took leave of the Frenchmen that there still remained, who with diligence determined to make as great speed after as they could. Thus, by means of contrary winds oftentimes, we prolonged our voyage in such manner that victuals scanted with us, so that we were divers times (or rather the most part) in despair of ever coming home, had not God of His goodness better provided for us than our deserving. In which state of great misery we were provoked to call upon Him by fervent prayer, which moved Him to hear us, so that we had a prosperous wind, which did set us so far shot as to be upon the bank of Newfoundland on St. Bartholomew's Eve, and we sounded thereupon, finding ground at a hundred-and-thirty fathoms, being that day somewhat becalmed, and took a great number of fresh codfish, which greatly relieved us; and being very glad thereof the next day we departed, and had lingering little gales for the space of four or five days, at the end of which we saw a couple of French ships, and had of them so much fish as would serve us plentifully for all the rest of the way, the Captain paying for the same both gold and silver, to the just value thereof, unto the chief owners of the said ships; but they, not looking for anything at all, were glad in themselves to meet with such good entertainment at sea as they had at our hands. After which departure from them with a good large wind on the 20th of September we came to Padstow, in Cornwall, God be thanked, in safety, with the loss of twenty persons in all the voyage, and with great profit to the venturers of the said voyage, as also to the whole realm, in bringing home both gold, silver, pearls, and other jewels great store. His name, therefore, be praised for evermore. Amen.

HAWKINS.—THIRD VOYAGE.

NARRATIVE BY HAWKINS HIMSELF.

The THIRD troublesome VOYAGE *made with the* JESUS *of Lubeck, the* MINION, *and four other ships, to the parts of* GUINEA *and the* WEST INDIES, *in the years* 1567 *and* 1568, *by* MASTER JOHN HAWKINS.

The ships departed from Plymouth, the 2nd day of October, Anno 1567, and had reasonable weather until the seventh day. At which time, forty leagues north from Cape Finisterre, there arose an extreme storm, which continued four days, in such sort, that the fleet was dispersed, and all our great boats lost; and the Jesus, our chief ship, in such case as not thought able to serve the voyage. Whereupon in the same storm we set our course homeward, determining to give over the voyage. But the eleventh day of the same month, the wind changed with fair weather, whereby we were animated to follow our enterprise, and so did, directing our course with the islands of the Canaries, where, according to an order before prescribed, all our ships before dispersed, met at one of those islands, called Gomera, where we took water, and departed from thence on the 4th day of November, towards the coast of Guinea, and arrived at Cape Verde, on the 18th of November: where we landed 150 men, hoping to obtain some negroes, where we got but few, and those with great hurt and damage to our men, which chiefly proceeded of their envenomed arrows. And although in the beginning they seemed to be but small hurts, yet there hardly escaped any that had blood drawn of them, but died in strange sort, with their mouths shut some ten days before they died, and after their wounds were whole; where I myself had one of the greatest wounds, yet, thanks be to God, escaped. From thence we passed the time upon the coast of Guinea, searching with all diligence the rivers from Rio Grande unto Sierra Leone, till the 12th of January, in which time we had not gotten together a hundred and fifty negroes. Yet notwithstanding, the sickness of our men and the late time of the year commanded us away: and thus having nothing wherewith to seek the coast of the West Indies, I was with the rest of our company in consultation to go to the coast of the Mine, hoping there to have obtained some gold for our wares, and thereby to have defrayed our charge. But even in that present instant, there came to us a negro, sent from a king, oppressed by other kings his neighbours, desiring our aid, with promise that as many negroes as by these wars might be obtained, as well of his part as of ours, should be at our pleasure. Whereupon we concluded to give aid, and sent 120 of our men, which on the 15th of January assaulted a town of the negroes of our ally's adversaries, which had in it 8,000 inhabitants, being very strongly impaled and fenced after their manner. But it was so well defended, that our men prevailed not, but lost six men and forty hurt: so that our men sent forthwith to me for more help. Whereupon, considering that the good success of this enterprise might highly further the commodity of our voyage, I went myself, and with the help of the king of our side, assaulted the town, both by land and sea, and very hardly with fire (their houses being covered with dry palm leaves) obtained the town, and put the inhabitants to flight, where we took 250 persons, men, women, and children, and by our friend the king of our side, there were taken 600 prisoners, whereof we hoped to have had our choice. But the negro (in which nation is seldom or never found truth) meant nothing less: for that night he removed his camp and prisoners, so that we were fain to content us with those few which we had gotten ourselves.

Now had we obtained between four and five hundred negroes, wherewith we thought it somewhat reasonable to seek the coast of the West Indies; and there, for our negroes, and other our merchandise, we hoped to obtain whereof to countervail our charges with some gains. Whereunto we proceeded with all diligence, furnished our watering, took fuel, and departed the coast of Guinea on the 3rd of February, continuing at the sea with a passage more hard than before hath been accustomed till the 27th day of March, which day we had sight of an island, called Dominica, upon the coast of the West Indies, in fourteen degrees. From thence we coasted from place to place, making our traffic with the Spaniards as we might, somewhat hardly, because the king had straitly commanded all his governors in those parts by no means to suffer any trade to be made with us. Notwithstanding, we had reasonable trade, and courteous entertainment, from the Isle of Margarita unto Cartagena, without anything greatly worth the noting, saving at Capo de la Vela, in a town called Rio de la Hacha, from whence come all the pearls. The treasurer, who had the charge there, would by no means agree to any trade, or suffer us to take water. He had fortified his town with divers bulwarks in all places where it might be entered, and furnished himself with an hundred arquebusiers, so that he thought by famine to have inforced us to have put on land our negroes. Of which purpose he had not greatly failed, unless we had by force entered the town ; which (after we could by no means obtain his favour) we were enforced to do, and so with two hundred men brake in upon their bulwarks, and entered the town with the loss only of two men of our part, and no hurt done to the Spaniards, because after their volley of shot discharged, they all fled. Thus having the town with some circumstance, as partly by the Spaniards' desire of negroes, and partly by friendship of the treasurer, we obtained a secret trade : whereupon the Spaniards resorted to us by night, and bought of us to the number of 200 negroes. In all other places where we traded the Spanish inhabitants were glad of us and traded willingly.

At Cartagena, the last town we thought to have seen on the coast, we could by no means obtain to deal with any Spaniard, the governor was so strait. And because our trade was so near finished, we thought not good either to adventure any landing, or to detract further time, but in peace departed from thence on the 24th of July, hoping to have escaped the time of their storms which then soon after began to reign, the which they call Furicanos. But passing by the west end of Cuba, towards the coast of Florida there happened to us on the 12th day of August an extreme storm which continued by the space of four days, which so beat the Jesus, that we cut down all her higher buildings. Her rudder also was sore shaken, and withal was in so extreme a leak that we were rather upon the point to leave her then to keep her any longer; yet, hoping to bring all to good pass, we sought the coast of Florida, where we found no place nor haven for our ships, because of the shallowness of the coast. Thus, being in greater despair, and taken with a new storm which continued other three days, we were enforced to take for our succour the port which serveth the city of Mexico, called

Saint John de Ullua, which standeth in nineteen degrees. In seeking of which port we took in our way three ships which carried passengers to the number of an hundred, which passengers we hoped should be a means to us the better to obtain victuals for our money, and a quiet place for the repairing of our fleet. Shortly after this on the 16th of September we entered the port of Saint John de Ullua. And in our entry the Spaniards thinking us to be the fleet of Spain, the chief officers of the country came aboard us. Which being deceived of their expectation were greatly dismayed: but immediately when they saw our demand was nothing but victuals, were recomforted. I found also in the same port twelve ships which had in them by the report two hundred thousand pound in gold and silver, all which (being in my possession, with the king's island as also the passengers before in my way thitherward stayed) I set at liberty, without the taking from them the weight of a groat. Only, because I would not be delayed of my dispatch, I stayed two men of estimation and sent post immediately to Mexico, which was two hundred miles from us, to the Presidents and Council there, shewing them of our arrival there by the force of weather, and the necessity of the repair of our ships and victuals, which wants we required as friends to king Philip to be furnished of for our money: and that the Presidents and Council there should with all convenient speed take order, that at the arrival of the Spanish fleet, which was daily looked for, there might no cause of quarrel rise between us and them, but for the better maintenance of amity, their commandment might be had in that behalf. This message being sent away on the 16th day of September at night, being the very day of our arrival, in the next morning, which was on the seventeeth day of the same month, we saw open of the haven thirteen great ships. And understanding them to be the fleet of Spain, I sent immediately to advertise the general of the fleet of my being there, doing him to understand, that before I would suffer them to enter the port, there should some order of conditions pass between us for our safe being there, and maintenance of peace. Now it is to be understood that this port is made by a little island of stones not three feet above the water in the highest place, and but a bow-shoot of length any way. This island standeth from the main land two bow-shoots or more. Also it is to be understood that there is not in all this coast any other place for ships to arrive in safety, because the north wind hath there such violence, that unless the ships be very safely moored with their anchors fastened upon this island, there is no remedy for these north winds but death. Also the place of the haven was so little, that of necessity the ships must ride one aboard the other, so that we could not give place to them, nor they to us. And here I began to bewail that which after followed, for now, said I, I am in two dangers, and forced to receive the one of them. That was, either I must have kept out the fleet from entering the port, the which with God's help I was very well able to do, or else suffer them to enter in with their accustomed treason, which they never failed to execute, where they may have opportunity to compass it by any means. If I had kept them out, then had there been present shipwreck of all the fleet, which amounted in value to six millions, which was in value of our money £1,800,000, which I considered I was not able to answer, fearing the Queen's Majesty's indignation in so weighty a matter. Thus with myself revolving the doubts, I thought rather better to abide the jut of the uncertainty than the certainty. The uncertain doubt I account was their treason which by good policy I hoped might be prevented, and therefore, as choosing the least mischief, I proceeded to conditions. Now was our first messenger come and returned from the fleet with report of the arrival of a Viceroy, so that he had authority, both in all this province of Mexico (otherwise called Nueva España) and in the sea, who sent us word that we should send our conditions, which of his part should (for the better maintenance of amity between the princes) be both favourably granted and faithfully performed ; with many fair words how passing the coast of the Indies he had understood of our honest behaviour towards the inhabitants where we had to do, as well elsewhere as in the same port, the which I let pass. Thus, following our demand, we required victuals for our money, and licence to sell as much ware as might furnish our wants, and that there might be of either part twelve gentlemen as hostages for the maintenance of peace : and that the island, for our better safety, might be in our own possession, during our abode there, and such ordnance as was planted in the same island, which were eleven pieces of brass : and that no Spaniard might land in the island with any kind of weapon. These conditions at the first he somewhat misliked, chiefly the guard of the island to be in our own keeping. Which if they had had, we had soon known our fare : for with the first north wind they had cut our cables and our ships had gone ashore. But in the end he concluded to our request, bringing the twelve hostages to ten, which with all speed of either part were received, with a writing from the Viceroy signed with his hand and sealed with his seal of all the conditions concluded, and forthwith a trumpet blown with commandment that none of either part should be mean to violate the peace upon pain of death : and, further, it was concluded that the two generals of the fleets should meet, and give faith each to other for the performance of the premises, which, was so done. Thus at the end of three days all was concluded and the fleet entered the port, saluting one another as the manner of the sea doth require. Thus, as I said before, Thursday we entered the port, Friday we saw the fleet, and on Monday at night they entered the port. Then we laboured two days placing the English ships by themselves and the Spanish by themselves, the captains of each part and inferior men of their parts promising great amity of all sides : which, even as with all fidelity it was meant on our part, so the Spaniards meant nothing less on their parts, but from the main land had furnished themselves with a supply of men to the number of one thousand, and meant the next Thursday, being the 23rd of September, at dinner-time to set upon us on all sides. The same Thursday, in the morning, the treason being at hand, some appearance shewed, as shifting of weapon from ship to ship, planting and bending of ordnance from the ships to the island where our men warded, passing to and fro of companies of men more than required for their necessary business, and many other ill likelihoods, which caused us to have a vehement suspicion. And therewithal we sent to the Viceroy to enquire what was meant by it, which sent immediately strait commandment to unplant all things suspicious, and also sent word that he in the faith of a Viceroy would be our defence from all villanies. Yet we being not satisfied with this answer, because we suspected a great number of men to be hid in a great ship of 900 tons which was moored near unto the Minion, sent again to the Viceroy the master of the Jesus, which had the Spanish tongue, and required to be satisfied if any such thing were or not. The Viceroy now seeing that the treason must be discovered, forthwith stayed our master, blew the trumpet, and of all sides set upon us. Our men which warded ashore being stricken with sudden fear, gave place, fled, and sought to recover succour of the ships. The Spaniards, being before provided for the purpose, landed in all places in multitudes from their ships, which they might easily do without boats, and slew all our men on shore without mercy; a few of them escaped aboard the Jesus. The great ship which had by the estimation three hundred men placed in her secretly, immediately fell aboard the Minion. But by

God's appointment, in the time of the suspicion we had, which was only one half-hour, the Minion was made ready to avoid, and so loosing her headfasts, and hauling away by the sternfasts, she was gotten out: thus with God's help she defended the violence of the first brunt of these three hundred men. The Minion being passed out, they came aboard the Jesus, which also with very much ado and the loss of many of our men were defended and kept out. Then were there also two other ships that assaulted the Jesus at the same instant, so that she had hard getting loose, but yet with some time we had cut our headfasts and gotten out by the sternfasts. Now when the Jesus and the Minion were gotten about two ships' length from the Spanish fleet, the fight began so hot on all sides that within one hour the admiral of the Spaniards was supposed to be sunk, their vice-admiral burned, and one other of their principal ships supposed to be sunk, so that the ships were little able to annoy us.

Then is it to be understood, that all the ordnance upon the island was in the Spaniards' hands, which did us so great annoyance, that it cut all the masts and yards of the Jesus, in such sort that there was no hope to carry her away. Also it sunk our small ships, whereupon we determined to place the Jesus on that side of the Minion, that she might abide all the battery from the land, and so be a defence for the Minion till night, and then to take such relief of victuals and other necessaries from the Jesus, as the time would suffer us, and to leave her. As we were thus determining, and had placed the Minion from the shot of the land, suddenly the Spaniards had fired two great ships which were coming directly with us. And having no means to avoid the fire, it bred among our men a marvellous fear, so that some said, Let us depart with the Minion. Other said, Let us see whether the wind will carry the fire from us. But to be short, the Minion's men which had always their sails in a readiness, thought to make sure work, and so without either the consent of the captain or master cut their sail, so that very hardly I was received into the Minion.

The most part of the men that were left alive in the Jesus, made shift and followed the Minion in a small boat. The rest which the little boat was not able to receive, were enforced to abide the mercy of the Spaniards, which I doubt was very little. So with the Minion only and the Judith, a small barque of fifty ton, we escaped. Which barque the same night forsook us in our great misery. We were now removed with the Minion from the Spanish ships two bow-shoots, and there rode all that night. The next morning we recovered an island a mile from the Spaniards, where there took us a north wind, and being left only with two anchors and two cables (for in this conflict we lost three cables and two anchors) we thought always upon death which ever was present, but God preserved us to a longer time.

The weather waxed reasonable; and on the Saturday we set sail, and having a great number of men and little victuals, our hope of life waxed less and less. Some desired to yield to the Spaniards; some rather desired to obtain a place where they might give themselves to the infidels: and some had rather abide with a little pittance the mercy of God at sea. So thus, with many sorrowful hearts, we wandered in an unknown sea by the space of fourteen days, till hunger enforced us to seek the land: for hides were thought very good meat, rats, cats, mice, and dogs, none escaped that might be gotten, parrots and monkeys, that were had in great price, were thought there very profitable if they served the turn one dinner. Thus in the end, on the 8th day of October, we came to the land in the bottom of the same bay of Mexico in twenty-three degrees and a half, where we hoped to have found inhabitants of the Spaniards, relief of victuals, and place for the repair of our ship, which was so sore beaten with shot from our enemies and bruised with shooting off our own ordnance, that our weary and weak arms were scarce able to defend and keep our water. But all things happened to the contrary; for we found neither people, victual, nor haven of relief, but a place where having fair weather with some peril we might land a boat. Our people being forced with hunger desired to be set on land, whereunto I consented.

And such as were willing to land, I put them apart; and such as were desirous to go homewards, I put apart; so that they were indifferently parted a hundred of one side and a hundred of the other side. These hundred men we set on land with all diligence in this little place beforesaid; which being landed, we determined there to take in fresh water, and so with our little remain of victuals to take the sea.

The next day having a-land with me fifty of our hundred men that remained for the speedier preparing of our water aboard, there arose an extreme storm, so that in three days we could by no means repair aboard our ship: the ship also was in such peril that every hour we looked for shipwreck.

But yet God again had mercy on us, and sent fair weather; we had aboard our water, and departed on the 16th day of October, after which day we had fair and prosperous weather till on the 16th day of November, which day God be praised we were clear from the coast of the Indies, and out of the channel and gulf of Bahama, which is between the Cape of Florida, and the islands of Jucayo. After this growing near to the cold country, our men being oppressed with famine, died continually, and they that were left, grew into such weakness that we were scantly able to manage our ship, and the wind being always ill for us to recover England, we determined to go with Galicia in Spain, with intent there to relieve our company and other extreme wants. And being arrived on the last day of December in a place near unto Vigo called Ponte Vedra, our men with excess of fresh meat grew into miserable diseases, and died a great part of them. This matter was borne out as long as it might be, but in the end although there were none of our men suffered to get a-land, yet by access of the Spaniards, our feebleness was known to them. Whereupon they ceased not to seek by all means to betray us, but with all speed possible we departed to Vigo, where we had some help of certain English ships and twelve fresh men, wherewith we repaired our wants as we might, and departing on the 20th day of January, 1569, arrived in Mount's Bay, in Cornwall, on the 25th of the same month, praised be God therefore.

If all the miseries and troublesome affairs of this sorrowful voyage should be perfectly and thoroughly written, there should need a painful man with his pen, and as great a time as he had that wrote the lives and deaths of the martyrs.

JOHN HAWKINS.

FROBISHER.

HAWKINS was the pioneer of the Slave Trade, and of the old Virginian and West Indian colonization which rested upon it. Frobisher was the pioneer of Arctic exploration, and of the long and fruitless quest of a North-West Passage to the eastern shores of Asia.

The object of the expedition of Columbus was a Western Passage to China. It resulted in the discovery of the vast continent of America, which bars the way. This barrier, however, might, perhaps, be turned, either at the south end or at the north, or at both; and the search for a Western Passage was thus transformed, and became a search for a South-West and a North-West Passage. The former was discovered by Magellan, a Portuguese in the Spanish service, in 1520. The North-West Passage remained neglected for half a century longer, and was first sought by the English.

The wealth and power derived by Spain and Portugal from their distant enterprises had by this time excited a strong emulation in England. The enormous extent of the North-West coasts of America was unknown. It was believed that the continent tapered to the north, and that a North-West Passage existed leading directly from the Atlantic to the Pacific, round Labrador, corresponding on the map to the South-West Passage already proved to exist round Patagonia. If such a passage were practicable, it would shorten the sea route to China by at least one half. It was peculiarly adapted for the use and advantage of England, and its exploration was discussed in that country, just as the exploration of a Western Passage had been discussed in Italy and Spain eighty years before. The tractates of Gilbert, Willes, and Best, all printed in Hakluyt, prove how strongly public attention was concentrated on the scheme.

Martin Frobisher, a Yorkshireman resident in London, became the Columbus of this project. For fifteen years he fruitlessly endeavoured to procure the means of testing it. At length he succeeded, through the patronage of the Earl of Warwick, and in 1576 he started for the north-west, in a little barque of twenty-five tons burden, his master being one Christopher Hall, intending to turn the most northerly point of Labrador. In about a month's time Hall made the coast of Greenland, and sailed north-west with the Greenland current. This course brought the Gabriel to land on the ice-bound shores to the north of Hudson's Straits, which lead into Hudson's Bay. These straits Frobisher never saw; but finding an inlet somewhat further to the north, up which he sailed for sixty leagues, he conceived this to be the passage of which he was in search—America lying, as he supposed, on his left, and Asia on his right (p. 66). Frobisher at once hastened home with the news, intending to return next year suitably provided for a long exploration. A narrative of this first voyage, gathered from his own lips, was prefixed to Best's narratives of the subsequent voyages. On the second and third voyages Best accompanied him as Lieutenant, or second in command. Hakluyt's collection contains narratives of all the voyages by other hands; but they are less lively and picturesque than those of Best, who seems to have enjoyed the confidence of his "General" in a high degree.

One of the sailors in the first voyage had brought back from Frobisher's Straits a bit of black stone, which an Italian alchymist, in defiance of the London goldsmiths, pronounced to contain gold. This falsehood proved the ruin of Frobisher's subsequent expeditions. He was ordered to abandon his explorations, and load his ships with this ore, which proved to be worthless pyrites. When the truth became known, Frobisher and his schemes fell into utter discredit. His third and most costly expedition was ruined by severe weather, against which, as the narrative abundantly shows, Frobisher's crews struggled with true English pluck and endurance. The further prosecution of the project was deferred, and the very site of Frobisher's Strait was soon forgotten. Davis, a few years afterwards, renamed it Lumley's Inlet; but the name of the first discoverer has been recently restored. Frobisher was the pioneer of Arctic exploration, though he did nothing to develope it. It was sufficient for him to have made known the difficulties which beset it: and these difficulties were first grappled with by Davis and Hudson.

FROBISHER.—FIRST VOYAGE.

NARRATIVE BY GEORGE BEST.*

WHICH thing being well considered, and familiarly known to our general Captain Frobisher, as well for that he is thoroughly furnished of the knowledge of the sphere and all other skills appertaining to the art of navigation; as also for the confirmation he hath of the same by many years' experience both by sea and land, and being persuaded of a new and nearer passage to Cathay than by Capo de Buona Sperança, which the Portuguese yearly use: he began first with himself to devise, and then with his friends to confer, and laid a plain plot unto them that that voyage was not only possible by the north-west, but also, he could prove, easy to be performed. And further, he determined and resolved with himself to go make full proof thereof, and to accomplish or bring true certificate of the truth, or else never to return again, knowing this to be the only thing of the world that was left yet undone, whereby a notable mind might be made famous and fortunate. But although his will were great to perform this notable voyage, whereof he had conceived in his mind a great hope by sundry sure reasons and secret intelligence, which here, for sundry causes, I leave untouched; yet he wanted altogether means and ability to set forward and perform the same. Long time he conferred with his private friends of these secrets, and made also many offers for the performing of the same in effect unto sundry merchants of our country, about fifteen years before he attempted the same, as by good witness shall well appear (albeit some evil willers, which challenge to themselves the fruits of other men's labours, have

---

* A more accurate idea of this voyage may be gathered from the dry narrative of Christopher Hall, master of the Gabriel, printed in Hakluyt. The present narrative was preceded by a treatise intended to prove all parts of the earth, even the poles, equally habitable.

greatly injured him in the reports of the same, saying that they have been the first authors of that action, and that they have learned him the way, which themselves as yet have never gone); but perceiving that hardly he was hearkened unto of the merchants—which never regard virtue without sure, certain, and present gains,—he repaired to the Court (from whence, as from the fountain of our common wealth, all good causes have their chief increase and maintenance), and there laid open to many great estates and learned men the plot and sum of his device. And amongst many honourable minds which favoured his honest and commendable enterprise, he was specially bound and beholding to the Right Honourable Ambrose Dudley, Earl of Warwick, whose favourable mind and good disposition hath always been ready to countenance and advance all honest actions with the authors and executers of the same; and so by means of my lord his honourable countenance he received some comfort of his cause, and by little and little, with no small expense and pain, brought his cause to some perfection, and had drawn together so many adventurers and such sums of money as might well defray a reasonable charge to furnish himself to sea withal.

He prepared two small barques of twenty and five-and-twenty tons a-piece, wherein he intended to accomplish his pretended voyage. Wherefore, being furnished with the foresaid two barques, and one small pinnace of ten tons burden, having therein victuals and other necessaries for twelve months' provision, he departed upon the said voyage from Blackwall, on the 15th of June,* anno domini 1576.

One of the barques wherein he went was named the Gabriel, and the other the Michael; and, sailing north-west from England, upon the 11th of July he had sight of an high and ragged land, which he judged to be Friesland† (whereof some authors have made mention), but durst not approach the same by reason of the great store of ice that lay along the coast, and the great

---

* Best is wrong. Hall quitted his moorings at Ratcliffe on the 7th, and left Deptford on the 8th. In passing the Royal Palace of Greenwich, says Hall, "we shot off an ordinance, and made the best show we could. Her Majesty, beholding the same, commended it, and bade us farewell, with shaking her hand at us out of the window."

† The land was Greenland. Friesland was the name given to the Faroe Islands in the voyage of the brothers Zeni. Hall saw the rocky spires of the coast "rising like pinnacles of steeples" in the afternoon sun.

mists that troubled them not a little. Not far from thence he lost company of his small pinnace, which, by means of the great storm, he supposed to be swallowed up of the sea, wherein he lost only four men.

Also the other barque, named the Michael, mistrusting the matter, conveyed themselves privily away from him, and returned home, with great report that he was cast away.

The worthy captain, notwithstanding these discomforts, although his mast was sprung, and his topmast blown overboard with extreme foul weather, continued his course towards the north-west, knowing that the sea at length must needs have an ending, and that some land should have a beginning that way; and determined, therefore, at the least to bring true proof what land and sea the same might be so far to the north-westwards, beyond any that man hath heretofore discovered. And on the 20th of July he had sight of an high land, which he called Queen Elizabeth's Foreland,* after her Majesty's name. And sailing more northerly along that coast, he descried another foreland, with a great gut, bay, or passage, dividing as it were two main lands or continents asunder. There he met with store of exceeding great ice all this coast along, and coveting still to continue his course to the northwards, was always by contrary winds detained overthwart these straits, and could not get beyond. Within a few days after, he perceived the ice to be well consumed and gone, either there engulfed in by some swift currents or indrafts, carried more to the southwards of the same straits, or else conveyed some other way; wherefore he determined to make proof of this place, to see how far that gut had continuance, and whether he might carry himself through the same into some open sea on the back-side, whereof he conceived no small hope; and so entered the same on the 21st day of July, and passed above fifty leagues therein, as he reported, having upon either hand a great main or continent. And that land upon his right hand as he sailed westward he judged to be the continent of Asia, and there to be divided from the firm of America, which lieth upon the left hand over against the same.

This place he named after his name, Frobisher's Straits, like as Magellanus at the south-west end of the world, having discovered the passage to the South Sea (where America is divided from the

---

* The island to the N.W. of Resolution Island.

continent of that land, which lieth under the South Pole), and called the same straits, Magellan's Straits.

After he had passed sixty leagues into this aforesaid strait, he went ashore, and found signs where fire had been made.

He saw mighty deer that seemed to be mankind, which ran at him, and hardly he escaped with his life in a narrow way, where he was fain to use defence and policy to save his life.

In this place he saw and perceived sundry tokens of the peoples resorting thither;* and, being ashore upon the top of a hill, he perceived a number of small things floating in the sea afar off, which he supposed to be porpoises, or seals, or some kind of strange fish; but coming nearer, he discovered them to be men in small boats made of leather; and before he could descend down from the hill, certain of those people had almost cut off his boat from him, having stolen secretly behind the rocks for that purpose; where he speedily hasted to his boat, and bent himself to his halberd, and narrowly escaped the danger, and saved his boat. Afterwards he had sundry conferences with them, and they came aboard his ship, and brought him salmon and raw flesh and fish, and greedily devoured the same before our men's faces; and, to show their agility, they tried many masteries upon the ropes of the ship after our mariners' fashion, and appeared to be very strong of their arms, and nimble of their bodies. They exchanged coats of seals and bears' skins, and such like, with our men; and received bells, looking-glasses, and other toys, in recompense thereof again. After great courtesy, and many meetings, our mariners, contrary to their captain's direction, began more easily to trust them; and five of our men going ashore were by them intercepted with their boat, and were never since heard of to this day again; so that the captain being destitute of boat, barque, and all company, had scarcely sufficient number to conduct back his barque again. He could now neither convey himself ashore to rescue his men (if he had been able) for want of a boat; and again the subtle traitors were so wary, as they would after that never come within our men's danger. The captain, notwithstanding, desirous of bringing some token from thence of his being there, was greatly discontented that he had not before apprehended some of them; and, therefore, to deceive the deceivers he wrought a pretty policy; for

---

* The natives were first seen on the 19th of August.

knowing well how they greatly delighted in our toys, and specially in bells, he rang a pretty lowbell, making signs that he would give him the same who would come and fetch it; and because they would not come within his danger for fear, he flung one bell unto them, which of purpose he threw short, that it might fall into the sea and be lost; and to make them more greedy of the matter he rang a louder bell, so that in the end one of them came near the ship's side to receive the bell, which, when he thought to take at the captain's hand, he was thereby taken himself; for the captain, being readily provided, let the bell fall, and caught the man fast, and plucked him with main force boat and all into his barque out of the sea. Whereupon, when he found himself in captivity, for very choler and disdain he bit his tongue in twain within his mouth; notwithstanding, he died not thereof, but lived until he came in England, and then he died of cold which he had taken at sea.

Now with this new prey (which was a sufficient witness of the captain's far and tedious travel towards the unknown parts of the world, as did well appear by this strange infidel, whose like was never seen, read, nor heard of before, and whose language was neither known nor understood of any), the said Captain Frobisher returned homewards, and arrived in England in Harwich the 2nd of October following, and thence came to London, 1576, where he was highly commended of all men for his great and notable attempt, but specially famous for the great hope he brought of the passage to Cathay.

And it is especially to be remembered that at their first arrival in those parts there lay so great store of ice all the coast along, so thick together, that hardly his boat could pass unto the shore. At length, after divers attempts, he commanded his company, if by any possible means they could get ashore, to bring him whatsoever thing they could first find, whether it were living or dead, stock or stone, in token of Christian possession, which thereby he took in behalf of the Queen's Most Excellent Majesty, thinking that thereby he might justify the having and enjoying of the same things that grew in these unknown parts.

Some of his company brought flowers, some green grass, and one brought a piece of black stone, much like to a sea-coal in colour, which by the weight seemed to be some kind of metal or mineral. This was a thing of no account in the judgment of the captain at first sight; and yet for novelty it was kept in respect of the place from whence it came.

After his arrival in London, being demanded of sundry his friends what thing he had brought them home out of that country, he had nothing left to present them withal but a piece of this black stone. And it fortuned a gentlewoman, one of the adventurers' wives, to have a piece thereof, which by chance she threw and burned in the fire, so long, that at the length being taken forth, and quenched in a little vinegar, it glistered with a bright marquesite of gold. Whereupon the matter being called in some question, it was brought to certain gold-finers in London to make assay thereof, who gave out that it held gold, and that very richly for the quantity.* Afterwards the same gold-finers promised great matters thereof if there were any store to be found, and offered themselves to adventure for the searching of those parts from whence the same was brought. Some that had great hope of the matter sought secretly to have a lease at Her Majesty's hands of those places, whereby to enjoy the mass of so great a public profit unto their own private gains.

In conclusion, the hope of more of the same gold ore to be found kindled a greater opinion in the hearts of many to advance the voyage again. Whereupon preparation was made for a new voyage against the year following, and the captain more specially directed by commission for the searching more of this gold ore than for the searching any further discovery of the passage. And being well accompanied with divers resolute and forward gentlemen, Her Majesty then lying at the Right Honourable the Lord of Warwick's house, in Essex, he came to take his leave; and kissing Her Highness's hands, with gracious countenance and comfortable words departed toward his charge.

---

* Best is here not quite accurate. The London goldsmiths pronounced the ore worthless. An Italian, Agnello, reported it to contain gold.

FROBISHER.—SECOND VOYAGE.

NARRATIVE BY GEORGE BEST.*

A true report of such things as happened in the SECOND VOYAGE *of* CAPTAIN FROBISHER, *pretended for the discovery of a new passage to* CATHAY, CHINA, *and the* WEST INDIES. *Anno Domini 1577.*

Being furnished with one tall ship of Her Majesty's, named The Aid, of 200 tons, and two other small barques, the one named The Gabriel, the other The Michael, about 30 tons apiece, being fitly appointed with men, munitions, victuals, and all things necessary for the voyage, the said Captain Frobisher, with the rest of his company, came aboard his ships riding at Blackwall, intending (with God's help) to take the first wind and tide serving him, the 25th day of May, in the year of Our Lord God 1577.

On Whit Sunday, being the 26th of May, Anno Domini 1577, early in the morning we weighed anchor at Blackwall, and fell that tide down to Gravesend, where we remained until Monday at night.

On Monday morning, the 27th of May, aboard the Aid, we received all the communion by the minister of Gravesend, and prepared us as good Christians towards God, and resolute men for all fortunes; and towards night we departed to Tilbury Hope.

Tuesday, the 28th of May, about nine of the clock at night, we arrived at Harwich, in Essex, and there stayed for the taking in of

---

* The narrative of Dionis Settle, also given by Hakluyt, adds nothing to Best's information. The same may be said of the Third Voyage by Thomas Ellis.

certain victuals until Friday, being the 30th of May; during which time came letters from the Lords of the Council, straightly commanding our general not to exceed his complement and number appointed him, which was 120 persons. Whereupon he discharged many proper men, which with unwilling minds departed.

He also dismissed all his condemned men, which he thought for some purposes very needful for the voyage; and towards night, upon Friday, the 31st of May, we set sail and put to the seas again; and sailing northward, along the east coasts of England and Scotland, the 7th day of June we arrived in Saint Magnus' Sound, in Orkney Island, called in Latin *Orcades*, and came to anchor on the south side of the bay; and this place is reckoned from Blackwall, where we set sail first,   leagues.*

Here, our company going on land, the inhabitants of these islands began to flee as from the enemy. Whereupon the lieutenant willed every man to stay together, and went himself into their houses to declare what we were, and the cause of our coming thither, which being understood, after their poor manner they friendly entreated us, and brought us for our money such things as they had. And here our gold-finers found a mine of silver.

Orkney is the principal of the Isles of the Orcades, and standeth in the latitude of fifty-nine degrees and a half. The country is much subject to cold, answerable for such a climate, and yet yieldeth some fruits, and sufficient maintenance for the people contented so poorly to live. There is plenty enough of poultry, store of eggs, fish, and fowl. For their bread they have oaten cakes, and their drink is ewes' milk, and in some parts ale. Their houses are but poor without and sluttish enough within, and the people in nature thereunto agreeable. For their fire they burn heath and turf, the country in most parts being void of wood. They have great want of leather, and desire our old shoes, apparel, and old ropes, before money, for their victuals, and yet are they not ignorant of the value of our coin. The chief town is called Kyrway. In this island hath been sometime an abbey or a religious house, called Saint Magnus, being on the west side of the isle, whereof this sound beareth name through which we passed. Their governor or chief lord is called the Lord Robert Steward,

---

* The distances and latitudes were expressed in cypher in the original MS., so as to keep the course secret.

who at our being there, as we understood, was in durance at Edinburgh, by the Regent's commandment of Scotland.

After we had provided us here of matter sufficient for our voyage, the 8th of June we set sail again, and, passing through Saint Magnus' Sound, having a merry wind by night, came clear and lost sight of all the land; and keeping our course west-north-west by the space of two days, the wind shifted upon us, so that we lay in traverse on the seas, with contrary winds, making good, as near as we could, our course to the westward, and sometimes to the northward, as the wind shifted. And hereabouts we met with three sail of English fishermen from Iceland, bound homeward, by whom we wrote our letters unto our friends in England. We traversed these seas by the space of twenty-six days without sight of any land, and met with much drift-wood and whole bodies of trees. We saw many monstrous fishes and strange fowls which seemed to live only by the sea, being there so far distant from any land. At length God favoured us with more prosperous winds: and after we had sailed four days with good wind in the poop, the 4th of July, the Michael, being foremost ahead, shot off a piece of ordnance, and struck all her sails, supposing that they descried land, which, by reason of the thick mists, they could not make perfect. Howbeit, as well our account as also the great alteration of the water, which became more black and smooth, did plainly declare we were not far off the coast. Our general sent his master aboard the Michael—who had been with him the year before—to bear in with the place to make proof thereof, who descried not the land perfect, but saw sundry huge islands of ice, which we deemed to be not past twelve leagues from the shore. About ten o'clock at night, being the 4th of July, the weather being more clear, we made the land perfect, and knew it to be Friesland. And the height being taken here, we found ourselves to be in the latitude of sixty degrees and a half, and were fallen with the southernmost part of this land. Between Orkney and Friesland are reckoned   leagues.

This Friesland showeth a ragged and high land, having the mountains almost covered over with snow—along the coast full of drift-ice—and seemeth almost inaccessible, and is thought to be an island in bigness not inferior to England, and is called by some authors West Friesland, I think because it lieth more west than any part of Europe. It extendeth in latitude to the northward very far, as seemed to us; and appeareth by a description set out by two brethren—Venetians—Nicholaus and Antonius Zeni, who, being driven off from Ireland by a violent tempest, made shipwreck here, and were the first known Christians that discovered this land, about 200 years since; and they have in their sea-cards set out every part thereof, and described the condition of the inhabitants, declaring them to be as civil and religious people as we. And for so much of this land as we have sailed along, comparing their card with the coast, we find it very agreeable. This coast seemeth to have good fishing: for we, lying becalmed, let fall a hook without any bait, and presently caught a great fish called a halibut, which served the whole company for a day's meat, and is dangerous meat for surfeiting. And sounding about five leagues off from the shore, our lead brought up in the tallow a kind of coral, almost white, and small stones as bright as crystal; and it is not to be doubted that this land may be found very rich and beneficial if it were thoroughly discovered, although we saw no creature there but little birds. It is a marvellous thing to behold of what great bigness and depth some islands of ice be here —some seventy, some eighty fathoms under water, besides that which is above, seeming islands more than half a mile in circuit. All these ice are in taste fresh, and seem to be bred in the sounds thereabouts, or in some land near the Pole, and with the wind and tides are driven along the coasts. We found none of these islands of ice salt in taste, whereby it appeareth that they were not congealed of the ocean sea-water, which is always salt, but of some standing or little moving lakes, or great fresh waters near the shore, caused either by melted snow from tops of mountains, or by continual access of fresh rivers from the land, and intermingling with the sea-water, bearing yet the dominion, by the force of extreme frost, may cause some part of salt water to freeze so with it, and so seem a little brackish; but otherwise the main sea freezeth not, and therefore there is no *Mare Glaciale*, or Frozen Sea, as the opinion hitherto hath been. Our General proved landing here twice, but by the sudden fall of mists, whereunto this coast is much subject, he was like to lose sight of his ships; and being greatly endangered with the driving ice along the coast, was forced aboard, and fain to surcease his pretence till a better opportunity might serve; and having spent four days and nights sailing along this land, finding the coast subject to such bitter cold and continual mists, he determined to spend no more time therein, but to bear out his course towards the straits called Frobisher's Straits, after the General's name; who being the first that ever passed beyond fifty-eight degrees to the northwards, for anything that hath been yet known of certainty, of Newfoundland, otherwise called the continent or firm land of America, discovered the said straits this last year, 1576.

Between Friesland and the straits we had one great storm, wherein the Michael was somewhat in danger, having her steerage broken and her topmasts blown overboard; and being not past fifty leagues short of the straits by our account, we struck sail and lay a hull, fearing the continuance of the storm, the wind being at the northeast; and having lost company of the barques in that flaw of wind, we happily met again the 17th day of July, having the evening before seen divers islands of fleeting ice, which gave an argument that we were not far from land. Our General, in the morning, from the maintop, the weather being reasonably clear, descried land; but to be better assured, he sent the two barques two contrary courses, whereby they might descry either the South or North Foreland, the Aid lying off and on at sea, with a small sail, by an island of ice, which was the mark for us to meet together again. And about noon, the weather being more clear, we made the North Foreland perfect, which otherwise is called Hall's Island,* and also the small island bearing the name of the said Hall, whence the ore was taken up which was brought into England this last year (1576), the said Hall being present at the finding and taking up thereof, who was then Master in the Gabriel, with Captain Frobisher. At our arrival here, all the seas about this coast were so covered over with huge quantity of great ice, that we thought these places might only deserve the name of *Mare Glaciale*, and be called the Icy Sea.

This North Foreland is thought to be divided from the continent of the Northerland by a little sound called Hall's Sound, which maketh it an island, and is thought little less than the Isle of Wight, and is the first entrance of the Straits upon the north side, and standeth in the latitude of sixty-two degrees and fifty minutes, and is reckoned from Friesland   leagues. God having blessed us with so happy a land-fall, we bare into the Straits which run in next hand, and somewhat further up to the northward, and came as near the shore as we might for the ice; and upon the

---

* Now Cape Enderby.

18th of July our General, taking the gold-finers with him, attempted to go on shore with a small rowing pinnace, upon the small island where the ore was taken up, to prove whether there were any store thereof to be found: but he could not get in all that island a piece so big as a walnut, where the first was found. But our men which sought the other islands thereabouts found them all to have good store of the ore: whereupon our General with these good tidings returned aboard about ten o'clock at night, and was joyfully welcomed of the company with a volley of shot. He brought eggs, fowls, and a young seal aboard, which the company had killed ashore; and having found upon those islands gins set to catch fowl, and sticks new cut, with other things, he well perceived that not long before some of the country people had resorted thither.

Having therefore found those tokens of the people's access in those parts, and being in his first voyage well acquainted with their subtle and cruel disposition, he provided well for his better safety; and on Friday, the 19th of July, in the morning early, with his best company of gentlemen and soldiers, to the number of forty persons, went on shore, as well to discover the inland and habitation of the people, as also to find out some fit harbour for our ships. And passing towards the shore with no small difficulty by reason of the abundance of ice which lay along the coast so thick together that hardly any passage through them might be discovered, we arrived at length upon the main of Hall's greater island, and found there also, as well as in the other small islands, good store of the ore. And leaving his boats here with sufficient guard, we passed up into the country about two English miles, and recovered the top of a high hill, on the top whereof our men made a column or cross of stones heaped up of a good height together in good sort, and solemnly sounded a trumpet, and said certain prayers kneeling about the ensign, and honoured the place by the name of Mount Warwick, in remembrance of the Right Honourable the Lord Ambrose Dudley, Earl of Warwick, whose noble mind and good countenance in this, as in all other good actions, gave great encouragement and good furtherance. This done, we retired our companies, not seeing anything here worth further discovery, the country seeming barren and full of ragged mountains, and in most parts covered with snow.

And thus marching towards our boats, we espied certain of the country people on the top of Mount Warwick with a flag, wafting us back again and making great noise, with cries like the mowing of bulls, seeming greatly desirous of conference with us. Whereupon the General, being therewith better acquainted, answered them again with the like cries; whereat, and with the noise of our trumpets, they seemed greatly to rejoice, skipping, laughing, and dancing for joy. And hereupon we made signs unto them, holding up two fingers, commanding two of our men to go apart from our companies, whereby they might do the like. So that forthwith two of our men and two of theirs met together a good space from company, neither party having their weapons about them. Our men gave them pins and points and such trifles as they had. And they likewise bestowed on our men two bowcases and such things as they had. They earnestly desired our men to go up into their country, and our men offered them like kindness aboard our ships; but neither part (as it seemed) admitted or trusted the other's courtesy. Their manner of traffic is thus,—they do use to lay down of their merchandise upon the ground, so much as they mean to part withal, and so looking that the other party with whom they make trade should do the like, they themselves do depart, and then if they do like of their mart they come again, and take in exchange the other's merchandise; otherwise, if they like not, they take their own and depart. The day being thus well near spent, in haste we retired our companies into our boats again, minding forthwith to search along the coast for some harbour fit for our ships; for the present necessity thereof was much, considering that all this while they lay off and on between the two lands, being continually subject as well to great danger of floating ice, which environed them, as to the sudden flaws which the coast seemeth much subject unto. But when the people perceived our departure, with great tokens of affection they earnestly called us back again, following us almost to our boats. Whereupon our General, taking his Master with him, who was best acquainted with their manners, went apart unto two of them, meaning, if they could lay sure hold upon them, forcibly to bring them aboard, with intent to bestow certain toys and apparel upon the one, and so to dismiss him with all arguments of courtesy, and retain the other for an interpreter. The General and his Master being met with their two companions together, after they had exchanged certain things the one with the other, one of the savages, for lack of better merchandise, cut off the tail of his coat (which is a chief ornament among them) and gave it unto our General for a present. But he presently, upon a watchword given with his Master, suddenly laid hold upon the two savages. But the ground under foot being slippery with the snow on the side of the hill, their handfast failed, and their prey escaping ran away and lightly recovered their bow and arrows, which they had hid not far from them behind the rocks. And being only two savages in sight, they so fiercely, desperately, and with such fury assaulted and pursued our General and his Master, being altogether unarmed, and not mistrusting their subtilty, that they chased them to their boats, and hurt the General in the buttock with an arrow, who the rather speedily fled back, because they suspected a greater number behind the rocks. Our soldiers (which were commanded before to keep their boats) perceiving the danger, and hearing our men calling for shot, came speedily to rescue, thinking there had been a greater number. But when the savages heard the shot of one of our calivers (and yet having first bestowed their arrows) they ran away, our men speedily following them. But a servant of my Lord of Warwick, called Nicholas Conger, a good footman, and uncumbered with any furniture, having only a dagger at his back, overtook one of them; and being a Cornish man and a good wrestler, shewed his companion such a Cornish trick, that he made his sides ache against the ground for a month after. And so being stayed, he was taken alive and brought away, but the other escaped. Thus with their strange and new prey our men repaired to their boats, and passed from the main to a small island of a mile in compass, where they resolved to tarry all night; for even now a sudden storm was grown so great at sea, that by no means they could recover their ships. And here every man refreshed himself with a small portion of victuals, which was laid into the boats for their dinners, having neither eat nor drunk all the day before. But because they knew not how long the storm might last, nor how far off the ships might be put to sea, nor whether they should ever recover them again or not, they made great spare of their victuals, as it greatly behoved them. For they knew full well that the best cheer the country could yield them was rocks and stones, a hard food to live withal, and the people more ready to eat them than to give them wherewithal to eat. And thus, keeping very good watch and ward, they lay there all night upon hard cliffs of snow and ice, both wet, cold, and comfortless.

These things thus happening with the company on land, the danger of the ships at sea was no less perilous. For within one hour after the General's departing in the morning, by negligence of the cook in over-heating, and the workman in making the chimney, the Aid was set on fire, and had been the confusion of the whole if, by chance a boy espying it, it had not been speedily with great labour and God's help well extinguished.

This day also were divers storms and flaws, and by nine o'clock at night the storm was grown so great, and continued such until the morning, that it put our ships at sea in no small peril; for having mountains of fleeting ice on every side, we went roomer for one, and loosed for another,—some scraped us, and some happily escaped us,—that the least of a thousand were as dangerous to strike as any rock, and able to have split asunder the strongest ship of the world. We had a scope of clear without ice (as God would), wherein we turned, being otherwise compassed on every side about. But so much was the wind and so little was our sea-room, that being able to bear only our forecourse we cast so oft about, that we made fourteen boards in eight glasses running, being but four hours. But God being our best steersman, and by the industry of Charles Jackman and Andrew Dyer, the master's mates, both very expert mariners, and Richard Cox, the master gunner, with other very careful sailors, then within board, and also by the help of the clear nights, which are without darkness, we did happily avoid those present dangers, whereat since we have more marvelled than in the present danger feared, for that every man within board, both better and worse, had enough to do with his hands to haul ropes, and with his eyes to look out for danger. But the next morning, being the 20th of July, as God would, the storm ceased, and the General, espying the ships with his new captive and whole company, came happily aboard, and reported what had passed ashore, whereupon altogether upon our knees we gave God humble and hearty thanks for that it had pleased Him from so speedy peril to send us such speedy deliverance; and so from this northern shore we struck over towards the southerland.

On the 21st of July, we discovered a bay which ran into the land, that seemed a likely harbour for our ships; wherefore our General rowed thither with his boats, to make proof thereof, and with his gold-finers to search for ore, having never assayed anything on the south shore as yet, and the first small island, which we landed upon. Here all the sands and cliffs did so glitter and had so bright a marquesite, that it seemed all to be gold; but upon trial made, it proved no better than black-lead, and verified the proverb, "All is not gold that glistereth."

Upon the 22nd of July we bare into the said sound, and came to anchor a reasonable breadth off the shore; where, thinking ourselves in good security, we were greatly endangered with a piece of drift ice, which the ebb brought forth of the sounds and came thwart us ere we were aware. But the gentlemen and soldiers within board taking great pains at this pinch at the capstan, overcame the most danger thereof, and yet for all that might be done, it struck on our stern such a blow, that we feared lest it had stricken away our rudder, and being forced to cut our cable in the hawse, we were fain to set our foresail to run further up within, and if our steerage had not been stronger than in the present time we feared, we had run the ship upon the rocks, having a very narrow channel to turn in; but, as God would, all came well to pass. And this was named Jackman's Sound, after the name of the Master's mate, who had first liking unto the place.

Upon a small island within this sound, called Smith's Island (because he first set up his forge there), was found a mine of silver, but was not won out of the rocks without great labour. Here our gold-finers made assay of such ore as they found upon the northerland, and found four sorts thereof to hold gold in good quantity. Upon another small island here was also found a great dead fish, which as it should seem, had been embayed with ice, and was in proportion round like to a porpoise, being about twelve foot long, and in bigness answerable, having a horn of two yards long growing out of the snout or nostrils. This horn is wreathed and straight, like in fashion to a taper made of wax, and may truly be thought to be the sea unicorn. This horn is to be seen and reserved as a jewel by the queen's majesty's commandment, in her wardrobe of robes.

On Tuesday, the 23rd of July, our general with his best company of gentlemen, soldiers and sailors, to the number of seventy persons in all, marched with ensign displayed, upon the continent of the southerland (the supposed continent of America) where, commanding a trumpet to sound a call for every man to repair to the ensign, he declared to the whole company how much the cause imported for the service of her majesty, our country, our

credits, and the safety of our own lives, and therefore required
every man to be conformable to order, and to be directed by
those he should assign. And he appointed for leaders Captain
Fenton, Captain Yorke, and his Lieutenant George Best: which
done, we cast ourselves into a ring, and altogether upon our
knees, gave God humble thanks for that it had pleased him of
his great goodness to preserve us from such imminent dangers,
beseeching likewise the assistance of his holy spirit, so to deliver
us in safety into our country, whereby the light and truth of these
secrets being known, it might redound to the more honour of his
holy name, and consequently to the advancement of our common
wealth. And so, in as good sort as the place suffered, we
marched towards the tops of the mountains, which were no less
painful in climbing than dangerous in descending, by reason of their
steepness and ice. And having passed about five miles, by such
unwieldy ways, we returned unto our ships without sight of any
people, or likelihood of habitation. Here divers of the gentlemen desired our General to suffer them, to the number of twenty
or thirty persons, to march up thirty or forty leagues in the
country, to the end they might discover the inland, and do some
acceptable service for their country. But he, not contented
with the matter he sought for, and well considering the short
time he had in hand, and the greedy desire our country hath
to a present savour and return of gain, bent his whole endeavour
only to find a mine to freight his ships, and to leave the rest
(by God's help) hereafter to be well accomplished. And therefore
on the 26th of July he departed over to the northland, with the
two barques, leaving the Aid riding in Jackman's Sound, and
meant (after he had found convenient harbour, and freight there
for his ships) to discover further for the passage. The barques
came the same night to anchor in a sound upon the northland, where the tides did run so swift, and the place was so
subject to indrafts of ice, that by reason thereof they were
greatly endangered; and having found a very rich mine, as they
supposed, and got almost twenty tons of ore together, upon the
28th of July the ice came driving into the sound where the
barques rode, in such sort, that they were therewith greatly
distressed. And the Gabriel, riding astern the Michael, had her
cable galled asunder in the hawse with a piece of driving ice,
and lost another anchor; and having but one cable and anchor
left, for she had lost two before, and the ice still driving upon

her, she was (by God's help) well fenced from the danger of the rest, by one great island of ice, which came aground hard ahead of her; which, if it had not so chanced, I think surely she had been cast upon the rocks with the ice. The Michael moored anchor upon this great ice, and rode under the lee thereof: but about midnight, by the weight of itself, and the setting of the tides, the ice broke within half of the barque's length, and made unto the company within board a sudden and fearful noise. The next flood toward the morning we weighed anchor, and went further up the straits, and leaving our ore behind us which we had digged, for haste left the place by the name of Beare's Sound, after the Master's name of the Michael, and named the island Leicester's Island. In one of the small islands here we found a tomb, wherein the bones of a dead man lay together, and our savage captive being with us, and being demanded by signs whether his countrymen had not slain this man and eat his flesh so from the bones, he made signs to the contrary, and that he was slain with wolves and wild beasts. Here also was found hid under stones good store of fish, and sundry other things of the inhabitants; as sledges, bridles, kettles of fish-skins, knives of bone, ahd such other like. And our savage declared unto us the use of all those things. And taking in his hand one of those country bridles, he caught one of our dogs and hampered him handsomely therein, as we do our horses, and with a whip in his hand, he taught the dog to draw in a sledge as we do horses in a coach, sitting himself thereupon like a guide: so that we might see they use dogs for that purpose that we do our horses. And we found since by experience, that the lesser sort of dogs they feed fat, and keep them as domestic cattle in their tents for their eating, and the greater sort serve for the use of their sledges.

On the 29th of July, about five leagues from Beare's Sound, we discovered a bay which, being fenced on each side with small islands lying off the main, which break the force of the tides, and make the place free from any indrafts of ice, did prove a fit harbour for our ships, where we came to anchor under a small island, which now together with the sound is called by the name of that right honourable and virtuous lady, Anne Countess of Warwick. And this is the furtherest place that this year we have entered up within the straits, and is reckoned from the Cape of the Queen's Foreland, which is the entrance of the straits, not above thirty leagues. Upon this island was found good store of the ore, which in the washing held gold to our thinking plainly to be seen: whereupon it was thought best rather to load here, where there was store and indifferent good, than to seek further for better, and spend time with jeopardy. And therefore our General setting the miners to work, and shewing first a good precedent of a painful labourer and a good captain in himself, gave good examples for others to follow him: whereupon every man, both better and worse, with their best endeavours willingly laid to their helping hands. And the next day, being the 30th of July, the Michael was sent over to Jackman's Sound, for the Aid and the whole company to come thither. Upon the main-land, over against the Countess's Island, we discovered and beheld to our great marvel the poor caves and houses of those country people, which serve them (as it should seem) for their winter dwellings, and are made two fathoms underground, in compass round, like to an oven, being joined fast one by another, having holes like to a fox or coney burrow, to keep and come together. They undertrenched these places with gutters, so that the water, falling from the hills above them, may slide away without their annoyance: and are seated commonly in the foot of a hill, to shield them better from the cold winds, having their door and entrance ever open towards the south. From the ground upwards they build with whale's bones, for lack of timber, which bending one over another, are handsomely compacted in the top together, and are covered over with sealskins, which, instead of tiles, fence them from the rain. In which house they have only one room, having the one half of the floor raised with broad stones a foot higher than the other, whereon strewing moss, they make their nests to sleep in. They defile these dens most filthily with their beastly feeding, and dwell so long in a place (as we think) until their sluttishness loathing them, they are forced to seek a sweeter air, and a new seat, and are (no doubt) a dispersed and wandering nation, as the Tartarians, and live in hordes and troops, without any certain abode, as may appear by sundry circumstances of our experience.

Here our captive, being ashore with us to declare the use of such things as we saw, stayed himself alone behind the company, and did set up five small sticks round in a circle one by another, with one small bone placed just in the midst of all: which thing when one of our men perceived, he called us back to behold the matter, thinking that he had meant some charm or witchcraft therein. But the best conjecture we could make thereof was, that he would thereby his countrymen should understand, that for our five men which they betrayed the last year (whom he signified by the five sticks) he was taken and kept prisoner, which he signified by the bone in the midst. For afterwards when we showed him the picture of his countryman, which the last year was brought into England (whose counterfeit we had drawn, with boat and other furniture, both as he was in his own and also in English apparel) he was upon the sudden much amazed thereat: and beholding advisedly the same with silence a good while, as though he would strain courtesy whether should begin the speech (for he thought him no doubt a lively creature) at length began to question with him, as with his companion, and finding him dumb and mute, seemed to suspect him, as one disdainful, and would with a little help have grown into choler at the matter; until at last, by feeling and handling, he found him but a deceiving picture. And then with great noise and cries, ceased not wondering, thinking that we could make men live or die at our pleasure.

And thereupon calling the matter to his remembrance, he gave us plainly to understand by signs, that he had knowledge of the taking of our five men the last year, and confessing the manner of each thing, numbered the five men upon his five fingers, and pointed unto a boat in our ship, which was like unto that wherein our men were betrayed. And when we made him signs that they were slain and eaten, he earnestly denied, and made signs to the contrary.

The last of July the Michael returned with the Aid to us from the southerland, and came to anchor by us in the Countess of Warwick's Sound, and reported that since we departed from Jackman's Sound there happened nothing among them there greatly worth the remembrance, until the 30th of July, when certain of our company being ashore upon a small island within the said Jackman's Sound, near the place where the Aid rode, did espy a long boat with divers of the country people therein, to the number of eighteen or twenty persons, whom so soon as our men perceived, they returned speedily aboard, to give notice thereof unto our company. They might perceive these people climbing up to the top of a hill, where, with a flag, they wafted unto our ship, and made great outcries and noises, like so many bulls. Hereupon our men did presently man forth a small skiff, having not above six or seven persons therein, which rowed near the place where those people were, to prove if they could have any conference with them; but after this small boat was sent a greater, being well appointed for their rescue, if need required.

As soon as they espied our company coming near them, they took their boats and hasted away, either for fear, or else for policy, to draw our men from rescue further within their danger; wherefore our men construing that their coming thither was but to seek advantage, followed speedily after them; but they rowed so swiftly away that our men could come nothing near them. Howbeit they failed not of their best endeavour in rowing; and having chased them above two miles into the sea, returned into their ships again.

The morning following, being the 1st of August, Captain Yorke, with the Michael, came into Jackman's Sound, and declared unto the company there that the last night past he came to anchor in a certain bay (which since was named Yorke's Sound) about four leagues distant from Jackman's Sound, being put to leeward of that place for lack of wind, where he discovered certain tents of the country people; where going with his company ashore he entered into them, but found the people departed, as it should seem, for fear of their coming. But amongst sundry strange things which in these tents they found, there was raw and new-killed flesh of unknown sorts, with dead carcases and bones of dogs, and I know not what. They also beheld (to their greatest marvel) a doublet of canvas made after the English fashion, a shirt, a girdle, three shoes for contrary feet, and of unequal bigness, which they well conjectured to be the apparel of our five poor countrymen, which were intercepted the last year by these country people, about fifty leagues from this place, further within the straits. Whereupon our men being in good hope that some of them might be here, and yet living: the captain, devising for the best, left his mind behind him in writing, with pen, ink, and paper also, whereby our poor captive countrymen, if it might come to their hands, might know their friends' minds, and of their arrival, and likewise return their answer. And so, without taking anything away in their tents, leaving there also looking-glasses, points, and other of our toys (the better to allure them by such friendly means) departed aboard his barque, with intent to make haste to the Aid, to give notice unto the company of all such things as he had there discovered; and so meant to return to these tents again, hoping that he might by force or policy entrap or entice the people to some friendly conference. Which things when he had delivered to the whole company there, they determined forthwith to go in hand with the matter. Hereupon Captain Yorke with the Master of the Aid and his mate (who the night before had been at the tents, and came over from the other side in the Michael, with him) being accompanied with the gentlemen and soldiers to the number of thirty or forty persons, in two small rowing pinnaces made towards the place, where the night before they discovered the tents of those people, and setting Charles Jackman, being the Master's mate, ashore with a convenient number, for that he could best guide them to the place, they marched overland, meaning to compass them on the one side, whilst the captain with his boats might entrap them on the other side; but landing at last at the place where the night before they left them they found them with their tents removed. Notwithstanding, our men which marched up into the country, passing over two or three mountains, by chance espied certain tents in a valley underneath them near unto a creek by the sea side, which because it was not the place where the guide had been the night before, they judged them to be another company, and besetting them about, determined to take them if they could. But they having quickly descried our company, launched one great and another small boat, being about sixteen or eighteen persons, and, very narrowly escaping, put themselves to sea. Whereupon our soldiers discharged their calivers, and followed them, thinking the noise thereof being heard to our boats at sea, our men there would make what speed they might to that place; and thereupon indeed our men which were in the boats (crossing upon them in the mouth of the sound whereby their passage was let from getting sea room, wherein it had been impossible for us to overtake them by rowing), forced them to put themselves ashore upon a point of land within the said sound (which upon the occasion of the slaughter there, was since named "the bloody point,") whereunto our men so speedily followed, that they had little leisure left them to make any escape. But so soon as they landed, each of them brake his oar, thinking by that means to prevent us in carrying away their boats for want of oars, and desperately returning upon our men, resisted them manfully in their landing, so long as their arrows and darts lasted, and after gathering up those arrows which our men shot at them,—yea, and plucking our arrows out of their bodies,—encountered afresh again, and maintained their cause until both weapons and life failed them. And when they found they were mortally wounded, being ignorant what mercy meaneth, with deadly fury they cast themselves headlong from off the rocks into the sea, least perhaps their enemies should receive glory or prey of their dead carcases, for they supposed us belike to be cannibals or eaters of man's flesh. In this conflict one of our men was dangerously hurt in the belly with one of their arrows, and of them were slain five or six, the rest by flight escaping among the rocks; saving two women, whereof the one being old and ugly, our men thought she had been a devil or some witch, and therefore let her go; the other, being young and cumbered with a sucking child at her back, hiding herself behind the rocks, was espied by one of our men, who supposing she had been a man, shot through the hair of her head, and pierced through the child's arm, whereupon she cried out, and our surgeon meaning to heal her child's arm, applied salves thereunto. But she, not acquainted with such kind of surgery, plucked those salves away, and by continual licking with her own tongue, not much unlike our dogs, healed up the child's arm. And because the day was well near spent our men made haste unto the rest of our company which on the other side of the water remained at the tents, where they found by the apparel, letter, and other English furniture, that they were the same company which Captain Yorke discovered the night before, having removed themselves from the place where he left them.

And now, considering their sudden flying from our men, and their desperate manner of fighting, we began to suspect that we had heard the last news of our men which the last year were betrayed of these people; and considering also their ravenous and bloody disposition in eating any kind of raw flesh or carrion howsoever stinking, it is to be thought that they had slain and devoured our men; for the doublet which was found in their tents had many holes therein, being made with their arrows and darts.

But now the night being at hand, our men, with their captives and such poor stuff as they found in their tents, returned towards their ships, when, being at sea, there arose a sudden flaw of wind, which was not a little dangerous for their small boats; but as God would, they came all safely aboard. And with these good news they returned, as before mentioned, into the Countess of Warwick's Sound, unto us. And between Jackman's Sound—from whence they came—and the Countess of Warwick's Sound, between land

and land, being thought the narrowest place of the straits, were judged nine leagues over at the least, and Jackman's Sound being upon the southerland, lieth directly almost over against the Countess's Sound, as is reckoned scarce thirty leagues within the straits from the Queen's Cape, which is the entrance of the Straits of the Southerland. This cape being named Queen Elizabeth's Cape, standeth in the latitude of sixty-two degrees and a half to the northwards of Newfoundland, and upon the same continent for anything that is yet known to the contrary.

Having now got a woman captive for the comfort of our man, we brought them both together, and every man with silence desired to behold the manner of their meeting and entertainment, the which was more worth the beholding than can be well expressed by writing. At their first encountering they beheld each the other very wistfully a good space, without speech or word uttered, with great change of colour and countenance, as though it seemed the grief and disdain of their captivity had taken away the use of their tongues and utterance. The woman at the first very suddenly, as though she disdained or regarded not the man, turned away and began to sing, as though she minded another matter; but being again brought together, the man broke up the silence first, and with stern and staid countenance, began to tell a long solemn tale to the woman, whereunto she gave good hearing, and interrupted him nothing till he had finished; and afterwards, being grown into more familiar acquaintance by speech, they were turned together, so that I think the one would hardly have lived without the comfort of the other. And for so much as we could perceive, albeit they lived continually together, yet they did never use as man and wife, though the woman spared not to do all necessary things that appertained to a good housewife indifferently for them both, as in making clean their cabin, and every other thing that appertained to his ease; for when he was sea-sick she would make him clean, she would kill and flay the dogs for their eating, and dress his meat.

* * * * * * *

On Monday, the 6th of August, the Lieutenant, with all the soldiers, for the better guard of the miners and the other things on shore, pitched their tents in the Countess's Island, and fortified the place for their better defence as well as they could, and were to the number of forty persons, when, being all at labour, they might perceive upon the top of a hill over against them, a number of the country people, wafting with a flag, and making great outcries unto them, and were of the same company which had encountered lately our men upon the other shore, being come to complain of their late losses, and to entreat, as it seemed, for the restitution of the woman and child, which our men in the late conflict had taken and brought away. Whereupon the General, taking the savage captive with him, and setting the woman—where they might best perceive her—in the highest place of the island, went over to talk with them. This captive, at his first encounter of his friends, fell so out into tears that he could not speak a word in a great space; but after a while, overcoming his kindness, he talked at full with his companions, and bestowed friendly upon them such toys and trifles as we had given him: whereby we noted that they are very kind one to another, and greatly sorrowful for the loss of their friends. Our General, by signs, required his five men, which they took captive the last year, and promised them not only to release those which he had taken, but also to reward them with great gifts and friendship. Our savage made signs in answer from them that our men should be delivered us, and were yet living, and made signs likewise unto us that we should write our letters unto them, for they knew very well the use we have of writing, and received knowledge thereof, either of our poor captive countrymen which they betrayed, or else by this our new captive, who hath seen us daily write and repeat again such words of his language as we desired to learn; but they for this night, because it was late, departed without any letter, although they called earnestly in haste for the same. And the next morning early, being the 7th of August, they called again for the letter; which being delivered unto them, they speedily departed, making signs with three fingers, and pointing to the sun, that they meant to return within three days, until which time we heard no more of them; and about the time appointed they returned, in such sort as you shall afterwards hear.

This night, because the people were very near unto us, the Lieutenant caused the trumpet to sound a call, and every man in the island repairing to the Ensign, he put them in mind of the place, so far from their country, wherein they lived, and the danger of a great multitude, which they were subject unto, if good watch and ward were not kept—for at every low water the enemy might come almost dry-foot from the main unto us; wherefore he willed every man to prepare him in good readiness upon all sudden occasions; and so, giving the watch their charge, the company departed to rest.

I thought the Captain's letter well worth the remembering, not for the circumstance of curious inditing, but for the substance and good meaning therein contained, and therefore have repeated here the same as by himself it was hastily written.

The Form of MR. MARTIN FROBISHER'S *Letter to the English Captives.*

"In the name of God, in whom we all believe, who, I trust, hath preserved your bodies and souls amongst these infidels, I commend me unto you. I will be glad to seek by all means you can devise for your deliverance, either with force or with any commodities within my ships, which I will not spare for your sakes, or anything else I can do for you. I have aboard, of theirs, a man, a woman, and a child, which I am contented to deliver for you, but the man which I carried away from hence the last year is dead in England. Moreover, you may declare unto them that if they deliver you not, I will not leave a man alive in their country. And thus, if one of you can come to speak with me, they shall have either the man, woman, or child in pawn for you. And thus unto God, whom I trust you do serve, in haste I leave you, and to Him we will daily pray for you. This Tuesday morning, the 7th of August, anno 1577.

"Yours to the uttermost of my power,
"MARTIN FROBISHER.

"I have sent you by these bearers, pen, ink, and paper, to write back unto me again, if personally you cannot come to certify me of your estate."

Now had the General altered his determination for going any further into the straits at this time, for any further discovery of the passage, having taken a man and a woman of that country, which he thought sufficient for the use of language, and having also met with these people here which intercepted his men the last year (as the apparel and English furniture which was found in their tents very well declared), he knew it was but a labour lost to seek them further off, when he had found them there at hand. And considering also the short time he had in hand, he thought it best to bend his whole endeavour for the getting of mine, and to leave the passage further to be discovered hereafter; for his commission directed him in this voyage only for the searching of the ore, and to defer the further discovery of the passage until another time.

On Thursday, the 9th of August, we began to make a small fort, for our defence in the Countess's Island, and entrenched a corner of a cliff, which on three parts, like a wall of good height, was compassed and well fenced with the sea, and we finished the rest with casks of the earth to good purpose : and this was called Best's Bulwark, after the Lieutenant's name who first devised the same. This was done for that we suspected more lest the desperate men might oppress us with multitude, than any fear we had of their force, weapons, or policy of battle, but as wisdom would us in such place, so far from home, not to be of ourselves altogether careless. So the signs which our captive made unto us of the coming down of his Governor or Prince, which he called Catchoe, gave us occasion to foresee what might ensue thereof, for he showed by signs that this Catchoe was a man of higher stature far than any of our nation is, and he is accustomed to be carried upon men's shoulders.

About midnight, the Lieutenant caused a false alarm to be given in the island, to prove as well the readiness of the company there ashore, as also what help might be hoped for upon the sudden from the ships, if need so required ; and every part was found in good readiness upon such a sudden.

On Saturday, the 11th of August, the people showed themselves again, and called unto us from the side of a hill over against us. The General, with good hope to hear of his men, and to have answer of his letter, went over unto them, where they presented themselves not above three in sight, but were hidden indeed in greater numbers behind the rocks, and making signs of delay with us, to entrap some of us to redeem their own, did only seek advantage to train our boat about a point of land from sight of our company ; whereupon our men, justly suspecting them, kept aloof without their danger, and yet set one of our company ashore, which took up a great bladder which one of them offered us, and leaving a looking-glass in the place, came into the boat again. In the meanwhile, our men which stood in the Countess's Island to behold, who might better discern them than those of the boat, by reason they were on higher ground, made a great outcry unto our men in the boat, for that they saw divers of the savages creeping behind the rocks towards our men ; whereupon the General presently returned without tidings of his men.

Concerning this bladder which we received, our captive made signs that it was given him to keep water and drink in, but we suspected rather it was given him to swim and shift away withal, for he and the woman sought divers times to escape, having loosed our boats from astern our ships, and we never a boat left to pursue them withal, and had prevailed very far, had they not been very timely espied and prevented therein.

After our General's coming away from them they mustered themselves in our sight, upon the top of a hill, to the number of twenty in a rank, all holding hands over their heads, and dancing with great noise and songs together: we supposed they made this dance and show for us to understand, that we might take view of their whole companies and force, meaning belike that we should do the same. And thus they continued upon the hill-tops until night, when hearing a piece of our great ordnance, which thundered in the hollowness of the high hills, it made unto them so fearful a noise, that they had no great will to tarry long after. And this was done more to make them know our force than to do them any hurt at all.

On Sunday, the 12th of August, Captain Fenton trained the company, and made the soldiers maintain skirmish among themselves, as well for their exercise, as for the country people to behold in what readiness our men were always to be found, for it was to be thought, that they lay hid in the hills thereabout, and observed all the manner of our proceedings.

On Wednesday, the 14th of August, our General with two small boats well appointed, for that he suspected the country people to lie lurking thereabout, went up a certain bay within the Countess's Sound to search for ore, and met again with the country people, who so soon as they saw our men made great outcries, and with a white flag made of bladders sewed together with the guts and sinews of beasts, wafted us amain unto them, but showed not above three of their company. But when we came near them, we might perceive a great multitude creeping behind the rocks, which gave us good cause to suspect their traitorous meaning: whereupon we made them signs, that if they would lay their weapons aside, and come forth, we would deal friendly with them, although their intent was manifested unto us: but for all the signs of friendship we could make them they came still creeping towards us behind the rocks to get more advantage of us, as though we had no eyes to see them, thinking belike that our single wits could not discover so bare devises and simple drifts of theirs. Their spokesman earnestly persuaded us with many enticing shows, to come eat and sleep ashore, with great arguments of courtesy, and clapping his bare hands over his head in token of peace and innocency, willed us to do the like. But the better to allure our hungry stomachs, he brought us a trim bait of raw flesh, which for fashion sake with a boat-hook we caught into our boat: but when the cunning cater perceived his first cold morsel could nothing sharpen our stomachs, he cast about for a new train of warm flesh to procure our appetites. Wherefore he caused one of his fellows in halting manner, to come forth as a lame man from behind the rocks, and the better to declare his kindness in carving, he hoisted him upon his shoulders, and bringing him hard to the water-side where we were, left him there limping as an easy prey to be taken of us. His hope was that we would bite at his bait, and speedily leap ashore within their danger, whereby they might have apprehended some of us, to ransom their friends home again, which before we had taken. The gentlemen and soldiers had great will to encounter them ashore, but the General more careful by process of time to win them, than wilfully at the first to spoil them, would in no wise admit that any man should put himself in hazard ashore, considering the matter he now intended was for the ore, and not for the conquest: notwithstanding, to prove this cripple's footmanship, he gave liberty for one to shoot: whereupon the cripple, having a parting blow, lightly recovered a rock, and went away a true and no fained cripple, and hath learned his lesson for ever halting afore such cripples again. But his fellows which lay hid before, full quickly then appeared in their likeness, and maintained the skirmish with their slings, bows and arrows very fiercely, and came as near as the water suffered them: and with as desperate mind as hath been seen in any men, without fear of shot or anything, followed us all along the coast; but all their shot fell short of us, and are of little danger. They had belayed all the coast along for us, and being dispersed so, were not well to be numbered, but we might discern of them above an hundred persons, and had cause to suspect a greater number. And thus without loss or hurt we returned to our ships again.

Now our work growing to an end, and having, only with five poor miners, and the help of a few gentlemen and soldiers, brought aboard almost two hundred tons of ore in the space of twenty days, every man therewithal well comforted, determined lustily to work afresh for a *bon voyage*, to bring our labour to a speedy and happy end.

And upon Wednesday at night, being the 21st of August, we fully finished the whole work. And it was now good time to leave, for as the men were well wearied, so their shoes and clothes were well worn, their baskets' bottoms torn out, their tools broken, and the ships reasonably well filled. Some with over-straining themselves received hurts not a little dangerous, some having their bellies broken, and others their legs made lame. And about this time the ice began to congeal and freeze about our ships-sides at night, which gave us a good argument of the sun's declining southward, and put us in mind to make more haste homeward.

It is not a little worth the memory, to the commendation of the gentlemen and soldiers herein, who, leaving all reputation apart, with so great willingness and with courageous stomachs, have themselves almost overcome in so short a time the difficulty of this so great a labour. And this to be true, the matter, if it be well weighed without further proof, now brought home doth well witness.

On Thursday, the 22nd of August, we plucked down our tents, and every man hasted homeward, and making bonfires upon the top of the highest mount of the island, and marching with ensign displayed round about the island, we gave a volley of shot for a farewell, in honour of the Right Honourable Lady Anne, Countess of Warwick, whose name it beareth: and so departed aboard.

On the 23rd of August, having the wind large at west, we set sail from out of the Countess's Sound homeward; but the wind calming we came to anchor within the point of the same sound again.

On the 24th of August, about three o'clock in the morning, having the wind large at west, we set sail again, and by nine o'clock at night, we left the Queen's Foreland astern of us, and being cleared of the straits, we bare further into the main ocean, keeping our course more southerly, to bring ourselves the sooner under the latitude of our own climate.

The wind was very great at sea, so that we lay a hull all night, and had snow half a foot deep on the hatches.

From the 24th until the 28th we had very much wind, but

large, keeping our course south-south-east, and had like to have lost the barques, but by good hap we met again. The height being taken, we were in   degrees and a half.

On the 29th of August the wind blew much at north-east, so that we could bear but only a bunt of our foresail, and the barques were not able to carry any sail at all.

The Michael lost company of us and shaped her course towards Orkney, because that way was better known unto them, and arrived at Yarmouth.

On the 30th of August, with the force of the wind, and a surge of the sea, the master of the Gabriel and the boatswain were stricken both overboard, and hardly was the boatswain recovered, having hold on a rope hanging overboard in the sea, and yet the barque was laced fore and after with ropes a breast high within board.

This Master was called William Smith, being but a young man and a very sufficient mariner, who being all the morning before exceeding pleasant, told his Captain he dreamt that he was cast overboard, and that the boatswain had him by the hand, and could not save him, and so immediately upon the end of his tale, his dream came right evilly to pass, and indeed the boatswain in like sort held him by one hand, having hold on a rope with the other, until his force failed, and the Master drowned. The height being taken we found ourselves to be in the latitude of   degrees and a half, and reckoned ourselves from the Queen's Cape homeward about two hundred leagues.

On the last of August, about midnight, we had two or three great and sudden flaws or storms.

On the 1st of September the storm was growing very great, and continued almost the whole day and night, and lying a hull to tarry for the barques our ship was much beaten with the seas, every sea almost overtaking our poop, so that we were constrained with a bunt of our sail to try it out, and ease the rolling of our ship. And so the Gabriel not able to bear any sail to keep company with us, and our ship being higher in the poop, and a tall ship, whereon the wind had more force to drive, went so fast away that we lost sight of them, and left them to God and their good fortune of sea. On the 2nd of September in the morning, it pleased God in his goodness to send us a calm, whereby we perceived the rudder of our ship torn in twain, and almost ready to fall away. Wherefore, taking the benefit of the time, we flung half-a-dozen couple of our best men overboard, who taking great pains under water, driving planks, and binding with ropes, did well strengthen and mend the matter, who returned the most part more than half-dead out of the water, and, as God's pleasure was, the sea was calm until the work was finished. On the 5th of September, the height of the sun being taken, we found ourselves to be in the latitude of   degrees and a-half. In this voyage commonly we took the latitude of the place by the height of the sun, because the long day taketh away the light not only of the polar, but also of all other fixed stars. And here the north star is so much elevated above the horizon, that with the staff it is hardly to be well observed, and the degrees in the Astrolabe are too small to observe minutes. Therefore we always used the staff and the sun as fittest instruments for this use.

Having spent four or five days in traverse of the seas with contrary wind, making our souther way good as near as we could, to raise our degrees to bring ourselves with the latitude of Scilly, we took the height the 10th of September, and found ourselves in the latitude of   degrees and ten minutes. On the 11th of September, about six o'clock at night, the wind came good south-west, we veered sheet and set our course south-east.

And upon Thursday, the 12th of September, taking the height, we were in the latitude of   and a-half, and reckoned ourselves not past one hundred and fifty leagues short of Scilly, the weather fair, the wind large at west-south-west, we kept our course south-east.

On the thirteenth day, the height being taken, we found ourselves to be in the latitude of   degrees, the wind west-south-west, then being in the height of Scilly, and we kept our course east, to run in with the sleeve or channel so called, being our narrow seas, and reckoned us short of Scilly twelve leagues.

On Sunday, the 15th of September, about four o'clock, we began to sound with our lead, and had ground at sixty-one fathom depth, white small sandy ground, and reckoned us upon the back of Scilly, and set our course east and by north, east-north-east, and north-east among.

On the 16th of September, about eight o'clock in the morning, sounding, we had sixty-five fathom, oozy sand, and thought ourselves athwart of St. George's Channel, a little within the banks, and bearing a small sail all night, we made many soundings, which were about forty fathom, and so shallow that we could not well tell where we were.

On the 17th of September, we sounded, and had forty fathom, and were not far off the Land's-End, finding branded sand with small worms and cockle-shells, and were shot between Scilly and the Land's-End; and being within the bay, we were not able to double the point with a south-and-by-east way, but were fain to make another board, the wind being at south-west and by west, and yet could not double the point to come clear of the Lands-End, to bear along the Channel; and the weather cleared up when we were hard aboard the shore, and we made the Land's-End perfect, and so put up along St. George's Channel. And the weather being very foul at sea, we coveted some harbour, because our steerage was broken, and so came to anchor in Padstow Road, in Cornwall. But riding there a very dangerous road, we were advised by the country to put to sea again, and of the two evils, to choose the less, for there was nothing but present peril where we rode; whereupon we plied along the Channel to get to Lundy, from whence we were again driven, (being but an open road, where our anchor came home), and with force of weather put to sea again, and about the 23rd of September arrived at Milford Haven, in Wales, which being a very good harbour, made us happy men, that we had received such long-desired safety.

About one month after our arrival here, by order from the Lords of the Council, the ship came up to Bristol, where the ore was committed to keeping in the castle there. Here we found the Gabriel, one of the barques, arrived in good safety, who having never a man within board very sufficient to bring home the ship, after the master was lost, by good fortune, when she came upon the coast, met with a ship of Bristol at sea, who conducted her in safety thither.

Here we heard good tidings also of the arrival of the other barque called the Michael, in the north parts, which was not a little joyful unto us, that it pleased God so to bring us to a safe meeting again; and we lost in all the voyage only one man, besides one that died at sea, which was sick before he came aboard, and was so desirous to follow his enterprise that he rather chose to die therein, than not to be one to attempt so notable a voyage.

FROBISHER—THIRD VOYAGE.

NARRATIVE BY GEORGE BEST.

The THIRD VOYAGE *of* CAPTAIN FROBISHER, *pretended for the discovery of* CATHAY, *by* META INCOGNITA, *Anno Domini 1578.*

THE General being returned from the second voyage, immediately after his arrival in England repaired with all haste to the Court, being then at Windsor, to advertise her Majesty of his prosperous proceeding and good success in this last voyage, and of the plenty of gold ore, with other matters of importance which he had in these septentrional parts discovered. He was courteously entertained, and heartily welcomed of many noblemen, but especially for his great adventure commended of her Majesty, at whose hands he received great thanks, and most gracious countenance, according to his deserts. Her Highness also greatly commended the rest of the gentlemen in this service, for their great forwardness in this so dangerous an attempt; but especially she rejoiced very much that among them there was so good order of government, so good agreement, every man so ready in his calling, to do whatsoever the General should command, which due commendation graciously of her Majesty remembered, gave so great encouragement to all the captains and gentlemen, that they, to continue Her Highness's so good and honourable opinion of them, have since neither spared labour, limb, nor life, to bring this matter (so well begun) to a happy and prosperous end. And finding that the matter of the gold ore had appearance and made show of great riches and profit, and the hope of the passage to Cathay by this last voyage greatly increased, her Majesty appointed special Commissioners chosen for this purpose, gentlemen of great judgment, art, and skill, to look thoroughly into the cause, for the true trial and due examination thereof, and for the full handling of all matters thereunto appertaining. And because that place and country hath never heretofore been discovered, and therefore had no special name by which it might be called and known, her Majesty named it very properly Meta Incognita, as a mark and bound utterly hitherto unknown. The commissioners, after sufficient trial and proof made of the ore, and having understood by sundry reasons and substantial grounds, the possibility and likelihood of the passage, advertised Her Highness that the cause was of importance, and the voyage greatly worthy to be advanced again.. Whereupon preparation was made of ships and all other things necessary, with such expedition, as the time of the year then required. And because it was assuredly made account of, that the commodity of mines, there already discovered, would at the least countervail in all respects the adventurers' charge, and give further hope and likelihood of greater matters to follow: it was thought needful, both for the better guard of those parts already found, and for further discovery of the inland and secrets of those countries, and also for further search of the passage of Cathay (whereof the hope continually more and more increaseth) that certain numbers of chosen soldiers and discreet men for those purposes should be assigned to inhabit there. Whereupon there was a strong fort or house of timber, artificially framed, and cunningly devised by a notable learned man here at home, in ships to be carried thither, whereby those men that were appointed to winter and stay there the whole year, might as well be defended from the danger of the snow and cold air, as also fortified from the force or offence of those country people, which perhaps otherwise with too great multitudes might oppress them. And to this great adventure and notable exploit many well-minded and forward young gentlemen of our country willingly have offered themselves. And first Captain Fenton, Lieutenant-General for Captain Frobisher, and in charge of the company with him there, Captain Best, and Captain Filpot, unto whose good discretions the government of that service was chiefly commended, who, as men not regarding peril in respect of the profit and common wealth of their country, were willing to abide the first brunt and adventure of those dangers among a savage and brutish kind of people, in a place hitherto ever thought for extreme cold not habitable. The whole number of men which had offered, and were appointed to inhabit Meta Incognita all the year, were one hundred persons, whereof forty should be mariners for the use of ships, thirty miners for gathering the gold ore together for the next year, and thirty soldiers for the better guard of the rest, within which last number are included the gentlemen, gold-finers, bakers, carpenters, and all necessary persons. To each of the captains was assigned one ship, as well for the further searching of the coast and country there, as for to return and bring back their companies again, if the necessity of the place so urged, or by miscarrying of the fleet the next year, they might be disappointed of their further provision. Being therefore thus furnished with all necessaries, there were ready to depart upon the said voyage fifteen sail of good ships, whereof the whole number was to return again with their loading of gold ore in the end of the summer, except those three ships which should be left for the use of those Captains which should inhabit there the whole year. And being in so good readiness the General with all the Captains came to the Court, then lying at Greenwich, to take their leave of her Majesty, at whose hands they all received great encouragement, and gracious countenance. Her Highness, besides other good gifts, and greater promises, bestowed on the General a fair chain of gold, and the rest of the Captains kissed her hand, took their leave, and departed every man towards their charge.

The said fifteen sail of ships arrived and met together at Harwich on the 27th of May, 1578, where the General and the other Captains made view, and mustered their companies. And every several Captain received from the General certain Articles of Direction for the better keeping of order and company together in the way, which Articles are as followeth:—

Articles and Orders to be observed for the Fleet, set down by CAPTAIN FROBISHER, GENERAL, *and delivered in writing to every Captain, as well for keeping company, as for the course, the 31st of May.*

1. IMPRIMIS, to banish swearing, dice, and card-playing, and filthy communication, and to serve God twice a-day, with the ordinary service usual in Churches of England, and to clear the glass, according to the old order of England.

2. The Admiral shall carry the light, and after his light be once put out no man to go ahead of him, but every man to fit his sails to follow as near as they may without endangering one another.

3. That no man shall by day or by night depart further from the Admiral than the distance of one English mile, and as near as they may without danger one of another.

4. If it chance to grow thick, and the wind contrary, either by day or by night, that the Admiral be forced to cast about, before her casting about she shall give warning by shooting off a piece: and to her shall answer the Vice-Admiral and the Rear-Admiral, each of them with a piece if it be by night or in a fog; and that the Vice-Admiral shall answer first and the Rear-Admiral last.

5. That no man in the Fleet, descrying any sail or sails, give upon any occasion any chase before he have spoken with the Admiral.

6. That every evening all the Fleet come up and speak with the Admiral, at seven o'clock, or between that and eight; and if the weather will not serve them all to speak with the Admiral, then some shall come to the Vice-Admiral, and receive the order of their course of Master Hall, Chief Pilot of the Fleet, as he shall direct them.

7. If to any man in the Fleet there happen any mischance, they shall presently shoot off two pieces by day, and if it be by night, two pieces, and shew two lights.

8. If any man in the Fleet come up in the night, and hail his fellow, knowing him not, he shall give him this watchword, "Before the world was God." The other shall answer him (if he be one of our Fleet), "After God came Christ his Son." So that if any be found amongst us, not of our own company, he that first descrieth any such sail or sails, shall give warning to the Admiral by himself or any other that he can speak to, that sails better than he, being nearest unto him.

9. That every ship in the Fleet in the time of fogs, which continually happen with little winds, and most part calms, shall keep a reasonable noise with trumpet, drum, or otherwise, to keep themselves clear one of another.

10. If it fall out so thick or misty that we lay it to hull, the Admiral shall give warning with a piece, and putting out three lights one over another, to the end that every man may take in his sails, and at his setting of sails again do the like, if it be not clear.

11. If any man discover land by night, that he give the like warning that he doth for mischances, two lights and two pieces, if it be by day one piece, and put out his flag, and strike all his sails he hath aboard.

12. If any ship shall happen to lose company by force of weather, then any such ship or ships shall get her into the latitude of   , and so keep that latitude until they get to Friesland. And after they be past the west parts of Friesland, they shall get

them into the latitude of   , and   , and not to the northward of   ; and being once entered within the Straits, all such ships shall every watch shoot off a good piece, and look out well for smoke and fire which those that get in first shall make every night, until all the Fleet be come together.

13. That upon the sight of an ensign in the mast of the Admiral (a piece being shot off) the whole Fleet shall repair to the Admiral, to understand such conference as the General is to have with them.

14. If we chance to meet with any enemies, that four ships shall attend upon the Admiral—viz., the Francis of Foy, the Moon, the barque Dennis, and the Gabriel; and four upon my Lieutenant-General in the Judith—viz., the Hopewell, the Armenal, the Bear, and the Salomon; and the other four upon the Vice-Admiral—the Anne Francis, the Thomas of Ipswich, the Emmanuel, and the Michael.

15. If there happen any disordered person in the Fleet, that he be taken and kept in safe custody until he may conveniently be brought aboard the Admiral, and there to receive such punishment as his or their offences shall deserve.

By me, MARTIN FROBISHER.

Having received these Articles of Direction, we departed from Harwich on the 31st of May; and sailing along the south part of England westward, we at length came by the coast of Ireland at Cape Clear on the 6th of June, and gave chase there to a small barque which was supposed to be a pirate or rover on the seas; but it fell out indeed that they were poor men of Bristol, who had met with such company of Frenchmen as had spoiled and slain many of them, and left the rest so sore wounded that they were like to perish in the sea, having neither hand nor foot whole to help themselves with, nor victuals to sustain their hungry bodies. Our General, who well understood the office of a soldier and an Englishman, and knew well what the necessity of the sea meaneth, pitying much the misery of the poor men, relieved them with surgery and salves to heal their hurts, and with meat and drink to comfort their pining hearts; some of them having neither eaten nor drunk more than olives and stinking water in many days before, as they reported. And after this good deed done, having a large wind, we kept our course upon our said voyage without staying for the taking in of fresh water, or any other provision, whereof many of the fleet were not throughly furnished. And sailing towards the north-west parts from Ireland, we met with a great current from out of the south-west, which carried us (by our reckoning) one point to the north-eastwards of our said course, which current seemed to us to continue itself towards Norway, and other the north-east parts of the world, whereby we may be induced to believe that this is the same which the Portugals meet at the Cape of Good Hope, where striking over from thence to the Straits of Magellan, and finding no passage there for the narrowness of the said Straits, runneth along into the great Bay of Mexico, where also having a let of land, it is forced to strike back again towards the north-east, as we not only here, but in another place also, further to the northwards, by good experience this year have found, as shall be hereafter in this place more at large declared.

Now had we sailed about fourteen days without sight of land or any other living thing, except certain fowls, as willmots, noddies, gulls, &c., which there seem only to live by sea.

On the 20th of June, at two o'clock in the morning, the General descried land, and found it to be West Friesland, now named West England. Here the General and other gentlemen went ashore, being the first known Christians that we have true notice of that ever set foot upon that ground. And therefore the General took possession thereof to the use of our Sovereign Lady the Queen's Majesty, and discovered here a goodly harbour for the ships, where were also certain little boats of that country. And being there landed they espied certain tents and people of that country, which were (as they judge) in all sorts, very like those of Meta Incognita, as by their apparel, and other things which we found in their tents, appeared.

The savage and simple people so soon as they perceived our men coming towards them, (supposing there had been no other world but theirs) fled fearfully away, as men much amazed at so strange a sight, and creatures of human shape, so far in apparel, complexion, and other things different from themselves. They left in their tents all their furniture for haste behind them, where amongst other things were found a box of small nails, and certain red herrings, boards of fir-tree well cut, with divers other things artificially wrought: whereby it appeareth, that they have trade with some civil people, or else are indeed themselves artificial workmen. Our men brought away with them only two of their dogs, leaving in recompense bells, looking-glasses, and divers of our country toys behind them. This country, no doubt, promiseth good hope of great commodity and riches, if it may be well discovered. The description whereof you shall find more at large in the second voyage. Some are of opinion that this West England is firm land with the north-east parts of Meta Incognita, or else with Greenland. And their reason is, because the people, apparel, boats, and other things are so like to theirs; and another reason is, the multitude of islands of ice, which lay between it and Meta Incognita, doth argue, that on the north side there is a bay, which cannot be but by conjoining of the two lands together.

And having a fair and large wind we departed from thence towards Frobisher's Straits on the 23rd of June. But first we gave name to a high cliff in West England, the last that was in our sight, and for a certain similitude we called it Charing Cross. Then we bore southerly towards the sea, because to the northwards of this coast we met with much driving ice, which by reason of the thick mists and weather might have been some trouble unto us. On Monday, the last of June, we met with many great whales, as they had been porpoises. This same day the Salamander, being under both her corses and bonnets, happened to strike a great whale with her full stem, with such a blow that the ship stood still, and stirred neither forward nor backward. The whale thereat made a great and ugly noise, and cast up his body and tail, and so went under water, and within two days after there was found a great whale dead, swimming above water, which we supposed was that which the Salamander struck.

On the 2nd of July, early in the morning, we had sight of the Queen's Foreland, and bare in with the land all the day, and passing through a great quantity of ice, by night were entered somewhat within the Straits, perceiving no way to pass further in, the whole place being frozen over from the one side to the other, and as it were with many walls, mountains, and bulwarks of ice, choked up the passage, and denied us entrance. And yet do I not think that this passage or sea hereabouts is frozen over at any time of the year: albeit it seemed so unto us by the abundance of ice gathered together, which occupied the whole place. But I do rather suppose these ice to be bred in the hollow sounds and freshets thereabouts; which, by the heat of the summer's sun, being loosed, do empty themselves with the ebbs into the sea, and so gather in great abundance there together.

And to speak somewhat here of the ancient opinion of the

frozen sea in these parts: I do think it to be rather a bare conjecture of men, than that ever any man hath made experience of any such sea. And that which they speak of *Mare glaciale*, may be truly thought to be spoken of these parts; for this may well be called indeed the icy sea, but not the frozen sea, for no sea consisting of salt water can be frozen, as I have more at large herein shewed my opinion in my second voyage, for it seemeth impossible for any sea to be frozen which hath his course of ebbing and flowing, especially in those places where the tides do ebb and flow above ten fathoms. And also all these aforesaid ice, which we sometimes met a hundred miles from land, being gathered out of the salt sea, are in taste fresh, and being dissolved become sweet and wholesome water.

And the cause why this year we have been more cumbered with ice than at other times before, may be by reason of the easterly and southerly winds, which brought us more timely thither now than we looked for, which blowing from the sea directly upon the place of our Straits, hath kept in the ice, and not suffered them to be carried out by the ebb to the main sea, where they would in more short time have been dissolved. And all these fleeting ice are not only so dangerous in that they wind and gather so near together, that a man may pass sometimes ten or twelve miles as it were upon one firm island of ice; but also for that they open and shut together again in such sort with the tides and sea-gate, that whilst one ship followeth the other with full sails, the ice which was open unto the foremost will join and close together before the latter can come to follow the first, whereby many times our ships were brought into great danger, as being not able so suddenly to take in our sails, or stay the swift way of our ships.

We were forced many times to stem and strike great rocks of ice, and so as it were make way through mighty mountains. By which means some of the fleet, where they found the ice to open, entered in, and passed so far within the danger thereof, with continual desire to recover their port, that it was the greatest wonder of the world that they ever escaped safe, or were ever heard of again. For even at this present we missed two of the fleet, that is, the Judith, wherein was the Lieutenant-General Captain Fenton; and the Michael, whom both we supposed had been utterly lost, having not heard any tidings of them in more than twenty days before. And one of our fleet named the barque Dennis, being of an 100 tons burden, seeking way in amongst the ice, received such a blow with a rock of ice that she sunk down therewith in the sight of the whole fleet. Howbeit, having signified her danger by shooting off a piece of great ordnance, new succour of other ships came so readily unto them, that the men were all saved with boats. Within this ship that was drowned there was parcel of our house which was to be erected for them that should stay all the winter in Meta Incognita.

This was a more fearful spectacle for the fleet to behold, for that the outrageous storm which presently followed, threatened them the like fortune and danger; for the fleet being thus compassed (as aforesaid) on every side with ice, having left much behind them, through which they passed, and finding more before them, through which it was not possible to pass, there arose a sudden terrible tempest at the south-east, which blowing from the main sea directly upon the place of the Straits, brought together all the ice a sea-board of us upon our backs, and thereby debarred us of turning back to recover sea-room again; so that being thus compassed with danger on every side, sundry men with sundry devices sought the best way to save themselves. Some of the ships, where they could find a place more clear of ice, and get a little berth of sea-room, did take in their sails, and there lay adrift. Other some fastened and moored anchor upon a great island of ice, and rode under the lee thereof, supposing to be better guarded thereby from the outrageous winds, and the danger of the lesser fleeting ice. And again some were so fast shut up, and compassed in amongst an infinite number of great countries and islands of ice, that they were fain to submit themselves and their ships to the mercy of the unmerciful ice, and strengthened the sides of their ships with junks of cables, beds, masts, planks, and such like, which being hanged overboard on the sides of their ships, might the better defend them from the outrageous sway and strokes of the said ice. But as in greatest distress men of best valour are best to be discerned, so it is greatly worthy commendation and noting with what invincible mind every Captain encouraged his company, and with what incredible labour the painful mariners and poor miners (unacquainted with such extremities) to the everlasting renown of our nation, did overcome the brunt of these so great and extreme dangers; for some, even without board upon the ice, and some within board upon the sides of their ships, having poles, pikes, pieces of timber, and oars in their hands, stood almost day and night without any rest, bearing off the force, and breaking the sway of the ice with such incredible pain and peril, that it was wonderful to behold, which otherwise no doubt had stricken quite through and through the sides of their ships, notwithstanding our former provision; for planks of timber of more than three inches thick, and other things of greater force and bigness, by the surging of the sea and billows, with the ice were shivered and cut in sunder, at the sides of our ships, so that it will seem more than credible to be reported of. And yet (that which is more) it is faithfully and plainly to be proved, and that by many substantial witnesses, that our ships, even those of greatest burdens, with the meeting of contrary waves of the sea, were heaved up between islands of ice, a foot well near out of the sea, above their watermark, having their knees and timbers within board both bowed and broken therewith.

And amidst these extremes, whilst some laboured for defence of the ships, and sought to save their bodies, other some of more milder spirit sought to save the soul by devout prayer and meditation to the Almighty, thinking indeed by no other means possible than by a Divine miracle to have their deliverance; so that there was none that were either idle, or not well occupied; and he that held himself in best security had (God knoweth) but only bare hope remaining for his best safety. Thus all the gallant fleet and miserable men, without hope of ever getting forth again, distressed with these extremities, remained here all the whole night and part of the next day, excepting four ships—that is, the Anne Francis, the Moon, the Francis of Foy, and the Gabriel, which being somewhat a-seaboard of the fleet, and being fast ships by a wind, having a more scope of clear, tried it out all the time of the storm under sail, being hardly able to bear a coast of each.

And albeit, by reason of the fleeting ice, which were dispersed here almost the whole sea over, they were brought many times to the extremest point of peril, mountains of ice ten thousand times escaping them scarce one inch, which to have stricken had been their present destruction, considering the swift course and way of the ships, and the unwieldiness of them to stay and turn as a man would wish, yet they esteemed it their better safety, with such peril, to seek sea-room, than, without hope of ever getting liberty, to lie striving against the stream and beating amongst the icy mountains, whose hugeness and monstrous greatness was such that no man could credit but such as, to their pains, saw and felt it. And these four ships by the next day at noon got out to sea, and were first clear of the ice; who now, enjoying their own liberty, began anew to sorrow and fear for their fellows' safeties; and, devoutly kneeling about their mainmast, they gave unto God humble thanks, not only for themselves, but besought Him likewise highly for their friends' deliverance. And even now whilst amidst these extremities this gallant fleet and valiant men were altogether over-laboured and fore-watched with the long and fearful continuance of the aforesaid dangers, it pleased God with His eyes of mercy to look down from heaven to send them help in good time, giving them the next day a more favourable wind at the west-north-west, which did not only disperse and drive forth the ice before them, but also gave them liberty of more scope and searoom; and they were by night of the same day following perceived of the other four ships, where, to their greatest comfort, they enjoyed again the fellowship one of another. Some in mending the sides of their ships, some in setting up their topmasts, and mending their sails and tacklings; again, some complaining of their false stem borne away, some in stopping their leaks, some in recounting their dangers past, spent no small time and labour. So that I dare well avouch there were never men more dangerously distressed, nor more mercifully by God's providence delivered. And hereof both the torn ships and the forwearied bodies of the men arrived do bear most evident mark and witness. And now the whole fleet plied off to seaward, resolving there to abide until the sun might consume, or the force of wind disperse, these ice from the place of their passage. And being a good berth off the shore, they took in their sails and lay adrift.

On the 7th of July, as men nothing yet dismayed, we cast about towards the inward, and had sight of land, which rose in form like the Northerland of the Straits, which some of the fleet, and those not the worst mariners, judged to be the North Foreland; howbeit, other some were of contrary opinion. But the matter was not well to be discerned by reason of the thick fog which a long time hung upon the coast, and the new-falling snow, which yearly altereth the shape of the land, and taketh away sometimes the mariner's marks. And by reason of the dark mists, which continued by the space of twenty days together, this doubt grew the greater and the longer perilous. For whereas indeed we thought ourselves to be upon the north-east side of Frobisher's Straits, we were now carried to the south-westwards of the Queen's Foreland, and, being deceived by a swift current coming from the north-east, were brought to the south-westwards of our said course many miles more than we did think possible could come to pass. The cause whereof we have since found, and it shall be at large hereafter declared.

Here we made a point of land which some mistook for a place in the Straits called Mount Warwick. But how we should be so far shot up so suddenly within the said Straits the expertest mariners began to marvel, thinking it a thing impossible that they could be so far overtaken in their accounts, or that any current could deceive them here which they had not by former experience proved and found out. Howbeit, many confessed that they found a swifter course of flood than before time they had observed. And truly it was wonderful to hear and see the rushing and noise that the tides do make in this place, with so violent a force that our ships lying a-hull were turned sometimes round about even in a moment, after the manner of a whirlpool, and the noise of the stream no less to be heard afar off than the waterfall of London Bridge.

But whilst the fleet lay thus doubtful amongst great store of ice, in a place they knew not, without sight of sun, whereby to take the height, and so to know the true elevation of the pole, and without any clear of light to make perfect the coast, the General, with the captains and masters of his ships, began doubtfully to question of the matter, and sent his pinnace aboard to hear each man's opinion, and specially of James Beare, Master of the Anne Francis, who was known to be a sufficient and skilful mariner, and, having been there the year before, had well observed the place, and drawn out charts of the coast. But the rather this matter grew the more doubtful, for that Christopher Hall, chief pilot of the voyage, delivered a plain and public opinion, in the hearing of the whole fleet, that he had never seen the foresaid coast before, and that he could not make it for any place of Frobisher's Straits, as some of the fleet supposed; and yet the lands do lie and trend so like, that the best mariners therein may be deceived.

On the 10th of July, the weather still continuing thick and dark, some of the ships in the fog lost sight of the Admiral and the rest of the fleet, and, wandering to and fro, with doubtful opinion whether it were best to seek back again to seaward through great store of ice, or to follow on a doubtful course in a sea, bay, or straits they knew not, or along a coast whereof, by reason of the dark mists, they could not discern the dangers, if by chance any rock or broken ground should lie off the place, as commonly in these parts it doth. The Vice-Admiral Captain Yorke, considering the aforesaid opinion of the pilot Hall, who was with him in the Thomas Allen, having lost sight of the fleet, turned back to sea again, having two other ships in company with him. Also the Captain of the Anne Francis, having likewise lost company of the fleet, and being all alone, held it for best to turn it out to sea again until they might have clear weather to take the sun's altitude, and with incredible pain and peril got out of the doubtful place into the open sea again, being so narrowly distressed by the way by means of continual fog and ice, that they were many times ready to leap upon an island of ice to avoid the present danger, and so hoping to prolong life awhile meant rather to die a pining death. Some hoped to save themselves on chests, and some determined to tie the hatches of the ships together, and to bind themselves with their furniture fast thereunto, and so to be towed with the shipboat ashore, which otherwise could not receive half of the company, by which means, if happily they had arrived, they should either have perished for lack of food to eat, or else should themselves have been eaten of those ravenous, bloody, and men-eating people. The rest of the fleet following the course of the General, which led them the way, passed up above sixty leagues within the said doubtful and supposed straits, having always a fair continent upon their starboard side, and a continuance still of an open sea before them.

The General albeit with the first perchance he found out the error, and that this was not the old straits, yet he persuaded the fleet always that they were in their right course and known straits. Howbeit, I suppose he rather dissembled his opinion therein than otherwise, meaning by that policy (being himself led with an honourable desire of further discovery) to induce the fleet to follow him, to see a further proof of that place. And, as some of the company reported, he hath since confessed that if it had not been for the charge and care he had of the fleet and fraughted ships, he both would and could have gone through to the South Sea called *Mar del Sur*, and dissolved the long doubt of the passage which we seek to find to the rich country of Cathay.

1. Of which mistaken straits, considering the circumstance, we have great cause to confirm our opinion, to like and hope well of the passage in this place. For the foresaid bay or sea, the further we sailed therein the wider we found it, with great likelihood of endless continuance. And where in other places we were much troubled with ice, as in the entrance of the same, so after we had

sailed fifty or sixty leagues therein we had no let of ice, or other thing at all, as in other places we found.

2. Also this place seemeth to have a marvellous great indraft, and draweth into it most of the drift ice and other things which do float in the sea, either to the north or eastwards of the same, as by good experience we have found.

3. For here also we met with boards, laths, and divers other things driving in the sea, which was of the wreck of the ship called the barque Dennis, which perished amongst the ice as beforesaid, being lost at the first attempt of the entrance overthwart the Queen's Foreland in the mouth of Frobisher's Straits, which could by no means have been so brought thither, neither by wind nor tide, being lost so many leagues off, if by force of the said current the same had not been violently brought. For if the same had been brought thither by tide of flood, look how far the said flood had carried it, the ebb would have re-carried it as far back again, and by the wind it could not so come to pass, because it was then sometimes calm, and most times contrary. And some mariners do affirm that they have diligently observed, that there runneth in this place nine hours' flood to three ebb, which may thus come to pass by force of the said current: for whereas the sea in most places of the world doth more or less ordinarily ebb and flow once every twelve hours, with six hours' ebb and six hours' flood, so also would it do there, were it not for the violence of this hastening current, which forceth the flood to make appearance to begin before his ordinary time one hour and a half, and also to continue longer than his natural course by another hour and a half, until the force of the ebb be so great that it will no longer be resisted: according to the saying, "*Naturam expellas furca licet, usque recurret.*" "Although nature and natural courses be forced and resisted never so much, yet at last they will have their own sway again."

4. Moreover it is not possible that so great course of floods and current, so high swelling tides with continuance of so deep waters, can be digested here without unburdening themselves into some open sea beyond this place, which argueth the more likelihood of the passage to be hereabouts. Also we suppose these great indrafts do grow and are made by the reverberation and reflection of that same current, which at our coming by Ireland, met and crossed us, of which in the first part of this discourse I spoke, which coming from the bay of Mexico, passing by and washing

the south-west parts of Ireland, reboundeth over to the north-east parts of the world, as Norway, Iceland, &c., where not finding any passage to an open sea, but rather being there increased by a new access, and another current meeting with it from the Scythian sea, passing the bay of Saint Nicholas westwards, it doth once again rebound back, by the coasts of Greenland, and from thence upon Frobisher's Straits, being to the south-westwards of the same.

5. And if that principle of philosophy be true, that "*Inferiora corpora reguntur à superioribus,*" that is, "if inferior bodies be governed, ruled, and carried after the manner and course of the superiors," then the water being an inferior element, must needs be governed after the superior heaven, and so follow the course of *Primum mobile* from east to west.

6. But every man that hath written or considered anything of this passage, hath more doubted the return by the same way by reason of a great downfall of water, which they imagine to be thereabouts (which we also by experience partly find) than any mistrust they have of the same passage at all. For we find (as it were) a great downfall in this place, but yet not such but that we may return, although with much ado. For we were easier carried in one hour than we could get forth again in three. Also by another experience at another time, we found this current to deceive us in this sort: That whereas we supposed it to be fifteen leagues off, and lying a-hull, we were brought within two leagues of the shore contrary to all expectation.

Our men that sailed furthest in the same mistaken Straits (having the mainland upon their starboard side) affirm that they met with the outlet or passage of water which cometh through Frobisher's Straits, and followeth as all one into this passage. Some of our company also affirm that they had sight of a continent upon their larboard side, being sixty leagues within the supposed Straits: howbeit, except certain islands in the entrance hereof we could make no part perfect thereof. All the foresaid tract of land seemeth to be more fruitful and better stored of grass, deer, wild fowl, as partridges, larks, sea-mews, gulls, willmots, falcons, and tassel gentils, ravens, bears, hares, foxes, and other things, than any other part we have yet discovered, and is more populous. And here Luke Ward, a gentleman of the company, traded merchandise, and did exchange knives, bells, looking-glasses, &c., with those country people, who brought him fowl, fish, bear's-skins, and such like, as their country yieldeth, for the same. Here also they saw of those greater boats of the country, with twenty persons in a-piece.

Now after the General had bestowed these many days here, not without many dangers, he returned back again. And by the way sailing along this coast (being the backside of the supposed continent of America) and the Queen's Foreland, he perceived a great sound to go through into Frobisher's Straits. Whereupon he sent the Gabriel, on the 21st of July, to prove whether they might go through and meet again with him in the Straits, which they did: and, as we imagined before, so the Queen's Foreland proved an island, as I think most of these supposed continents will. And so he departed towards the Straits, thinking it were high time now to recover his port, and to provide the fleet of their lading, whereof he was not a little careful, as shall by the process and his resolute attempts appear. And in his return with the rest of the fleet he was so intangled by reason of the dark fog amongst a number of islands and broken ground that lie off this coast, that many of the ships came over the top of rocks, which presently after they might perceive to lie dry, having not half-a-foot of water more than some of their ships did draw. And by reason they could not with a small gale of wind stem the force of the flood, whereby to get clear off the rocks, they were fain to let an anchor fall with two bent of cable together, at an hundred and odd fathoms deep, where otherwise they had been by the force of the tides carried upon the rocks again, and perished: so that if God in these fortunes (as a merciful guide, beyond the expectation of man) had not carried us through, we had surely perished amidst these dangers. For being many times driven hard aboard the shore without any sight of land, until we were ready to make shipwreck thereon, being forced commonly with our boats to sound before our ships, least we might light thereon before we could discern the same; it pleased God to give us a clear of sun and light for a short time to see and avoid thereby the danger, having been continually dark before, and presently after. Many times also by means of fog and currents being driven near upon the coast, God lent us even at the very pinch one prosperous breath of wind or other, whereby to double the land and avoid the peril, and when that we were all without hope of help, every man recommending himself to death, and crying out, "Lord, now help or never, now Lord look down from heaven and save us sinners, or else our safety cometh too late:" even then the mighty maker of heaven, and our merciful God, did deliver us : so that they who have been partakers of these dangers do even in their souls confess, that God even by miracle hath sought to save them, whose name be praised evermore.

Long time now the Anne Francis had lain beating off and on all alone before the Queen's Foreland, not being able to recover their port for ice, albeit many times they dangerously attempted it, for yet the ice choked up the passage, and would not suffer them to enter. And having never seen any of the fleet since twenty days past, when by reason of the thick mists they were severed in the mistaken Straits, they did now this present 23rd of July overthwart a place in the Straits called Hatton's Headland, where they met with seven ships of the fleet again, which good hap did not only rejoice them for themselves, in respect of the comfort which they received by such good company, but especially that by this means they were put out of doubt of their dear friends, whose safeties long time they did not a little suspect and fear. At their meeting they hailed the Admiral after the manner of the sea, and with great joy welcomed one another with a thundering volley of shot. And now every man declared at large the fortunes and dangers which they had passed.

On the 24th of July we met with the Francis of Foy, who with much ado fought way back again through the ice from out of the mistaken Straits, where (to their great peril) they proved to recover their port. They brought the first news of the Vice-Admiral Captain York, who many days with themselves, and the Buss of Bridgewater was missing. They reported that they left the Vice-Admiral reasonably clear of the ice, but the other ship they greatly feared, whom they could not come to help, being themselves so hardly distressed as never men more. Also they told us of the Gabriel, who having got through from the backside and western point of the Queen's Foreland into Frobisher's Straits, fell into their company about the Cape of Good Hope.

And upon the 27th day of July, the ship of Bridgewater got out of the ice and met with the fleet which lay off and on under Hatton's Headland. They reported of their marvellous accidents and dangers, declaring their ship to be so leak that they must of necessity seek harbour, having their stem so beaten within their huddings, that they had much ado to keep themselves above water. They had (as they say) five hundred strokes at the pump in less than half a watch, being scarce two hours ; their men being so over-wearied therewith, and with the former dangers, that they desired help of men from the other ships. Moreover they declared that there was nothing but ice and danger where they had been, and that the Straits within were frozen up, and that it was the most impossible thing of the world, to pass up into the Countess of Warwick's Sound, which was the place of our port.

The report of these dangers by these ships thus published amongst the fleet, with the remembrance of the perils past, and those present before their face, brought no small fear and terror into the hearts of many considerate men, so that some began privily to murmur against the General for this wilful manner of proceeding. Some desired to discover some harbour thereabouts to refresh themselves and reform their broken vessels for awhile, until the north and north-west winds might disperse the ice, and make the place more free to pass. Other some forgetting themselves, spake more undutifully in this behalf, saying, that they had as lief be hanged when they came home, as without hope of safety to seek to pass, and so to perish amongst the ice.

The General, not opening his ears to the peevish passion of any private person, but chiefly respecting the accomplishment of the cause he had undertaken (wherein the chief reputation and fame of a General and Captain consisteth), and calling to his remembrance the short time he had in hand to provide so great number of ships their loading, determined with this resolution to pass and recover his port, or else there to bury himself with his attempt. Notwithstanding, somewhat to appease the feeble passions of the fearful sort, and the better to entertain time for a season, whilst the ice might the better be dissolved, he hailed on the fleet with belief that he would put them into harbour; thereupon whilst the ships lay off and on under Hatton's Headland, he sought to go in with his pinnaces amongst the islands there, as though he meant to search for harbour, where indeed he meant nothing less, but rather sought if any ore might be found in that place, as by the sequel appeared.

In the meantime whilst the fleet lay thus doubtful without any certain resolution what to do, being hard aboard the lee-shore, there arose a sudden and terrible tempest at the south-southeast, whereby the ice began marvellously to gather about us. Whereupon every man, as in such case of extremity he thought best, sought the wisest way for his own safety. The most part of the fleet which were further shot up within the Straits, and so far to the leeward, as that they could not double the land, following the course of the General, who led them the way, took in their sails, and laid it a-hull amongst the ice, and so passed over the storm, and had no extremity at all, but for a short time in the same place. Howbeit the other ships which plied out to seaward, had an extreme storm for a longer season. And the nature of the place is such, that it is subject diversely to divers winds, according to the sundry situation of the great Alps and mountains there, every mountain causing a general blast and pirry after the manner of a Levant.

In this storm, being the 26th of July, there fell so much snow, with such bitter cold air, that we could not scarce see one another for the same, nor open our eyes to handle our ropes and sails, the snow being above half-a-foot deep upon the hatches of our ship, which did so wet through our poor mariners' clothes, that he that had five or six shifts of apparel had scarce one dry thread to his back, which kind of wet and coldness, together with the over-labouring of the poor men amongst the ice, bred no small sickness amongst the fleet, which somewhat discouraged some of the poor men, who had not experience of the like before, every man persuading himself that the winter there must needs be extreme, where they found so unseasonable a summer. And yet, notwithstanding this cold air, the sun many times hath a marvellous force of heat amongst those mountains, insomuch that when there is no breath of wind to bring the cold air from the dispersed ice upon us, we shall be weary of the blooming heat, and then suddenly with a pirry of wind which cometh down from the hollowness of the hills, we shall have such a breath of heat brought upon our faces as though we were entered within some bath-stove or hot-house, and when the first of the pirry and blast is past, we shall have the wind suddenly anew blow cold again.

In this storm the Anne Francis, the Moon, and the Thomas of Ipswich, who found themselves able to hold it up with a sail, and could double about the Cape of the Queen's Foreland, plied out to the seaward, holding it for better policy and safety to seek sea-room, than to hazard the continuance of the storm, the danger of the ice, and the lee-shore. And being uncertain at this time of the General's private determination, the weather being so dark that they could not discern one another, nor perceive which may be wrought, betook themselves to this course for best and safest.

The General, notwithstanding the great storm, following his own former resolution, sought by all means possible, by a shorter way, to recover his port, and where he saw the ice ever so little open, he got in at one gap and out at another, and so himself valiantly led the way through before to induce the fleet to follow after, and with incredible pain and peril at length got through the ice, and upon the 31st of July recovered his long-wished port after many attempts and sundry times being put back, and came to anchor in the Countess of Warwick's Sound, in the entrance whereof, when he thought all peril past, he encountered a great island of ice, which gave the Aid such a blow, having a little before weighed her anchor a-cock-bill, that it struck the anchor-fluke through the ship's bows under the water, which caused so great a leak, that with much ado they preserved the ship from sinking.

At their arrival here they perceived two ships at anchor within the harbour, whereat they began much to marvel and greatly to rejoice, for those they knew to be the Michael, wherein was the Lieutenant-General, Captain Fenton, and the small bark called the Gabriel, who so long time were missing, and never heard of before, whom every man made the last reckoning never to hear of again. Here every man greatly rejoiced of their happy meeting, and welcomed one another after the sea manner with their great ordnance, and when each party had ripped up their sundry fortunes and perils past, they highly praised God, and altogether upon their knees gave Him due humble and hearty thanks, and Master Wolfall, a learned man, appointed by Her Majesty's Council to be their minister and preacher, made unto them a godly sermon, exhorting them especially to be thankful to God for their strange and miraculous deliverance in those so dangerous places, and putting them in mind of the uncertainty of man's life, willed them to make themselves always ready as resolute men to enjoy and accept thankfully whatsoever adventure his divine providence should appoint. This Master Wolfall, being well seated and settled at home in his own country, with a good and large living, having a good honest woman to wife, and very towardly children, being of good reputation among the best, refused not to take in hand this painful voyage, for the only care he had to save souls, and to reform those infidels, if it were possible, to Christianity; and also partly for the great desire he had that this notable voyage, so well begun, might be brought to perfection; and therefore he was contented to stay there the whole year if occasion had served, being in every necessary action as forward as the resolutest men of all. Wherefore in this behalf he may rightly be called a true pastor and minister of God's word, which for the profit of his flock spared not to venture his own life.

But to return again to Captain Fenton's company, and to speak somewhat of their dangers (albeit they be more than by writing can be expressed): they reported that from the night of the first storm which was about the 1st of July until seven days before the General's arrival, which was the 26th of the same, they never saw one day or hour wherein they were not troubled with continual danger and fear of death, and were twenty days almost together fast amongst the ice. They had their ship stricken through and through on both sides, their false stem borne quite away, and could go from their ship in some places upon the ice very many miles, and might easily have passed from one island of ice to another even to the shore; and if God had not wonderfully provided for them and their necessity, and time had not made them more cunning and wise to seek strange remedies for strange kinds of dangers, it had been impossible for them ever to have escaped; for among other devices, wheresoever they found any island of ice of greater bigness than the rest (as there be some of more than half a mile compass about, and almost forty fathom high) they commonly coveted to recover the same, and thereof to make a bulwark for their defence, whereon having moored anchor, they rode under the lee thereof for a time, being thereby guarded from the danger of the lesser driving ice. But when they must needs forego this new found fort by means of other ice, which at length would undermine and compass them round about, and when that by heaving of the billow they were therewith liked to be bruised in pieces, they used to make fast the ship unto the most firm and broad piece of ice they could find, and binding her nose fast thereunto, would fill all their sails, whereon the wind having great power, would force forward the ship, and so the ship bearing before her the ice, and so one ice driving forward another, should at length get scope and sea-room; and having by this means at length put their enemies to flight, they occupied the clear place for a pretty season among sundry mountains and alps of ice. One there was found by measure to be sixty-five fathom above water, which, for a kind of similitude, was called Solomon's Porch. Some think those islands eight times so much under water as they are above, because of their monstrous weight. But now I remember I saw very strange wonders: men walking, running, leaping and shooting upon the main seas, forty miles from any land, without any ship or other vessel under them. Also I saw fresh rivers running amidst the salt sea a hundred miles from land; which if any man will not believe, let him know that many of our company leaped out of their ships upon islands of ice, and running there up and down, did shoot at butts upon the ice, and with their calivers did kill great seals, which use to lie and sleep upon the ice; and this ice melting above at the top by reflection of the sun, came down in sundry streams, which, uniting together, made a pretty brook able to drive a mill. The said Captain Fenton recovered his port ten days before any man, and spent good time in searching for mines, and he found good store thereof. He also discovered about ten miles up into the country, where he perceived neither town, village, nor likelihood of habitation, but it seemeth (as he saith) barren as the other parts which as yet we have entered upon; but their victuals and provisions went so scant with them, that they had determined to return homeward within seven days after if the fleet had not then arrived.

The General, after his arrival in the Countess's Sound, spent no time in vain, but immediately at his first landing called the chief captains of his council together, and consulted with them for the speedier execution of such things as then they had in hand. As, first, for searching and finding out good mineral for the miners to be occupied on. Then to give good orders to be observed of the whole company on shore. And lastly, to consider for the erecting up of the fort and house for the use of them which were to abide there the whole year. For the better handling of these, and all other like important causes in this service, it was ordained from Her Majesty and the council that the General should call unto him certain of the chief captains and gentlemen in council to confer, consult, and determine of all occurrences in this service, whose names are as here they follow:—Captain Fenton, Captain Yorke, Captain Best, Captain Carew, and Captain Philpot. And in sea causes to have as assistants Christopher Hall and Charles Jackman, being both very good pilots and sufficient mariners, whereof the one was chief pilot of the voyage and the other for the discovery. From the place of our habitation westward Master Selman was appointed notary, to register the whole manner of proceeding in these affairs, that true relation thereof might be made if it pleased Her Majesty to require it.

On the 1st of August every captain, by order from the General and his council, was commanded to bring ashore unto the Countess's Island all such gentlemen, soldiers, and miners as were under their charge, with such provision as they had of victuals, tents, and things necessary for the speedy getting together of mines and freight for the ships. The muster of the men being taken, and the victuals, with all other things viewed and considered, every man was set to his charge as his place and office required. The miners were appointed where to work and the mariners discharged their ships. On the 2nd of August were published and proclaimed upon the Countess of Warwick's Island, with sound of trumpet, certain orders of the General and his council, appointed to be observed of the company during the time of their abiding there. In the meantime, while the mariners plied their work, the captains sought out new mines, the gold-finers made trial of the ore, the mariners discharged their ships, the gentlemen for example's sake laboured heartily and honestly encouraged the inferior sort to work. So that the small time of that little leisure that was left to tarry was spent in vain.

On the 2nd of August the Gabriel arrived, who came from the Vice-Admiral, and being distressed sore with ice, put into harbour near unto Mount Oxford. And now was the whole fleet arrived safely at their port excepting four, besides the ship that was lost— that is, the Thomas Allen, the Anne Francis, the Thomas of Ipswich, and the Moon, whose absence was some let unto the works and other proceedings, as well for that these ships were furnished with the better sort of miners as with other provision for the habitation.

On the 9th of August the General with the captains of his council assembled together, and began to consider and take order for the erecting up of the house or fort for them that were to inhabit there the whole year, and that presently the masons and carpenters might go in hand therewith. First, therefore, they perused the bills of lading, what every man received into his ship, and found that there was arrived only the east side and the south side of the house, and yet not that perfect and entire; for many pieces thereof were used for fenders in many ships, and so broken in pieces whilst they were distressed in the ice. Also after due examination had, and true account taken, there was found want of drink and fuel to serve one hundred men, which was the number appointed first to inhabit there, because their greatest store was in the ships which were not yet arrived. Then Captain Fenton, seeing the scarcity of the necessary things aforesaid, was contented, and offered himself to inhabit there with sixty men. Whereupon they caused the carpenters and masons to come before them, and demanded in what time they would take upon them to erect up a less house for sixty men. They required eight or nine weeks, if there were timber sufficient, whereas now they had but six-and-twenty days in all to remain in that country. Wherefore it was fully agreed upon and resolved by the General and his council that no habitation should be there this year. And therefore they willed Master Selman the registrar to set down this decree with all their contents, for the better satisfying of Her Majesty, the Lords of the Council, and the adventurers.

The Anne Francis, since she was parted from the fleet in the last storm before spoken of, could never recover above five leagues within the Straits, the wind being sometime contrary, and most times the ice compassing them round about. And from that time, being about the 27th of July, they could neither hear nor have sight of any of the fleet until the 3rd of August, when they descried a sail near unto Mount Oxford, with whom when they had spoken they could understand no news of any of the fleet at all. And this was the Thomas of Ipswich, who had lain beating off and on at sea with very foul weather and contrary winds ever since that aforesaid storm without sight of any man. They kept company not long together, but were forced to lose one another again, the Moon being consort always with the Anne Francis, and keeping very good company, plied up together into the Straits, with great desire to recover their long wished-for port. And they attempted as often, and passed as far as possible the wind, weather, and ice gave them leave, which commonly they found very contrary. For when the weather was clear and without fog then commonly the wind was contrary. And when it was either easterly or southerly, which would serve their turns, then had they so great a fog and dark mist therewith that either they could not discern way through the ice, or else the ice lay so thick together that it was impossible for them to pass. And on the other side, when it was calm, the tides had force to bring the ice so suddenly about them, that commonly then they were most therewith distressed, having no wind to carry them from the danger thereof.

And by the 6th of August, being with much ado got up as high as Leicester Point they had good hope to find the southern shore clear, and so to pass up towards their port. But being there becalmed and lying a-hull openly upon the great bay which cometh out of the mistaken straits before spoken of, they were so suddenly compassed with ice round about by means of the swift tides which run in that place, that they were never afore so hardly beset as now. And, in seeking to avoid these dangers in the dark weather, the Anne Francis lost sight of the other two ships, who, being likewise hardly distressed, signified their danger, as they since reported, by shooting off their ordnance, which the other could not hear, nor, if they had heard, could have given them any remedy, being so busily occupied to wind themselves out of their own troubles.

The flee-boat called the Moon was here heaved above the water with the force of the ice, and received a great leak thereby. Likewise the Thomas of Ipswich and the Anne Francis were sore bruised at that instant, having their false stems borne away and their ship-sides strucken quite through.

Now, considering the continual dangers and contraries and the little leisure that they had left to tarry in these parts, besides that every night the ropes of their ships were so frozen that a man could not handle them without cutting his hands, together with the great doubt they had of the fleet's safety, thinking it an impossibility for them to pass unto their port, as well for that they saw themselves as for that they heard by the former report of the ships which had proved before, who affirmed that the Straits were all frozen over within, they thought it now very high time to consider of their estates and safeties that were yet left together. And hereupon the captains and masters of these ships desired the Captain of the Anne Francis to enter into consideration with them of these matters. Wherefore Captain Tanfield, of the Thomas of Ipswich, with his pilot Richard Cox, and Captain Upcote, of the Moon, with his master, John Lakes, came aboard the Anne Francis on the 8th of August to consult of these causes. And being assembled together in the Captain's cabin, sundry doubts were there alleged. For the fearfuller sort of mariners, being over-tired with the continued labour of the former dangers, coveted to return homeward, saying that they would not again tempt God so much, who had given them so many warnings and delivered them from so wonderful dangers, that they rather desired to lose wages, freight and all, than to continue and follow such desperate fortunes. Again, their ships were so leaky and the men so weary, that, to amend the one and refresh the other, they must of necessity seek into harbour.

But on the other side it was argued again to the contrary that to seek into harbour thereabouts was but to subject themselves to double dangers. If happily they escaped the dangers of the rocks in their entering, yet, being in, they were nevertheless subject there to the danger of the ice which with the swift tides and currents is carried in and out in most harbours thereabouts, and may thereby gall their cables asunder, drive them upon the shore, and bring them to much trouble. Also the coast is so much subject to broken ground and rocks, especially in the mouth and entrance of every harbour, that albeit the Channel be sounded over and over again, yet are you never the nearer to discern the dangers. For the bottom of the sea holding like shape and form as the land, being full of hills, dales, and ragged rocks, suffereth you not by your soundings to know and keep a true guess of the depth. For you shall sound upon the side or hollowness of one hill or rock under water and have a hundred, fifty, or forty fathom deep; and before the next cast, ere you shall be able to heave your lead again, you shall be upon the top thereof, and come aground to your utter confusion.

Another reason against going to harbour was that the cold air did threaten a sudden freezing up of the sounds, seeing that every night there was new congealed ice, even of that water which remained within the ships. And therefore it should seem to be more safe to lie off and on at sea than for lack of wind to bring them forth of harbour, to hazard by sudden frosts to be shut up the whole year.

After many such dangers and reasons alleged, and large debating of these causes on both sides, the Captain of the Anne Francis delivered his opinion unto the company to this effect :—First, concerning the question of returning home, he thought it so much dishonourable as not to grow in any farther question; and again, to return home at length (as at length they must needs) and not to be able to bring a certain report of the fleet, whether they were living or lost, or whether any of them had recovered their port or not in the Countess's Sound (as it was to be thought the most part would if they were living), he said that it would be so great an argument either of want of courage or discretion in them, as he resolved rather to fall into any danger than so shamefully consent to return home, protesting that it should never be spoken of him that he would ever return without doing his endeavour to find the fleet and know the certainty of the General's safety. He put his company in remembrance of a pinnace of five tons burden which he had within his ship, which was carried in pieces and unmade up, for the use of those which should inhabit there the whole year, the which, if they could find means to join together, he offered himself to prove before therewith, whether it were possible for any boat to pass for ice, whereby the ship might be brought in after, and might also thereby give true notice if any of the fleet were arrived at their port or not.

But notwithstanding, for that he well perceived that the most part of his company were addicted to put into harbour, he was willing the rather for these causes somewhat to incline thereunto. As first, to search along the same coast and the Sounds thereabouts, he thought it to be to good purpose, for that it was likely to find some of the fleet there, which, being leaky and sore bruised with the ice, were the rather thought likely to be put into an ill harbour, being distressed with foul weather in the last storm, than to hazard their uncertain safeties amongst the ice; for about this place they lost them, and left the fleet then doubtfully questioning of harbour.

It was likely, also, that they might find some fit harbour thereabouts, which might be behoveful for them against another time. It was not likewise impossible to find some ore or mines thereabouts wherewithal to freight their ships, which would be more commodious in this place for the nearness to seaward and for a better outlet than further within the Straits, being likely here always to load in a shorter time, howsoever the Strait should be pestered with ice within, so that if it might come to pass that thereby they might either find the fleet, mine, or convenient harbour, any of these three would serve their present turns, and give some hope and comfort unto their companies, which now were altogether comfortless. But if that all fortune should fall out so contrary that they could neither recover their port nor any of these aforesaid helps, that yet they would not depart the coast as long as it was possible for them to tarry there, but would lie off and on at sea athwart the place. Therefore his final conclusion was set down thus —First, that the Thomas of Ipswich and the Moon should consort and keep company together carefully with the Anne Francis, as near as they could, and, as true Englishmen and faithful friends, should supply one another's want in all fortunes and dangers. In the morning following, every ship to send off his boat with a sufficient pilot to search out and sound the harbours for the safe bringing in of their ships. And being arrived in harbour, where they might find convenient place for the purpose, they resolved forthwith to join and set together the pinnace, wherewithal the Captain of the Anne Francis might, according to his former determination, discover up into the Straits.

After these determinations thus set down, the Thomas of Ipswich the night following lost company of the other ships, and afterward shaped a contrary course homeward, which fell out, as it manifestly appeared, very much against their Captain Master Tanfield's mind, as by due examination before the Lords of Her Majesty's Most Honourable Privy Council it hath since been proved, to the great discredit of the Pilot Cox, who specially persuaded his company, against the opinion of the said Captain, to return home.

And, as the Captain of the Anne Francis doth witness, even at their conference together Captain Tanfield told him that he did not a little suspect the said Pilot Cox, saying that he had opinion in the man neither of honest duty, manhood, nor constancy. Notwithstanding the said ship's departure, the Captain of the Anne Francis, being desirous to put in execution his former resolutions, went with the ship's boat (being accompanied also with the Moon's skiff) to prove amongst the islands which lie under Hatton's Headland if any convenient harbour, or any knowledge of the fleet, or any good ore were there to be found. The ships lying off and on at sea the while under sail, searching through many sounds, they saw them all full of many dangers and broken ground; yet one there was, which seemed an indifferent place to harbour in, and which they did very diligently sound over, and searched again.

Here the said Captain found a great black island, whereunto he had good liking; and certifying the company thereof, they were somewhat comforted, and with the good hope of his words, rowed cheerfully unto the place, where, when they arrived, they found such plenty of black ore of the same sort which was brought into England this last year, that if the goodness might answer the great plenty thereof, it was to be thought that it might reasonably suffice all the gold-gluttons of the world. This island the Captain, for cause of his good hap, called after his own name Best's Blessing, and with these good tidings returned aboard his ship on the 9th of

August, about ten o'clock at night. He was joyfully welcomed of his company, who before were discomforted, and greatly expected some better fortune at his hands.

The next day, being the 10th of August, the weather reasonably fair, they put into the foresaid harbour, having their boat for their better security sounding before their ship. But, for all the care and diligence that could be taken in sounding the Channel over and again, the Anne Francis came aground upon a sunken rock within the harbour, and lay thereon more than half dry until the next flood, when, by God's almighty providence, contrary almost to all expectation, they came afloat again, being forced all that time to underset their ship with their main-yard, which otherwise was likely to overset and put thereby in danger the whole company. They had above two thousand strokes together at the pump before they could make their ship free of the water again, so sore she was bruised by lying upon the rocks. The Moon came safely, and rode at anchor by the Anne Francis, whose help in their necessity they could not well have missed.

Now whilst the mariners were rummaging their ships and mending that which was amiss, the miners followed their labour for getting together of sufficient quantity of ore, and the carpenters endeavoured to do their best for the making up of the boat or pinnace, which to bring to pass, they wanted two special and most necessary things—that is, certain principal timbers that are called knees, which are the chief strength of any boat, and also nails wherewithal to join the planks together. Whereupon, having by chance a smith amongst them (and yet unfurnished of his necessary tools to work and make nails withal), they were fain of a gun-chamber to make an anvil to work upon, and to use a pickaxe instead of a sledge to bear withal, and also to occupy two small bellows instead of one pair of greater smith's bellows. And for lack of small iron for the easier making of the nails, they were forced to break their tongs, gridiron, and fire-shovel in pieces.

On the 11th of August the Captain of the Anne Francis, taking the master of his ship with him, went up to the top of Hatton's Headland, which is the highest land of all the Straits, to the end to descry the situation of the country underneath, and to take a true plot of the place, whereby also to see what store of ice was yet left in the Straits, as also to search what mineral matter or fruit that soil might yield. And the rather for the honour the said Captain doth owe to that honourable name which himself gave thereunto the last year, in the highest part of this headland he caused his company to make a column or cross of stone in token of Christian possession. In this place there is plenty of black ore and divers pretty stones.

On the 17th of August the captains with their companies chased and killed a great white bear, which adventured and gave a fierce assault upon twenty men being weaponed. And he served them for good meat many days. On the 18th of August, the pinnace with much ado being set together, the said Captain Best determined to depart up the Straits, to prove and make trial, as before was pretended, some of his company greatly persuading him to the contrary, and specially the carpenter that set the same together, who said he would not adventure himself therein for five hundred pounds, for that the boat hung together but only by the strength of the nails, and lacked some of the principal knees and timbers. These words somewhat discouraged some of the company which should have gone therein. Whereupon the Captain, as one not altogether addicted to his own self-will, but somewhat foreseeing how it might be afterwards spoken if contrary fortune should happen him ("Lo, he hath followed his own opinion and desperate resolutions, and so thereafter it is befallen him"), calling the master and mariners of best judgment together, declared unto them how much the cause imported him in his credit to seek out the General, as well to confer with him of some causes of weight as otherwise to make due examination and trial of the goodness of the ore, whereof they had no assurance but by guess of the eye, and it was well like the other; which so to carry home, not knowing the goodness thereof, might be as much as if they should bring so many stones. And therefore he desired them to deliver their plain and honest opinion, whether the pinnace were sufficient for him so to adventure in or no. It was answered that by careful heed-taking thereunto among the ice and the foul weather, the pinnace might suffice. And hereupon the master's mate of the Anne Francis, called John Gray, manfully and honestly offering himself unto his Captain in this adventure and service, gave cause to others of his mariners to follow the attempt.

And upon the 19th of August the said Captain, being accompanied with Captain Upcote, of the Moon, and eighteen persons in the small pinnace, having convenient portion of victuals and things necessary, departed upon the said pretended voyage, leaving their ship at anchor in a good readiness for the taking in of their freight.

And having little wind to sail withal, they plied along the southern shore, and passed above thirty leagues, having the only help of man's labour with oars, and so intending to keep that shore aboard until they were got up to the farthest and narrowest of the Straits, minded there to cross over, and to search likewise along the northerland unto the Countess's Sound, and from thence to pass all that coast along, whereby if any of the fleet had been distressed by wreck of rock or ice by that means they might be perceived of them, and so they thereby to give them such help and relief as they could. They did greatly fear and ever suspect that some of the fleet were surely cast away and driven to seek sour sallets amongst the cold cliffs.

And being shot up about forty leagues within the Straits, they put over towards the northern shore, which was not a little dangerous for their small boats; and by means of a sudden flaw were driven and fain to seek harbour in the night amongst all the rocks and broken ground of Gabriel's Islands, a place so named within the Straits above the Countess of Warwick's Sound. And by the way where they landed they did find certain great stones set up by the country people, as it seemed, for marks, where they also made many crosses of stone, in token that Christians had been there. On the 22nd of August they had sight of the Countess's Sound, and made the place perfect from the top of a hill, and, keeping along the northern shore, perceived the smoke of a fire under a hill's side, whereof they diversely deemed. When they came nearer the place they perceived people which wafted unto them, as it seemed, with a flag or ensign. And because the country people had used to do the like when they perceived any of our boats to pass by, they suspected them to be the same. And coming somewhat nearer, they might perceive certain tents, and discern this ensign to be of mingled colours, black and white, after the English fashion. But because they could see no ship, nor likelihood of harbour within five or six leagues about, and knew that none of our men were wont to frequent those parts, they could not tell what to judge thereof; but imagined that some of the ships, being carried so high with the storm and mists, had made shipwreck amongst the ice or the broken islands there, and were spoiled by the country people, who might use the sundry-coloured flag for a policy, to bring them likewise within their danger. Whereupon the said Captain with his companies resolved to recover the same ensign, if it were so, from those base people, or else to lose their lives and all together. In the end they discerned them to be their countrymen, and then they deemed them to have lost their ships, and so to be gathered together for their better strength. On the other side, the company ashore feared that the Captain, having lost his ship, came to seek forth the fleet for his relief in his poor pinnace: so that their extremities caused each part to suspect the worst.

The Captain, now with his pinnace being come near the shore, commanded his boat carefully to be kept afloat, lest in their necessity they might win the same from him, and seek first to save themselves. For every man in that case is next himself. They hailed one another according to the manner of the sea, and demanded what cheer. And either party answered the other that all was well. Whereupon there was a sudden and joyful outshout, with great flinging up of caps, and a brave volley of shot to welcome one another. And truly it was a most strange case to see how joyful and glad every party was to see themselves meet in safety again after so strange and incredible dangers. Yet, to be short, as their dangers was great so their God was greater. And here the company were working upon new mines, which Captain York, being here arrived not long before, had found out in this place, and it is named the Countess of Sussex Mine.

After some conference with our friends here, the Captain of the Anne Francis departed towards the Countess of Warwick's Sound, to speak with the General, and to have trial made of such metal as he had brought thither by the gold-finers. And so he determined to dispatch again towards his ship. And having spoken with the General, he received orders for all causes and direction as well for the bringing up of his ship to the Countess's Sound, as also to freight his ship with the same ore which he had himself found, which, upon trial made, was supposed to be very good.

On the 23rd of August the said Captain met together with the other captains (Commissioners in Council with the General) aboard the Aid, where they considered and consulted of sundry causes, which being particularly registered by the notary, were appointed where and how to be done against another year.

On the 24th of August the General, with two pinnaces and good numbers of men, went to Beare's Sound, commanding the said Captain with his pinnace to attend the service, to see if he could encounter or apprehend any of the people; for sundry times they shewed themselves busy thereabouts, sometimes with seven or eight boats in one company, as though they minded to encounter with our company, which were working there at the mines in no great numbers. But when they perceived any of our ships to ride in that road (being belike more amazed at the countenance of a ship, and a more number of men) they did never shew themselves there again at all. Wherefore our men sought with their pinnaces to compass about the island where they did use, supposing there suddenly to intercept some of them. But before our men could come near, having belike some watch in the top of the mountains, they conveyed themselves privily away, and left (as it should seem) one of their great darts behind them for haste, which we found near to a place of their caves and housing. Therefore, though our General were very desirous to have taken some of them to have brought into England, they, being now grown more wary by their former losses, would not at any time come within our dangers. About midnight of the same day the Captain of the Anne Francis departed thence and set his course over the Straits towards Hatton's Headland, being about fifteen leagues over, and returned aboard his ship on the 25th of August, to the great comfort of his company, who long expected his coming, where he found his ships ready rigged and laden. Wherefore he departed from thence again the next morning towards the Countess's Sound, where he arrived on the 28th of the same. By the way he set his miners ashore at Beare's Sound for the better despatch and gathering the ore together, for that some of the ships were behindhand with their freight, the time of the year passing suddenly away.

On the 30th of August the Anne Francis was brought aground, and had eight great leaks mended which she had received by means of the rocks and ice. On this day the masons finished a house which Captain Fenton caused to be made of lime and stone upon the Countess of Warwick's Island, to the end we might prove against the next year, whether the snow could overwhelm it, the frost break it up, or the people dismember the same. And the better to allure those brutish and uncivil people to courtesy against other times of our coming, we left therein divers of our country toys, as bells and knives, wherein they specially delight, one for the necessary use, and the other for the great pleasure thereof. Also pictures of men and women in lead, men on horseback, looking-glasses, whistles, and pipes. Also in the house was made an oven, and bread left baked therein for them to see and taste. We buried the timber of our pretended fort. Also here we sowed peas, corn, and other grain, to prove the fruitfulness of the soil against the next year.

Master Wolfall on Winter's Furnace preached a goodly sermon, which being ended, he celebrated also a communion upon the land, at the partaking whereof was the Captain of the Anne Francis, and many other gentlemen and soldiers, mariners, and miners with him. The celebration of the divine mystery was the first sign, seal, and confirmation of Christ's name, death, and passion ever known in these quarters. The said Master Wolfall made sermons, and celebrated the communion at sundry other times, in several and sundry ships, because the whole company could never meet together in any one place. The fleet now being in some good readiness for their lading, the General calling together the gentlemen and captains to consult, told them that he was very desirous that some further discovery should be attempted, and that he would not only by God's help bring home his ships laden with ore, but also meant to bring some certificate of a further discovery of the country, which thing to bring to pass (having sometime therein consulted) they found very hard and almost invincible. And considering that already they had spent some time in searching out the trending and fashion of the mistaken Straits, therefore it could not be said, but that by this voyage they have notice of a further discovery, and that the hope of the passage thereby is much furthered and increased, as appeared before in the discourse thereof. Yet notwithstanding if any means might be further devised, the captains were contented and willing, as the General should appoint and command, to take any enterprise in hand. Which, after long debating, was found a thing very impossible, and that rather consultation was to be had of returning homeward, especially for these causes following:
—First, the dark foggy mists, the continual falling snow and stormy weather which they commonly were vexed with, and now daily ever more and more increased, have no small argument of the winter drawing near. And also the frost every night was so hard congealed within the Sound, that if by evil hap they should be long kept in with contrary winds, it was greatly to be feared, that they should be shut up there fast the whole year, which being utterly unprovided, would be their utter destruction. Again, drink was so scant throughout all the fleet by means of the great leakage,

that not only the provision which was laid in for the habitation was wanting and wasted, but also each ship's several provisions spent and lost, which many of our company to their great grief found in their return, since, for all the way homewards, they drank nothing but water. And the great cause of this leakage and wasting was, for that the great timber and sea-coal, which lay so weighty upon the barrels, brake, bruised, and rotted the hoops asunder. Yet notwithstanding these reasons alleged the General himself (willing the rest of the gentlemen and captains every man to look to his several charge and lading, that against a day appointed, they should be all in readiness to set homeward) went in a pinnace, and discovered further northward in the Straits, and found that by Beare's Sound and Hall's Island the land was not firm, as it was first supposed, but all broken islands in manner of an Archipelago, and so with other secret intelligence to himself, he returned to the fleet. Where, presently upon his arrival at the Countess's Sound, he began to take order for their returning homeward, and first caused certain Articles to be proclaimed, for the better keeping of orders and courses in their return, which Articles were delivered to every captain.

Having now received Articles and directions for our return homewards, all other things being in forwardness and in good order, on the last day of August the whole fleet departed from the Countess's Sound, excepting the Judith, and the Anne Francis, who stayed for the taking in of fresh water, and came the next day and met the fleet lying off and on, athwart Beare's Sound, who stayed for the General, which then was gone ashore to despatch the two barques and the Buss of Bridgewater, for their loading, whereby to get the companies and other things aboard. The Captain of the Anne Francis, having most part of his company ashore, on the 1st of September, went also to Beare's Sound in his pinnace to fetch his men aboard; but the wind grew so great immediately upon their landing, that the ships at sea were in great danger, and some of them forcibly put from their anchors, and greatly feared to be utterly lost, as the Hopewell, wherein was Captain Carew, and others, who could not tell on which side their danger was most: for having mighty rocks threatening on the one side, and driving islands of cutting ice on the other side, they greatly feared to make shipwreck, the ice driving so near them that it touched their bowsprit. And by means of the sea that was grown so high, they were not able to put to sea with their small pinnaces to recover their ships. And again, the ships were not able to tarry or lie athwart for them, by means of the outrageous winds and swelling seas. The General willed the Captain of the Anne Francis, with his company, for that night to lodge aboard the Buss of Bridgewater, and went himself with the rest of his men aboard the barques. But their numbers were so great, and the provision of the barques so scant, that they pestered one another exceedingly. They had great hope that the next morning the weather would be fair, whereby they might recover their ships. But in the morning following it was much worse, for the storm continued greater, the sea being more swollen, and the fleet gone quite out of sight. So that now their doubts began to grow great: for the ship of Bridgewater which was of greatest receipt, and whereof they had best hope and made most account, rode so far to leeward of the harbour's mouth, that they were not able for the rocks (that lay between the wind and them) to lead it out to sea with a sail. And the barques were already so pestered with men, and so slenderly furnished with provision, that they had scarce meat for six days for such numbers.

The General in the morning departed to sea in the Gabriel to seek the fleet, leaving the Buss of Bridgewater and the Michael behind in Beare's Sound. The Buss set sail, and thought by turning in the narrow channel within the harbour to get to windward: but being put to leeward more, by that means was fain to come to anchor for her better safety, amongst a number of rocks, and there left in great danger of ever getting forth again. The Michael set sail to follow the General, and could give the Buss no relief, although they earnestly desired the same. And the Captain of the Anne Francis was left in hard election of two evils: either to abide his fortune with the Buss of Bridgewater, which was doubtful of ever getting forth, or else to be towed in his small pinnace at the stern of the Michael through the raging seas, for that the barque was not able to receive or relieve half his company, wherein his danger was not a little perilous.

So after he resolved to commit himself with all his company unto that fortune of God and sea, and was dangerously towed at the stern of the barque for many miles, until at length they espied the Anne Francis under sail, hard under their lee, which was no small comfort unto them. For no doubt, both those and a great number more had perished for lack of victuals, and convenient room in the barques without the help of the said ship. But the

honest care that the Master of the Anne Francis had of his captain, and the good regard of duty towards his General, suffered him not to depart, but honestly abode to hazard a dangerous road all the night long, notwithstanding all the stormy weather, when all the fleet besides departed. And the pinnace came no sooner aboard the ship, and the men entered, but she presently shivered and fell in pieces and sunk at the ship's stern, with all the poor mens' furniture: so weak was the boat with towing, and so forcible was the sea to bruise her in pieces. But (as God would) the men were all saved.

At this present in this storm many of the fleet were dangerously distressed, and were severed almost all asunder. Yet, thanks be to God, all the fleet arrived safely in England about the 1st of October, some in one place and some in another. But amongst other, it was most marvellous how the Buss of Bridgewater got away, who being left behind the fleet in great danger of never getting forth, was forced to seek a way northward through an unknown channel full of rocks, upon the backside of Beare's Sound, and there by good hap found out a way into the North sea, a very dangerous attempt: save that necessity, which hath no law, forced them to try masteries. This aforesaid North Sea, is the same which lieth upon the backside of Frobisher's Straits, where first the General himself in his pinnaces, and after some other of our company have discovered (as they affirm) a great foreland, where they would have also a great likelihood of the greatest passage towards the South Sea, or *Mar del Sur.*

The Buss of Bridgewater, as she came homeward, to the southeastward of Friesland, discovered a great island in the latitude of fifty-seven degrees and a half, which was never yet found before, and sailed three days along the coast, the land seeming to be fruitful, full of woods, and a champaign country.

There died in the whole fleet in all this voyage not above forty persons, which number is not great, considering how many ships were in the fleet, and how strange fortunes we passed.

A general and brief description of the country, and condition of the people which are found in Meta Incognita.

Having now sufficiently and truly set forth the whole circumstance, and particular handling of every occurrence in the three voyages of our worthy general Captain Frobisher, it shall not be from the purpose to speak somewhat in general of the nature of this country called Meta Incognita, and the condition of the savages there inhabiting.

First, therefore, touching the topographical description of the place. It is now found in the last voyage, that Queen Elizabeth's Cape being situate in latitude at sixty-one degrees and a-half, which before was supposed to be part of the firm land of America, and also all the rest of the south side of Frobisher's Straits, are all several islands and broken land, and likewise so will all the north side of the said Straits fall out to be, as I think. And some of our company being entered above sixty leagues within the mistaken straits in the third voyage mentioned, thought certainly that they had descried the firm land of America towards the south, which I think will fall out so to be.

These broken lands and islands being very many in number, do seem to make there an archipelago, which, as they all differ in greatness, form, and fashion one from another, so are they in goodness, colour, and soil, much unlike. They are all very high lands, mountains, and in most parts covered with snow even all the summer long. The northern lands have less store of snow, more grass, and are more plain countries; the cause whereof may be, for that the southern islands receive all the snow, that the cold winds and piercing air bring out of the north. And contrarily the north parts receive more warm blasts of milder air from the south, whereupon may grow the cause why the people covet to inhabit more upon the northwards than the south, as far as we can yet by our experience perceive they do. These people I judge to be a kind of Tartar, or rather a kind of Samoed, of the same sort and condition of life that the Samoeds be to the north-eastwards beyond Muscovy, who are called Samoeds, which is as much to say, in the Muscovy tongue, as "eaters of themselves," and so the Russians, their borderers, do name them. And by late conference with a friend of mine (with whom I did sometime travel in the parts of Muscovy) who hath great experience of those Samoeds and people of the north-east, I find that in all their manner of living, those people of the north-east and these of the north-west are like. They are of the colour of a ripe olive, which how it may come to pass, being born in so cold a climate, I refer to the judgment of others, for they are naturally born children of the same colour and complexion that all the Americans are, which dwell under the equinoctial line.

They are men very active and nimble. They are a strong people and very warlike, for in our sight upon the tops of the hills they would often muster themselves, and, after the manner of a skirmish, trace their ground very nimbly, and manage their bows and darts with great dexterity. They go clad in coats made of the skins of beasts, as of seals, deer, bears, foxes, and hares. They have also some garments of feathers, being made of the cases of fowls, finely sewed and compact together, of all which sorts we brought home with us into England which we found in their tents. In summer they use to wear the hairy side of their coats outward, and sometimes go naked for too much heat; and in winter (as by signs they have declared) they wear four or five fold upon their bodies with the hair, for warmth, turned inwards. Hereby it appeareth, that the air there is not indifferent, but either it is fervent hot or else extreme cold, and far more excessive in both qualities than the reason of the climate should yield, for there it is colder, being under sixty-two degrees in latitude, than it is at Wardhouse, in the voyage to St. Nicholas in Muscovy, being at about seventy-two degrees in latitude. The reason hereof perhaps may be, that this Meta Incognita is much frequented and vexed with eastern and north-eastern winds, which from the sea and ice bringeth often an intolerable cold air, which was also the cause that this year our Straits were so long shut up with so great store of ice. But there is great hope and likelihood, that further within the Straits it will be more constant and temperate weather.

These people are in nature very subtle and sharp witted, ready to conceive our meaning by signs, and to make answer well to be understood again. And if they have not seen the thing whereof you ask them, they will wink, or cover their eyes with their hands, as who would say, it hath been hid from their sight. If they understand you not whereof you ask them, they will stop their ears. They will teach us the names of each thing in their language which we desire to learn, and are apt to learn anything of us. They delight in music above measure, and will keep time and stroke to any tune which you shall sing, both with their voice, head, hand, and feet, and will sing the same tune aptly after you. They will row with our oars in our boats, and keep a true stroke with our mariners, and seem to take great delight therein. They live in caves of the earth, and hunt for their dinners or prey, even as the bear or other wild beasts do. They eat raw flesh and fish, and refuse no meat howsoever it be stinking. They are desperate in their fight, sullen of nature, and ravenous in their manner of feeding.

Their sullen and desperate nature doth herein manifestly appear, that a company of them being environed by our men on the top of a high cliff, so that they could by no means escape our hands, finding themselves in this case distressed, chose rather to cast themselves headlong down the rocks into the sea, and so be bruised and drowned, rather than to yield themselves to our men's mercies.

For their weapons to offend their enemies or kill their prey withal, they have darts, slings, bows, and arrows headed with sharp stones, bones, and some with iron. They are exceeding friendly and kind-hearted one to the other, and mourn greatly at the loss or harm of their fellows, and express their grief of mind, when they part one from another, with a mournful song and dirges.

* * * * * *

And in all the space of two or three months, while the man lived in company of the woman, there was never anything seen or perceived between them, more than might have passed between brother and sister; but the woman was in all things very serviceable for the man, attending him carefully when he was sick, and he likewise in all the meats which they did eat together, would carve unto her of the sweetest, fattest, and best morsels they had. They wondered much at all our things, and were afraid of our horses and other beasts out of measure. They began to grow more civil, familiar, pleasant, and docile amongst us in very short time.

They have boats made of leather, and covered clean over, saving one place in the middle to sit in, planked within with timber, and they use to row therein with one oar, more swiftly a great deal than we in our boats can do with twenty. They have one sort of greater boats wherein they can carry about twenty persons, and have a mast with a sail thereon, which sail is made of thin skins or bladders sewed together with the sinews of fishes. They are good fishermen, and in their small boats, being disguised with their coats of seal skins, they deceive the fish, who take them rather for their fellow seals than for deceiving men. They are good marksmen. With their dart or arrow they will commonly kill a duck, or any other fowl in the head, and commonly in the eye. When they shoot at a great fish with any of their darts, they use to tie a bladder thereunto, whereby they may the better find them again, and the fish not able to carry it so easily away (for that the bladder doth buoy the dart) will at length be weary, and die therewith. They use to traffic and exchange their commodities with some other people, of whom they have such things as their miserable country, and ignorance of art to make, denieth them to have, as bars of iron, heads of iron for their darts, needles made four square, certain buttons of copper, which they use to wear upon their foreheads for ornament, as our ladies in the Court of England do use great pearls. Also they have made signs unto us, that they have seen gold, and such bright plates of metals, which are used for ornaments amongst some people with whom they have conference. We found also in their tents a Guinea-bean of red colour, the which doth usually grow in the hot countries, whereby it appeareth they trade with other nations which dwell far off, or else themselves are great travellers. They have nothing in use among them to make fire withal, saving a kind of heath and moss which groweth there.

And they kindle their fire with continual rubbing and fretting one stick against another, as we do with flints. They draw with dogs in sleds upon the ice, and remove their tents therewithal wherein they dwell in summer, when they go hunting for their prey and provision against winter. They do sometimes parboil their meat a little and seethe the same in kettles made of beasts' skins; they have also pans cut and made of stone very artificially; they use pretty gins wherewith they take fowl. The women carry their sucking children at their backs, and do feed them with raw flesh, which first they do a little chew in their own mouths. The women have their faces marked or painted over with small blue spots, they have black and long hair on their heads, and trim the same in a decent order. The men have but little hair on their faces, and very thin beards. For their common drink they eat ice to quench their thirst withal. Their earth yieldeth no grain or fruit of sustenance for man, or almost for beast, to live upon; and the people will eat grass and shrubs of the ground, even as our kine do. They have no wood growing in their country thereabouts, and yet we find they have some timber among them, which we think doth grow far off to the southwards of this place, about Canada, or some other part of Newfoundland; for there belike, the trees standing on the cliffs of the sea-side, by the weight of ice and snow in winter overcharging them with weight, when the summer's thaw cometh above, and also the sea underfretting them beneath, which winneth daily of the land, they are undermined and fall down from those cliffs into the sea, and with the tides and currents are driven to and fro upon the coasts further off, and by conjecture are taken up here by these country people to serve them to plank and strengthen their boats withal, and to make darts, bows, and arrows, and such other things necessary for their use. And of this kind of drift wood we find all the seas over great store, which being cut or sawed asunder, by reason of long driving in the sea is eaten of worms, and full of holes, of which sort theirs is found to be.

We have not yet found any venomous serpent or other hurtful thing in these parts, but there is a kind of small fly or gnat that stingeth and offendeth sorely, leaving many red spots in the face, and other places where she stingeth. They have snow and hail in the best time of their summer, and the ground frozen three fathoms deep.

These people are great enchanters, and use many charms of witchcraft; for when their heads do ache they tie a great stone with a string unto a stick, and with certain prayers and words done to the stick, they lift up the stone from ground, which sometimes with all a man's force they cannot stir, and sometimes again they lift as easily as a feather, and hope thereby with certain ceremonious words to have ease and help. And they made us by signs to understand, lying grovelling with their faces upon the ground, and making a noise downward, that they worship the devil under them.

They have great store of deer, bears, hares, foxes, and innumerable numbers of sundry sorts of wild fowl, as sea-mews, gulls, willmots, ducks, &c., whereof our men killed in one day fifteen hundred. They have also store of hawks, as falcons, tassels, &c., whereof two alighted, upon one of our ships at their return, and were brought into England, which some think will prove very good. There are also great store of ravens, larks, and partridges, whereof the country people feed. All these fowls are far thicker clothed with down and feathers and have

thicker skins than any in England have; for as that country is colder, so nature hath provided a remedy thereunto. Our men have eaten of their bears, hares, partridges, larks, and of their wild fowl, and find them reasonable good meat, but not so delectable as ours. Their wild fowl must be all flain, their skins are so thick; and they taste best fried in pans. The country seemeth to be much subject to earthquakes. The air is very subtle, piercing and searching, so that if any corrupted or infected body, especially with the disease called *Morbus Gallicus* come there, it will presently break forth and shew itself, and cannot there by any kind of salve or medicine be cured. Their longest summer's day is of great length, without any dark night, so that in July all the night long we might perfectly and easily write and read whatsoever had pleased us, which lightsome nights were very beneficial unto us, being so distressed with abundance of ice as we were. The sun setteth to them in the evening at a quarter of an hour after ten of the clock, and riseth again in the morning at three-quarters of an hour after one of the clock, so that in summer their sun shineth to them twenty hours and a-half, and in the night is absent three hours and a-half. And although the sun be absent these three hours and a half, yet it is not dark that time, for that the sun is never above three or four degrees under the edge of their horizon; the cause is, that the tropic of Cancer doth cut their horizon at very uneven and oblique angles. But the moon at any time of the year being in Cancer, having north latitude, doth make a full revolution above their horizon, so that sometimes they see the moon above twenty-four hours together. Some of our company, of the more ignorant sort, thought we might continually have seen the sun and the moon, had it not have been for two or three high mountains.

The people are now become so wary, and so circumspect by reason of their former losses, that by no means we can apprehend any of them, although we attempted often in this last voyage. But to say truth, we could not bestow any great time in pursuing them, because of our great business in lading and other things.

DRAKE.

FRANCIS DRAKE, the first of the English Buccaneers, was one of the twelve children of Edward Drake, of Tavistock, in Devonshire, a staunch Protestant who had fled his native place to avoid persecution, and had then become a ship's chaplain. Drake, like Columbus, had been a seaman by profession from boyhood; and, as the reader is aware (p. 6), he had served as a young man, in command of the Judith, under Hawkins. During the ten years which elapsed between the disastrous third voyage of the latter and the date of the present famous voyage (1567-1577) young Drake steadily gained experience as a seaman, and pursued his adopted calling of plundering the Spaniards. Hawkins had confined himself to smuggling: Drake advanced from this to piracy. This practice was authorized by law in the middle ages for the purpose of recovering debts or damages from the subjects of another nation. The English, especially those of the west country, were the most formidable pirates in the world; and the whole nation was by this time roused against Spain in consequence of the ruthless war waged against Protestantism in the Netherlands by Philip the Second. Drake had accounts of his own to settle with the Spaniards. Though Elizabeth had not declared for the revolted States, and pursued a shifting policy, her interests and theirs were identical; and it was with the view of cutting off those supplies of gold and silver from America which enabled Philip to bribe politicians and pay soldiers, in pursuit of his policy of aggression, that the Famous Voyage was authorized by English statesmen. Drake had recently made more than one successful voyage of plunder to the American coast; and on the 11th of February, 1573, the Indians of Panama had conducted him to the top of a lofty hill, on the top of which was a tree of giant growth, in which steps were hewn for ascent. Drake ascended the tree, and from a stage constructed near the top he beheld, for the first time, the great Pacific Ocean, in which no English vessel had ever yet sailed. Drake then and there resolved to be the pioneer of England in the Pacific; and on this resolution he solemnly besought the blessing of God. Nearly four years elapsed before it was executed; for it was not until November, 1577, that Drake embarked on his Famous Voyage, in the course of which he proposed to plunder Peru itself. The Peruvian ports were unfortified. The Spaniards knew them to be by nature absolutely secured from attack on the north; and they never dreamed that the English pirates would be daring enough to pass the terrible Straits of Magellan and attack them from the south. Such was the plan of Drake; and it was executed with complete success. Laden with a rich booty of Peruvian treasure, he deemed it unsafe to return by the way that he came. He therefore resolved to strike across the Pacific, and for this purpose made the latitude in which this voyage was usually performed by the Spanish Government vessels which sailed annually from Acapulco to the Philippines. Drake thus reached the coast of California, where the Indians, delighted beyond measure by presents of clothing and trinkets, invited him to remain and rule over them. Drake took possession of the country in the name of the Queen, and refitted his vessel in preparation for the unknown perils of the Pacific. The place where he landed must have been either the great bay of San Francisco or the small bay of Bodega, which lies a few leagues farther north. The great seaman had already coasted five degrees more to the northward before finding a suitable harbour.* He believed himself to be the first European who had coasted these shores; but it is now well known that Spanish explorers had preceded him.

Drake's circumnavigation of the globe was thus no deliberate feat of seamanship, but the necessary result of circumstances. The voyage made in more than one way a great epoch in English nautical history. It encouraged Englishmen to extend their enterprises in defiance of the attitude of Spain, and thus contributed to the occupation of North America; and it also proved the possibility of opening a trade round the Cape of Good Hope to India and the Malay Archipelago. Drake had not only defied the Spaniards in America; he had been the first Englishman to visit the rich Oriental islands which the Portuguese had first reached, and which had now fallen, together with Portugal, into the avaricious grasp of Spain.

The account which follows was written by Francis Pretty, one of the crew of Drake's vessel, at the request of Hakluyt. It is a plain and even meagre narrative, but no additional facts of any importance are contained in the more diffuse relation of Francis Fletcher, the chaplain. The trial and execution of Doughty in Port St. Julian form a characteristic episode. When the Pelican lay off Java, it would seem that Fletcher was near meeting the same fate. Drake found him

---

* Davis and Sir William Monson erroneously state that Drake went as far north as forty-eight degrees. The true reading is forty-three. Drake never reached the mouth of the Columbia river.

guilty of mutiny; but, instead of beheading him, he contented himself with excommunication. Calling the ship's company together, he caused the rebellious chaplain to be chained by the leg to the hatches, and then "sitting cross-legged on a chest, and a pair of pantofles in his hand," he said, "Francis Fletcher, I do here excommunicate thee out of the Church of God, and from all the benefits and graces thereof; and I renounce thee to the devil and all his angels." A "posy" was then bound round Fletcher's arm, which read thus:—"Francis Fletcher, the falsest knave that liveth." Drake swore that the chaplain should hang if he took it off, or ever appeared before the mast.

Drake's old ship, the Pelican, named, after the Famous Voyage, the Golden Hind, was long an object of veneration to the seamen of Deptford. When she was broken up, John Davis caused a chair to be made out of her, and presented it to the University of Oxford. This interesting relic is still preserved over the Bodleian Library. Cowley's fine lines, written while sitting and drinking in it, are well-known:—

> Great Relic! thou, too, in this port of ease,
> Hast still one way of making voyages:
> The breath of fame, like an auspicious gale,
> (The greater trade-wind, which does never fail)
> Shall drive thee round the world, and thou shalt run
> As long around it as the sun.
> The straits of time too narrow are for thee—
> Launch forth into an undiscover'd sea,
> And steer the endless course of vast eternity:
> Take for thy sail, this verse, and for thy pilot, me.

DRAKE'S FAMOUS VOYAGE.

NARRATIVE BY FRANCIS PRETTY.

The FAMOUS VOYAGE *of* SIR FRANCIS DRAKE, *into the South Sea, and therehence about the whole globe of the earth, begun in the year of our Lord, 1577.*

ON the 15th day of November, in the year of Our Lord 1577, Mr. Francis Drake, with a fleet of five ships and barques, and to the number of 164 men, gentlemen and sailors, departed from Plymouth, giving out his pretended voyage for Alexandria; but the wind falling contrary, he was forced the next morning to put into Falmouth Haven, in Cornwall, where such and so terrible a tempest took us, as few men have seen the like, and was indeed so vehement that all our ships were like to have gone to wreck; but it pleased God to preserve us from that extremity, and to afflict us only for that present with these two particulars: The mast of our Admiral, which was the Pelican, was cut overboard for the safeguard of the ship, and the Marigold was driven ashore, and somewhat bruised: for the repairing of which damages we returned again to Plymouth, and having recovered those harms, and brought the ships again to good state, we set forth the second time from Plymouth, and set sail on the 13th day of December following.

On the 25th day of the same month we fell with the Cape Cantin, upon the coast of Barbary, and coasting along, the 27th day we found an island called Mogador, lying one mile distant from the main, between which island and the main we found a very good and safe harbour for our ships to ride in, as also very good entrance, and void of any danger. On this island our General erected a pinnace, whereof he brought out of England with him four already framed. While these things were in doing, there came to the water's side some of the inhabitants of the country, shewing forth their flags of truce, which being seen of our General, he sent his ship's boat to the shore to know what they would: they being willing to come aboard, our men left there one man of our company for a pledge, and brought two of theirs aboard our ship, which by signs shewed our General that the next day they would bring some provision, as sheep, capons, and hens, and such like: whereupon our General bestowed amongst them some linen cloth and shoes, and a javelin, which they very joyfully received, and departed for that time. The next morning they failed not to come again to the water's side, and our General again setting out our boat, one of our men leaping over-rashly ashore, and offering friendly to embrace them, they set violent hands on him, offering a dagger to his throat if he had made any resistance, and so laying him on a horse carried him away; so that a man cannot be too circumspect and wary of himself among such miscreants. Our pinnace being finished, we departed from this place on the 30th and last day of December, and coasting along the shore we did descry, not contrary to our expectation, certain canters, which were Spanish fishermen, to whom we gave chase and took three of them, and proceeding further we met with three caravels, and took them also.

On the 17th day of January we arrived at Cape Blanco, where we found a ship riding at anchor, within the Cape, and but two simple mariners in her, which ship we took and carried her further into the harbour, where we remained four days, and in that space our General mustered and trained his men on land in warlike manner, to make them fit for all occasions. In this place we took of the fishermen such necessaries as we wanted, and they could yield us, and leaving here one of our little barques, called the Benedict, we took with us one of theirs which they called canters, being of the burden of 40 tons or thereabouts. All these things being finished we departed this harbour on the 22nd of January, carrying along with us one of the Portugal caravels, which was bound to the islands of Cape de Verde for salt, whereof good store is made in one of those islands. The master or pilot of that caravel did advertise our General that upon one of those islands called Mayo, there was great store of dried cabritos,* which a few inhabitants there dwelling did

---

* Goats.

yearly make ready for such of the king's ships as did there touch, being bound for his country of Brazil or elsewhere. We fell with this island on the 27th of January, but the inhabitants would in no case traffic with us, being thereof forbidden by the king's edict; yet the next day our General sent to view the island, and the likelihoods that might be there of provision of victuals, about threescore and two men under the conduct and government of Master Winter and Master Doughty, and marching towards the chief place of habitation in this island (as by the Portugal we were informed) having travelled to the mountains the space of three miles, and arriving there somewhat before the daybreak, but arrested ourselves to see day before us, which appearing, we found the inhabitants to be fled; but the place, by reason that it was manured, we found to be more fruitful than the other part, especially the valleys among the hills.

Here we gave ourselves a little refreshing, as by very ripe and sweet grapes, which the fruitfulness of the earth at that season of the year yielded us; and that season being with us the depth of winter, it may seem strange that those fruits were then there growing; but the reason thereof is this, because they being between the tropic and the equinoctial, the sun passeth twice in the year through their zenith over their heads, by means whereof they have two summers, and being so near the heat of the line they never lose the heat of the sun so much, but the fruits have their increase and continuance in the midst of winter. The island is wonderfully stored with goats and wild hens, and it hath salt also without labour, save only that the people gather it into heaps, which continually in great quantity is increased upon the sands by the flowing of the sea, and the receiving heat of the sun kerning the same, so that of the increase thereof they keep a continual traffic with their neighbours.

Amongst other things we found here a kind of fruit called cocoas, which because it is not commonly known with us in England, I thought good to make some description of it. The tree beareth no leaves nor branches, but at the very top the fruit groweth in clusters, hard at the top of the stem of the tree, as big every several fruit as a man's head; but having taken off the outermost bark, which you shall find to be very full of strings or sinews, as I may term them, you shall come to a hard shell, which may hold in quantity of liquor a pint commonly, or some a quart, and some less; within that shell of the thickness of half-an-inch good, you shall have a kind of hard substance and very white, no less good and sweet than almonds; within that again a certain clear liquor, which being drunk, you shall not only find it very delicate and sweet, but most comfortable and cordial.

After we had satisfied ourselves with some of these fruits, we marched further into the island, and saw great store of cabritos alive, which were so chased by the inhabitants that we could do no good towards our provision, but they had laid out, as it were, to stop our mouths withal, certain old dried cabritos, which being but ill, and small and few, we made no account of. Being returned to our ships, our General departed hence the 31st of this month, and sailed by the island of Santiago, but far enough from the danger of the inhabitants, who shot and discharged at us three pieces, but they all fell short of us, and did us no harm. The island is fair and large, and, as it seemeth, rich and fruitful, and inhabited by the Portugals, but the mountains and high places of the island are said to be possessed by the Moors, who having been slaves to the Portugals, to ease themselves, made escape to the desert places of the island, where they abide with great strength. Being before this island, we espied two ships under sail, to the one of which we gave chase, and in the end boarded her with a ship-boat without resistance, which we found to be a good prize, and she yielded unto us good store of wine; which prize our General committed to the custody of Master Doughty, and retaining the pilot, sent the rest away with his pinnace, giving them a butt of wine and some victuals, and their wearing clothes, and so they departed. The same night we came with the island called by the Portuguese Ilha del Fogo, that is, the burning island; in the north side whereof is a consuming fire. The matter is said to be of sulphur, but, notwithstanding, it is like to be a commodious island, because the Portugals have built, and do inhabit there. Upon the south-side thereof lieth a most pleasant and sweet island, the trees whereof are always green and fair to look upon, in respect whereof they call it Ilha Brava, that is, the brave island. From the banks thereof into the sea do run in many places reasonable streams of fresh water easy to be come by, but there was no convenient road for our ships; for such was the depth that no ground could be had for anchoring, and it is reported, that ground was never found in that place, so that the tops of Fogo burn not so high in the air, but the roots of Brava are quenched as low in the sea.

Being departed from these islands, we drew towards the line, where we were becalmed the space of three weeks, but yet subject to divers great storms, terrible lightnings and much thunder; but with this misery we had the commodity of great store of fish, as dolphins, bonitos, and flying-fishes, whereof some fell into our ships, wherehence they could not rise again for want of moisture, for when their wings are dry they cannot fly.

From the first day of our departure from the islands of Cape de Verde, we sailed fifty-four days without sight of land, and the first land that we fell with was the coast of Brazil, which we saw on the 5th of April, in the height of 33 degrees towards the Pole Antarctic, and being discovered at sea by the inhabitants of the country, they made upon the coast great fires for a sacrifice (as we learned) to the devils, about which they use conjurations, making heaps of sand, and other ceremonies, that when any ship shall go about to stay upon their coast, not only sands may be gathered together in shoals in every place, but also that storms and tempests may arise, to the casting away of ships and men, whereof (as it is reported) there have been divers experiments.

On the 7th day in a mighty great storm, both of lightning, rain, and thunder, we lost the canter which we called the Christopher; but the eleventh day after, by our General's great care in dispersing his ships, we found her again, and the place where we met our General called the Cape of Joy, where every ship took in some water. Here we found a good temperature and sweet air, a very fair and pleasant country with an exceeding fruitful soil, where were great store of large and mighty deer, but we came not to the sight of any people; but travelling further into the country we perceived the footing of people in the clay-ground, shewing that they were men of great stature. Being returned to our ships we weighed anchor, and ran somewhat further, and harboured ourselves between the rock and the main, where by means of the rock that broke the force of the sea, we rode very safe, and upon this rock we killed for our provision certain sea-wolves, commonly called with us seals. From hence we went our course to 36 degrees, and entered the great river of Plate, and ran into 54 and 53½ fathoms of fresh water, where we filled our water by the ship's side; but our General finding here no good harbour, as he thought he should, bore out again to sea on the 27th of April, and in bearing out we lost sight of our fly-boat, wherein Master Doughty was. But we sailing along, found a fair and reasonable good bay, wherein were many and the same profitable islands, one whereof had so many seals as would at the least have laden all our ships, and the rest of the islands are, as it were, laden with fowls, which is wonderful to see, and they of divers sorts. It is a place very plentiful of victuals, and hath in it no want of fresh water. Our General, after certain days of his abode in this place, being on shore in an island, the people of the country shewed themselves unto him, leaping and dancing, and entered into traffic with him, but they would not receive anything at any man's hands, but the same must be cast upon the ground. They are of clean, comely, and strong bodies, swift on foot, and seem to be very active.

On the 18th day of May, our General thought it needful to have a care of such ships as were absent, and therefore endeavouring to seek the fly-boat wherein Master Doughty was, we espied her again the next day; and whereas certain of our ships were sent to discover the coast and to search an harbour, the Marigold and the canter being employed in that business, came unto us and gave us understanding of a safe harbour that they had found, wherewith all our ships bare, and entered it, where we watered and made new provision of victuals, as by seals, whereof we slew to the number of two or three hundred in the space of an hour. Here our General in the Admiral rode close aboard the fly-boat, and took out of her all the provision of victuals and what else was in her, and hauling her to the land, set fire to her, and so burnt her to save the iron work; which being a-doing, there came down of the country certain of the people naked, saving only about their waist the skin of some beast, with the fur or hair on, and something also wreathed on their heads. Their faces were painted with divers colours, and some of them had on their heads the similitude of horns, every man his bow, which was an ell in length, and a couple of arrows. They were very agile people and quick to deliver, and seemed not to be ignorant in the feats of war, as by their order of ranging a few men might appear. These people would not of a long time receive any thing at our hands; yet at length our General being ashore, and they dancing after their accustomed manner about him, and he once turning his back towards them, one leaped suddenly to him, and took his cap with his gold band off his head, and ran a little distance from him, and shared it with his fellow, the cap to the one, and the band to the other. Having despatched all our business in this place, we departed and set sail, and immediately upon our setting forth we lost our canter, which was absent three or four days; but when our General had her again, he took out the necessaries, and so gave her over, near to the Cape of Good Hope. The next day after, being the 20th of June, we harboured ourselves again in a very good harbour, called by Magellan, Port St. Julian, where we found a gibbet standing upon the main, which we supposed to be the place where Magellan did execution upon some of his disobedient and rebellious company.

On the 22nd of June our General went ashore to the main, and in his company John Thomas, and Robert Winterhie, Oliver the Master-Gunner, John Brewer, Thomas Hood, and Thomas Drake. And entering on land, they presently met with two or three of the country people. And Robert Winterhie having in his hands a bow and arrows, went about to make a shoot of pleasure, and, in his draught, his bowstring brake, which the rude savages taking as a token of war, began to bend the force of their bows against our company, and drove them to their shifts very narrowly.

In this port our General began to enquire diligently of the actions of Master Thomas Doughty, and found them not to be such as he looked for, but tending rather to contention or mutiny, or some other disorder, whereby (without redress) the success of the voyage might greatly have been hazarded. Whereupon the company was called together and made acquainted with the particulars of the cause, which were found partly by Master Doughty's own confession, and partly by the evidence of the fact, to be true; which, when our General saw, although his private affection for Master Doughty (as he then in the presence of us all sacredly protested) was great, yet the care he had of the state of the voyage, of the expectation of Her Majesty, and of the honour of his country did more touch him (as indeed it ought) than the private respect of one man. So that the cause being thoroughly heard, and all things done in good order as near as might be to the course of our laws in England, it was concluded that Master Doughty should receive punishment according to the quality of the offence. And he, seeing no remedy but patience for himself, desired before his death to receive the communion, which he did at the hands of Master Fletcher, our Minister, and our General himself accompanied him in that holy action. Which being done, and the place of execution made ready, he having embraced our

General, and taken his leave of all the company, with prayers for the Queen's Majesty and our realm, in quiet sort laid his head to the block, where he ended his life. This being done, our General made divers speeches to the whole company, persuading us to unity, obedience, love, and regard of our voyage, and for the better confirmation thereof, willed every man the next Sunday following to prepare himself to receive the communion, as Christian brethren and friends ought to do, which was done in very reverent sort. And so with good contentment every man went about his business.

On the 17th of August we departed the port of St. Julian, and on the 20th we fell in with the Straits of Magellan, going into the South Sea, at the cape or headland whereof we found the body of a dead man, whose flesh was clean consumed. On the 21st day we entered the Straits, which we found to have many turnings, and as it were shuttings-up, as if there were no passage at all, by means whereof we had the wind often against us, so that some of the fleet recovering a cape or point of land, others should be forced to turn back again, and to come to an anchor where they could. In this Strait there be many fair harbours, with store of fresh water, but yet they lack their best commodity, for the water there is of such depth, that no man shall find ground to anchor in, except it be in some narrow river or corner, or between some rocks, so that if any extreme blasts or contrary winds do come (whereunto the place is much subject) it carrieth with it no small danger. The land on both sides is very huge and mountainous, the lower mountains whereof, although they be monstrous and wonderful to look upon for their height, yet there are others which in height exceed them in a strange manner, reaching themselves above their fellows so high, that between them did appear three regions of clouds. These mountains are covered with snow. At both the southerly and easterly parts of the Straits there are islands, among which the sea hath his indraught into the Straits, even as it hath in the main entrance of the Strait. This Strait is extreme cold, with frost and snow continually; the trees seem to stoop with the burden of the weather, and yet are green continually, and many good and sweet herbs do very plentifully grow and increase under them. The breadth of the Straits is in some places a league, in some other places two leagues and three leagues, and in some other four leagues, but the narrowest place hath a league over.

On the 24th of August we arrived at an island in the Straits, where we found great store of fowl which could not fly, of the bigness of geese, whereof we killed in less than one day three thousand, and victualled ourselves thoroughly therewith. On the 6th of September we entered the South Sea at the cape or head shore. On the 7th we were driven by a great storm from the entering into the South Sea, 200 leagues and odd in longitude, and one degree to the southward of the Straits, in which height, and so many leagues to the westward, the 15th of September, fell out the eclipse of the moon at the hour of six of the clock at night; but neither did the ecliptical conflict of the moon impair our state, nor her clearing again amend us a whit, but the accustomed eclipse of the sea continued in his force, we being darkened more than the moon sevenfold.

From the Bay (which we called the Bay of the Severing of Friends) we were driven back to the southward of the Straits in 57 degrees and a terce; in which height we came to an anchor among the islands, having there fresh and very good water, with herbs of singular virtue. Not far from hence we entered another bay, where we found people (both men and women) in their canoes naked, and ranging from one island to another to seek their meat, who entered traffic with us for such things as they had. We returning hence northward again, found on the 3rd of October three islands, in one of which was such plenty of birds as is scant credible to report. On the 8th of October we lost sight of one of our consorts, wherein Master Winter was, who as then we supposed, was put by a storm into the Straits again, which at our return home we found to be true, and he not perished, as some of our company feared. Thus being come into the height of the Straits again, we ran, supposing the coast of Chili to lie as the general maps have described it, namely north-west, which we found to lie and trend to the north-east and eastwards, whereby it appeareth that this part of Chili hath not been truly hitherto discovered, or at the least not truly reported for the space of twelve degrees at the least, being set down either of purpose to deceive, or of ignorant conjecture.

We continuing our course, fell the 29th of November with an island called La Mocha, where we cast anchor, and our General hoisting out our boat, went with ten of our company to shore, where we found people, whom the cruel and extreme dealings of the Spaniards have forced, for their own safety and liberty, to flee from the main, and to fortify themselves in the island. We being on land, the people came down to us to the water side with show of great courtesy, bringing to us potatoes, roots, and two very fat sheep, which our General received, and gave them other things for them, and had promise to have water there. But the next day repairing again to the shore, and sending two men to land with barrels to fill water, the people taking them for Spaniards (to whom they use to show no favour if they take them) laid violent hands on them, and, as we think, slew them.

Our General seeing this, stayed here no longer, but weighed anchor, and set sail towards the coast of Chili, and drawing towards it, we met near to the shore an Indian in a canoe, who thinking us to have been Spaniards, came to us and told us, that at a place called Santiago, there was a great Spanish ship laden from the kingdom of Peru, for which good news our General gave him divers trifles. Whereof he was glad, and went along with us and brought us to the place, which is called the port of Valparaiso. When we came thither we found, indeed, the ship riding at anchor, having in her eight Spaniards and three negroes, who, thinking us to have been Spaniards, and their friends, welcomed us with a drum, and made ready a Bottija of wine of Chili to drink to us. But as soon as we were entered, one of our company called Thomas Moon began to lay about him, and struck one of the Spaniards, and said unto him, "Abaxo perro!" that is in English, "Go down, dog!" One of these Spaniards, seeing persons of that quality in these seas, all to crossed and blessed himself. But, to be short, we stowed them under hatches, all save one Spaniard, who suddenly and desperately leapt overboard into the sea, and swam ashore to the the town of Santiago, to give them warning of our arrival.

They of the town being not above nine households, presently fled away and abandoned the town. Our General manned his boat and the Spanish ship's boat and went to the town, and, being come to it, we rifled it, and came to a small chapel, which we entered, and found therein a silver chalice, two cruets, and one altar-cloth, the spoil whereof our General gave to Mr. Fletcher, his minister. We found, also in this town a warehouse stored with wine of Chili and many boards of cedar-wood, all which wine we brought away with us, and certain of the boards to burn for firewood. And so, being come aboard, we departed the haven, having first set all the Spaniards on land, saving one John Griego, a Greek born, whom our General carried with him as pilot to bring him into the haven of Lima.

When we were at sea our General rifled the ship, and found in her good store of the wine of Chili, and 25,000 pesos of very pure and fine gold of Valdivia, amounting in value to 37,000 ducats of Spanish money, and above. So, going on our course, we arrived next at a place called Coquimbo, where our General sent fourteen of his men on land to fetch water. But they were espied by the Spaniards, who came with 300 horsemen and 200 footmen, and slew one of our men with a piece. The rest came aboard in safety, and the Spaniards departed. We went on shore again and buried our man, and the Spaniards came down again with a flag of truce; but we set sail, and would not trust them. From hence we went to a certain port called Tarapaca, where, being landed, we found by the sea side a Spaniard lying asleep, who had lying by him thirteen bars of silver, which weighed 4,000 ducats Spanish. We took the silver and left the man. Not far from hence, going on land for fresh water, we met with a Spaniard and an Indian boy driving eight llamas or sheep of Peru, which are as big as asses; everyone of which sheep had on his back two bags of leather, each bag containing 50 lbs. weight of fine silver. So that, bringing both the sheep and their burthen to the ship, we found in all the bags 800 weight of silver.

Herehence we sailed to a place called Arica, and, being entered the haven, we found there three small barques, which we rifled, and found in one of them fifty-seven wedges of silver, each of them weighing about 20 lbs. weight, and every of these wedges were of the fashion and bigness of a brickbat. In all these three barques we found not one person. For they, mistrusting no strangers, were all gone on land to the town, which consisteth of about twenty houses, which we would have ransacked if our company had been better and more in number. But our General, contented with the spoil of the ships, left the town and put off again to sea, and set sail for Lima, and, by the way, met with a small barque, which he boarded, and found in her good store of linen cloth. Whereof taking some quantity, he let her go.

To Lima we came on the 13th of February, and, being entered the haven, we found there about twelve sail of ships lying fast moored at anchor, having all their sails carried on shore; for the masters and merchants were here most secure, having never been assaulted by enemies, and at this time feared the approach of none such as we were. Our General rifled these ships, and found in one of them a chest full of reals of plate, and good store of silks and linen cloth, and took the chest into his own ship, and good store of the silks and linen. In which ship he had news of another ship called the Cacafuego, which was gone towards Payta, and that the same ship was laden with treasure. Whereupon we stayed no longer here, but, cutting all the cables of the ships in the haven, we let them drive whither they would, either to sea or to the shore, and with all speed we followed the Cacafuego toward Payta, thinking there to have found her; but before we arrived there she was gone from thence towards Panama, whom our General still pursued, and by the way met with a barque laden with ropes and tackle for ships, which he boarded and searched, and found in her 80 lbs. weight of gold, and a crucifix of gold with goodly great emeralds set in it, which he took, and some of the cordage also for his own ship.

From hence we departed, still following the Cacafuego; and our General promised our company that whosoever should first descry her should have his chain of gold for his good news. It fortuned that John Drake, going up into the top, descried her at about three o'clock, and at about six o'clock we came to her and boarded her, and shot at her three pieces of ordnance, and struck down her mizen, and, being entered, we found in her great riches, as jewels and precious stones, thirteen chests full of reals of plate, fourscore pounds weight of gold, and six-and-twenty tons of silver. The place where we took this prize was called Cape de San Francisco, about 150 leagues from Panama. The pilot's name of this ship was Francisco, and amongst other plate that our General found in this ship he found two very fair gilt bowls of silver, which were the pilot's, to whom our General said, "Señor Pilot, you have here two silver cups; but I must needs have one of them," which the pilot, because he could not otherwise choose, yielded unto, and gave the other to the steward of our General's ships. When this pilot departed from us, his boy said thus unto our General, "Captain, our ship shall be called no more the Cacafuego, but the Cacaplata, and your ship shall be called the Cacafuego," which pretty speech of the pilot's boy ministered matter of laughter to us, both then and long after. When our General had done what he would with this Cacafuego, he cast her off, and we went on our course still towards the west, and not long after met with a ship laden with linen cloth and fine China dishes of white earth, and great store of China silks, of all which things we took as we listed. The owner himself of this ship was in her, who was a Spanish gentleman, from whom our General took a faulcon of gold, with a great emerald in the breast thereof; and the pilot of the ship he took also with him, and so cast the ship off.

This pilot brought us to the haven of Aguatulco, the town whereof, as he told us, had but seventeen Spaniards in it. As soon as we were entered this haven, we landed, and went presently to the town and to the Town-house, where we found a judge sitting in judgment, being associated with three other officers, upon three negroes that had conspired the burning of the town. Both which judges and prisoners we took, and brought them a-shipboard, and caused the chief judge to write his letter to the town to command all the townsmen to avoid, that we might safely water there, which being done, and they departed, we ransacked the town, and in one house we found a pot, of the quantity of a bushel, full of reals of plate, which we brought to our ship. And here one Thomas Moon, one of our company, took a Spanish gentleman as he was flying out of the town, and, searching him, he found a chain of gold about him, and other jewels, which he took, and so let him go. At this place our General, among other Spaniards, set ashore his Portuguese pilot which he took at the Islands of Cape Verde out of a ship of St. Mary Port, of Portugal; and having set them ashore we departed hence, and sailed to the Island of Canno, where our General landed, and brought to shore his own ship, and discharged her, mended and graved her, and furnished our ship with water and wood sufficiently.

And while we were here we espied a ship and set sail after her, and took her, and found in her two pilots and a Spanish Governor, going for the Islands of the Philippines. We searched the ship, and took some of her merchandise, and so let her go. Our General at this place and time, thinking himself, both in respect of his private injuries received from the Spaniards, as also of their contempts and indignities offered to our country and Prince in general, sufficiently satisfied and revenged; and supposing that her Majesty at his return would rest contented with this service, purposed to continue no longer upon the Spanish coast, but began to consider and to consult of the best way for his country.

He thought it not good to return by the Straits, for two special causes—the one, lest the Spaniards should there wait and attend for him in great number and strength, whose hands, he, being left but one ship, could not possibly escape. The other cause was the dangerous situation of the mouth of the Straits in the South Sea, where continual storms reigning and blustering, as he found by experience, besides the shoals and sands upon the coast, he thought it not a good course to adventure that way. He resolved, therefore, to avoid these hazards, to go forward to the Islands of the Moluccas, and there hence to sail the course of the Portuguese by the Cape of Buena Esperanza. Upon this resolution he began to think of his best way to the Moluccas, and finding himself, where he now was, becalmed, he saw that of necessity he must be forced to take a Spanish course—namely to sail somewhat northerly to get a wind. We therefore set sail, and sailed 600 leagues at the least for a good wind; and thus much we sailed from the 16th of April till the 3rd of June.

On the 5th of June, being in forty-three degrees towards the Arctic Pole, we found the air so cold, that our men being grievously pinched with the same, complained of the extremity thereof, and the further we went, the more the cold increased upon us. Whereupon we thought it best for that time to seek the land, and did so, finding it not mountainous, but low plain land, till we came within thirty-eight degrees towards the line. In which height it pleased God to send us into a fair and good bay, with a good wind to enter the same. In this bay we anchored, and the people of the country having their houses close by the waterside, shewed themselves unto us, and sent a present to our General. When they came unto us, they greatly wondered at the things that we brought, but our General (according to his natural and accustomed humanity) courteously entreated them, and liberally bestowed on them necessary things to cover their nakedness, whereupon they supposed us to be gods, and would not be persuaded to the contrary: the presents which they sent to our General, were feathers, and cauls of net-work. Their houses are digged round about with earth, and have from the uttermost brims of the circle, clifts of wood set upon them, joined close together at the top like a spire steeple, which by reason of that closeness are very warm. Their bed is the ground with rushes strewed on it, and lying about the house, they have the fire in the midst. The men go naked, the women take bulrushes, and comb them after the manner of hemp, and thereof make their loose garments, which being knit about their middles, hang down about their hips, having also about their shoulders a skin of deer, with the hair upon it. These women are very obedient and serviceable to their husbands.

After they were departed from us, they came and visited us the second time, and brought with them feathers and bags of tobacco for presents; and when they came to the top of the hill (at the bottom whereof we had pitched our tents) they stayed themselves, where one appointed for speaker wearied himself by making a long oration, which done, they left their bows upon the hill, and came down with their presents. In the meantime the women remaining upon the hill, tormented themselves lamentably, tearing their flesh from their cheeks, whereby we perceived that they were about a sacrifice. In the meantime our General with his company went to prayer, and to reading of the Scriptures, at which exercise they were attentive, and seemed greatly to be affected with it; but when they were come unto us, they restored again unto us those things which before we bestowed upon them. The news of our being there spread through the country, the people that inhabited round about came down, and amongst them the King himself, a man of goodly stature, and comely personage, with many other tall and warlike men; before whose coming were sent two Ambassadors to our General, to signify that their King was coming, in doing of which message, their speech was continued about half-an-hour. This ended, they by signs requested our General to send something by their hand to their King, as a token that his coming might be in peace; wherein our General having satisfied them, they returned with glad tidings to their King, who marched to us with a princely majesty, the people crying continually after their manner, and as they drew near unto us, so did they strive to behave themselves in their actions with comeliness. In the fore-front was a man of goodly personage, who bore the sceptre or mace before the King, whereupon hanged two crowns, a less and a bigger, with three chains of a marvellous length; the crowns were made of knit-work wrought artificially with feathers of divers colours; the chains were made of a bony substance, and few be the persons among them that are admitted to wear them, and of that number also the persons are stinted, as some ten, some twelve, &c. Next unto him which bore the sceptre, was the King himself, with his guard about his person, clad with coney skins, and other skins; after them followed the naked common sort of people, every one having his face painted, some with white, some with black, and other colours, and having in their hands one thing or another for a present, not so much as their children, but they also brought their presents.

In the meantime our General gathered his men together, and marched within his fenced place, making against their approaching, a very warlike show. They being trooped together in their order, and a general salutation being made, there was presently a general silence. Then he that bore the sceptre before the King, being informed by another, whom they assigned to that office, with a manly and lofty voice proclaimed that which the other spake to him in secret, continuing half-an-hour; which ended, and a general amen as it were given, the King with the whole number of men and women (the children excepted) came down without any weapon, who descending to the foot of the hill, set themselves in order. In coming towards our bulwarks and tents, the sceptre-bearer began a song, observing his measures in a dance, and that with a stately countenance, whom the King with his guard, and every degree of persons following, did in like manner sing and dance, saving only the women, which danced and kept silence. The General permitted them to enter within our bulwarks, where they continued their song and dance a reasonable time. When they had satisfied themselves, they made signs to our General to sit down, to whom the King and divers others made several orations, or rather supplications, that he would take their province and kingdom into his hand, and become their King, making signs that they would resign unto him their right and title of the whole land, and become his subjects. In which, to persuade us the better, the King and the rest, with one consent, and with great reverence, joyfully singing a song, did set the crown upon his head, enriched his neck with all their chains, and offered him many other things, honouring him by the name of Hioh, adding thereunto as it seemed, a sign of triumph; which thing our General thought not meet to reject, because he knew not what honour and profit it might be to our country. Wherefore in the name, and to the use of her majesty, he took the sceptre, crown, and dignity of the said country into his hands, wishing that the riches and treasure thereof might so conveniently be transported to the enriching of her kingdom at home, as it abounded in the same.

The common sort of people leaving the King and his guard with our General, scattered themselves together with their sacrifices among our people, taking a diligent view of every person: and such as pleased their fancy (which were the youngest), they enclosing them about offered their sacrifices unto them with lamentable weeping, scratching, and tearing their flesh from their faces with their nails, whereof issued abundance of blood. But we used signs to them of disliking this, and stayed their hands from force, and directed them upwards to the living God, whom only they ought to worship. They shewed unto us their wounds, and craved help of them at our hands, whereupon we gave them lotions, plaisters, and ointments agreeing to the state of their griefs, beseeching God to cure their diseases. Every third day they brought their sacrifices unto us, until they understood our meaning, that we had no pleasure in them; yet they could not be long absent from us, but daily frequented our company to the hour of our departure, which departure seemed so grievous unto them, that their joy was turned into sorrow. They entreated us, that being absent we would remember them, and by stealth provided a sacrifice, which we misliked.

Our necessary business being ended, our General with his company travelled up into the country to their villages, where we found herds of deer by thousands in a company, being most large, and fat of body. We found the whole country to be a warren of a strange kind of coneys, their bodies in bigness as be the Barbary coneys, their heads as the heads of ours, the feet of a want, and the tail of a rat, being of great length. Under her chin is on either side a bag, into the which she gathereth her meat, when she hath filled her belly abroad. The people eat their bodies, and make great account of their skins, for their King's coat was made of them.

Our General called this country New Albion, and that for two causes, the one in respect of the white banks and cliffs, which lie towards the sea, and the other, because it might have some affinity with our country in name, which sometimes was so called. There is no part of earth here to be taken up, wherein there is not some probable show of gold or silver.

At our departure hence our General set up a monument of our being there, as also of her majesty's right and title to the same, namely a plate, nailed upon a fair great post, whereupon was engraved her majesty's name, the day and year of our arrival there, with the free giving up of the province and people into her majesty's hands, together with her highness's picture and arms, in a piece of six-pence of current English money, under the plate, whereunder was also written the name of our General.

It seemeth that the Spaniards hitherto had never been in this part of the country, neither did ever discover the land by many degrees to the southwards of this place.

After we had set sail from hence, we continued without sight of land till the 13th of October following, which day in the morning we fell with certain islands eight degrees to the northward of the line, from which islands came a great number of canoes, having in some of them four, in some six, and in some also fourteen men, bringing with them cocoas and other fruits. Their canoes were hollow within, and cut with great art and cunning, being very smooth within and without, and bearing a glass as if it were a horn daintily burnished, having a prow and a stern of one sort, yielding inwards circle-wise, being of a great height, and full of certain white shells for a bravery, and on each side of them lie out two pieces of timber about a yard and a-half long, more or less, according to the smallness or bigness of the boat. These people have the nether part of their ears cut into a round circle, hanging down very low upon their cheeks, whereon they hang things of a reasonable weight. The nails of their hands are an inch long, their teeth are as black as pitch, and they renew them often, by eating of an herb with a kind of powder, which they always carry about them in a cane for the same purpose.

Leaving this island the night after we fell in with it, on the 18th of October we lighted upon divers others, some whereof made a great show of inhabitants. We continued our course by the islands of Tagulanda,* Zelon, and Zewarra, being friends to the Portugals, the first whereof hath growing in it great store of cinnamon. On the 14th of November we fell in with the islands of Molucca. Which day at night (having directed our course to run with Tidore) in coasting along the island of Mutyr,† belonging to the King of Ternate, his Deputy or Vice-King seeing us at sea, came with his canoe to us without all fear, and came aboard, and after some conference with our General, willed him in any wise to run in with Ternate, and not with Tidore, assuring him that the King would be glad of his coming, and would be ready to do what he would require, for which purpose he himself would that

---

* Tagulandang, to the north-east of Celebes.
† Now Motir, one of the Ternate Moluccas.

night be with the King, and tell him the news, with whom if he once dealt, we should find that as he was a King, so his word should stand; adding further, that if he went to Tidore before he came to Ternate, the King would have nothing to do with us, because he held the Portugals as his enemy; whereupon our General resolved to run with Ternate, where the next morning early we came to anchor, at which time our General sent a messenger to the King, with a velvet cloak for a present and token of his coming to be in peace, and that he required nothing but traffic and exchange of merchandise, whereof he had good store, in such things as he wanted.

In the meantime the Vice-King had been with the King according to his promise, signifying unto him what good things he might receive from us by traffic; whereby the King was moved with great liking towards us, and sent to our General, with special message, that he should have what things he needed and would require, with peace and friendship, and moreover that he would yield himself and the right of his island to be at the pleasure and commandment of so famous a prince as we served. In token whereof he sent to our General a signet, and within short time after came in his own person, with boats and canoes, to our ship, to bring her into a better and safer road than she was in at that present. In the meantime, our General's messenger being come to the Court, was met by certain noble personages with great solemnity, and brought to the King, at whose hands he was most friendly and graciously entertained.

The King purposing to come to our ship, sent before four great and large canoes, in every one whereof were certain of his greatest statesmen that were about him, attired in white lawn of cloth of Calicut, having over their heads, from the one end of the canoe to the other, a covering of thin perfumed mats, borne up with a frame made of reeds for the same use, under which everyone did sit in his order according to his dignity, to keep him from the heat of the sun, divers of whom being of good age and gravity, did make an ancient and fatherly show. There were also divers young and comely men attired in white, as were the others; the rest were soldiers, which stood in comely order round about on both sides, without whom sat the rowers in certain galleries, which being three on a side all along the canoes, did lie off from the side thereof three or four yards, one being orderly built lower than another, in every of which galleries were the number of fourscore rowers. These canoes were furnished with warlike munition, every man for the most part having his sword and target, with his dagger, besides other weapons, as lances, calivers, darts, bows and arrows; also every canoe had a small cast base mounted at the least one full yard upon a stock set upright. Thus coming near our ship, in order, they rowed about us one after another, and passing by, did their homage with great solemnity, the great personages beginning with great gravity and fatherly countenance signifying that the King had sent them to conduct our ship into a better road. Soon after the King himself repaired, accompanied with six grave and ancient persons, who did their obeisance with marvellous humility. The King was a man of tall stature, and seemed to be much delighted with the sound of our music, to whom as also to his nobility, our General gave presents, wherewith they were passing well contented.

At length the King craved leave of our General to depart, promising the next day to come aboard, and in the meantime to send us such victuals as were necessary for our provision; so that the same night we received of them meal, which they call sago, made of the tops of certain trees, tasting in the mouth like sour curds, but melteth like sugar, whereof they make certain cakes, which may be kept the space of ten years and yet then good to be eaten. We had of them store of rice, hens, unperfect and liquid sugar, sugar-canes, and a fruit which they call figo, with store of cloves.

The King having promised to come aboard, broke his promise, but sent his brother to make his excuse, and to entreat our General to come on shore, offering himself pawn aboard for his safe return. Whereunto our General consented not, upon mislike conceived of the breach of his promise, the whole company also utterly refusing it. But to satisfy him, our General sent certain of his gentlemen to the Court, to accompany the King's brother, reserving the Vice-King for their safe return. They were received of another brother of the King and other statesmen, and were conducted with great honour to the castle. The place that they were brought unto was a large and fair house, where were at the least one thousand persons assembled.

The King being yet absent, there sat in their places sixty grave personages, all which were said to be of the King's Council. There were besides four grave persons, apparelled all in red, down to the ground, and attired on their heads like the Turks, and these were said to be Romans, and Ligiers* there to keep continual traffic with the people of Ternate. There were also two Turks Ligiers in this place, and one Italian. The King at last came in guarded with twelve lances, covered over with a rich canopy with embossed gold. Our men, accompanied with one of their captains called Moro, rising to meet him, he graciously did welcome and entertain them. He was attired after the manner of the country, but more sumptuously than the rest. From his waist down to the ground was all cloth of gold, and the same very rich; his legs were bare, but on his feet were a pair of shoes, made of Cordovan skin. In the attire of his head were finely wreathed hooped rings of gold, and about his neck he had a chain of perfect gold, the links whereof were great and one fold double. On his fingers he had six very fair jewels, and sitting in his chair of state, at his right hand stood a page with a fan in his hand, breathing and gathering the air to the King. The same was in length two feet, and in breadth one foot, set with eight sapphires, richly embroidered, and knit to a staff three feet in length, by the which the page did hold and move it. Our gentlemen having delivered their message and received order accordingly, were licenced to depart, being safely conducted back again by one of the king's council. This island is the chief of all the islands of Molucca, and the king hereof is king of seventy islands besides. The king with his people are Moors in religion, observing certain new moons, with fastings; during which fasts they neither eat nor drink in the day, but in the night.

After that our gentlemen were returned, and that we had here by the favour of the king received all necessary things that the place could yield us; our General considering the great distance, and how far he was yet off from his country, thought it not best here to linger the time any longer, but weighing his anchors, set out of the island, and sailed to a certain little island to the southwards of Celebes, where we graved our ship, and continued there in that and other business, twenty-six days. This island is thoroughly grown with wood of a large and high growth, very straight, and without boughs, save only in the head or top, whose leaves are not much differing from our broom in England. Amongst these trees night by night, through the whole land, did shew themselves an

---

* Agents or factors

infinite swarm of fiery worms flying in the air, whose bodies being no bigger than our common English flies, make such a show and light as if every twig or tree had been a burning candle. In this place breedeth also wonderful store of bats, as big as large hens; of cray-fishes also here wanted no plenty, and they of exceeding bigness, one whereof was sufficient for four hungry stomachs at a dinner, being also very good and restoring meat, whereof we had experience; and they dig themselves holes in the earth like coneys.

When we had ended our business here we weighed, and set sail to run for the Moluccas; but having at that time a bad wind, and being amongst the islands, with much difficulty we recovered to the northward of the island of Celebes, where by reason of contrary winds, not able to continue our course to run westwards, we were enforced to alter the same to the southward again, finding that course also to be very hard and dangerous for us, by reason of infinite shoals which lie off and among the islands; whereof we had too much trial to the hazard and danger of our ship and lives. For, of all other days, upon the 9th of January, in the year 1580, we ran suddenly upon a rock, where we stuck fast from eight o'clock at night till four o'clock in the afternoon the next day, being indeed out of all hope to escape the danger; but our General as he had always hitherto shewed himself courageous, and of a good confidence in the mercy and protection of God; so now he continued in the same, and lest he should seem to perish wilfully, both he and we did our best endeavour to save ourselves, which it pleased God so to bless, that in the end we cleared ourselves most happily of the danger.

We lightened our ship upon the rocks of three tons of cloves, eight pieces of ordnance, and certain meal and beans; and then the wind (as it were in a moment by the special grace of God) changing from the starboard to the larboard of the ship, we hoisted our sails, and the happy gale drove our ship off the rock, into the sea again, to the no little comfort of all our hearts, for which we gave God such praise and thanks, as so great a benefit required.

On the 8th of February following, we fell in with the fruitful island of Barateue,* having in the mean time suffered many dangers by

---

* Borneo.

winds and shoals. The people of this island are comely in body and stature, and of a civil behaviour, just in dealing, and courteous to strangers, whereof we had the experience sundry ways, they being most glad of our presence, and very ready to relieve our wants in those things which their country did yield. The men go naked, saving their heads and privities, every man having something or other hanging at their ears. Their women are covered from the middle down to the foot, wearing a great number of bracelets upon their arms, for some had eight upon each arm, being made some of bone, some of horn, and some of brass, the lightest whereof, by our estimation, weighed two ounces apiece. With this people linen-cloth is good merchandise, and of good request, whereof they make rolls for their heads, and girdles to wear about them. Their island is both rich and fruitful—rich in gold, silver, copper, and sulphur, wherein they seem skilful and expert, not only to try the same, but in working it also artificially into any form and fashion that pleaseth them. Their fruits be divers and plentiful, as nutmegs, ginger, long pepper, lemons, cucumbers, cocoas, figs, sago, with divers other sorts; and among all the rest we had one fruit, in bigness, form and husk, like a bay berry, hard of substance and pleasant of taste, which being sodden becometh soft, and is a most good and wholesome victual, whereof we took reasonable store, as we did also of the other fruits and spices, so that to confess the truth, since the time that we first set out of our own country of England, we happened upon no place (Ternate only excepted) wherein we found more comforts and better means of refreshing.

At our departure from Barateue, we set our course for Java Major,* where arriving, we found great courtesy, and honourable entertainment. This island is governed by five kings, whom they call Rajas; as Raja Donaw, and Raja Mang Bange, and Raja Cabuccapollo, which live as having one spirit and one mind. Of these five we had four a-shipboard at once, and two or three often. They are wonderfully delighted in coloured clothes, as red and green; the upper part of their bodies are naked, save their heads, whereupon they wear a Turkish roll as do the Moluccians. From the middle downwards they wear a pintado of silk, trailing

---

* Java.

upon the ground, in colour as they best like. The Moluccians hate that their women should be seen of strangers; but these offer them of high courtesy, yea, the kings themselves. The people are of goodly stature and warlike, well provided of swords and targets, with daggers, all being of their own work, and most artificially done, both in tempering their metal, as also in the form, whereof we bought reasonable store. They have a house in every village for their common assembly; every day they meet twice, men, women, and children, bringing with them such victuals as they they think good, some fruits, some rice boiled, some hens roasted, some sago, having a table made three feet from the ground, whereon they set their meat, that every person sitting at the table may eat, one rejoicing in the company of another. They boil their rice in an earthen pot, made in the form of a sugar loaf, being full of holes, as our pots which we water our gardens withal, and it is open at the great end, wherein they put their rice dry, without any moisture. In the mean time they have ready another great earthen pot, set fast in a furnace, boiling full of water, whereinto they put their pot with rice, by such measure, that they swelling become soft at the first, and by their swelling stopping the holes of the pot, admit no more water to enter, but the more they are boiled, the harder and more firm substance they become, so that in the end they are a firm and good bread, of the which with oil, butter, sugar, and other spices, they make divers sorts of meats very pleasant of taste, and nourishing to nature.

*   *   *   *   *   *

Not long before our departure, they told us that not far off there were such great ships as ours, wishing us to beware; upon this our captain would stay no longer. From Java Major we sailed for the Cape of Good Hope, which was the first land we fell in withal; neither did we touch with it, or any other land, until we came to Sierra Leone, upon the coast of Guinea; notwithstanding we ran hard aboard the Cape, finding the report of the Portuguese to be most false, who affirm that it is the most dangerous Cape of the world, never without intolerable storms and present danger to travellers which come near the same. This Cape is a most stately thing, and the fairest Cape we saw in the whole circumference of the earth, and we passed by it on the 18th of June. From thence we continued our course to Sierra Leone, on the coast of Guinea, where we arrived on the 22nd of July, and found necessary provisions, great store of elephants, oysters upon trees of one kind, spawning and increasing infinitely, the oyster suffering no bud to grow. We departed thence on the 24th day.

We arrived in England on the 3rd of November, 1580, being the third year of our departure.

GILBERT.

WHILE Frobisher was wrestling with the elements in Davis's Straits, a west-country gentleman named Humphrey Gilbert was meditating the execution of a scheme no less daring than the permanent occupation of the North American coasts by the English. It was fifty years and more since the Italian navigator Verazzano, in the service of Francis of France, had explored these coasts and ascertained them to be continuous to the south with the great land which had been named after Amerigo Vespucci, and in the north with the "New-land" or Newfoundland of the Northmen, which had been revisited by Cabot in the time of Columbus, and whither the fishermen of Spain, Portugal, France, and England, now resorted every year. But this immense line of coast, unlike that of South America, was as yet unoccupied by Europeans. The Spaniards had destroyed the French settlements in Florida, but they failed to gain any footing there for themselves; and from Florida to Nova Scotia a fruitful virgin soil, in a temperate clime, invited the enterprising colonist. The French occupation had procured this land the name of New France. But the French occupation had failed; and in a few years this name was destined to be replaced. by the English name of Virginia.

Sir Humphrey Gilbert's mother had married as her second husband a sea-captain named Raleigh. Her youngest son,

Walter Raleigh, had been at Oxford, studying cosmography, reading in the Spanish historians the wondrous narrative of the discovery and conquest of the New World, and drinking in the opinions of some who believed that the destinies of the New World were not unalterably fixed by the Papal grant to Spain. That grant, however, had been so long acquiesced in that it was not easy to dispute it, unless upon some new ground; and accordingly an old story was now revived with a new meaning. John Cabot, a British seaman, had notoriously reached the mainland of America before Columbus himself. How far he had explored its coasts is unknown; but the probability is that he returned very shortly after making the land. But when the vast extent of North America became known, and its enormous value in the future became obvious, it was confidently alleged that Cabot had visited the whole coast from Florida to Labrador, and had thus acquired for England a title which superseded that of Spain and France. After Hawkins' survey of the coast in 1564 the attention of Englishmen was more and more strongly directed to these coasts. Tracts were written urging their occupation; the exploits of Hawkins and Drake had proved how powerless the Spaniards were to prevent it; and funds were raised for executing it. "The nakedness of the Spaniards, and their long-hidden secrets, whereby they went about to delude the world," wrote Hakluyt, in 1582, "are now espied." England was overflowing with poor, who might be advantageously planted in this new soil. "If we would behold," Hakluyt goes on, "with the eye of pity how all our prisons are pestered and filled with able men to serve their country, which for small robberies are daily hanged up in great numbers, even twenty at a clap out of one jail (as was seen at the last assizes at Rochester), we would hasten and further, every man to his power, the deducting of some colonies of our superfluous people into those temperate and fertile parts of America, which, being within six weeks' sailing of England, are yet unpossessed by any Christians, and seem to offer themselves unto us, stretching nearer unto Her Majesty's dominions than to any other part of Europe."* Following the line then usual in pulpit argument, the enthusiastic divine supported this view by the analogy of nature and of antiquity. Bees send forth swarmings from the old hive; colonies were "deducted" in antiquity by the Greeks and the Carthaginians. Hakluyt pointed to the successful colonization of Portuguese America, which was due to the suggestion of De Barros, a mere man of learning, like himself. Brazil was no longer a deserted coast. It had its nine baronies or lordships, its thirty ingenios or sugar-mills, each mill with its two or three hundred slaves, its judge and other civil officers, and its church and clergy. Why should not these little commonwealths be reproduced elsewhere? "An excellent learned man" of Portugal had protested to Hakluyt that, were he but younger, he would sell all that he had to furnish a convenient number of ships for the colonization of these northern parts of America.

When Hakluyt was writing thus, Raleigh's half-brother had already procured a grant, in the usual form, of such lands in these parts as he should discover and occupy. It was to last only six years, unless it took effect by actual occupation; and three of these years were expired. The time for action was come, and accordingly, in June, 1583, Gilbert sailed from Cawsand Bay with five vessels, with the general intention of discovering and colonizing the northern parts of America. It

---

* Hakluyt, Dedication to "Divers Voyages," pp. 1, 2.

was the first colonizing expedition which left the shores of Great Britain; and the narrative of the expedition by Hayes, who commanded one of Gilbert's vessels, forms the first page in the history of English colonization. Gilbert did no more than go through the empty form of taking possession of the island of Newfoundland, to which the English name formerly applied to the continent in general (see page 74) was now restricted; and the description of this island is the most interesting portion of Hayes' narrative. Gilbert dallied here too long. When he set sail to cross the Gulf of St. Lawrence and take possession of Cape Breton and Nova Scotia the season was too far advanced; one of his largest ships went down with all on board, including the Hungarian scholar Parmenius, who had come out as the historian of the expedition; the stores were exhausted and the crews dispirited; and Gilbert resolved on sailing home, intending to return and prosecute his discoveries the next spring. On the home voyage the little vessel in which he was sailing foundered; and the pioneer of English colonization found a watery grave. Few passages in English story are better known than that part of the present narrative which describes Gilbert as sitting abaft on the deck of the Squirrel, with a book in his hand, cheering those in the Hind by reiterating the old seaman's proverb, "We are as near to heaven by sea as by land" (p. 206). Gilbert was a man of courage, piety, and learning. He was, however, an indifferent seaman, and quite incompetent for the task of colonization to which he had set his hand. The misfortunes of his expedition induced Amadas and Barlow, who followed in his steps, to abandon the northward voyage and sail to the shores intended to be occupied by the easier but more circuitous route of the Canaries and the West Indies.

GILBERT'S VOYAGE.

A report of the VOYAGE *and success thereof, attempted in the year of Our Lord 1583, by* SIR HUMPHREY GILBERT, KNIGHT, *with other Gentlemen assisting him in that action, intended to discover and to plant Christian inhabitants in place convenient, upon those large and ample countries extended northward from the Cape of* FLORIDA, *lying under very temperate climes, esteemed fertile and rich in minerals, yet not in the actual possession of any Christian prince. Written by* MR. EDWARD HAYES, gentleman, *and principal actor in the same voyage, who alone continued unto the end, and, by God's special assistance, returned home with his retinue, safe and entire.*

MANY voyages have been pretended, yet hitherto never any thoroughly accomplished by our nation, of exact discovery into the bowels of those main, ample, and vast countries extended infinitely into the north from thirty degrees, or rather from twenty-five degrees of septentrional latitude, neither hath a right way been taken of planting a Christian habitation and regiment upon the same, as well may appear both by the little we yet do actually possess therein, and by our ignorance of the riches and secrets within those lands, which unto this day we know chiefly by the travel and report of other nations, and most of the French, who albeit they cannot challenge such right and interest unto the said countries as we, neither these many years have had opportunity nor means so great to discover and to plant (being vexed with the calamities of intestine wars) as we have had by the inestimable benefit of our long and happy peace. Yet have they both ways performed more, and had long since attained a sure possession and settled government of many provinces in those northerly parts of America, if their many attempts into those foreign and remote lands had not been impeached by their garboils at home.

The first discovery of these coasts (never heard of before) was well begun by John Cabot the father and Sebastian his son, an Englishman born, who were the first finders out of all that great tract of land stretching from the Cape of Florida unto those islands which we now call the Newfoundland; all which they brought and annexed unto the crown of England. Since when, if with like diligence the search of inland countries had been followed, as the discovery upon the coast and outparts thereof was performed by those two men, no doubt Her Majesty's territories and revenue had been mightily enlarged and advanced by this day. And, which is more, the seed of Christian religion had been sown amongst those pagans, which by this time might have brought forth a most plentiful harvest and copious congregation of Christians, which must be the chief intent of such as shall make any attempt that way. Or else whatsoever is builded upon other foundation shall never obtain happy success nor continuance.

And although we cannot precisely judge (which only belongeth to God) what have been the humours of men stirred up to great attempts of discovering and planting in those remote countries, yet the events do shew that either God's cause hath not been chiefly preferred by them, or else God hath not permitted so abundant grace as the light of His Word and knowledge of Him to be yet revealed unto those infidels before the appointed time. But most assuredly, the only cause of religion hitherto hath kept back, and will also bring forward at the time assigned by God, an effectual and complete discovery and possession by Christians both of those ample countries and the riches within them hitherto concealed; whereof notwithstanding God in His wisdom hath permitted to be revealed from time to time a certain obscure and misty knowledge, by little and little to allure the minds of men that way (which else will be dull enough in the zeal of His cause), and thereby to prepare us unto a readiness for the execution of His will against the due time ordained of calling those Pagans unto Christianity.

In the meanwhile it behoveth every man of great calling, in whom is any instinct of inclination unto this attempt, to examine his own motions, which, if the same proceed of ambition or avarice, he may assure himself it cometh not of God, and therefore cannot have confidence of God's protection and assistance against the violence (else irresistible) both of sea and infinite perils upon the land, whom God yet may use as an instrument to further His cause and glory some way, but not to build upon so bad a foundation. Otherwise, if his motives be derived from a virtuous and heroical mind, preferring chiefly the honour of God, compassion of poor infidels captived by the devil, tyrannising in most wonderful and dreadful manner over their bodies and souls; advancement of his honest and well-disposed countrymen, willing to accompany him in such honourable actions; relief of sundry people within this realm distressed; all these be honourable purposes, imitating the nature of the munificent God, wherewith He is well pleased, who will assist such an actor beyond expectation of man. And the same, who feeleth this inclination in himself, by all likelihood may hope, or rather confidently repose in the preordinance of God, that in this last age of the world (or likely never) the time is complete of receiving also these Gentiles into His mercy, and that God will raise him an instrument to effect the same. It seeming probable by event of precedent attempts made by the Spaniards and French sundry times, that the countries lying north of Florida God hath reserved the same to be reduced unto Christian civility by the English nation. For not long after that Christopher Columbus had discovered the islands and continent of the West Indies for Spain, John and Sebastian Cabot made discovery also of the rest from Florida northwards to the behoof of England.

And whensoever afterwards the Spaniards (very prosperous in all their southern discoveries) did attempt anything into Florida and those regions inclining towards the north, they proved most unhappy, and were at length discouraged utterly by the hard and lamentable success of many both religious and valiant in arms, endeavouring to bring those northerly regions also under the Spanish jurisdiction; as if God had prescribed limits unto the Spanish nation which they might not exceed; as by their own gests recorded may be aptly gathered.

The French, as they can pretend less title unto these northern parts than the Spaniard, by how much the Spaniard made the first discovery of the same continent so far northward as unto Florida, and the French did but review that before discovered by the English nation, usurping upon our right, and imposing names upon countries, rivers, bays, capes, or headlands as if they had been the first finders of those coasts; which injury we offered not unto the Spaniards, but left off to discover when we approached the Spanish limits. Even so God hath not hitherto permitted them to establish a possession permanent upon another's right, notwithstanding their manifold attempts, in which the issue hath been no less tragical than that of the Spaniards, as by their own reports is extant.

Then, seeing the English nation only hath right unto these countries of America from the Cape of Florida northwards by the privilege of first discovery, unto which Cabot was authorised by regal authority, and set forth by the expense of our late famous King Henry VII., which right also seemeth strongly defended on our behalf by the powerful hand of Almighty God withstanding the enterprises of other nations, it may greatly encourage us upon so just ground, as is our right, and upon so sacred an intent, as to plant religion (our right and intent being meet foundations for the same) to prosecute effectually the full possession of those so ample and pleasant countries appertaining unto the Crown of England; the same (as is to be conjectured by infallible arguments of the world's end approaching) being now arrived unto the time by God prescribed of their vocation, if ever their calling unto the knowledge of God may be expected. Which also is very probable by the revolution and course of God's Word and religion, which from the beginning hath moved from the east towards, and at last unto, the west, where it is like to end, unless the same begin again where it did in the east, which were to expect a like world again. But we are assured of the contrary by the prophecy of Christ, whereby we gather that after His Word preached throughout the world shall be the end. And as the Gospel when it descended westward began in the south, and afterward spread into the north of Europe, even so, as the same hath begun in the south countries of America, no less hope may be gathered that it will also spread into the north.

These considerations may help to suppress all dreads rising of hard events in attempts made this way by other nations, as also of the heavy success and issue in the late enterprise made by a worthy gentleman our countryman, Sir Humphrey Gilbert, Knight, who was the first of our nation that carried people to erect an habitation and government in those northerly countries of America. About which, albeit he had consumed much substance, and lost his life at last, his people also perishing for the most part: yet the mystery thereof we must leave unto God, and judge charitably both of the cause (which was just in all pretence) and of the person, who was very zealous in prosecuting the same, deserving honourable remembrance for his good mind and expense of life in so virtuous an enterprise. Whereby nevertheless, lest any man should be dismayed by example of other folks' calamity, and misdeem that God doth resist all attempts intended that way, I thought good, so far as myself was an eye-witness, to deliver the circumstance and manner of our proceedings in that action, in which the gentleman was so unfortunately encumbered with wants, and worse matched with many ill-disposed people, that his rare judgment and wisdom premeditated for those affairs, was subjected to tolerate abuses, and in sundry extremities to hold on a course more to uphold credit than likely in his own conceit happily to succeed.

The issue of such actions, being always miserable, not guided by God, who abhorreth confusion and disorder, hath left this for admonition (being the first attempt by our nation to plant) unto such as shall take the same cause in hand hereafter not to be discouraged from it; but to make men well advised how they handle His so high and excellent matters, as the carriage is of His Word into those very mighty and vast countries. An action doubtless not to be intermeddled with base purposes; as many have made the same but a colour to shadow actions otherwise scarce justifiable, which doth excite God's heavy judgments in the end, to the terrifying of weak minds from the cause, without pondering His just proceedings; and doth also incense foreign princes against our attempts, how just soever, who cannot but deem the sequel very dangerous unto the State (if in those parts we should grow to strength), seeing the very beginnings are entered with spoil.

And with this admonition denounced upon zeal towards God's cause, also towards those in whom appeareth disposition honourable unto this action of planting Christian people and religion in those remote and barbarous nations of America (unto whom I wish all happiness), I will now proceed to make relation briefly, yet particularly, of our voyage undertaken with Sir Humphrey Gilbert, begun, continued, and ended adversely.

When first Sir Humphrey Gilbert undertook the western discovery of America, and had procured from Her Majesty a very large commission to inhabit and possess at his choice all remote and heathen lands not in the actual possession of any Christian prince, the same commission exemplified with many privileges, such as in his discretion he might demand, very many gentlemen of good estimation drew unto him, to associate him in so commendable an enterprise, so that the preparation was expected to grow unto a puissant fleet, able to encounter a king's power by sea. Nevertheless, amongst a multitude of voluntary men, their dispositions were diverse, which bred a jar, and made a division in the end, to the confusion of that attempt even before the same was begun. And when the shipping was in a manner prepared, and men ready upon the coast to go aboard, at that time some brake consort, and followed courses degenerating from the voyage before pretended. Others failed of their promises contracted, and the greater number were dispersed, leaving the General with few of his assured friends, with whom he adventured to sea, where, having tasted of no less misfortune, he was shortly driven to retire home with the loss of a tall ship and (more to his grief) of a valiant gentleman, Miles Morgan.

Having buried, only in a preparation, a great mass of substance, whereby his estate was impaired, his mind yet not dismayed, he continued his former designment and purpose to revive this enterprise, good occasion serving. Upon which determination standing long, without means to satisfy his desire, at last he granted certain assignments out of his commission to sundry persons of mean ability, desiring the privilege of his grant, to plant and fortify in the north parts of America about the river of Canada, to whom, if God gave good success in the north parts (where then no matter of moment was expected), the same (he thought) would greatly advance the hope of the south, and be a furtherance unto his determination that way. And the worst that might happen in that course might be excused without prejudice unto him by the former supposition, that those north regions were of no regard, but chiefly a possession taken in any parcel of those heathen countries, by virtue of his grant, did invest him of territories extending every way two hundred leagues, which induced Sir Humphrey Gilbert to make those assignments, desiring greatly their expedition, because his commission did expire after six years, if in that space he had not gotten actual possession.

Time went away without anything done by his assignees, insomuch that at last he must resolve himself to take a voyage in person, for more assurance to keep his patent in force, which then almost was expired or within two years.

In furtherance of his determination, amongst others, Sir George Peckham, Knight, shewed himself very zealous to the action, greatly aiding him both by his advice and in the charge. Other gentlemen to their ability joined unto him, resolving to adventure their substance and lives in the same cause. Who beginning their preparation from that time, both of shipping, munition, victual, men, and things requisite, some of them continued the charge two years complete without intermission. Such were the difficulties and cross accidents opposing these proceedings, which took not end in less than two years, many of which circumstances I will omit.

The last place of our assembly, before we left the coast of England, was in Cawsand Bay, near unto Plymouth, then resolved to put unto the sea with shipping and provision, such as we had, before our store yet remaining, but chiefly the time and season of the year, were too far spent. Nevertheless, it seemed first very doubtful by what way to shape our course, and to begin our intended discovery, either from the south northward or from the north southward. The first—that is, beginning south—without all controversy was the likeliest, wherein we were assured to have commodity of the current, which from the Cape of Florida setteth northward, and would have furthered greatly our navigation, discovering from the foresaid Cape along towards Cape Breton, and all those lands lying to the north. Also, the year being far spent, and arrived to the month of June, we were not to spend time in northerly courses, where we should be surprised with timely winter, but to covet the south, which we had space enough then to have attained, and there might with less detriment have wintered that season, being more mild and short in the south than in the north, where winter is both long and rigorous. These and other like reasons alleged in favour of the southern course first to be taken to the contrary was inferred,—that forasmuch as both our victuals and many other needful provisions were diminished and left insufficient for so long a voyage and for the wintering of so many men, we ought to shape a course most likely to minister supply; and that was to take the Newfoundland in our way, which was but seven hundred leagues from our English coast. Where, being usually at that time of the year and until the fine of August, a multitude of ships repairing thither for fish, we should be relieved abundantly with many necessaries, which, after the fishing ended, they might well spare and freely impart unto us. Not staying long upon that Newland coast, we might proceed southward, and follow still the sun, until we arrived at places more temperate to our content.

By which reasons we were the rather induced to follow this northerly course, obeying unto necessity, which must be supplied. Otherwise, we doubted that sudden approach of winter, bringing with it continual fog, and thick mists, tempest and rage of weather, also contrariety of currents descending from the Cape of Florida unto Cape Breton and Cape Race, would fall out to be great and irresistible impediments unto our further proceeding for that year, and compel us to winter in those north and cold regions.

Wherefore suppressing all objections to the contrary, we resolved to begin our course northward, and to follow directly as we might, the trade way unto Newfoundland; from whence after our refreshing and reparation of wants, we intended without delay (by God's permission) to proceed into the south, not omitting any river or bay which in all that large tract of land appeared to our view worthy of search. Immediately we agreed upon the manner of our course and orders to be observed in our voyage; which were delivered in writing unto the captains and masters of every ship a copy in manner following:—

Every ship had delivered two bullets or scrolls, the one sealed up in wax, the other left open; in both which were included several watchwords. That open, serving upon our own coast or the coast of Ireland; the other sealed, was promised on all hands not to be broken up until we should be clear of the Irish coast; which from thenceforth did serve until we arrived and met all together in such harbours of the Newfoundland as were agreed for our rendezvous. The said watchwords being requisite to know our consorts whensoever by night, either by fortune of weather, our fleet dispersed should come together again; or one should hail another; or if by ill watch and steerage one ship should chance to fall aboard of another in the dark.

The reason of the bullet sealed was to keep secret that watchword while we were upon our own coast, lest any of the company stealing from the fleet might betray the same; which known to an enemy he might board us by night without mistrust, having our own watchword.

Orders agreed upon by the Captains and Masters to be observed by the Fleet of Sir Humphrey Gilbert.

1. The Admiral to carry his flag by day, and his light by night.
2. Item, if the Admiral shall shorten his sail by night, then to shew two lights until he be answered again by every ship shewing one light for a short time.
3. Item, if the Admiral after his shortening of sail, as aforesaid, shall make more sail again; then he to shew three lights one above another.
4. Item, if the Admiral shall happen to hull in the night, then to make a wavering light over his other light, wavering the light upon a pole.
5. Item, if the fleet should happen to be scattered by weather, or other mishap, then so soon as one shall descry another, to hoist both topsails twice, if the weather will serve, and to strike them twice again; but if the weather serve not, then to hoist the main-topsail twice, and forthwith to strike it twice again.
6. Item, if it shall happen a great fog to fall, then presently every ship to bear up with the Admiral, if there be wind; but if it be a calm, then every ship to hull, and so to lie at hull till it clear. And if the fog do continue long, then the Admiral to shoot off two pieces every evening, and every ship to answer it with one shot; and every man bearing to the ship that is to leeward so near as he may.
7. Item, every master to give charge unto the watch to look out well, for laying aboard one of another in the night, and in fogs.
8. Item, every evening every ship to hail the Admiral, and so to fall astern him, sailing through the ocean; and being on the coast, every ship to hail him both morning and evening.
9. Item, if any ship be in danger in any way, by leak or otherwise, then she to shoot off a piece, and presently to hang out one light, whereupon every man to bear towards her, answering her with one light for a short time, and so to put it out again; thereby to give knowledge that they have seen her token.
10. Item, whensoever the Admiral shall hang out her ensign in the main shrouds, then every man to come aboard her as a token of counsel.
11. Item, if there happen any storm or contrary wind to the fleet after the discovery, whereby they are separated; then every ship to repair unto their last good port, there to meet again.

The course.

The course first to be taken for the discovery is to bear directly to Cape Race, the most southerly Cape of Newfoundland; and there to harbour ourselves either in Rogneux or Fermous, being the first places appointed for our rendezvous, and the next harbours unto the northward of Cape Race: and therefore every ship separated from the fleet to repair to that place so fast as God shall permit, whether you shall fall to the southward or to the northward of it, and there to stay for the meeting of the whole fleet the space of ten days, and when you shall depart to leave marks. Beginning our course from Scilly, the nearest is by west-south-west (if the wind serve) until such time as we have brought ourselves in the latitude of 43 or 44 degrees, because the ocean is subject much to southerly winds in June and July. Then to take traverse from 45 to 47 degrees of latitude, if we be enforced by contrary winds; and not to go to the northward of the height of 47 degrees of septentrional latitude by no means, if God shall not enforce the contrary; but to do your endeavour to keep in the height of 46 degrees, so near as you can possibly, because Cape Race lieth about that height.

Notes.

If by contrary winds we be driven back upon the coast of England, then to repair unto Scilly for a place of our assembly or meeting.

If we be driven back by contrary winds that we cannot pass the coast of Ireland, then the place of our assembly to be at Beare Haven or Baltimore Haven.

If we shall not happen to meet at Cape Race, then the place of rendezvous to be at Cape Breton, or the nearest harbour unto the westward of Cape Breton.

If by means of other shipping we may not safely stay there, then to rest at the very next safe port to the westward; every ship leaving their marks behind them for the more certainty of the after comers to know where to find them.

The marks that every man ought to leave in such a case, were of the General's private device written by himself, sealed also in close wax, and delivered unto every ship one scroll, which was not to be opened until occasion required, whereby every man was certified what to leave for instruction of after comers; that every of us coming into any harbour or river might know who had been there, or whether any were still there up higher into the river, or departed, and which way.

Orders thus determined, and promises mutually given to be observed, every man withdrew himself unto his charge, the anchors being already weighed, and our ships under sail, having a soft gale of wind, we began our voyage upon Tuesday, the 11th day of June, in the year of our Lord 1583, having in our fleet (at our departure from Cawsand Bay) these ships, whose names and burthens, with the names of the captains and masters of them, I have also inserted, as followeth:—1. The Delight, *alias* the George, of burthen 120 tons, was Admiral; in which went the General, and William Winter, captain in her and part owner, and Richard Clarke, master. 2. The barque Raleigh, set forth by Mr. Walter Raleigh, of the burthen of 200 tons, was then Vice-Admiral; in which went Mr. Butler, captain, and Robert Davis, of Bristol, master. 3. The Golden Hind, of burthen 40 tons, was then Rear-Admiral; in which went Edward Hayes, captain and owner, and William Cox, of Limehouse, master. 4. The Swallow, of burthen 40 tons; in her was Captain Maurice Browne. 5. The Squirrel, of burthen 10 tons; in which went Captain William Andrews, and one Cade, master. We were in number in all about 260 men, among whom we had of every faculty good choice, as shipwrights, masons, carpenters, smiths, and such like, requisite to such an action; also mineral men and refiners. Besides, for solace of our people, and allurement of the savages, we were provided of music in good variety; not omitting the least toys, as Morris dancers, hobby-horse, and Maylike conceits to delight the savage people, whom we intended to win by all fair means possible. And to that end we were indifferently furnished of all petty haberdashery wares to barter with those simple people.

In this manner we set forward, departing (as hath been said) out of Cawsand Bay the 11th of June, being Tuesday, the weather and wind fair and good all day, but a great storm of thunder and wind fell the same night.

On the Thursday following, when we hailed one another in the evening (according to the order before specified) they signified unto us out of the Vice-Admiral, that both the Captain, and very many of the men were fallen sick; and about midnight the Vice-Admiral forsook us, notwithstanding we had the wind east, fair and good. But it was after credibly reported that they were infected with a contagious sickness, and arrived greatly distressed at Plymouth; the reason I could never understand. Sure I am, no cost was spared by their owner, Master Raleigh, in setting them forth; therefore I leave it unto God.

By this time we were in forty-eight degrees of latitude, not a little grieved with the loss of the most puissant ship in our fleet, after whose departure the Golden Hind succeeded in the place of Vice-Admiral, and removed her flag from the mizen into the foretop. From Saturday, the 15th of June, until the 28th, which was upon a Friday, we never had fair day without fog or rain, and winds bad, much to the west-north-west, whereby we were driven southward unto forty-one degrees scarce.

About this time of the year the winds are commonly west towards the Newfoundland, keeping ordinarily within two points of west to the south or to the north, whereby the course thither falleth out to be long and tedious after June, which in March April, and May, hath been performed out of England in twenty-two days and less. We had wind always so scant from west-north-west, and from west-south-west again, that our traverse was great, running south unto forty-one degrees almost, and afterwards north into fifty-one degrees. Also we were encumbered with much fog and mists in manner palpable, in which we could not keep so well together, but were dissevered, losing the company of the Swallow and the Squirrel upon the 20th day of July, whom we met again at several places upon the Newfoundland coast the 3rd of August, as shall be declared in place convenient. On Saturday, the 27th July, we might descry, not far from us, as it were mountains of ice driven upon the sea, being then in fifty degrees, which were carried southward to the weather of us, whereby may be conjectured that some current doth set that way from the north.

Before we come to Newfoundland, about fifty leagues on this side, we pass the bank, which are high grounds rising within the sea and under water, yet deep enough and without danger, being commonly not less than twenty-five and thirty fathom water upon them; the same (as it were some vein of mountains within the sea) do run along, and from the Newfoundland, beginning northward about fifty-two or fifty-three degrees of latitude, and do extend into the south infinitely. The breadth of this bank is somewhere more, and somewhere less; but we found the same about ten leagues over, having sounded both on this side thereof, and the other towards Newfoundland, but found no ground with almost two hundred fathom of line, both before and after we had passed the bank. The Portugals, and French chiefly, have a notable trade of fishing upon this bank, where are sometimes an hundred or more sail of ships, who commonly begin the fishing in April, and have ended by July. That fish is large, always wet, having no land near to dry, and is called cod-fish.

During the time of fishing, a man shall know without sounding when he is upon the bank, by the incredible multitude of sea-fowl hovering over the same, to prey upon the offal and garbage of fish thrown out by fishermen, and floating upon the sea.

On Tuesday, the 11th of June, we forsook the coast of England, so again on Tuesday, the 30th of July (seven weeks after) we got sight of land, being immediately embayed in the Grand Bay, or some other great bay, the certainty whereof we could not judge, so great haze and fog did hang upon the coast, as neither we might discern the land well, nor take the sun's height; but by our best computation we were then in the fifty-one degrees of latitude.

Forsaking this bay and uncomfortable coast (nothing appearing unto us but hideous rocks and mountains, bare of trees, and void of any green herb) we followed the coast to the south, with weather fair and clear. We had sight of an island named Penguin, of a fowl there breeding in abundance, almost incredible, which cannot fly, their wings not able to carry their body, being very large (not much less than a goose) and exceeding fat, which the Frenchmen use to take without difficulty upon that island, and to barrel them up with salt. But for lingering of time, we had made us there the like provision.

Trending this coast, we came to the island called Baccalaos, being not past two leagues from the main; to the south thereof lieth Cape St. Francis, five leagues distant from Baccalaos, between which goeth in a great bay, by the vulgar sort called the Bay of Conception. Here we met with the Swallow again, whom we had lost in the fog, and all her men altered into other apparel. Whereof it seemed their store was so amended, that for joy and congratulation of our meeting, they spared not to cast up into the air and overboard their caps and hats in good plenty. The Captain, albeit himself was very honest and religious, yet was he not appointed of men to his humour and desert; who for the most part were such as had been by us surprised upon the narrow seas of England, being pirates, and had taken at that instant certain Frenchmen laden, one barque with wines, and another with salt, both which we rescued, and took the man-of-war with all her men, which was the same ship now called the Swallow, following still their kind so oft, as (being separated from the General) they found opportunity to rob and spoil. And because God's justice did follow the same company, even to destruction, and to the overthrow also of the captain (though not consenting to their misdemeanour) I will not conceal anything that maketh to the manifestation and approbation of his judgments, for examples of others, persuaded that God more sharply took revenge upon them, and hath tolerated longer as great outrage in others, by how much these went under protection of his cause and religion, which was then pretended.

Therefore upon further enquiry it was known how this company met with a barque returning home after the fishing with his freight, and because the men in the Swallow were very near scanted of victuals, and chiefly of apparel, doubtful withal where or when to find and meet with their Admiral, they besought the Captain that they might go aboard this Newlander, only to borrow what might be spared, the rather because the same was bound homeward. Leave given, not without charge to deal favourably, they came aboard the fisherman, whom they rifled of tackle, sails, cables, victuals, and the men of their apparel, not sparing by torture (winding cords about their heads) to draw out else what they thought good. This done with expedition (like men skilful in such mischief) as they took their cock-boat to go aboard their own ship, it was overwhelmed in the sea, and certain of these men there drowned; the rest were preserved even by those silly souls whom they had before spoiled, who saved and delivered them aboard the Swallow. What became afterwards of the poor Newlander, perhaps destitute of sails and furniture sufficient to carry them home (whither they had not less to run than 700 leagues) God alone knoweth, who took vengeance not long after of the rest that escaped at this instant, to reveal the fact, and justify to the world God's judgments inflicted upon them, as shall be declared in place convenient.

Thus after we had met with the Swallow, we held on our course southward, until we came against the harbour called St. John, about five leagues from the former Cape of St. Francis, where before the entrance into the harbour, we found also the Frigate or Squirrel lying at anchor, whom the English merchants (that were and always be Admirals by turns interchangeably over the fleets of fishermen within the same harbour) would not permit to enter into the harbour. Glad of so happy meeting, both of the Swallow and Frigate in one day (being Saturday, the 3rd of August), we made ready our fights, and prepared to enter the harbour, any resistance to the contrary notwithstanding, there being within of all nations, to the number of thirty-six sail. But first the General despatched a boat to give them knowledge of his coming for no ill intent, having commission from Her Majesty for his voyage we had in hand; and immediately we followed with a slack gale, and in the very entrance (which is but narrow, not above two boats' length) the Admiral fell upon a rock on the larboard side by great oversight, in that the weather was fair, the rock much above water fast by the shore, where neither went any sea-gate. But we found such readiness in the English merchants to help us in that danger, that without delay there were brought a number of boats, which towed off the ship, and cleared her of danger.

Having taken place convenient in the road, we let fall anchors, the Captains and Masters repairing aboard our Admiral, whither also came immediately the Masters and owners of the fishing fleet of Englishmen, to understand the General's intent and cause of our arrival there. They were all satisfied when the General had showed his commission and purpose, to take possession of those lands to the behalf of the crown of England, and the advancement of the Christian religion in those paganish regions, requiring but their lawful aid for repairing of his fleet, and supply of some necessaries, so far as conveniently might be afforded him, both out of that and other harbours adjoining. In lieu whereof he made offer to gratify them with any favour and privilege, which upon their better advice they should demand, the like being not to be obtained hereafter for greater price. So craving expedition of his demand, minding to proceed further south without long detention in those parts, he dismissed them, after promise given of their best endeavour to satisfy speedily his so reasonable request. The merchants with their masters departed, they caused forthwith to be discharged all the great ordnance of their fleet in token of our welcome.

It was further determined that every ship of our fleet should deliver unto the merchants and masters of that harbour a note of all their wants: which done, the ships as well English as strangers, were taxed at an easy rate to make supply. And besides, commissioners were appointed, part of our own company and part of theirs, to go into other harbours adjoining (for our English merchants command all there) to levy our provision: whereunto the Portugals (above other nations) did most willingly and liberally contribute. In so much as we were presented (above our allowance) with wines, marmalades, most fine rusk or biscuit, sweet oils, and sundry delicacies. Also we wanted not of fresh salmons, trouts, lobsters, and other fresh fish brought daily unto us. Moreover as the manner is in fishing, every week to choose their Admiral anew, or rather they succeed in orderly course, and have weekly their Admiral's feast solemnized: even so the General, captains, and masters of our fleet were continually invited and feasted. To grow short, in our abundance at home, the entertainment had been delightful, but after our wants and tedious passage through the ocean, it seemed more acceptable and of greater contentation, by how much the same was unexpected in that desolate corner of the world: where at other times of the year, wild beasts and birds have only the fruition of all those countries, which now seemed a place very populous and much frequented.

The next morning being Sunday, and the 4th of August, the General and his company were brought on land by English merchants, who shewed unto us their accustomed walks unto a place they call the garden. But nothing appeared more than nature itself without art: who confusedly hath brought forth roses abundantly, wild, but odoriferous, and to sense very comfortable. Also the like plenty of raspberries, which do grow in every place.

Monday following, the General had his tent set up, who being accompanied with his own followers, summoned the merchants and masters, both English and strangers, to be present at his taking possession of those countries. Before whom openly was read and interpreted unto the strangers his commission: by virtue whereof he took possession in the same harbour of St. John, and 200 leagues every way, invested the Queen's Majesty with the title and dignity thereof, and delivered unto him (after the custom of England) a rod and a turf of the same soil, entering possession also for him, his heirs and assigns for ever: And signified unto all men, that from that time forward, they should take the same land as a territory appertaining to the Queen of England, and himself authorised under Her Majesty to possess and enjoy it. And to ordain laws for the government thereof, agreeable (so near as conveniently might be) unto the laws of England: under which all people coming thither hereafter, either to inhabit, or by way of traffic, should be subjected and governed. And especially at the same time for a beginning, he proposed and delivered three laws to be in force immediately. That is to say: the first for religion, which in public exercise should be according to the Church of England. The second for maintenance of Her Majesty's right and possession of those territories, against which if any thing were attempted prejudicial, the party or parties offending should be adjudged and executed as in case of high treason, according to the laws of England. The third, if any person should utter words sounding to the dishonour of Her Majesty, he should lose his ears, and have his ship and goods confiscate.

These contents published, obedience was promised by general voice and consent of the multitude, as well of Englishmen as strangers, praying for continuance of this possession and government begun. After this, the assembly was dismissed. And afterwards were erected not far from that place the arms of England engraved in lead, and infixed upon a pillar of wood. Yet further and actually to establish this possession taken in the right of Her Majesty, and to the behoof of Sir Humphrey Gilbert, knight, his heirs and assigns for ever: the General granted in fee farm divers parcels of land lying by the water side, both in this harbour of St. John, and elsewhere, which was to the owners a great commodity, being thereby assured (by their proper inheritance) of grounds convenient to dress and to dry their fish, whereof many times before they did fail, being prevented by them that came first into the harbour. For which grounds they did covenant to pay a certain rent and service unto Sir Humphrey Gilbert, his heirs or assigns for ever, and yearly to maintain possession of the same, by themselves or their assigns.

Now remained only to take in provision granted, according as every ship was taxed, which did fish upon the coast adjoining. In the meanwhile, the General appointed men unto their charge: some to repair and trim the ships, others to attend in gathering together our supply and provisions: others to search the commodities and singularities of the country, to be found by sea or land, and to make relation unto the General what either themselves could know by their own travail and experience, or by good intelligence of Englishmen or strangers, who had longest frequented the same coast. Also some observed the elevation of the pole, and drew plates of the country exactly graded. And by that I could gather by each man's several relation, I have drawn a brief description of the Newfoundland, with the commodities by sea or land already made, and such also as are in possibility and great likelihood to be made: Nevertheless the cards and plates that were drawing, with the due gradation of the harbours, bays, and capes, did perish with the Admiral: wherefore in the description following, I must omit the particulars of such things.

That which we do call the Newfoundland, and the Frenchmen Baccalaos, is an island, or rather (after the opinion of some) it consisteth of sundry islands and broken lands, situate in the north regions of America, upon the gulf and entrance of a great river called St. Lawrence in Canada. Into the which, navigation may be made both on the south and north side of this island. The land lieth south and north, containing in length between 300 and 400 miles, accounting from Cape Race (which is in forty-six degrees twenty-five minutes) unto the Grand Bay in fifty-two degrees of septentrional latitude. The land round about hath very many goodly bays and harbours, safe roads for ships, the like not to be found in any part of the known world.

The common opinion that is had of intemperature and extreme cold that should be in this country, as of some part it may be verified, namely the north, where I grant it is more cold than in countries of Europe, which are under the same elevation: even so it cannot stand with reason and nature of the clime, that the south parts should be so intemperate as the bruit hath gone. For as the same do lie under the climes of Breton, Anjou, Poictou in France, between forty-six and forty-nine degrees, so can they not so much differ from the temperature of those countries: unless upon the outcoast lying open unto the ocean and sharp winds, it must indeed be subject to more cold, than further within the land, where the mountains are interposed, as walls and bulwarks, to defend and to resist the asperity and rigour of the sea and weather. Some hold opinion, that the Newfoundland might be the more subject to cold, by how much it lieth high and near unto the middle region. I grant that not in Newfoundland alone, but in Germany, Italy and Africa, even under the equinoctial line, the mountains are extreme cold, and seldom uncovered of snow, in their culm and highest tops, which cometh to pass by the same reason that they are extended towards the middle region: yet in the countries lying beneath them, it is found quite contrary. Even so all hills having their descents, the valleys also and low grounds must be likewise hot or temperate, as the clime doth give in Newfoundland: though I am of opinion that the sun's reflection is much cooled, and cannot be so forcible in Newfoundland, nor generally throughout America, as in Europe or Africa: by how much the sun in his diurnal course from east to west, passeth over (for the most part) dry land and sandy countries, before he arriveth at the west of Europe or Africa, whereby his motion increaseth heat, with little or no qualification by moist vapours. Where, on the contrary he passeth from Europe and Africa unto America over the ocean, from whence it draweth and carrieth with him abundance of moist vapours, which do qualify and enfeeble greatly the sun's reverberation upon this country chiefly of Newfoundland, being so much to the northward. Nevertheless (as I said before) the cold cannot be so intolerable under the latitude of forty-six, forty-seven, and forty-eight (especially within land) that it should be unhabitable, as some do suppose, seeing also there are very many people more to the north by a great deal. And in these south parts there be certain beasts, ounces or leopards, and birds in like manner which in the summer we have seen, not heard of in countries of extreme and vehement coldness. Besides, as in the months of June, July, August and September, the heat is somewhat more than in England at those seasons: so men remaining upon the south parts near unto Cape Race, until after Hollandtide,* have not found the cold so extreme, nor much differing from the temperature of England. Those which have arrived there after November and December, have found the snow exceeding deep, whereat no marvel, considering the ground upon the coast is rough and uneven, and the snow is driven into the places most declining, as the like is to be seen with us. The like depth of snow happily shall not be found within land upon the plainer countries, which also are defended by the mountains, breaking off the violence of winds and weather. But admitting extraordinary cold in those south parts, above that with us here: it cannot be so great as in Swedeland, much less in Moscovia or Russia: yet are the same countries very populous, and the rigour of cold is dispensed with by the commodity of stoves, warm clothing, meats and drinks: all of which need not to be wanting in the Newfoundland, if we had intent there to inhabit.

In the south parts we found no inhabitants, which by all likelihood have abandoned those coasts, the same being so much frequented by Christians. But in the north are savages altogether

---

* All-hallow-tide.

harmless. Touching the commodities of this country, serving either, for sustentation of inhabitants or for maintenance of traffic, there are and may be made divers; so that it seemeth that nature hath recompensed that only defect and incommodity of some sharp cold, by many benefits; viz., with incredible quantity, and no less variety of kinds of fish in the sea and fresh waters, as trout, salmon, and other fish to us unknown; also cod, which alone draweth many nations thither, and is become the most famous fishing of the world. Abundance of whales, for which also is a very great trade in the bays of Placentia and the Grand Bay, where is made train oil of the whale; herring, the largest that have been heard of, and exceeding the Malstrond herring of Norway; but hitherto was never benefit taken of the herring fishing. There are sundry other fish very delicate, namely the bonitos, lobsters, turbot, with others infinite not sought after; oysters having pearl but not orient in colour; I took it, by reason they were not gathered in season.

Concerning the inland commodities, as well to be drawn from this land, as from the exceeding large countries adjoining, there is nothing which our east and northerly countries of Europe do yield, but the like also may be made in them as plentifully by time and industry; namely, rosin, pitch, tar, soap-ashes, deal-board, masts for ships, hides, furs, flax, hemp, corn, cables, cordage, linen cloth, metals, and many more. All which the countries will afford, and the soil is apt to yield. The trees for the most in those south parts, are fir-trees, pine, and cypress, all yielding gum and turpentine. Cherry trees bearing fruit no bigger than a small pea. Also pear-trees, but fruitless. Other trees of some sorts to us unknown. The soil along the coast is not deep of earth, bringing forth abundantly peason small, yet good feeding for cattle. Roses passing sweet, like unto our musk roses in form, raspases, a berry which we call hurts, good and wholesome to eat. The grass and herb doth fat sheep in very short space, proved by English merchants which have carried sheep thither for fresh victual and had them raised exceeding fat in less than three weeks. Peason which our countrymen have sown in the time of May, have come up fair, and been gathered in the beginning of August, of which our General had a present acceptable for the rareness, being the first fruits coming up by art and industry in that desolate and dishabited land. Lakes or pools of fresh water, both on the tops of mountains and in the valleys, in which are said to be muscles not unlike to have pearl, which I had put in trial, if by mischance falling unto me I had not been let from that and other good experiments I was minded to make. Fowl both of water and land in great plenty and diversity. All kinds of green fowl; others as big as bustards, yet not the same. A great white fowl called of some a gaunt. Upon the land divers sorts of hawks, as falcons, and others by report. Partridges most plentiful, larger than ours, grey and white of colour, and rough-footed like doves, which our men after one flight did kill with cudgels, they were so fat and unable to fly. Birds some like blackbirds, linnets, canary birds, and other very small. Beasts of sundry kinds, red deer, buffaloes, or a beast as it seemeth by the tract and foot very large, in manner of an ox. Bears, ounces or leopards, some greater and some lesser, wolves, foxes, which to the northward a little further are black, whose fur is esteemed in some countries of Europe very rich. Otters, beavers, martins. And in the opinion of most men that saw it, the General had brought unto him a sable alive, which he sent unto his brother, Sir John Gilbert, Knight, of Devonshire, but it was never delivered, as after I understood. We could not observe the hundredth part of creatures in those unhabited lands; but these mentioned may induce us to glorify the magnificent God, who hath superabundantly replenished the earth with creatures serving for the use of man, though man hath not used the fifth part of the same, which the more doth aggravate the fault and foolish sloth in many of our nation, choosing rather to live indirectly, and very miserably to live and die within this realm pestered with inhabitants, than to adventure as becometh men, to obtain an habitation in those remote lands, in which nature very prodigally doth minister unto men's endeavours, and for art to work upon. For besides these already recounted and infinite more, the mountains generally make shew of mineral substance; iron very common, lead, and somewhere copper. I will not aver of richer metals; albeit by the circumstances following, more than hope may be conceived thereof.

For amongst other charges given to inquire out the singularities of this country, the General was most curious in the search of metals, commanding the mineral-man and refiner especially to be diligent. The same was a Saxon born, honest, and religious, named Daniel, who after search brought at first some sort of ore, seeming rather to be iron than other metal. The next time he found ore, which with no small show of contentment he delivered unto the General, using protestation that if silver were the thing which might satisfy the General and his followers, there it was, advising him to seek no further; the peril whereof he undertook upon his life (as dear unto him as the crown of England unto her Majesty, that I may use his own words) if it fell not out accordingly.

Myself at this instant likelier to die than to live, by a mischance, could not follow this confident opinion of our refiner to my own satisfaction; but afterward demanding our General's opinion therein, and to have some part of the ore, he replied, "Content yourself, I have seen enough, and were it but to satisfy my private humour, I would proceed no further. The promise unto my friends, and necessity to bring also the south countries within compass of my patent near expired, as we have already done these north parts, do only persuade me further. And touching the ore, I have sent it aboard, whereof I would have no speech to be made so long as we remain within harbour; here being both Portugals, Biscayans, and Frenchmen, not far off, from whom must be kept any bruit or muttering of such matter. When we are at sea proof shall be made; if it be our desire, we may return the sooner hither again." Whose answer I judged reasonable, and contenting me well; wherewith I will conclude this narration and description of the Newfoundland, and proceed to the rest of our voyage, which ended tragically.

While the better sort of us were seriously occupied in repairing our wants, and contriving of matters for the commodity of our voyage, others of another sort and disposition were plotting of mischief. Some casting to steal away our shipping by night, watching opportunity by the Generals and Captains lying on the shore; whose conspiracies discovered, they were prevented. Others drew together in company, and carried away out of the harbours adjoining a ship laden with fish, setting the poor men on shore. A great many more of our people stole into the woods to hide themselves, attending time and means to return home by such shipping as daily departed from the coast. Some were sick of fluxes, and many dead; and in brief, by one means or other our company was diminished, and many by the General licensed to return home. Insomuch as after we had reviewed our people resolved to see an end of our voyage, we grew scant of men to furnish all our shipping; it seemed good therefore unto the General to leave the Swallow with such provision as might be spared for transporting home the sick people.

The Captain of the Delight or Admiral returned into England, in whose stead was appointed Captain Maurice Browne, before Captain of the Swallow; who also brought with him into the Delight all his men of the Swallow, which before have been noted of outrage perpetrated and committed upon fishermen there met at sea.

The General made choice to go in his frigate the Squirrel (whereof the captain also was amongst them that returned into England) the same frigate being most convenient to discover upon the coast, and to search into every harbour or creek, which a great ship could not do. Therefore the frigate was prepared with her nettings and fights, and overcharged with bases and such small ordnance, more to give a show, than with judgment to foresee unto the safety of her and the men, which afterward was an occasion also of their overthrow.

Now having made ready our shipping, that is to say, the Delight, the Golden Hind, and the Squirrel, and put aboard our provision, which was wines, bread or rusk, fish wet and dry, sweet oil, besides many other, as marmalades, figs, lemons barrelled, and such like. Also we had other necessary provisions for trimming our ships, nets and lines to fish withal, boats or pinnaces fit for discovery. In brief, we were supplied of our wants commodiously, as if we had been in a country or some city populous and plentiful of all things.

We departed from this harbour of St. John's upon Tuesday, the 20th of August, which we found by exact observation to be in 47 degrees 40 minutes. And the next day by night we were at Cape Race, 25 leagues from the same harbour. This Cape lieth south-south-west from St. John's; it is a low land, being off from the Cape about half a league; within the sea riseth up a rock against the point of the Cape, which thereby is easily known. It is in latitude 46 degrees 25 minutes. Under this Cape we were becalmed a small time, during which we laid out hooks and lines to take cod, and drew in less than two hours fish so large and in such abundance, that many days after we fed upon no other provision. From hence we shaped our course unto the island of Sablon, if conveniently it would so fall out, also directly to Cape Breton.

Sablon lieth to the seaward of Cape Breton about twenty-five leagues, whither we were determined to go upon intelligence we had of a Portugal (during our abode in St. John's) who was himself present when the Portugals above thirty years past did put into the same island both neat and swine to breed, which were since exceedingly multiplied. This seemed unto us very happy tidings, to have in an island lying so near unto the main, which we intended to plant upon, such store of cattle, whereby we might at all times conveniently be relieved of victual, and served of store to breed.

In this course we trended along the coast, which from Cape Race stretcheth into the north-west, making a bay which some called Trepassa. Then it goeth out again towards the west, and maketh a point, which with Cape Race lieth in manner east and west. But this point inclineth to the north, to the west of which goeth in the Bay of Placentia. We sent men on land to take view of the soil along this coast, whereof they made good report, and some of them had will to be planted there. They saw peas growing in great abundance everywhere.

The distance between Cape Race and Cape Breton is eighty-seven leagues; in which navigation we spent eight days, having many times the wind indifferent good, yet could we never attain sight of any land all that time, seeing we were hindered by the current. At last we fell into such flats and dangers, that hardly any of us escaped; where nevertheless we lost our Admiral with all the men and provisions, not knowing certainly the place. Yet for inducing men of skill to make conjecture, by our course and way we held from Cape Race thither (that thereby the flats and dangers may be inserted in sea cards, for warning to others that may follow the same course hereafter), I have set down the best reckonings that were kept by expert men, William Cox, Master of the Hind, and John Paul, his mate, both of Limehouse. Our course held in clearing us of these flats was east-south-east, and south-east, and south, fourteen leagues, with a marvellous scant wind.

Upon Tuesday, the 27th of August, toward the evening, our General caused them in his frigate to sound, who found white sand at thirty-five fathom, being then in latitude about forty-four degrees. On Wednesday, towards night, the wind came south, and we bare with the land all that night, west-north-west, contrary to the mind of Master Cox; nevertheless we followed the Admiral, deprived of power to prevent a mischief, which by no contradiction could be brought to hold another course, alleging they could not make the ship to work better, nor to lie otherways. The evening was fair and pleasant, yet not without token of storm to ensue, and most part of this Wednesday night, like the swan that singeth before her death, they in the Admiral, or Delight, continued in sounding of trumpets, with drums and fifes; also winding the cornets and hautboys, and in the end of their jollity, left with the battle and ringing of doleful knells. Towards the evening also we caught in the Golden Hind a very mighty porpoise, with a harping iron, having first stricken divers of them, and brought away part of their flesh sticking upon the iron, but could recover only that one. These also passing through the ocean in herds, did portend storm. I omit to recite frivolous reports by them in the frigate, of strange voices, the same night, which scared some from the helm.

On Thursday, the 29th of August, the wind rose, and blew vehemently at south and by east, bringing withal rain and thick mist, so that we could not see a cable's length before us; and betimes in the morning we were altogether run and folded in amongst flats and sands, amongst which we found shoal and deep in every three or four ships' length, after we began to sound: but first we were upon them unawares, until Master Cox looking out, discerned, in his judgment, white cliffs, crying "Land," withal, though we could not afterward descry any land, it being very likely the breaking of the sea white, which seemed to be white cliffs, through the haze and thick weather.

Immediately tokens were given unto the Delight, to cast about to seaward, which, being the greater ship, and of burthen 120 tons, was yet foremost upon the breach, keeping so ill watch, that they knew not the danger, before they felt the same, too late to recover it; for presently the Admiral struck aground, and had soon after her stern and hinder parts beaten in pieces; whereupon the rest (that is to say, the frigate, in which was the General, and the Golden Hind) cast about east-south-east, bearing to the south, even for our lives, into the wind's eye, because that way carried us to the seaward. Making out from this danger, we sounded one while seven fathoms, then five fathoms, then four fathoms and less, again deeper, immediately four fathoms, then but three fathoms, the sea going mightily and high. At last we recovered (God be thanked) in some despair, to sea room enough.

In this distress, we had vigilant eye unto the Admiral, whom we saw cast away, without power to give the men succour, neither could we espy any of the men that leaped overboard to save themselves, either in the same pinnace, or cock, or upon rafters, and such like means, presenting themselves to men in those extremities, for we desired to save the men by every possible means. But all in vain, since God had determined their ruin; yet all that day, and part of the next, we beat up and down as near unto the wreck as was possible for us, looking out if by good hap we might espy any of them.

This was a heavy and grievous event, to lose at one blow our chief ship freighted with great provision, gathered together with much travail, care, long time, and difficulty. But more was the loss of our men, which perished to the number almost of a hundred souls. Amongst whom was drowned a learned man, a Hungarian,* born in the city of Buda, called thereof Budæus, who of piety and zeal to good attempts, adventured in this action, minding to record in the Latin tongue, the gests and things worthy of remembrance, happening in this discovery, to the honour of our nation, the same being adorned with the eloquent style of this orator and rare poet of our time.

Here also perished our Saxon refiner and discoverer of inestimable riches, as it was left amongst some of us in undoubted hope. No less heavy was the loss of the Captain, Maurice Browne, a virtuous, honest, and discreet gentleman, overseen only in liberty given late before to men that ought to have been restrained, who shewed himself a man resolved, and never unprepared for death, as by his last act of this tragedy appeared, by report of them that escaped this wreck miraculously, as shall be hereafter declared. For when all hope was passed of recovering the ship, and that men began to give over, and to save themselves, the Captain was advised before to shift also for his life, by the pinnace at the stern of the ship; but refusing that counsel, he would not give example with the first to leave the ship, but used all means to exhort his people not to despair, nor so to leave off their labour, choosing rather to die than to incur infamy by forsaking his charge, which then might be thought to have perished through his default, shewing an ill precedent unto his men, by leaving the ship first himself. With this mind he mounted upon the highest deck, where he attended imminent death, and unavoidable; how long,

---

* Stephen Parmenius.

I leave it to God, who withdraweth not his comfort from his servants at such times.

In the mean season, certain, to the number of fourteen persons, leaped into a small pinnace (the bigness of a Thames barge, which was made in Newfoundland) cut off the rope wherewith it was towed, and committed themselves to God's mercy, amidst the storm, and rage of sea and winds, destitute of food, not so much as a drop of fresh water. The boat seeming overcharged in foul weather with company, Edward Headly, a valiant soldier, and well reputed of his company, preferring the greater to the lesser, thought better that some of them perished than all, made this motion to cast lots, and them to be thrown overboard upon whom the lots fell, thereby to lighten the boat, which otherways seemed impossible to live, offered himself with the first, content to take his adventure gladly: which nevertheless Richard Clarke, that was master of the Admiral, and one of this number, refused, advising to abide God's pleasure, who was able to save all, as well as a few.

The boat was carried before the wind, continuing six days and nights in the ocean, and arrived at last with the men (alive, but weak) upon the Newfoundland, saving that the foresaid Headly, (who had been late sick) and another called of us Brasile, of his travel into those countries, died by the way, famished, and less able to hold out than those of better health. For such was these poor men's extremity, in cold and wet, to have no better sustenance than their own urine, for six days together.

Thus whom God delivered from drowning, he appointed to be famished, who doth give limits to man's times, and ordaineth the manner and circumstance of dying: whom again he will preserve, neither sea nor famine can confound. For those that arrived upon the Newfoundland, were brought into France by certain Frenchmen, then being upon the coast.

After this heavy chance, we continued in beating the sea up and down, expecting when the weather would clear up that we might yet bear in with the land, which we judged not far off either the continent or some island. For we many times, and in sundry places found ground at fifty, forty-five, forty fathoms, and less. The ground coming upon our lead, being sometime oozy sand and other while a broad shell, with a little sand about it.

Our people lost courage daily after this ill success, the weather continuing thick and blustering, with increase of cold, winter drawing on, which took from them all hope of amendment, settling an assurance of worse weather to grow upon us every day. The leeside of us lay full of flats and dangers inevitable, if the wind blew hard at south. Some again doubted we were ingulfed in the Bay of St. Lawrence, the coast full of dangers, and unto us unknown. But above all, provision waxed scant, and hope of supply was gone with loss of our Admiral.

Those in the frigate were already pinched with spare allowance, and want of clothes chiefly: Whereupon they besought the General to return to England, before they all perished. And to them of the Golden Hind, they made signs of their distress, pointing to their mouths, and to their clothes thin and ragged: then immediately they also of the Golden Hind grew to be of the same opinion and desire to return home.

The former reasons having also moved the General to have compassion of his poor men, in whom he saw no want of good will, but of means fit to perform the action they came for, resolved upon retiring: and calling the captain and master of the Hind, he yielded them many reasons, enforcing this unexpected return, withal protesting himself greatly satisfied with that he had seen and knew already. Reiterating these words, "Be content, we have seen enough, and take no care of expense past: I will set you forth royally the next spring, if God send us safe home. Therefore I pray you let us no longer strive here, where we fight against the elements."

Omitting circumstance, how unwillingly the captain and master of the Hind condescended to this motion, his own company can testify: yet comforted with the General's promise of a speedy return at spring, and induced by other apparent reasons, proving an impossibility to accomplish the action at that time, it was concluded on all hands to retire.

So upon Saturday in the afternoon of the 31st of August, we changed our course, and returned back for England, at which very instant, even in winding about, there passed along between us and towards the land which we now forsook a very lion to our seeming, in shape, hair, and colour, not swimming after the manner of a beast by moving of his feet, but rather sliding upon the water with his whole body (excepting the legs) in sight, neither yet diving under, and again rising above the water, as the manner is of whales, dolphins, tunnies, porpoises, and all other fish: but confidently showing himself above water without hiding: notwithstanding, we presented ourselves in open view and gesture to amaze him, as all creatures will be commonly at a sudden gaze and sight of men. Thus he passed along turning his head to and fro, yawning and gaping wide, with ugly demonstration of long teeth, and glaring eyes, and to bid us a farewell (coming right against the Hind) he sent forth a horrible voice, roaring or bellowing as doth a lion, which spectacle we all beheld so far as we were able to discern the same, as men prone to wonder at every strange thing, as this doubtless was, to see a lion in the ocean sea, or fish in shape of a lion. What opinion others had thereof, and chiefly the General himself, I forbear to deliver: But he took it for *Bonum Omen*, rejoicing that he was to war against such an enemy, if it were the devil. The wind was large for England at our return, but very high, and the sea rough, insomuch as the frigate wherein the General went was almost swallowed up.

Monday in the afternoon we passed in the sight of Cape Race, having made as much way in little more than two days and nights back again, as before we had done in eight days from Cape Race unto the place where our ship perished. Which hindrance thitherward, and speed back again, is to be imputed unto the swift current, as well as to the winds, which we had more large in our return. This Monday the General came aboard the Hind, to have the surgeon of the Hind to dress his foot, which he hurt by treading upon a nail: At what time we comforted each other with hope of hard success to be all past, and of the good to come. So agreeing to carry out lights always by night, that we might keep together, he departed into his frigate, being by no means to be entreated to tarry in the Hind, which had been more for his security. Immediately after followed a sharp storm, which we overpassed for that time, praised be God.

The weather fair, the General came aboard the Hind again, to make merry together with the captain, master, and company, which was the last meeting, and continued there from morning until night. During which time there passed sundry discourses, touching affairs past, and to come, lamenting greatly the loss of his great ship, more of the men, but most of all his books and notes, and what else I know not, for which he was out of measure grieved, the same doubtless being some matter of more importance than his books, which I could not draw from him: yet by circumstances I gathered the same to be the ore which Daniel the Saxon had brought unto him in the Newfoundland. Whatsoever it was, the remembrance touched him so deep as, not able to contain himself, he beat his boy in great rage, even at the same time, so long after the miscarrying of the great ship, because upon a fair bay, when we were becalmed upon the coast of the Newfoundland, near unto Cape Race, he sent his boy aboard the Admiral, to fetch certain things: amongst which, this being chief, was yet forgotten and left behind. After which time he could never conveniently send again aboard the great ship, much less he doubted her ruin so near at hand.

Herein my opinion was better confirmed diversely, and by sundry conjectures, which maketh me have the greater hope of this rich mine. For whereas the General had never before good conceit of these north parts of the world: now his mind was wholly fixed upon the Newfoundland. And as before he refused not to grant assignments liberally to them that required the same into these north parts, now he became contrarily affected, refusing to make any so large grants, especially of St. John's, which certain English merchants made suit for, offering to employ their money and travel upon the same: yet neither by their own suit, nor of others of his own company, whom he seemed willing to pleasure, it could be obtained. Also laying down his determination in the spring following for disposing of his voyage then to be re-attempted: he assigned the captain and master of the Golden Hind unto the south discovery, and reserved unto himself the north, affirming that this voyage had won his heart from the south, and that he was now become a northern man altogether.

Last, being demanded what means he had at his arrival in England to compass the charges of so great preparation as he intended to make the next spring, having determined upon two fleets, one for the south, another for the north, "Leave that to me," he replied, "I will ask a penny of no man. I will bring good tidings unto Her Majesty, who will be so gracious to lend me 10,000 pounds," willing us therefore to be of good cheer; for he did thank God, he said, with all his heart for that he had seen, the same being enough for us all, and that we needed not to seek any further. And these last words he would often repeat, with demonstration of great fervency of mind, being himself very confident and settled in belief of inestimable good by this voyage, which the greater number of his followers nevertheless mistrusted altogether, not being made partakers of those secrets, which the General kept unto himself. Yet all of them that are living may be witnesses of his words and protestations, which sparingly I have delivered.

Leaving the issue of this good hope unto God, who knoweth the truth only, and can at His good pleasure bring the same to light, I will hasten to the end of this tragedy, which must be knit up in the person of our General. And as it was God's ordinance upon him, even so the vehement persuasion and entreaty of his friends could nothing avail to divert him of a wilful resolution of going through in his frigate, which was overcharged upon their decks with fights, nettings, and small artillery, too cumbersome for so small a boat, that was to pass through the ocean sea at that season of the year, when by course we might expect much storm of foul weather, whereof, indeed, we had enough.

But when he was entreated by the captain, master, and other his well-willers of the Hind not to venture in the frigate, this was his answer:—"I will not forsake my little company going homeward, with whom I have passed so many storms and perils." And in very truth he was urged to be so over hard by hard reports given of him that he was afraid of the sea, albeit this was rather rashness than advised resolution, to prefer the wind of a vain report to the weight of his own life. Seeing he would not bend to reason, he had provision out of the Hind, such as was wanting aboard his frigate. And so we committed him to God's protection, and set him aboard his pinnace, we being more than 300 leagues onward of our way home.

By that time we had brought the Islands of Azores south of us; yet we then keeping much to the north, until we had got into the height and elevation of England, we met with very foul weather and terrible seas, breaking short and high, pyramid-wise. The reason whereof seemed to proceed either of hilly grounds high and low within the sea (as we see hills and vales upon the land), upon which the seas do mount and fall, or else the cause proceedeth of diversity of winds, shifting often in sundry points, all which having power to move the great ocean, which again is not presently settled, so many seas do encounter together, as there had been diversity of winds. Howsoever it cometh to pass, men which all their lifetime had occupied the sea never saw more outrageous seas. We had also upon our mainyard an apparition of a little fire by night, which seamen do call Castor and Pollux. But we had only one, which they take an evil sign of more tempest. The same is usual in storms.

On Monday, the 9th of September, in the afternoon, the frigate was near cast away, oppressed by waves, yet at that time recovered; and giving forth signs of joy, the General sitting abaft with a book in his hand, cried out to us in the Hind (so oft as we did approach within hearing), "We are as near to heaven by sea as by land," reiterating the same speech, well beseeming a soldier resolute in Jesus Christ, as I can testify he was.

On the same Monday night, about twelve o'clock, or not long after, the frigate being ahead of us in the Golden Hind, suddenly her lights were out, whereof as it were in a moment we lost the sight, and withal our watch cried the General was cast away, which was too true; for in that moment the frigate was devoured and swallowed up of the sea. Yet still we looked out all that night and ever after, until we arrived upon the coast of England, omitting no small sail at sea, unto which we gave not the tokens between us agreed upon to have perfect knowledge of each other, if we should at any time be separated.

In great torment of weather and peril of drowning it pleased God to send safe home the Golden Hind, which arrived in Falmouth on the 22nd of September, being Sunday, not without as great danger escaped in a flaw, coming from the south-east, with such thick mist that we could not discern land to put in right with the haven.

From Falmouth we went to Dartmouth, and lay there at anchor before the Range, while the Captain went aland to enquire if there had been any news of the frigate, which, sailing well, might happily have been before us. Also to certify Sir John Gilbert, brother unto the General, of our hard success, whom the Captain desired (while his men were yet aboard him, and were witnesses of all occurrences in that voyage) it might please him to take the examination of every person particularly, in discharge of his and their faithful endeavour. Sir John Gilbert refused so to do, holding himself satisfied with report made by the Captain, and not altogether despairing of his brother's safety, offered friendship and courtesy to the Captain and his company, requiring to have his barque brought into the harbour; in furtherance whereof a boat was sent to help to tow her in.

Nevertheless, when the Captain returned aboard his ship, he found his men bent to depart every man to his home; and then the wind serving to proceed higher upon the coast, they demanded money to carry them home, some to London, others to Harwich, and elsewhere (if the barque should be carried into Dartmouth and they discharged so far from home), or else to take benefit of the wind, then serving to draw nearer home, which should be a less charge unto the Captain, and great ease unto the men, having else far to go.

Reason accompanied with necessity persuaded the Captain, who sent his lawful excuse and cause of this sudden departure unto Sir John Gilbert, by the boat of Dartmouth, and from thence the Golden Hind departed and took harbour at Weymouth. All the men tired with the tediousness of so unprofitable a voyage to their seeming, in which their long expense of time, much toil and labour, hard diet, and continual hazard of life was unrecompensed; their Captain nevertheless by his great charges impaired greatly thereby, yet comforted in the goodness of God, and His undoubted providence following him in all that voyage, as it doth always those at other times whosoever have confidence in Him alone. Yet have we more near feeling and perseverance of His powerful hand and protection when God doth bring us together with others into one same peril, in which He leaveth them and delivereth us, making us thereby the beholders, but not partakers of their ruin.

Even so, amongst very many difficulties, discontentments, mutinies, conspiracies, sicknesses, mortality, spoilings, and wrecks by sea, which were afflictions, more than in so small a fleet or so short a time may be supposed, howbeit true in every particularity, as partly by the former relation may be collected, and some I suppressed with silence for their sakes living, it pleased God to support this company, of which only one man died of a malady inveterate, and long infested, the rest kept together in reasonable contentment and concord, beginning, continuing, and ending the voyage, which none else did accomplish, either not pleased with the action, or impatient of wants, or prevented by death.

Thus have I delivered the contents of the enterprise and last action of Sir Humphrey Gilbert, Knight, faithfully, for so much as I thought meet to be published, wherein may always appear (though he be extinguished) some sparks of his virtues, he remaining firm and resolute in a purpose by all pretence honest and godly, as was this, to discover, possess, and to reduce unto the service of God and Christian piety those remote and heathen countries of America not actually possessed by Christians, and most rightly appertaining unto the Crown of England: unto the which, as his zeal deserveth high commendation, even so he may justly be taxed of temerity and presumption (rather) in two respects.

First, when yet there was only probability, not a certain and determinate place of habitation selected, neither any demonstration of commodity there *in esse*, to induce his followers, nevertheless, he both was too prodigal of his own patrimony and too careless of other men's expenses to employ both his and their substance upon a ground imagined good. The which falling, very like his associates were promised, and made it their best reckoning to be salved some other way, which pleased not God to prosper in his first and great preparation.

Secondly, when by his former preparation he was enfeebled of ability and credit to perform his designments, as it were impatient to abide in expectation better opportunity and means, which God might raise, he thrust himself again into the action, for which he was not fit, presuming the cause pretended on God's behalf would carry him to the desired end. Into which, having thus made re-entry, he could not yield again to withdraw, though he saw no encouragement to proceed, lest his credit, foiled in his first attempt, in a second should utterly be disgraced. Between extremities he made a right adventure, putting all to God and good fortune, and, which was worst, refused not to entertain every person and means whatsoever, to furnish out this expedition, the success whereof hath been declared.

But such is the infinite bounty of God, who from every evil deriveth good. For besides that fruit may grow in time of our travelling into those north-west lands, the crosses, turmoils, and afflictions, both in the preparation and execution of this voyage, did correct the intemperate humours which before we noted to be in this gentleman, and made unsavory and less delightful his other manifold virtues. Then as he was refined, and made nearer drawing unto the image of God, so it pleased the Divine will to resume him unto Himself, whither both his and every other high and noble mind have always aspired.

AMADAS AND BARLOW.

TAKING advantage of the death of his half-brother, Raleigh obtained in March, 1584, a new lease, for six years, of North American enterprise. He resolved that there should be little delay in giving it effect. Before April was over, two barques had quitted Plymouth for the purpose of taking possession of some fitting spot for a colony between Florida and Newfoundland. Raleigh directed that the northern route of Gilbert should be abandoned. American enterprise had thus early divided itself, in accordance with the physical condition of the Atlantic Ocean, into northern and southern. Gilbert, as we have seen, had declared himself in favour of the former: and his choice was justified, in the next generation, by the success which attended the French colonists on the St. Lawrence, and the English in New England. But Raleigh had derived from his reading of the Spanish histories a strong predilection for the richer and more romantic south: and accordingly his two skippers, Philip Amadas and Arthur Barlow, took the old route by the Canaries, and made the continent of North America in the latitude of North Carolina. They touched successively at the island of Wocokon (Ocracoke) at the entrance of Pamlico Sound, and at that of Roanoke, farther northward, near the mouth of Albemarle Sound, spent some weeks in viewing the country and trafficking with the natives, and then returned to England, with the report embodied in

P

the narrative of Barlow which is here printed. The Queen was delighted with the prospect of an English settlement in this desirable land, and gave it the name of Virginia. In the next year (1585) Grenville, Lane, and Hariot, sailed for Roanoke, with a hundred and eighty persons, and there established the first English colony in America. It proved to be only temporary. Instead of cultivating the soil, the emigrants spent their time in the fruitless quest of the precious metals; their stores failed, and no provisions reached them from home; and, finally, the remnant of the colony was brought back to England by Drake in 1586, in the circumstances which appear in the next narrative. This original settlement of "Virginia" was made within the limits of what afterwards became the State of North Carolina. The shores of the James River and of Chesapeake Bay, afterwards so famous under the name bestowed by Elizabeth on her American colony, remained unvisited for twenty years longer.

AMADAS AND BARLOW'S VOYAGE.

The First Voyage made to the coasts of AMERICA, *with two barques, wherein were Captains* MR. PHILIP AMADAS, *and* MR. ARTHUR BARLOW, *who discovered part of the country now called* VIRGINIA, *Anno Domini 1584. Written by one of the said captains, and sent to* SIR WALTER RALEIGH, *knight, at whose charge and direction the said voyage was set forth.*

ON the 27th day of April, in the year of our redemption 1584, we departed the west of England, with two barques well furnished with men and victuals, having received our last and perfect directions by your letters, confirming the former instructions and commandments delivered by yourself at our leaving the river of Thames. And I think it a matter both unnecessary for the manifest discovery of the country, as also for tediousness sake, to remember unto you the diurnal of our course, sailing thither and returning; only I have presumed to present unto you this brief discourse, by which you may judge how profitable this land is likely to succeed, as well to yourself (by whose direction and charge, and by whose servants this our discovery hath been performed), as also to Her Highness and the Commonwealth, in which we hope your wisdom will be satisfied, considering that as much by us hath been brought to light as by those small means and number of men we had could any way have been expected, or hoped for.

On the 10th of May we arrived at the Canaries, and the 10th of June in this present year, we were fallen with the islands of the West Indies, keeping a more south-easterly course than was needful, because we doubted that the current of the Bay of Mexico, disboguing between the Cape of Florida and Havana, had been of greater force than afterwards we found it to be. At which islands we found the air very unwholesome, and our men grew for the most part ill-disposed: so that having refreshed ourselves with sweet water and fresh victual, we departed the twelfth day of our arrival here. These islands, with the rest adjoining, are so well known to yourself, and to many others, as I will not trouble you with the remembrance of them.

On the 2nd of July we found shoal water, where we smelt so sweet and so strong a smell, as if we had been in the midst of some delicate garden, abounding with all kind of odoriferous flowers, by which we were assured that the land could not be far distant. And keeping good watch and bearing but slack sail, the 4th of the same month we arrived upon the coast, which we supposed to be a continent and firm land, and we sailed along the same 120 English miles before we could find any entrance, or river issuing into the sea. The first that appeared unto us we entered, though not without some difficulty, and cast anchor about three arquebuse-shot within the haven's mouth, on the left hand of the same; and after thanks given to God for our safe arrival thither, we manned our boats, and went to view the land next adjoining, and to take possession of the same in the right of the Queen's Most Excellent Majesty, as rightful Queen and Princess of the same, and after delivered the same over to your use, according to Her Majesty's grant and letters patent, under Her Highness's great Seal. Which being performed, according to the ceremonies used in such enterprises, we viewed the land about us, being, whereas we first landed, very sandy and low towards the water's side, but so full of grapes as the very beating and surge of the sea overflowed them; of which we found such plenty, as well there as in all places else, both on the sand and on the green soil on the hills, as in the plains, as well on every little shrub, as also climbing towards the tops of high cedars, that I think in all the world the like abundance is not to be found: and myself having seen those parts of Europe that most abound, find such difference as were incredible to be written.

We passed from the sea side towards the tops of those hills next adjoining, being but of mean height; and from thence we beheld the sea on both sides to the north and to the south, finding no end of any both ways. This land lay stretching itself to the west, which after we found to be but an island of twenty miles long, and not above six miles broad. Under the bank or hill whereon we stood, we beheld the valleys replenished with goodly cedar trees, and having discharged our arquebuse-shot, such a flock of cranes (the most part white) arose under us, with such a cry redoubled by many echoes, as if an army of men had shouted altogether.

This island had many goodly woods full of deer, coneys, hares and fowl, even in the midst of summer, in incredible abundance. The woods are not such as you find in Bohemia, Muscovy, or Hercynia, barren and fruitless, but the highest and reddest cedars of the world, far bettering the cedars of the Azores, of the Indies, or Libanus, pines, cypress, sassafras, the lentisk, or the tree that beareth the mastic, the tree that beareth the rind of black cinnamon, of which Master Winter brought from the Straits of Magellan, and many other of excellent smell and quality. We remained by the side of this island two whole days before we saw any people of the country. The third day we espied one small boat rowing towards us, having in it three persons. This boat came to the island side, four arquebuse-shot from our ships; and there two of the people remaining, the third came along the shore side towards us, and we being then all within board, he walked up and down upon the point of the land next unto us. Then the Master and the Pilot of the Admiral, Simon Ferdinando, and the Captain, Philip Amadas, myself, and others, rowed to the land, whose coming this fellow attended, never making any show of fear or doubt. And after he had spoken of many things not understood by us, we brought him, with his own good liking, aboard the ships, and gave him a shirt, a hat, and some other things, and made him taste of our wine, and our meat, which he liked very well; and, after having viewed both barques, he departed, and went to his own boat again, which he had left in a little cove or creek adjoining. As soon as he was two bow-shot into the water he fell to fishing, and in less than half-an-hour he had laden his boat as deep as it could swim, with which he came again to the point of the land, and there he divided his fish into two parts, pointing one part to the ship and the other to the pinnace; which, after he had (as much he might) requited the former benefits received, departed out of our sight.

The next day there came unto us divers boats, and in one of them the King's brother accompanied with forty or fifty men, very handsome and goodly people, and in their behaviour as mannerly and civil as any of Europe. His name was Granganimeo, and the King is called Wingina; the country, Wingandacoa; and now by Her Majesty, Virginia. The manner of his coming was in this sort:—He left his boats altogether, as the first man did, a little from the ships by the shore, and came along to the place over against the ships, followed with forty men. When he came to the place, his servants spread a long mat upon the ground, on which he sat down, and at the other end of the mat four others of his company did the like; the rest of his men stood round about him somewhat afar off. When we came to the shore to him, with our weapons, he never moved from his place, nor any of the other four, nor never mistrusted any harm to be offered from us; but, sitting still, he beckoned us to come and sit by him, which we performed; and, being set, he made all signs of joy and welcome, striking on his head and his breast and afterwards on ours, to shew we were all one, smiling and making shew the best he could of all love and familiarity. After he had made a long speech unto us we presented him with divers things, which he received very joyfully and thankfully. None of the company durst speak one word all the time; only the four which were at the other end spake one in the other's ear very softly.

The King is greatly obeyed, and his brothers and children reverenced. The King himself in person was at our being there sore wounded in a fight which he had with the King of the next country, called Piemacum, and was shot in two places through the body, and once clean through the thigh, but yet he recovered; by reason whereof, and for that he lay at the chief town of the country, being six day's journey off, we saw him not at all.

After we had presented this his brother with such things as we thought he liked, we likewise gave somewhat to the other that sat with him on the mat. But presently he arose and took all from them and put it into his own basket, making signs and tokens that all things ought to be delivered unto him, and the rest were but his servants and followers. A day or two after this we fell to trading with them, exchanging some things that we had for chamois, buff, and deer skins. When we shewed him all our packet of merchandise, of all things that he saw a bright tin dish most pleased him, which he presently took up and clapt it before his breast, and after made a hole in the brim thereof and hung it about his neck, making signs that it would defend him against his enemies' arrows. For those people maintain a deadly and terrible war with the people and King adjoining. We exchanged our tin dish for twenty skins, worth twenty crowns or twenty nobles; and a copper kettle for fifty skins, worth fifty crowns. They offered us good exchange for our hatchets and axes and for knives, and would have given anything for swords; but we would not depart with any. After two or three days the King's brother came aboard the ships and drank wine, and eat of our meat and of our bread, and liked exceedingly thereof. And after a few days overpassed, he brought his wife with him to the ships, his daughter, and two or three children. His wife was very well-favoured, of mean stature, and very bashful. She had on her back a long cloak of leather, with the fur side next to her body, and before her a piece of the same. About her forehead she had a band of white coral, and so had her husband many times. In her ears she had bracelets of pearls hanging down to her middle (whereof we delivered your worship a little bracelet), and those were of the bigness of good peas. The rest of her women of the better sort had pendants of copper hanging in either ear, and some of the children of the King's brother and other noblemen have five or six in either ear; he himself had upon his head a broad plate of gold or copper; for, being unpolished, we knew not what metal it should be, neither would he by any means suffer us to take it off his head, but feeling it, it would bow very easily. His apparel was as his wife's, only the women wear their hair long on both sides, and the men but on one. They are of colour yellowish, and their hair black for the most part; and yet we saw children that had very fine auburn and chestnut-coloured hair.

After that these women had been there, there came down from all parts great store of people, bringing with them leather, coral, divers kinds of dyes very excellent, and exchanged with us. But when Granganimeo, the King's brother, was present, none durst trade but himself, except such as wear red pieces of copper on their heads like himself; for that is the difference between the noblemen and the governors of countries, and the meaner sort. And we both noted there, and you have understood since by these men which we brought home, that no people in the world carry more respect to their King, nobility, and governors than these do. The King's brother's wife, when she came to us (as she did many times), was followed with forty or fifty women always. And when she came into the ship she left them all on land, saving her two daughters, her nurse, and one or two more. The King's brother always kept this order: as many boats as he would come withal to the ships, so many fires would he make on the shore afar off, to the end we might understand with what strength and company he approached. Their boats are made of one tree, either of pine or pitch-trees, a wood not commonly known to our people, nor found growing in England. They have no edge-tools to make them withal; if they have any they are very few, and those, it seems, they had twenty years since, which, as those two men declared, was out of a wreck which happened upon their coast of some Christian ship, being beaten that way by some storm and outrageous weather, whereof none of the people were saved, but only the ship, or some part of her, being cast upon the sand, out of whose sides they drew the nails and the spikes, and with those they made their best instruments. The manner of making their boats is thus: they burn down some great tree, or take such as are windfallen, and, putting gum and rozin upon one side thereof, they set fire into it, and when it hath burnt it hollow they cut out the coal with their shells, and ever where they would burn it deeper or wider they lay on gums, which burn away the timber, and by this means they fashion very fine boats, and such as will transport twenty men. Their oars are like scoops, and many times they set with long poles, as the depth serveth.

The King's brother had great liking of our armour, a sword, and divers other things which we had; and offered to lay a great box of pearl in gage for them; but we refused it for this time, because we would not make them know that we esteemed thereof, until we had understood in what places of the country the pearl grew, which now your worship doth very well understand.

He was very just of his promise: for many times we delivered him merchandise upon his word, but ever he came within the day and performed his promise. He sent us every day a brace or two of fat bucks, coneys, hares, fish the best of the world. He sent us divers kinds of fruits, melons, walnuts, cucumbers, gourds, peas, and divers roots, and fruits very excellent good, and of their country corn, which is very white, fair, and well tasted, and groweth three times in five months: in May they sow, in July they reap; in June they sow, in August they reap; in July they sow, in September they reap. Only they cast the corn into the ground, breaking a little of the soft turf with a wooden mattock or pickaxe. Ourselves proved the soil, and put some of our peas in the ground, and in ten days they were of fourteen inches high. They have also beans very fair, of divers colours, and wonderful plenty, some growing naturally and some in their gardens; and so have they both wheat and oats.

The soil is the most plentiful, sweet, fruitful, and wholesome of all the world. There are above fourteen several sweet-smelling timber-trees, and the most part of their underwoods are bays and suchlike. They have those oaks that we have, but far greater and better. After they had been divers times aboard our ships, myself with seven more went twenty mile into the river that runneth toward the city of Skicoak, which river they call Occam; and the evening following we came to an island which they call Roanoke, distant from the harbour by which we entered seven leagues; and at the north end thereof was a village of nine houses built of cedar and fortified round about with sharp trees to keep out their enemies, and the entrance into it made like a turnpike very artificially. When we came towards it, standing near unto the water's side, the wife of Granganimeo, the King's brother, came running out to meet us very cheerfully and friendly. Her husband was not then in the village. Some of her people she commanded to draw our boat on shore, for the beating of the billow. Others she appointed to carry us on their backs to the dry ground, and others to bring our oars into the house for fear of stealing. When we were come into the outer room (having five rooms in her house) she caused us to sit down by a great fire, and after took off our clothes and washed them and dried them again. Some of the women plucked off our stockings and washed them, some washed our feet in warm water, and she herself took great pains to see all things ordered in the best manner she could, making great haste to dress some meat for us to eat.

After we had thus dried ourselves, she brought us into the inner room, where she set on the board standing along the house some wheat-like fermenty, sodden venison, and roasted, fish sodden, boiled, and roasted, melons raw and sodden, roots of divers kinds, and divers fruits. Their drink is commonly water, but while the grape lasteth they drink wine, and for want of casks to keep it all the year after they drink water; but it is sodden with ginger in it, and black cinnamon, and sometimes sassafras, and divers other wholesome and medicinal herbs and trees. We were entertained with all love and kindness, and with as much bounty (after their manner) as they could possibly devise. We found the people most gentle, loving, and faithful, void of all guile and treason, and such as live after the manner of the golden age. The people only care how to defend themselves from the cold in their short winter, and to feed themselves with such meat as the soil affordeth; their meat is very well sodden, and they make broth very sweet and savory. Their vessels are earthen pots, very large, white, and sweet; their dishes are wooden platters of sweet timber. Within the place where they feed was their lodging, and within that their idol, which they worship, of whom they speak incredible things. While we were at meat, there came in at the gates two or three men with their bows and arrows from hunting, whom when we espied we began to look one towards the other, and offered to reach our weapons : but as soon as she espied our mistrust, she was very much moved, and caused some of her men to run out, and take away their bows and arrows and brake them, and withal beat the poor fellows out of the gate again. When we departed in the evening and would not tarry all night, she was very sorry, and gave us into our boat our supper half-dressed, pots and all, and brought us to our boat's-side, in which we lay all night, removing the same a pretty distance from the shore; she perceiving our jealousy, was much grieved, and sent divers men and thirty women to sit all night on the bank-side by us, and sent us into our boats fine mats to cover us from the rain, using very many words to entreat us to rest in their houses; but because we were few men, and if we had miscarried the voyage had been in very great danger, we durst not adventure anything, although there was no cause of doubt; for a more kind and loving people there cannot be found in the world, as far as we have hitherto had trial.

Beyond this island there is the mainland, and over against this island falleth into this spacious water the great river called Occam by the inhabitants, on which standeth a town called Pomeiock, and six days journey from the same is situate their greatest city called Skicoak, which this people affirm to be very great; but the savages were never at it, only they speak of it by the report of their fathers and other men, whom they have heard affirm it to be above one hour's journey about.

Into this river falleth another great river called Cipo, in which there is found great store of muscles, in which there are pearls; likewise there descendeth into this Occam another river called Nomopana, on the one side whereof standeth a great town called Chawanook, and the Lord of that town and country is called

Pooneno. This Pooneno is not subject to the king of Wingandacoa, but is a free Lord. Beyond this country is there another king, whom they call Menatonon, and these three kings are in league with each other. Towards the south-west, four days' journey, is situate a town called Secotan, which is the southernmost town of Wingandacoa, near unto which six-and-twenty years past there was a ship cast away, whereof some of the people were saved, and those were white people, whom the country people preserved.

And after ten days remaining in an out island unhabited, called Wocokon, they, with the help of some of the dwellers of Secotan, fastened two boats of the country together, and made masts unto them, and sails of their shirts, and having taken into them such victuals as the country yielded, they departed after they had remained in this out island three weeks; but shortly after it seemed they were cast away, for the boats were found upon the coast, cast a-land in another island adjoining. Other than these, there was never any people appareled, or white of colour, either seen or heard of amongst these people, and these aforesaid were seen only of the inhabitants of Secotan, which appeared to be very true, for they wondered marvellously when we were amongst them at the whiteness of our skins, ever coveting to touch our breasts, and to view the same. Besides they had our ships in marvellous admiration, and all things else were so strange unto them, as it appeared that none of them had ever seen the like. When we discharged any piece, were it but an arquebuse, they would tremble thereat for very fear, and for the strangeness of the same, for the weapons which themselves use are bows and arrows. The arrows are but of small canes, headed with a sharp shell or tooth of a fish sufficient enough to kill a naked man. Their swords be of wood hardened; likewise they use wooden breastplates for their defence. They have beside a kind of club, in the end whereof they fasten the sharp horns of a stag, or other beast. When they go to wars they carry about with them their idol, of whom they ask counsel, as the Romans were wont of the oracle of Apollo. They sing songs as they march towards the battle, instead of drums and trumpets. Their wars are very cruel and bloody, by reason whereof, and of their civil dissensions which have happened of late years amongst them, the people are marvellously wasted, and in same places the country left desolate.

Adjoining to this country aforesaid, called Secotan, beginneth a country called Pomovik, belonging to another king, whom they call Piemacum, and this king is in league with the next king adjoining towards the setting of the sun, and the country Newsiok, situate upon a goodly river called Neus. These kings have mortal war with Wingina, king of Wingandacoa; but about two years past there was a peace made between the king Piemacum and the Lord of Secotan, as these men which we have brought with us to England have given us to understand; but there remaineth a mortal malice in the Secotans, for many injuries and slaughters done upon them by this Piemacum. They invited divers men, and thirty women of the best of his country, to their town to a feast, and when they were altogether merry, and praying for their idol (which is nothing else but a mere delusion of the devil) the Captain or Lord of the town came suddenly upon them, and slew them every one, reserving the women and children; and these two have oftentimes since persuaded us to surprise Piemacum's town, having promised and assured us that there will be found in it great store of commodities. But whether their persuasion be to the end they may be revenged of their enemies, or for the lové they bear to us, we leave that to the trial hereafter.

Beyond this island called Roanoke, are many islands very plentiful of fruits and other natural increases, together with many towns and villages along the side of the continent, some bounding upon the islands, and some stretching up further into the land.

When we first had sight of this country, some thought the first land we saw to be the continent; but after we entered into the haven, we saw before us another mighty long sea, for there lieth along the coast a tract of islands 200 miles in length, adjoining to the ocean sea, and between the islands two or three entrances. When you are entered between them (these islands being very narrow for the most part, as in some places six miles broad, in some places less, in few more), then there appeareth another great sea, containing in breadth in some places forty, in some fifty, in some twenty miles over, before you come unto the continent; and in this enclosed sea there are above a hundred islands of divers bignesses, whereof one is sixteen miles long, at which we were, finding it a most pleasant and fertile ground, replenished with goodly cedars, and divers other sweet woods, full of currants, of flax, and many other notable commodities, which we at that time had no leisure to view. Besides this island there are many, as I have said, some of two, of three, of four, of five miles, some more, some less, most beautiful and pleasant to behold, replenished with deer, coneys, hares, and divers beasts, and about them the goodliest and best fish in the world, and in greatest abundance.

Thus, Sir, we have acquainted you with the particulars of our discovery made this present voyage, as far forth as the shortness of the time we there continued would afford us to take view of; and so contenting ourselves with this service at this time, which we hope hereafter to enlarge, as occasion and assistance shall be given, we resolved to leave the country, and to apply ourselves to return for England, which we did accordingly, and arrived safely in the west of England about the midst of September.

And whereas we have above certified you of the country taken in possession by us to Her Majesty's use, and so to yours by Her Majesty's grant, we thought good for the better assurance thereof, to record some of the particular gentlemen, and men of account, who then were present, as witnesses of the same, that thereby all occasion of cavil to the title of the country, in Her Majesty's behalf, may be prevented, which otherwise, such as like not the action may use and pretend, whose names are:—

Master Philip Amadas, Master Arthur Barlow, Captains.

William Greenville, John Wood, James Bromewich, Henry Greene, Benjamin Wood, Simon Ferdinando, Nicholas Petman, John Hughes, of the company.

We brought home also two of the savages, being lusty men, whose names were Wanchese and Manteo.

DRAKE.

WHILE Raleigh, after his half-brother's death, was busy with his projected colonization of "Virginia," (that is, the first convenient site to the north of Florida, in the future State of North Carolina), the American question suddenly entered on a new phase. In 1585 Philip of Spain laid an embargo on all British subjects, their ships and goods, that might be found in his dominions. Elizabeth at once authorized general reprisals on the goods of Spaniards, and active hostilities were planned on a scale commensurate with the national resources. She equipped an armada of twenty-five vessels, manned by 2,300 men, and despatched it under the command of Drake to plunder Spanish America. Spain drew from the New World the means of supporting her cruel and arrogant domination in Europe; and practical reasoners like Raleigh were continually forcing this fact on the attention of English statesmen. The superiority of the Englishman to the Spaniard at sea had, by this time, been abundantly demonstrated. The two nations were now at open war, and it was necessary to deal a blow where a blow would be most effectual. To strike at Spain in America was to compel her to withdraw her ships and soldiers from Europe, to relieve the pressure on the Netherlands, and to secure England from the peril of direct invasion; for, unless this were done, Spanish America must

fall an easy prey to the buccaneering admirals of England.
Designs for colonization were thus thrown into the background. The difficulties of planting colonies were great, and
the success uncertain, whereas the old Spanish settlements
offered an easy and seducing booty. It was better to win
25,000 dollars, as Drake did, by the ransom of St. Domingo
city, than to throw away the same sum in futile attempts at
colonizing the wilds of Virginia. During eighteen years the
wise plans of Hakluyt were for the most part neglected, and
the English mind was dazzled with Drake's profitable piracies
and Raleigh's golden dream of a Third American Empire,
yet undiscovered, and equal in riches to Mexico and Peru.

Drake's armament of 1585 was the greatest that had ever
crossed the Atlantic. After plundering the vessels in the
Vigo river, he sailed for the West Indies by way of the
Canaries and Cape Verde Islands, crossed the Atlantic in
eighteen days, and arrived at Dominica. At daybreak, on
New Year's Day, 1586, Drake's soldiers landed in Española, a
few miles to the west of the capital, and before evening
Carlisle and Powell had entered the town, which the colonists
only saved from total destruction by the payment of a heavy
ransom. Drake's plan was to do exactly the same at
Carthagena and Nombre de Dios, and thence to strike across
the peninsula and secure Panama, the key of the wealth of
Peru. But the sojourn at Carthagena, after its capture, was
fatal to the progress of the enterprise. The troops and seamen
died of yellow fever in great numbers; and after consultation
with the military commander, Drake resolved on sailing home
at once by way of Florida, not omitting to plunder its petty
settlements by the way. The spoils of the campaign, though
short of the original expectation, were ample in themselves;
and Drake's armada accordingly returned to England, carrying

with them the remnant of the colony which had been left by Sir Richard Grenville in "Virginia."

In after years, Drake was severely blamed by English politicians for not securing all the Spanish settlements in America while their defenceless state made them an easy prey. Had Nombre de Dios and Panama been taken and permanently garrisoned, Spanish America, it was argued, with all its wealth and promise, must have been won for England. The Spaniards profited by the experience of 1586. Nine years afterwards, when the art of carrying on a great war on the ocean was better understood, Drake and Hawkins sailed with the intention of accomplishing the conquest of the isthmus. But the Spanish harbours had now been rendered impregnable. The campaign not only failed, but cost England the lives of her two greatest admirals, in the persons of Drake and Hawkins. The latter had died off Porto Rico early in the campaign. Drake died of dysentery off Porto Bello. Frobisher had died of his wounds, at Plymouth, in the previous year.

DRAKE.—SECOND VOYAGE.

A summary and true discourse of SIR FRANCIS DRAKE'S *West Indian Voyage, begun in the year 1585. Wherein were taken the cities of* SANTIAGO, SANTO DOMINGO, CARTHAGENA, *and the town of* ST. AUGUSTINE, *in* FLORIDA. *Published by* MR. THOMAS CATES.

THIS worthy knight, for the service of his prince and country, having prepared his whole fleet, and gotten them down to Plymouth, in Devonshire, to the number of twenty-five sail of ships and pinnaces, and having assembled of soldiers and mariners to the number of 2,300 in the whole, embarked them and himself at Plymouth aforesaid, the 12th day of September, 1585, being accompanied with these men of name and charge which hereafter follow:—

Master Christopher Carleil, Lieutenant-General, a man of long experience in the wars as well by sea as land, who had formerly carried high offices in both kinds in many fights, which he discharged always very happily, and with great good reputation; Anthony Powell, Sergeant-Major; Captain Matthew Morgan, and Captain John Sampson, Corporals of the Field.

These officers had commandment over the rest of the Land-Captains, whose names hereafter follow:—

Captain Anthony Platt, Captain Edward Winter, Captain John Goring, Captain Robert Pew, Captain George Barton, Captain John Merchant, Captain William Cecil, Captain Walter Biggs, Captain John Hannam, Captain Richard Stanton.

Captain Martin Frobisher, Vice-Admiral, a man of great experience in seafaring actions, who had carried the chief charge of many ships himself, in sundry voyages before, being now shipped in the Primrose; Captain Francis Knolles, Rear-Admiral in the galleon Leicester; Master Thomas Venner, Captain in the Elizabeth Bonadventure, under the General; Master Edward Winter, Captain in the Aid; Master Christopher Carleil, the Lieutenant-General, Captain of the Tiger; Henry White, Captain of the Sea-Dragon; Thomas Drake, Captain of the Thomas; Thomas Seeley, Captain of the Minion; Baily, Captain of the barque Talbot; Robert Cross, Captain of the barque Bond; George Fortescue, Captain of the barque Bonner; Edward Careless, Captain of the Hope; James Erizo, Captain of the White Lion; Thomas Moon, Captain of the Francis; John Rivers, Captain of the Vantage; John Vaughan, Captain of the Drake; John Varney, Captain of the George; John Martin, Captain of the Benjamin; Edward Gilman, Captain of the Scout; Richard Hawkins, Captain of the galliot called the Duck; Bitfield, Captain of the Swallow.

After our going hence, which was the 14th of September, in the year of Our Lord 1585, and taking our course towards Spain, we had the wind for a few days somewhat scant, and sometimes calm. And being arrived near that part of Spain which is called the Moors, we happened to espy divers sails, which kept their course close by the shore, the weather being fair and calm. The General caused the Vice-Admiral to go with the pinnaces well manned to see what they were, who upon sight of the said pinnaces approaching near unto them, abandoned for the most part all their ships (being Frenchmen) laden all with salt, and bound homewards into France, amongst which ships (being all of small burthen) there was one so well liked, which also had no man in her, as being brought unto the General, he thought good to make stay of her for the service, meaning to pay for her, as also accordingly he performed at our return, which barque was called the Drake. The rest of these ships (being eight or nine) were dismissed without anything at all taken from them. Who being afterwards put somewhat further off from the shore, by the contrariety of the wind, we happened to meet with some other French ships, full laden with Newland fish, being upon their return homeward from the said Newfoundland; whom the General after some speech had with them (and seeing plainly that they were Frenchmen) dismissed, without once suffering any man to go aboard of them.

The day following standing in with the shore again, we descried another tall ship of twelve score tons or thereabouts, upon whom Master Carleil, the Lieutenant-General, being in the Tiger, undertook the chase, whom also anon after the Admiral followed, and the Tiger having caused the said strange ship to strike her sails, kept her there without suffering anybody to go aboard until the Admiral was come up; who forthwith sending for the Master, and divers others of their principal men, and causing them to be severally examined, found the ship and goods to be belonging to the inhabitants of St. Sebastian, in Spain, but the mariners to be for the most part belonging to St. John de Luz, and the Passage. In this ship was great store of dry Newland fish, commonly called with us Poor John, whereof afterwards (being thus found a lawful prize) there was distribution made into all the ships of the fleet, the same being so new and good, as it did very greatly bestead us in the whole course of our voyage. A day or two after the taking of this ship we put in within the Isles of Bayona,* for lack of favourable wind; where we had no sooner anchored some part of the fleet, but the General commanded all the pinnaces with the shipboats to be manned, and every man to be furnished with such arms as were needful for that present service; which being done, the General put himself into his galley, which was also well furnished, and rowing towards the city of Bayona, with intent, and the favour of the Almighty, to surprise it. Before we had advanced one half-league of our way there came a messenger, being an English merchant, from the Governor, to see what strange fleet we were, who came to our General, conferred a while with him, and after a small time spent, our General called for Captain Sampson, and willed him to go to the Governor of the city, to resolve him of two points. The first, to know if there were any wars between Spain and England; the second, why our merchants with their goods were embargoed or arrested? Thus departed Captain Sampson with the said messenger to the city, where he found the Governor and people much amazed of such a sudden accident.

The General, with the advice and counsel of Mr. Carleil, his Lieutenant-General, who was in the galley with him, thought not good to make any stand, till such time as they were within the shot of the city, where they might be ready upon the return of Captain Sampson, to make a sudden attempt if cause did require before it were dark.

---

* The Cies Islets, at the mouth of the Vigo River.

Captain Sampson returned with his message in this sort:—First, touching peace or wars, the Governor said he knew of no wars, and that it lay not in him to make any, he being so mean a subject as he was. And as for the stay of the merchants with their goods, it was the king's pleasure, but not with intent to endamage any man. And that the king's counter-commandment was (which had been received in that place some seven-night before) that English merchants with their goods should be discharged; for the more verifying whereof, he sent such merchants as were in the town of our nation, who trafficked those parts, which being at large declared to our General by them, counsel was taken what might best be done. And for that the night approached, it was thought needful to land our forces, which was done in the shutting up of the day; and having quartered ourselves to our most advantage, with sufficient guard upon every strait, we thought to rest ourselves for that night there. The Governor sent us some refreshing, as bread, wine, oil, apples, grapes, marmalade, and such like. About midnight the weather began to overcast, insomuch that it was thought meeter to repair aboard, than to make any longer abode on land, and before we could recover the fleet a great tempest arose, which caused many of our ships to drive from their anchor-hold, and some were forced to sea in great peril, as the barque Talbot, the barque Hawkins, and the Speedwell, which Speedwell only was driven into England, the others recovered us again. The extremity of the storm lasted three days, which no sooner began to assuage, but Mr. Carleil, our Lieutenant-General, was sent with his own ship and three others, as also with the galley and with divers pinnaces, to see what he might do above Vigo, where he took many boats and some caravels, diversely laden with things of small value, but chiefly with household stuff, running into the high country, and amongst the rest he found one boat laden with the principal church stuff of the High Church of Vigo, where also was their great cross of silver, of very fair embossed work, and double-gilt all over, having cost them a great mass of money. They complained to have lost in all kind of goods above thirty thousand ducats in this place.

The next day the General with his whole fleet went from up the Isles of Bayona to a very good harbour above Vigo, where Mr. Carleil stayed his coming, as well for the more quiet riding of his ships, as also for the good commodity of fresh watering which the place there did afford full well. In the meantime the Governor of

Galicia had reared such forces as he might; his numbers by estimate were some two thousand foot and three hundred horse, and marched from Bayona to this part of the country, which lay in sight of our fleet; where, making a stand, he sent to parley with our General, which was granted by our General, so it might be in boats upon the water; and for safety of their persons there were pledges delivered on both sides; which done, the Governor of Galicia put himself with two others into our Vice-Admiral's skiff, the same having been sent to the shore for him, and in like sort our General went in his own skiff; where by them it was agreed we should furnish ourselves with fresh water, to be taken by our own people quietly on the land, and have all other such necessaries, paying for the same, as the place would afford.

When all our business was ended we departed, and took our way by the Islands of Canary, which are esteemed some three hundred leagues from this part of Spain, and falling purposely with Palma, with intention to have taken our pleasure of that place, for the full digesting of many things into order, and the better furnishing our store with such several good things as it affordeth very abundantly, we were forced by the vile sea-gate, which at that present fell out, and by the naughtiness of the landing-place, being but one, and that under the favour of many platforms well furnished with great ordnance, to depart with the receipt of many their cannon-shot, some into our ships and some besides, some of them being in very deed full cannon high. But the only or chief mischief was the dangerous sea-surge, which at shore all along plainly threatened the overthrow of as many pinnaces and boats as for that time should have attempted any landing at all.

Now seeing the expectation of this attempt frustrated by the causes aforesaid, we thought it meeter to fall with the Isle Hierro, to see if we could find any better fortune, and coming to the island we landed a thousand men in a valley under a high mountain, where we stayed some two or three hours, in which time the inhabitants, accompanied with a young fellow born in England, who dwelt there with them, came unto us, shewing their state to be so poor that they were all ready to starve, which was not untrue; and therefore without anything gotten, we were all commanded presently to embark, so as that night we put off to sea south-southeast along towards the coast of Barbary.

Upon Saturday in the morning, being the 13th of November, we fell with Cape Blank, which is a low land and shallow water, where we catched store of fish, and doubling the Cape, we put into the bay, where we found certain French ships of war, whom we entertained with great courtesy, and there left them. This afternoon the whole fleet assembled, which was a little scattered about their fishing, and put from thence to the Isles of Cape de Verde, sailing till the 16th of the same month in the morning, on which day we descried the Island of Santiago, and in the evening we anchored the fleet between the town called the Playa or Praya and Santiago, where we put on shore one thousand men or more, under the leading of Mr. Christopher Carleil, Lieutenant-General, who directed the service most like a wise commander. The place where we had first to march did afford no good order, for the ground was mountainous and full of dales, being a very stony and troublesome passage; but such was his industrious disposition, as he would never leave, until we had gotten up to a fair plain, where we made stand for the assembling of the army. And when we were all gathered together upon the plain, some two miles from the town, the Lieutenant-General thought good not to make attempt till daylight, because there was not one that could serve for guide or giving knowledge at all of the place. And therefore after having well rested, even half an hour before day, he commanded the army to be divided into three special parts, such as he appointed, whereas before we had marched by several companies, being thereunto forced by the badness of the way as is aforesaid.

Now by the time we were thus ranged into a very brave order, daylight began to appear, and being advanced hard to the wall, we saw no enemy to resist; whereupon the Lieutenant-General appointed Captain Sampson with thirty shot, and Captain Barton with other thirty, to go down into the town which stood in the valley under us, and might very plainly be viewed all over from that place where the whole army was now arrived; and presently after these Captains were sent the great ensign, which had nothing in it but the plain English cross, to be placed towards the sea, that our fleet might see Saint George's Cross flourish in the enemy's fortress. Order was given that all the ordnance throughout the town and upon all the platforms, which were about fifty pieces already charged, should be shot off in honour of the Queen's Majesty's Coronation Day, being the 17th of November, after the yearly custom of England, which was so answered again by the ordnance out of all the ships in the fleet which now was come near, as it was strange to hear such a thundering noise last so long together. In this meanwhile the Lieutenant-General held still the most part of his force on the hill-top, till such time as the town was quartered out for the lodging of the whole army, which being done every Captain took his own quarter, and in the evening was placed such a sufficient guard upon every part of the town that we had no cause to fear any present enemy.

Thus we continued in the city the space of fourteen days, taking such spoils as the place yielded, which were, for the most part, wine, oil, meal, and some such like things for victuals, as vinegar, olives, and some such other trash, as merchandise for their Indian trades. But there was not found any treasure at all, or anything else of worth besides.

The situation of Santiago is somewhat strange, in form like a triangle, having on the east and west sides two mountains of rock and cliff, as it were hanging over it, upon the top of which two mountains were builded certain fortifications to preserve the town from any harm that might be offered, as in a plot is plainly shewn. From thence on the south side of the town is the main sea, and on the north side, the valley lying between the foresaid mountains, wherein the town standeth; the said valley and town both do grow very narrow, insomuch that the space between the two cliffs of this end of the town is estimated not to be above ten or twelve score over.

In the midst of the valley cometh down a rivulet, rill, or brook of fresh water, which hard by the seaside maketh a pond or pool, whereout our ships were watered with very great ease and pleasure. Somewhat above the town on the north side between the two mountains, the valley waxeth somewhat larger than at the town's end, which valley is wholly converted into gardens and orchards, well replenished with divers sorts of fruits, herbs, and trees, as lemons, oranges, sugar-canes, cocoa or cocoa-nuts, plantains, potato-roots, cucumbers, small and round onions, garlic, and some other things not now remembered, amongst which the cocoa-nuts and plantains are very pleasant fruits; the said cocoa hath a hard shell and a green husk over it, as hath our walnut, but it far exceedeth in greatness, for this cocoa in his green husk is bigger than any man's two fists. Of the hard shell many drinking cups are made here in England, and set in silver as I have often seen. Next within this hard shell is a white rind resembling in show very much even as any thing may do, to the white of an egg when it is hard boiled; and within this white of the nut lieth a water, which is whitish and very clear, to the quantity of half a pint or thereabouts, which water and white rind before spoken of are both of a very cool fresh taste, and as pleasing as anything may be. I have heard some hold opinion that it is very restorative.

The plantain groweth in pods, somewhat like to beans, but is bigger and longer, and much more thick together on the stalk, and when it waxeth ripe, the meat which filleth the rind of the cod becometh yellow, and is exceeding sweet and pleasant.

In this time of our being there happened to come a Portugal to the western fort, with a flag of truce, to whom Captain Sampson was sent with Captain Goring; who coming to the said messenger, he first asked them what nation they were: they answered Englishmen. He then required to know if wars were between England and Spain, to which they answered that they knew not, but if he would go to their General he could best resolve him of such particulars, and for his assurance of passage and repassage these Captains made offer to engage their credits, which he refused for that he was not sent from his Governor. Then they told him if his Governor did desire to take a course for the common benefit of the people and country his best way were to come and present himself unto our noble and merciful Governor, Sir Francis Drake, whereby he might be assured to find favour, both for himself and the inhabitants; otherwise within three days we should march over the land, and consume with fire all inhabited places, and put to the sword all such living souls as we should chance upon; so thus much he took for the conclusion of his answer, and departing, he promised to return the next day, but we never heard more of him.

On the 24th of November, the General accompanied with the Lieutenant-General and six hundred men, marched forth to a village twelve miles within the land, called Saint Domingo, where the Governor and the Bishop with all the better sort were lodged, and by eight of the clock we came to it, finding the place abandoned, and the people fled into the mountains. So we made stand a while to ease ourselves, and partly to see if any would come to speak to us.

After we had well rested ourselves, the General commanded the troops to march away homewards, in which retreat the enemy shewed themselves, both horse and foot, though not such force as durst encounter us; and so in passing sometime at the gaze with them, it waxed late and towards night before we could recover home to Santiago.

On Monday, the 26th of November, the General commanded all the pinnaces with the boats to use all diligence to embark the army into such ships as every man belonged. The Lieutenant-General in like sort commanded Captain Goring and Lieutenant Tucker, with one hundred shot to make a stand in the market-place, until our forces were wholly embarked, the Vice-Admiral making stay with his pinnace (and certain boats in the harbour) to bring the said last company aboard the ships. Also the General willed forthwith the galley with two pinnaces to take into them the company of Captain Barton, and the company of Captain Biggs, under the leading of Captain Sampson, to seek out such munition as was hidden in the ground, at the town of Praya, or Playa, having been promised to be shewed it by a prisoner, which was taken the day before.

The Captains aforesaid coming to the Playa, landed their men, and having placed the troop in their best strength, Captain Sampson took the prisoner, and willed him to show that he had promised, the which he could not, or at least would not; but they searching all suspected places, found two pieces of ordnance, one of iron, another of brass. In the afternoon the General anchored with the rest of the fleet before the Playa, coming himself ashore, willing us to burn the town and make all haste aboard, the which was done by six o'clock the same day, and ourselves embarked again the same night, and so we put off to sea south-west.

But before our departure from the town of Santiago, we established orders for the better government of the army, every man mustered to his Captain, and oaths were ministered to acknowledge Her Majesty supreme Governor, as also every man to do his uttermost endeavour to advance the service of the action, and to yield due obedience unto the directions of the General and his officers. By this provident counsel, and laying down this good foundation beforehand, all things went forward in a due course, to the achieving of our happy enterprise.

In all the time of our being here, neither the Governor for the said King of Spain (which is a Portugal), neither the Bishop, whose authority is great, neither the inhabitants of the town, or island, ever came at us (which we expected they should have done), to entreat us to leave them some part of their needful provisions, or at the least to spare the ruining of their town at our going away.

The cause of this their unreasonable distrust (as I do take it) was the fresh remembrance of the great wrongs that they had done to old Mr. William Hawkins, of Plymouth, in the voyage he made four or five years before, when as they did both break their promise, and murdered many of his men, whereof I judge you have understood, and therefore it is needless to be repeated. But since they came not at us, we left written in sundry places, as also in the Spital House (which building only was appointed to be spared) the great discontentment and scorn we took at this their refraining to come unto us, as also at the rude manner of killing, and savage kind of handling the dead body of one of our boys found by them straggling all alone, from whom they had taken his head and heart, and had straggled the other bowels about the place, in a most brutish and beastly manner.

In revenge whereof at our departing we consumed with fire all the houses, as well in the country which we saw, as in the town of Santiago.

From hence putting off to the West Indies, we were not many days at sea but there began among our people such mortality as in a few days there were dead above two or three hundred men. And until some seven or eight days after our coming from Santiago, there had not died any one man of sickness in all the fleet. The sickness showed not his infection wherewith so many were stricken until we were departed thence, and then seized our people with extreme hot burning and continual agues, whereof very few escaped with life, and yet those for the most part not without great alteration and decay of their wits and strength for a long time after. In some that died were plainly shown the small spots, which are often found upon those that be infected with the plague. We were not above eighteen days in passage between the sight of Santiago aforesaid, and the island of Dominica, being the first island of the West Indies that we fell withal, the same being inhabited with savage people, which go all naked, their skin coloured with some painting of a reddish tawny, very personable and handsome strong men, who do admit little conversation with the Spaniards; for as some of our people might understand them, they had a Spaniard or two prisoners with them, neither do I think that there is any safety for any of our nation or any other to be within the limits of their commandment, albeit they used us very kindly for those few hours of time which we spent with them, helping our folks to fill and carry on their bare shoulders fresh water from the river to our ships' boats, and fetching from their houses great store of tobacco, as also a kind of bread which they fed on, called cassavi, very white and savoury, made of the roots of cassavi. In recompense whereof we bestowed liberal rewards of glass, coloured beads, and other things, which we had found at Santiago, wherewith (as it seemed) they rested very greatly satisfied, and shewed some sorrowful countenance when they perceived that we would depart.

From hence we went to another island westward of it, called Saint Christopher's Island, wherein we spent some days of Christmas, to refresh our sick people, and to cleanse and air our ships. In which island were not any people at all that we could hear of.

In which time by the General it was advised and resolved, with the consent of the Lieutenant-General, the Vice-Admiral, and all the rest of the Captains, to proceed to the great island of Hispaniola, as well for that we knew ourselves then to be in our best strength, as also the rather allured thereunto, by the glorious fame of the city of St. Domingo, being the ancientest and chief inhabited place in all the tract of country thereabouts. And so proceeding in this determination, by the way we met a small frigate, bound for the same place, the which the Vice-Admiral took, and having duly examined the men that were in her, there was one found by whom we were advertized, the haven to be a barred haven, and the shore or land thereof to be well fortified, having a castle thereupon furnished with great store of artillery, without the danger whereof was no convenient landing-place within ten English miles of the city, to which the said pilot took upon him to conduct us.

All things being thus considered on, the whole forces were commanded in the evening to embark themselves in pinnaces, boats, and other small barques appointed for this service. Our soldiers being thus embarked, the General put himself into the barque Francis as Admiral, and all this night we lay on the sea, bearing small sail until our arrival to the landing place, which was about the breaking of the day, and so we landed, being New Year's Day, nine or ten miles to the westward of that brave city of St. Domingo; for at that time nor yet is known to us any landing-place, where the sea-surge doth not threaten to overset a pinnace or boat. Our General having seen us all landed in safety, returned to his fleet, bequeathing us to God, and the good conduct of Master Carleil, our Lieutenant-General; at which time, being about eight o'clock, we began to march, and about noon-time, or towards one o'clock, we approached the town, where the gentlemen and those of the better sort, being some hundred and fifty brave horses, or rather more, began to present themselves; but our small shot played upon them, which were so sustained with good proportion of pikes in all parts, as they finding no part of our troops unprepared to receive them (for you must understand they viewed all round about) they were thus driven to give us leave to proceed towards the two gates of the town, which were the next to the seaward. They had manned them both, and planted their ordnance for that present and sudden alarm without the gate, and also some troops of small shot in ambuscade upon the highway side. We divided our whole force, being some thousand or twelve hundred men, into two parts, to enterprise both the gates at one instant, the Lieutenant-General having openly vowed to Captain Powell (who led the troop that entered the other gate) that with God's good favour he would not rest until our meeting in the market-place.

Their ordnance had no sooner discharged upon our near approach, and made some execution amongst us, though not much, but the Lieutenant-General began forthwith to advance both his voice of encouragement and pace of marching; the first man that was slain with the ordnance being very near unto himself; and thereupon hasted all that he might, to keep them from the recharging of the ordnance. And notwithstanding their ambuscades, we marched or rather ran so roundly into them, as pell-mell we entered the gates, and gave them more care every man to save himself by flight, than reason to stand any longer to their broken fight. We forthwith repaired to the market-place; but to be more truly understood, a place of very fair spacious square ground, whither also came as had been agreed Captain Powell with the other troop; which place with some part next unto it, we strengthened with barricades, and there as the most convenient place assured ourselves, the city being far too spacious for so small and weary a troop to undertake to guard. Somewhat after midnight, they who had the guard of the castle, hearing us busy about the gates of the said castle, abandoned the same; some being taken prisoners, and some fleeing away by the help of boats to the other side of the haven, and so into the country.

The next day we quartered a little more at large, but not into the half part of the town, and so making substantial trenches, and planting all the ordnance, that each part was correspondent to other, we held this town the space of one month.

In the which time happened some accidents, more than are well remembered for the present, but amongst other things, it chanced that the General sent on his message to the Spaniards a negro boy with a flag of white, signifying truce, as is the Spanish ordinary manner to do there, when they approach to speak to us; which boy unhappily was first met withal by some of those who had been belonging as officers for the king in the Spanish galley, which with the town was lately fallen into our hands, who without all order or reason, and contrary to that good usage wherewith we had entertained their messengers, furiously struck the poor boy through the body with one of their horseman's staves; with which wound the boy returned to the General; and after he had declared the manner of this wrongful cruelty, died forthwith in his presence. Wherewith the General being greatly passioned, commanded the Provost Martial to cause a couple of friars, then prisoners, to be carried to the same place where the boy was struck, accompanied with sufficient guard of our soldiers, and there presently to be hanged, despatching at the same instant another poor prisoner, with this reason wherefore this execution was done, and with this message further, that until the party who had thus murdered the General's messenger were delivered into our hands to receive condign punishment, there should no day pass wherein there should not two prisoners be hanged, until they were all consumed which were in our hands. Whereupon the day following, he that had been Captain of the King's Galley, brought the offender to the town's end, offering to deliver him into our hands; but it was thought to be a more honourable revenge to make them there, in our sight, to perform the execution themselves, which was done accordingly.

During our being in this town, as formerly also at Santiago, there had passed justice upon the life of one of our own company for an odious matter, so here likewise was there an Irishman hanged for the murdering of his corporal.

In this time also passed many treaties between their Commissioners and us, for ransom of their city; but upon disagreements we still spent the early mornings in firing the outmost houses; but they being built very magnificently of stone, with high lofts gave us no small travail to ruin them. And albeit for divers days together we ordained each morning by daybreak, until the heat began at nine o'clock, that two hundred mariners did naught else but labour to fire and burn the said houses without our trenches, whilst the soldiers in a like proportion stood forth for their guard; yet did we not, or could not in this time consume so much as one-third part of the town, which town is plainly described and set forth in a certain map. And so in the end, what wearied with firing, and what hastened by some other respects, we were contented to accept of twenty-five thousand ducats of five shillings and six-pence the piece, for the ransom of the rest of the town.

Amongst other things which happened and were found at St. Domingo, I may not omit to let the world know one very notable mark and token of the insatiable ambition of the Spanish king and his nation, which was found in the king's house, wherein the chief governor of that city and country is appointed always to lodge, which was this:—In the coming to the hall or other rooms of this house, you must first ascend up by a fair large pair of stairs, at the head of which stairs is a handsome spacious place to walk in, somewhat like unto a gallery, wherein upon one of the walls, right over against you as you enter the said place, so as your eye cannot escape the sight of it, there is described and painted in a very large escutcheon the arms of the King of Spain, and in the lower part of the said escutcheon, there is likewise described a globe, containing in it the whole circuit of the sea and the earth, whereupon is a horse standing on his hinder part within the globe, and the other fore-part without the globe, lifted up as it were to leap, with a scroll painted in his mouth, wherein was written these words in Latin, "Non sufficit orbis," which is as much to say, as the world sufficeth not. Whereof the meaning was required to be known of some of those of the better sort, that came in commission to treat upon the ransom of the town, who would shake their heads, and turn aside their countenance, in some smiling sort, without answering anything, as greatly ashamed thereof. For by some of our company it was told them, that if the Queen of England would resolutely prosecute the wars against the King of Spain, he should be forced to lay aside that proud and unreasonable reaching vein of his; for he should find more than enough to do to keep that which he had already, as by the present example of their lost town they might for a beginning perceive well enough.

Now to the satisfying of some men, who marvel greatly that such a famous and goodly-builded city, so well inhabited of gallant people, very brave in their apparel (whereof our soldiers found good store for their relief), should afford no greater riches than was found there. Herein it is to be understood that the Indian people, which were the natives of this whole island of Hispaniola (the same being near hand as great as England), were many years since clean consumed by the tyranny of the Spaniards, which was the cause that, for lack of people to work in the mines, the gold and silver mines of this island are wholly given over, and thereby they are fain in this island to use copper money, whereof was found very great quantity. The chief trade of this place consisteth of sugar and ginger, which groweth in the island, and of hides of oxen and kine, which in this waste country of the island are bred in infinite numbers, the soil being very fertile. And the said beasts are fed up to a very large growth, and so killed for nothing so much as for the hides aforesaid. We found here great store of strong wine, sweet oil, vinegar, olives, and other such-like provisions, as excellent wheat-meal packed up in wine-pipes and other casks, and other commodities likewise, as woollen and linen cloth and some silks, all which provisions are brought out of Spain, and served us for great relief. There was but a little plate or vessel of silver, in comparison of the great pride in other things of this town, because in these hot countries they use much of those earthen dishes finely painted or varnished, which they call porcelain, which is had out of the East Indies; and for their drinking they use glasses altogether, whereof they make excellent good and fair in the same place. But yet some plate we found, and many other good things, as their household garniture, very gallant and rich, which had cost them dear, although unto us they were of small importance.

From St. Domingo we put over to the main or firm land, and, going all along the coast, we came at last in sight of Carthagena, standing upon the seaside, so near as some of our barques in passing along approached within the reach of their culverin shot, which they had planted upon certain platforms. The harbour-mouth lay some three miles toward the westward of the town, whereinto we entered at about three or four o'clock in the afternoon without any resistance of ordnance or other impeachment planted upon the same. In the evening we put ourselves on land towards the harbour-mouth, under the leading of Master Carleil, our Lieutenant-General, who, after he had digested us to march forward about midnight, as easily as foot might fall, expressly commanded us to keep close by the sea-wash of the shore for our best and surest way, whereby we were like to go through, and not to miss any more of the way, which once we had lost within an hour after our first beginning to march, through the slender knowledge of him that took upon him to be our guide, whereby the night spent on, which otherwise must have been done by resting. But as we came within some two miles of the town, their horsemen, which were some hundred, met us, and, taking the alarm, retired to their townward again upon the first volley of our shot that was given them; for the place where we encountered being woody and bushy, even to the water-side, was unmeet for their service.

At this instant we might hear some pieces of artillery discharged, with divers small shot, towards the harbour, which gave us to understand, according to the order set down in the evening before by our General, that the Vice-Admiral, accompanied with Captain Venner, Captain White, and Captain Crosse, with other sea captains, and with divers pinnaces and boats, should give some attempt unto the little fort standing on the entry of the inner haven, near adjoining to the town, though to small purpose, for that the place was strong, and the entry (very narrow) was chained over; so as there could be nothing gotten by the attempt more than the giving of them an alarm on that other side of the haven, being a mile and a-half from the place we now were at. In which attempt the Vice-Admiral had the rudder of his skiff stricken through with a saker shot, and a little or no harm received elsewhere.

The troops being now in their march, half-a-mile behither the town or less, the ground we were on grew to be straight, and not above fifty paces over, having the main sea on the one side of it and the harbour water or inner sea (as you may term it) on the other side, which in the plot is plainly shewed. This strait was fortified clean over with a stone wall and a ditch without it, the said wall being as orderly built with flanking in every part as can be set down. There was only so much of this strait unwalled as might serve for the issuing of the horsemen or the passing of carriage in time of need. But this unwalled part was not without a very good barricade of wine-butts or pipes, filled with earth, full and thick as they might stand on end one by another, some part of them standing even within the main sea.

This place of strength was furnished with six great pieces, demi-culverins and sakers, which shot directly in front upon us as we approached. Now within this wall upon the inner side of the strait they had brought likewise two great galleys with their prows to the shore, having planted in them eleven pieces of ordnance, which did beat all cross the strait, and flanked our coming on. In these two galleys were planted three or four hundred small shot, and on the land, in the guard only of this place, three hundred shot and pikes.

They, in this their full readiness to receive us, spared not their shot both great and small. But our Lieutenant-General, taking the advantage of the dark (the daylight as yet not broken out) approached by the lowest ground, according to the express direction which himself had formerly given, the same being the sea-wash shore, where the water was somewhat fallen, so as most of all their shot was in vain. Our Lieutenant-General commanded our shot to forbear shooting until we were come to the wall-side, and so with pikes roundly together we approached the place, where we soon found out the barricades of pipes or butts to be the meetest place for our assault, which, notwithstanding it was well furnished with pikes and shots, was without staying attempted by us. Down went the butts of earth, and pell-mell came our swords and pikes together, after our shots had first given their volley, even at the enemy's nose. Our pikes were somewhat longer than theirs, and our bodies better armed; for very few of them were armed. With which advantage our swords and pikes grew too hard for them, and they driven to give place. In this furious entry the Lieutenant-General slew with his own hands the chief ensign-bearer of the Spaniards, who fought very manfully to his life's end.

We followed into the town with them, and, giving them no leisure to breathe, we won the market-place, albeit they made head and fought awhile before we got it, and so we being once seized and assured of that, they were content to suffer us to lodge within the town, and themselves to go to their wives, whom they had carried into other places of the country before our coming thither. At every street's end they had raised very fine barricades of earthworks, with trenches without them, as well made as ever we saw any work done; at the entering whereof was some little resistance, but soon overcome it was, with few slain or hurt. They had joined with them many Indians, whom they had placed in corners of advantage, all bowmen, with their arrows most villainously empoisoned, so as if they did but break the skin, the party so touched died without great marvel. Some they slew of our people with their arrows; some they likewise mischiefed to death with certain pricks of small sticks sharply pointed, of a foot and a-half long, the one end put into the ground, the other empoisoned, sticking fast up, right against our coming in the way as we should approach from our landing towards the town, whereof they had planted a wonderful number in the ordinary way; but our keeping the sea-wash shore, missed the greatest part of them very happily.

I overpass many particular matters, as the hurting of Captain Sampson at sword blows in the first entering, unto whom was committed the charge of the pikes of the vanguard by his lot and turn, as also of the taking of Alonzo Bravo, the chief commander of that place, by Captain Goring, after the said Captain had first hurt him with his sword; unto which Captain was committed the charge of the shot of the said vanguard. Captain Winter was likewise by his turn of the vanguard in this attempt, where also the Lieutenant-General marched himself; the said Captain Winter, through a great desire to serve by land, having now exchanged his charge at sea with Captain Cecil for his band of footmen. Captain Powell, the Serjeant-Major, had by his turn the charge of the four companies which made the battle. Captain Morgan, who at St. Domingo was of the vanguard, had now by turn his charge upon the companies of the rearward. Every man, as well of one part as of another, came so willingly on to the service, as the enemy was not able to endure the fury of such hot assault.

We stayed here six weeks, and the sickness with mortality before spoken of still continued among us, though not with the same fury as at the first; and such as were touched with the said sickness, escaping death, very few or almost none could recover their strength; yea, many of them were much decayed in their memory, insomuch that it was grown an ordinary judgment, when one was heard to speak foolishly, to say he had been sick of the *Calentura*, which is the Spanish name of their burning ague; for, as I told you before, it is a very burning and pestilent ague. The original cause thereof is imputed to the evening or first night air, which they term *La serena*, wherein they say and hold very firm opinion that whoso is then abroad in the open air shall certainly be infected to the death, not being of the Indian or native race of those country people. By holding their watch our men were thus subjected to the infectious air, which at Santiago was most dangerous and deadly of all other places.

With the inconvenience of continual mortality we were forced to give over our intended enterprise, to go with Nombre de Dios, and so overland to Panama, where we should have struck the stroke for the treasure, and full recompense of our tedious travails. And thus at Carthagena we took our first resolution to return homewards, the form of which Resolution I thought good here to put down under the principal captain's hands as followeth:—

A Resolution of the Land-Captains, what course they think most expedient to be taken. Given at CARTHAGENA, *the 27th day of February, 1586.*

Whereas it hath pleased the General to demand the opinions of his Captains what course they think most expedient to be now undertaken, the land Captains being assembled by themselves together, and having advised hereupon do in three points deliver the same.

The first, touching the keeping of the town against the force of the enemy, either that which is present, or that which may come out of Spain, is answered thus:—

"We hold opinion, that with this troop of men which we have presently with us in land service, being victualled and munitioned, we may well keep the town, albeit that of men able to answer present service, we have not above 700. The residue being some 150 men, by reason of their hurts and sickness, are altogether unable to stand us in any stead: wherefore hereupon the sea captains are likewise to give their resolution, how they will undertake the safety and service of the ships upon the arrival of any Spanish fleet."

The second point we make to be this, whether it be mete to go presently homeward, or else to continue further trial of our fortune in undertaking such like enterprises as we have done already, and thereby to seek after that bountiful mass of treasure for recompense of our travels, which was generally expected at our coming forth of England: wherein we answer:—

"That it is well known how both we and the soldiers are entered into this action as voluntary men, without any impress or gage from Her Majesty or anybody else: and forasmuch as we have hitherto discharged the parts of honest men, so that now by the great blessing and favour of our good God there have been taken three such notable towns, wherein by the estimation of all men would have been found some very great treasures, knowing that Santiago was the chief city of all the islands and traffics thereabouts, St. Domingo the chief city of Española, and the head government not only of that island, but also of Cuba, and of all the islands about it, as also of such inhabitations of the firm land, as were next unto it, and a place that is both magnificently built and entertaineth great trades of merchandise; and now lastly the city of Carthagena, which cannot be denied to be one of the chief places of most especial importance to the Spaniard of all the cities which be on this side of the West Indies: we do therefore consider, that since all these cities, with their goods and prisoners taken in them, and the ransoms of the said cities being all put together, are found far short to satisfy that expectation which by the generality of the enterprisers was first conceived; and being further advised of the slenderness of our strength, whereunto we be now reduced, as well in respect of the small number of able bodies, as also not a little in regard of the slack disposition of the greater part of those which remain, very many of the better minds and men being either consumed by death or weakened by sickness and hurts; and lastly, since that as yet there is not laid down to our knowledge any such enterprise as may seem convenient to be undertaken with such few as we are presently able to make, and withal of such certain likelihood, as with God's good success which it may please him to bestow upon us, the same may promise to yield us any sufficient contentment: we do therefore conclude hereupon, that it is better to hold sure as we may the honour already gotten, and with the same to return towards our gracious sovereign and country, from whence it shall please Her Majesty to set us forth again with her orderly means and entertainment, we are most ready and willing to go through with anything that the uttermost of our strength and endeavour shall be able to reach unto; but therewithal we do advise and protest that it is far from our thoughts, either to refuse, or so much as to seem to be weary of anything, which for the present shall be further required or directed to be done by us from our General."

The third and last point is concerning the ransom of this city of

Carthagena, for the which, before it was touched with any fire, there was made an offer of some 27,000 or 28,000 pounds sterling:—

"Thus much we utter herein as our opinions agreeing (so it be done in good sort) to accept this offer aforesaid, rather than to break off by standing still upon our demands of £100,000, which seems a matter impossible to be performed for the present by them, and to say truth, we may now with much honour and reputation better be satisfied with that sum offered by them at the first (if they will now be contented to give it) than we might at that time with a great deal more, inasmuch as we have taken our full pleasure both in the uttermost sacking and spoiling of all their household goods and merchandise, as also in that we have consumed and ruined a great part of their town with fire. And thus much further is considered herein by us, that as there be in the voyage a great many poor men, who have willingly adventured their lives and travels, and divers amongst them having spent their apparel and such other little provisions as their small means might have given them leave to prepare, which being done upon such good and allowable intention as this action hath always carried with it, meaning, against the Spaniard, our greatest and most dangerous enemy: so surely we cannot but have an inward regard so far as may lie in us, to help either in all good sort towards the satisfaction of this their expectation, and by procuring them some little benefit to encourage them and to nourish this ready and willing disposition of theirs both in them and in others by their example against any other time of like occasion. But because it may be supposed that herein we forget not the private benefit of ourselves, and are thereby the rather moved to incline ourselves to this composition, we do therefore think good for the clearing of ourselves of all such suspicion, to declare hereby, that what part or portion soever it be of this ransom or composition for Carthagena which should come unto us, we do freely give and bestow the same wholly upon the poor men, who have remained with us in the voyage, meaning as well the sailor as the soldier, wishing with all our hearts it were such or so much as might seem a sufficient reward for their painful endeavour. And for the firm confirmation thereof, we have thought meet to subsign those presents with our own hands in the place and time aforesaid.

"Captain Christopher Carleil, Lieutenant-General; Captain Goring, Captain Sampson, Captain Powell, &c."

But while we were yet there it happened one day, that our watch called the sentinel, upon the church-steeple, had discovered in the sea a couple of small barques or boats, making in with the harbour of Carthagena, whereupon Captain Moon and Captain Varney, with John Grant, the master of the Tiger, and some other seamen, embarked themselves in a couple of small pinnaces, to take them before they should come nigh the shore, at the mouth of the harbour, lest by some straggling Spaniards from the land, they might be warned by signs from coming in, which fell out accordingly, notwithstanding all the diligence that our men could use: for the Spanish boats, upon the sight of our pinnaces coming towards them, ran themselves ashore, and so their men presently hid themselves in bushes hard by the sea-side, amongst some others that had called them by signs thither. Our men presently without any due regard had to the quality of the place, and seeing no man of the Spaniards to shew themselves, boarded the Spanish barques or boats, ånd so standing all open in them, were suddenly shot at by a troop of Spaniards out of the bushes; by which volley of shot there were slain Captain Varney, which died presently, and Captain Moon, who died some few days after, besides some four or five others that were hurt: and so our folks returned without their purpose, not having any sufficient number of soldiers with them to fight on shore. For those men they carried were all mariners to row, few of them armed, because they made account with their ordnance to have taken the barques well enough at sea which they might full easily have done, without any loss at all, if they had come in time to the harbour mouth, before the Spaniards' boats had gotten so near the shore.

During our abode in this place, as also at St. Domingo, there passed divers courtesies between us and the Spaniards, as feasting, and using them with all kindness and favour; so as amongst others there came to see the General the Governor of Carthagena, with the Bishop of the same, and divers other gentlemen of the better sort. This town of Carthagena we touched in the outparts, and consumed much with fire, as we had done St. Domingo upon discontentments, and for want of agreeing with us in their first treaties touching their ransom, which at the last was concluded between us, should be 110,000 ducats for that which was yet standing, the ducat valued at five shillings and sixpence sterling.

This town, though not half so big as St. Domingo, gives, as you see, a far greater ransom, being in very deed of far more importance, by reason of the excellency of the harbour and the situation thereof, to serve the trade of Nombre de Dios and other places, and is inhabited with far more richer merchants. The other is chiefly inhabited with lawyers and brave gentlemen, being the chief or highest appeal of their suits in law of all the islands about it and of the mainland coast next unto it. And it is of no such account as Carthagena, for these and some other like reasons which I could give you over long to be now written.

The warning which this town received of our coming towards them from St. Domingo, by the space of twenty days before our arrival here, was cause that they had both fortified and every way prepared for their best defence. As also that they had carried and conveyed away all their treasure and principal substance.

The ransom of an hundred and ten thousand ducats thus concluded on, as is aforesaid, the same being written, and expressing for nothing more than the town of Carthagena, upon the payment of the said ransom we left the said town and drew some part of our soldiers into the priory or abbey, standing a quarter of an English mile below the town upon the harbour water-side, the same being walled with a wall of stone, which we told the Spaniards was yet ours, and not redeemed by their composition; whereupon they, finding the defect of their contract, were contented to enter into another ransom for all places, but specially for the said house, as also the blockhouse or castle, which is upon the mouth of the inner harbour. And when we asked as much for the one as for the other, they yielded to give a thousand crowns for the abbey, leaving us to take our pleasure upon the blockhouse, which they said they were not able to ransom, having stretched themselves to the uttermost of their powers; and therefore the said blockhouse was by us undermined, and so with gunpowder blown up in pieces. While this latter contract was in making, our whole fleet of ships fell down towards the harbour-mouth, where they anchored the third time and employed their men in fetching of fresh water aboard the ships for our voyage homewards, which water was had in a great well that is in the island by the harbour-mouth; which island is a very pleasant place as hath been seen, having in it many sorts of goodly and very pleasant fruits, as the orange-trees and others, being set orderly in walks of great length together. Insomuch as the whole island being some two or three miles about, is cast into grounds of gardening and orchards.

After six weeks' abode in this place, we put to sea the last of March, where, after two or three days, a great ship which we had taken at St. Domingo, and thereupon was called the New Year's Gift, fell into a great leak, being laden with ordnance, hides, and other spoils, and in the night she lost the company of our fleet, which, being missed the next morning by the General, he cast about with the whole fleet, fearing some great mischance to be happened unto her, as in very deed it so fell out; for her leak was so great that her men were all tired with pumping. But at the last, having found her and the barque Talbot in her company, which stayed by great hap with her, they were ready to take their men out of her for the saving of them. And so the General, being fully advertised of their great extremity, made sail directly back again to Carthagena with the whole fleet, where, having staid eight or ten days more about the unlading of this ship and the bestowing thereof and her men into other ships, we departed once again to sea, directing our course toward the Cape St. Anthony, being the westermost part of Cuba, where we arrived on the 27th of April. But because fresh water could not presently be found, we weighed anchor and departed, thinking in few days to recover the Matanzas, a place to the eastward of Havana.

After we had sailed some fourteen days we were brought to Cape St. Anthony again through lack of favourable wind; but then our scarcity was grown such as need made us look a little better for water, which being found in sufficient quantity, being indeed, as I judge, none other than rain-water newly fallen and gathered up by making pits in a plot of marsh ground some three hundred paces from the seaside.

I do wrong if I should forget the good example of the General at this place, who, to encourage others, and to hasten the getting of fresh water aboard the ships, took no less pain himself than the meanest; as also at St. Domingo, Carthagena, and all other places, having always so vigilant a care and foresight in the good ordering of his fleet, accompanying them, as it is said, with such wonderful travail of body, as doubtless had he been the meanest person, as he was the chiefest, he had yet deserved the first place of honour; and no less happy do we account him for being associated with Mr. Carleil, his Lieutenant-General, by whose experience, prudent counsel, and gallant performance he achieved so many and happy enterprises of the war, by whom also he was very greatly assisted in setting down the needful orders, laws, and course of justice, and the due administration of the same upon all occasions.

After three days spent in watering our ships, we departed now the second time from this Cape of St. Anthony on the 13th of May, and, proceeding about the Cape of Florida, we never touched anywhere; but, coasting along Florida, and keeping the shore still in sight, on the 28th of May, early in the morning, we descried on the shore a place built like a beacon, which was indeed a scaffold upon four long masts raised on end for men to discover to the seaward, being in the latitude of thirty degrees, or very near thereunto. Our pinnaces manned and coming to the shore, we marched up along the river-side to see what place the enemy held there; for none amongst us had any knowledge thereof at all.

Here the General took occasion to march with the companies himself in person, the Lieutenant-General having the vanguard; and, going a mile up, or somewhat more, by the river-side, we might discern on the other side of the river over against us a fort which newly had been built by the Spaniards; and some mile, or thereabout, above the fort was a little town or village without walls, built of wooden houses, as the plot doth plainly shew. We forthwith prepared to have ordnance for the battery; and one piece was a little before the evening planted, and the first shot being made by the Lieutenant-General himself at their ensign, struck through the ensign, as we afterwards understood by a Frenchman which came unto us from them. One shot more was then made, which struck the foot of the fort wall, which was all massive timber of great trees like masts. The Lieutenant-General was determined to pass the river this night with four companies, and there to lodge himself entrenched as near to the fort as that he might play with his muskets and smallest shot upon any that should appear, and so afterwards to bring and plant the battery with him; but the help of mariners for that sudden to make trenches could not be had, which was the cause that this determination was remitted until the next night.

In the night the Lieutenant-General took a little rowing skiff and a half-a-dozen well armed, as Captain Morgan and Captain Sampson, with some others besides the rowers, and went to view what guard the enemy kept, as also to take knowledge of the ground. And albeit he went as covertly as might be, yet the enemy, taking the alarm, grew fearful that the whole force was approaching to the assault, and therefore with all speed abandoned the place after the shooting of some of their pieces. They thus gone, and he being returned unto us again, but nothing knowing of their flight from their fort, forthwith came a Frenchman, being a piper (who has been prisoner with them) in a little boat, playing on his pipe the tune of the Prince of Orange's song; and being called unto by the guard, he told them before he put foot out of the boat what he was himself, and how the Spaniards had gone from the fort, offering either to remain in hands there, or else to return to the place with them that would go.

Upon this intelligence the General, the Lieutenant-General, with some of the captains in one skiff and the Vice-Admiral with some others in his skiff, and two or three pinnaces furnished of soldiers with them, put presently over towards the fort, giving order for the rest of the pinnaces to follow. And in our approach some of the enemy, bolder than the rest, having stayed behind their company, shot off two pieces of ordnance at us; but on shore we went, and entered the place without finding any man there.

When the day appeared, we found it built all of timber, the walls being none other than whole masts or bodies of trees set upright and close together in manner of a pale, without any ditch as yet made, but wholly intended with some more time; for they had not as yet finished all their work, having begun the same some three or four months before; so as, to say the truth, they had no reason to keep it, being subject both to fire and easy assault.

The platform whereon the ordnance lay was whole bodies of long pine-trees, whereof there is great plenty, laid across one on another and some little earth amongst. There were in it thirteen or fourteen great pieces of brass ordnance and a chest unbroken up, having in it the value of some two thousand pounds sterling by estimation of the King's treasure to pay the soldiers of that place, who were a hundred and fifty men.

The Fort thus won, which they called St. John's Fort, and the day opened, we assayed to go to the town, but could not by reason of some rivers and broken ground which was between the two places; and therefore being enforced to embark again into our pinnaces, we went thither upon the great main river, which is called as also the town, by the name of St. Augustine.

At our approaching to land, there were some that began to shew themselves, and to bestow some few shot upon us, but presently withdrew themselves. And in their running thus away, the Sergeant-Major finding one of their horses ready saddled and bridled, took the same to follow the chase; and so overgoing all his company, was (by one laid behind a bush) shot through the head; and falling down therewith, was by the same and two or three more, stabbed in three or four places of his body with swords and daggers, before any could come near to his rescue. His death was much lamented, being in very deed an honest, wise gentleman, and soldier of good experience, and of as great courage as any man might be.

In this place called St. Augustine, we understood the king did keep, as is before said, one hundred and fifty soldiers, and at another place some dozen leagues beyond to the northwards, called St. Helena, he did there likewise keep an hundred and fifty more, serving there for no other purpose than to keep all other nations from inhabiting any part of all that coast; the government whereof was committed to one Pedro Melendez, marquis, nephew to that Melendez the Admiral, who had overthrown Mr. John Hawkins in the Bay of Mexico some seventeen or eighteen years ago. This Governor had charge of both places, but was at this time in this place, and one of the first that left the same.

Here it was resolved in full assembly of captains, to undertake the enterprise of St. Helena, and from thence to seek out the inhabitation of our English countrymen in Virginia, distant from thence some six degrees northward. When we came thwart of St. Helena, the shoals appearing dangerous, and we having no pilot to undertake the entry, it was thought meetest to go hence alongst. For the Admiral had been the same night in four fathom and a half, three leagues from the shore; and yet we understood by the help of a known pilot, there may and do go in ships of greater burden and draught than any we had in our fleet. We passed thus along the coast hard aboard the shore, which is shallow for a league or two from the shore, and the same is low and broken land for the most part. On the 9th of June upon sight of one special great fire (which are very ordinary all along this coast, even from the Cape of Florida hither) the General sent his skiff to the shore, where they found some of our English countrymen (that had been sent thither the year before by Sir Walter Raleigh) and brought them aboard: by whose direction we proceeded along to the place which they make their port. But some of our ships being of great draught, unable to enter, anchored without the harbour in a wild road at sea, about two miles from shore. From whence the General wrote letters to Mr. Ralfe Lane, being governor of those English in Virginia, and then at his fort about six leagues from the road in an Island which they called Roanoke wherein especially he shewed how ready he was to supply his necessities and wants, which he understood of, by those he had first talked withal.

The morrow after, Mr. Lane himself and some of his company coming unto him, with the consent of his captains he gave them the choice of two offers, that is to say: Either he would leave a ship, a pinnace, and certain boats with sufficient masters and mariners, together furnished with a month's victuals, to stay and make further discovery of the country and coasts, and so much victual likewise as might be sufficient for the bringing of them all (being an hundred and three persons) into England, if they thought good after such time, with any other thing they would desire, and that he might be able to spare.

Or else if they thought they had made sufficient discovery already, and did desire to return into England, he would give them passage. But they, as it seemed, being desirous to stay, accepted very thankfully and with great gladness, that which was offered first. Whereupon the ship being appointed and received into charge by some of their own company sent into her by Mr. Lane, before they had received from the rest of the fleet the provision appointed them, there arose a great storm (which they said was extraordinary and very strange) that lasted three days together, and put all our fleet in great danger, to be driven from their anchoring upon the coast; for we broke many cables, and lost many anchors; and some of our fleet which had lost all (of which number was the ship appointed for Mr. Lane and his company) was driven to put to sea in great danger, in avoiding the coast, and could never see us again until we met in England. Many also of our small pinnaces and boats were lost in this storm.

Notwithstanding, after all this, the General offered them (with consent of his captains) another ship with some provisions, although not such a one for their turns, as might have been spared them before, this being unable to be brought into their harbour. Or else if they would, to give them passage into England, although he knew he should perform it with greater difficulty than he might have done before. But Mr. Lane, with those of the chiefest of his company which he had then with him, considering what should be best for them to do, made request unto the General under their hands, that they might have passage for England:

the which being granted, and the rest sent for out of the country and shipped, we departed from that coast on the 18th of June. And so, God be thanked, both they and we in good safety arrived at Portsmouth on the 28th of July, 1586, to the great glory of God, and to no small honour to our Prince, our country, and ourselves. The total value of that which was got in this voyage is esteemed at three score thousand pounds, whereof the companies which have travelled in the voyage were to have twenty thousand pounds, the adventurers the other forty. Of which twenty thousand pounds (as I can judge) will redound some six pounds to the single share. We lost some seven hundred and fifty men in the voyage; above three parts of them only by sickness. The men of name that died and were slain in this voyage, which I can presently call to remembrance, are these:—Captain Powell, Captain Varney, Captain Moon, Captain Fortescue, Captain Biggs, Captain Cecil, Captain Hannam, Captain Greenfield; Thomas Tucker, a lieutenant; Alexander Starkey, a lieutenant; Mr. Escot, lieutenant; Mr. Waterhouse, a lieutenant; Mr. George Candish, Mr. Nicholas Winter, Mr. Alexander Carleil, Mr. Robert Alexander, Mr. Scroope, Mr. James Dier, Mr. Peter Duke. With some other, whom for haste I cannot suddenly think on.

The ordnance gotten of all sorts, brass and iron, were about two hundred and forty pieces, whereof the two hundred and some more were brass, and were thus found and gotten:—At Santiago some two or three and fifty pieces. In St. Domingo about four score, whereof was very much great ordnance, as whole cannon, demi-cannon, culverins, and such like. In Carthagena some sixty and three pieces, and good store likewise of the greater sort. In the Fort of St. Augustin were fourteen pieces. The rest was iron ordnance, of which the most part was gotten at St. Domingo, the rest at Carthagena.

CAVENDISH.

THOMAS CAVENDISH, a young Suffolk gentleman of good family, who had squandered the savings of a long minority, and dissipated the substance of a large fortune in the extravagances of Elizabeth's Court, bethought him of repairing his shattered wealth by an American voyage in imitation of that which had immortalized Francis Drake. Accordingly, in July, 1586, he left Plymouth with three vessels, following Drake's track by way of the Canaries and the Guinea Coast to the shores of Brazil, which was reached in December. Early in the New Year (1587) Cavendish made the Straits of Magellan, which it took him over six weeks to traverse. He then coasted along the western shore of South America in search of plunder. His success was quite equal to his expectations. Before he reached the coast of California he had sunk many Spanish vessels, and collected a considerable cargo of silver and American produce; but Cavendish had resolved to strike a yet more daring blow for fortune. He would await, on the Californian coast, the arrival of the great galleon from the Philippines, laden with the spoils of Asia; and on the 4th of November, 1587, while Cavendish was beating up and down on the headland of California, the great flag-ship of the Pacific hove in sight. It was the Santa Anna, with 120,000 dollars in gold aboard, besides quantities of Oriental silks, satins, and damask, and rich spices and perfumes. Cavendish speedily laid her aboard, and captured her after an obstinate fight of several hours. Having put her crew on shore, emptied her of all her treasures, and burnt her to the water's edge, Cavendish sailed due west across the Pacific, and reached the Philippines in the middle of January, 1588, or a year and a-half after quitting Plymouth. Having touched at several islands of the Malay archipelago, especially Java, where he took pains to obtain exact information as to the condition and resources of the island, and found the natives and the Portuguese equally ready to welcome a deliverer from the despotism of Spain; and thence, after a run of nine weeks across the Indian Ocean, he made the Cape of Good Hope. Cavendish did not land until he reached the Island of St. Helena, of which the narrative gives an interesting description. Two months from St. Helena brought him back to Plymouth, after a voyage which had lasted over two years.

Three years elapsed before Cavendish sailed on his second expedition. It was as disastrous as the first had been prosperous. He was late in the season, and unusually bad weather prevented him from making the Straits until April, 1592. Cavendish did not reach the Pacific. The Desire, commanded by Davis, with whom sailed the writer of the narrative here printed, was forced back up the Straits by stress of weather, and followed the Admiral back to the coast of Brazil; and, after months of unexampled suffering and distress, her crew reached the coast of Ireland. Cavendish himself was spared the mortification of an inglorious return; for he died at sea shortly before his ship reached the shores of England. Cavendish was the second English circumnavigator of the globe. Beyond this circumstance his voyages have no special historical significance. But the dramatic nature of their incidents fixed them firmly in the public mind. They served to stimulate and confirm the spirit of English enterprize in the American and East Indian seas; and the name of the bold and unfortunate Suffolk gentleman-adventurer will always occupy an important place on the roll of English worthies.

CAVENDISH.—FIRST VOYAGE.

The admirable and prosperous Voyage of the Worshipful MR. THOMAS CAVENDISH, *of* TRIMLEY, *in the County of* SUFFOLK, *Esquire, into the South Sea, and from thence round about the circumference of the whole earth; begun in the year of our Lord 1586, and finished 1588. Written by* MR. FRANCIS PRETTY, *lately of* EYE, *in* SUFFOLK, *a gentleman employed in the same action.*

WE departed out of Plymouth on Thursday, the 21st of July, 1586, with three sails, to wit, the Desire, a ship of 120 tons, the Content, of 60 tons, and the Hugh Gallant, a barque of 40 tons, in which small fleet were 123 persons of all sorts, with all kind of furniture and victuals sufficient for the space of two years, at the charges of the Worshipful Mr. Thomas Cavendish. of Trimley, in the county of Suffolk, Esquire, being our General. On Tuesday, the 26th of the same month, we were forty-five leagues from Cape Finisterre, where we met with five sails of Biscayans, coming from the Grand Bay in Newfoundland, as we supposed, which our Admiral shot at, and fought with them three hours, but we took none of them by reason the night grew on. On the 1st of August we came in sight of Forteventura, one of the Isles of the Canaries, about 10 o'clock in the morning.

On Sunday, being the 7th of August, we were gotten as high as Rio del Oro, on the coast of Barbary. On Monday, the 19th, we fell with Cape Blanco; but the wind blew so much at the north, that we could not get up where the canters do use to ride and fish; therefore we lay off six hours west-south-west, because of the sand which lieth off the Cape south-west and by south. On the 15th of the same month we were in the height of Cape

Verde, by estimation fifty leagues off the same. On the 18th, Sierra Leone did bear east of us, being forty-five leagues from us; and the same day the wind shifted to the north-west, so that by the 20th day of the said month we were in six degrees and a-half to the northward from the equinoctial line. On the 23rd we put room for Sierra Leone, and the 25th day we fell with the point on the south side of Sierra Leone, which Mr. Brewer knew very well, and went in before with the Content, which was Vice-Admiral; and we had no less than five fathoms water when we had least, and had for fourteen leagues in southwest all the way running into the harbour of Sierra Leone, sixteen, fourteen, twelve, ten, and eight fathoms of water.

On the 26th of the said month we put into the harbour, and in going in we had (by the southernmost point, when we had least) five fathoms water fair by the rock as it lieth at the said point; and after we came two or three cables' lengths within the said rock, we never had less than ten fathoms, until we came up to the road, which is about a league from the point, borrowing always on the south side until you come up to the watering-place, in which bay is the best road; but you must ride far into the bay because there run marvellous great tides in the offing, and it floweth into the road next of anything at a south-east and by east moon. It is out of England to this place 930 leagues, which we ran from the 21st of July to the 26th of this month of August.

On Saturday, being the 27th day, there came two negroes aboard our Admiral from the shore, and made signs unto our General that there was a Portugal ship up within the harbour: so the Hugh Gallant, being the Rear-Admiral, went up three or four leagues, but for want of a pilot they sought no farther; for the harbour runneth three or four leagues up more, and is of a marvellous breadth and very dangerous, as we learned afterwards by a Portugal.

On Sunday, the 28th, the General sent some of his company on shore, and there as they played and danced all the forenoon among the negroes, to the end to have heard some good news of the Portugal ship, toward their coming aboard they espied a Portugal, which lay hid among the bushes, whom we took and brought away with us the same night, and he told us it was very dangerous going up with our boats for to seek the ship that was at the town. Whereupon we went not to seek her, because we knew he told us the truth; for we bound him and made him fast, and so examined him. Also he told us that his ship was there cast away, and that there were two more of his company among the negroes. The Portugal's name was Emmanuel, and was by his occupation a caulker, belonging to the Port of Portugal.*

On Monday morning, being the 29th day, our General landed with seventy men, or thereabouts, and went up to their town, where we burnt two or three houses, and took what spoil we would, which was but little; but all the people fled, and in our retiring aboard in a very little plain at their town's end they shot their arrows at us out of the woods, and hurt three or four of our men. Their arrows were poisoned, but yet none of our men miscarried at that time, thanked be God. Their town is marvellous artificially builded with mud walls, and built round, with their yards paled in and kept very clean as well in their streets as in their houses. These negroes use good obedience to their king, as one of our men said, which was with them in pawn for the negroes which came first. There were in their town by estimation about one hundred houses.

On the 1st of September there went many of our men on shore at the watering-place, and did wash shirts very quietly all the day, and the second day they went again, and the negroes were in ambush round about the place; and the carpenter of the Admiral going into the wood to do some special business, espied them by good fortune. But the negroes rushed out upon our men so suddenly, that in retiring to our boats many of them were hurt; among whom one William Pickman, a soldier, was shot into the thigh, who plucking the arrow out broke it, and left the head behind, and he told the surgeons that he plucked out all the arrow, because he would not have them lance his thigh; whereupon the poison wrought so that night, that he was marvellously swollen, and the next morning he died, the piece of the arrow with the poison being plucked out of his thigh.

On the 3rd day of the said month, divers of our fleet went up four miles within the harbour with our boat, and caught great store of fish, and went on shore and took lemons from the trees, and coming aboard again saw two buffes. On the 6th day we departed from Sierra Leone, and went out of the harbour, and stayed one

---

* Oporto.

tide three leagues from the point of the mouth of the harbour in six fathoms, and it floweth south-south-west. On Wednesday, being the 7th of the same month, we departed from one of the islands of Cape Verde, alias the islands of Madrabumba, which is ten leagues distant from the point of Sierra Leone, and about five o'clock the same night we anchored two miles off the island, in six fathoms water, and landed the same night, and found plantains only upon the island. On the 8th day one of our boats went out and sounded round about the island, and they passed through a sound at the west end of the island, where they found five fathoms round about the island, until they came into the very gut of the sound, and then for a cast or two they had but two fathoms, and presently after six fathoms, and so deeper and deeper. And at the east end of the island there was a town, where negroes do use at sometimes, as we perceived by their provision.

There is no fresh water on all the south side, as we could perceive, but on the north side three or four very good places of fresh water; and all the whole island is a wood, save certain little places where their houses stand, which are environed round about with plantain trees, whereof the fruit is excellent meat. This place is subject marvellous much to thunder, rain, and lightning in this month. I think the reason is, because the sun is so near the line equinoctial. On Saturday, the 10th, we departed from the said island, about three o'clock in the afternoon, the wind being at the south-west.

The last of October, running west-south-west, about twenty-four leagues from Cape Frio, in Brazil, we fell with a great mountain which had a high round knob on the top of it, standing from it like a town, with two little islands from it.

On the 1st of November we went in between the island of St. Sebastian and the main land, and had our things on shore, and set up a forge, and had our cask on shore; our coopers made hoops, and so we remained there until the 23rd day of the same month, in which time we fitted our things, built our pinnace, and filled our fresh water; and while our pinnace was in building, there came a canoe from the River of Janeiro, meaning to go to St. Vincent, wherein were six naked slaves of the country people, which did row the canoe, and one Portugal. And the Portugal knew Christopher Hare, Master of the Admiral, for that Mr. Hare had been at St. Vincent, in the Minion, of London, in the year 1581; and thinking to have John Whithall, the Englishman which dwelleth at St. Vincent, come unto us, which is twenty leagues from this harbour with some other, thereby to have had some fresh victuals, we suffered the Portugal to go with a letter unto him, who promised to return or send some answer within ten days, for that we told him we were merchants, and would traffic with them; but we never received answer from him any more; and seeing that he came not according to appointment, our business being despatched, we weighed anchor, and set sail from St. Sebastian on the 23rd of November.

On the 16th day of December we fell in with the coast of America in 47 degrees and a third, the land bearing west from us about six leagues off: from which place we ran along the shore until we came into 48 degrees. It is a steep beach all along. On the 17th day of December, in the afternoon, we entered into an harbour, where our Admiral went in first (wherefore our General named the said harbour Port Desire), in which harbour is an island or two, where there is wonderful great store of seals, and another island of birds, which are grey gulls. These seals are of a wonderful great bigness, huge, and monstrous of shape, and for the fore-part of their bodies cannot be compared to anything better than to a lion: their head, and neck, and fore-parts of their bodies are full of rough hair: their feet are in manner of a fin, and in form like unto a man's hand; they breed and cast every month, giving their young milk, yet continually get they their living in the sea, and live altogether upon fish: their young are marvellous good meat, and being boiled or roasted, are hardly to be known from lamb or mutton. The old ones be of such bigness and force, that it is as much as four men are able to do to kill one of them with great cowle-staves: and he must be beaten down with striking on the head of him: for his body is of that bigness that four men could never kill him, but only on the head. For being shot through the body with an arquebuse or a musket, yet he will go his way into the sea, and never care for it at the present. Also the fowls that were there were very good meat, and great store of them: they have burrows in the ground like coneys, for they cannot fly. They have nothing but down upon their pinions: they also fish and feed in the sea for their living, and breed on shore.

This harbour is a very good place to trim ships in, and to bring them on ground, and grave them in: for there ebbeth and floweth much water: therefore we graved and trimmed all our ships there.

On the 24th of December, being Christmas Eve, a man and a boy of the Rear-Admiral went some forty score from our ships unto a very fair green valley at the foot of the mountains, where was a little pit or well which our men had digged and made some two or three days before to get fresh water, for there was none in all the harbour; and this was but brackish: therefore this man and boy came thither to wash their linen: and being in washing at the said well, there were great store of Indians which were come down, and found the said man and boy in washing. These Indians being divided on each side of the rocks, shot at them with their arrows and hurt them both, but they fled presently, being about fifty or threescore, though our General followed them with but sixteen or twenty men. The man's name which was hurt was John Garge, the boy's name was Lutch: the man was shot clean through the knee, the boy into the shoulder: either of them having very sore wounds. Their arrows are made of little canes, and their heads are of a flint stone, set into the cane very artificially: they seldom or never see any Christians: they are as wild as ever was a buck or any other wild beast; for we followed them, and they ran from us as it had been the wildest thing in the world. We took the measure of one of their feet, and it was 18 inches long. Their use is when any of them die, to bring him or them to the cliffs by the sea-side, and upon the top of them they bury them, and in their graves are buried with them their bows and arrows, and all their jewels which they have in their life-time, which are fine shells which they find by the sea-side, which they cut and square after an artificial manner; and all is laid under their heads. The grave is made all with great stones of great length and bigness, being set all along full of the dead man's darts which he used when he was living. And they colour both their darts and their graves with a red colour which they use in colouring of themselves.

On the 28th of December we departed out of the Port of Desire, and went to an island which lieth three leagues to the southward of it; where we trimmed our saved penguins with salt for victual all that and the next day, and departed along the coast south-west and by south. On the 30th day we fell with a rock which lieth about five leagues from the land, much like unto Eddystone, which lieth off the sound of Plymouth, and we sounded, and had 8 fathoms rocky ground, within a mile thereof: the rock bearing west-south-west. We went coasting along south-south-west, and found great store of seals all along the coast. This rock standeth in 48 degrees and a-half to the southward of the line.

On the 2nd day of January we fell with a very fair white cape, which standeth in 51 degrees, and had 7 fathoms water a league off the land. On the 3rd day of the aforesaid month we fell with another great white cape, which standeth in 52 degrees and 45 minutes; from which cape there runneth a low beach about a league to the southward, and this beach reacheth to the opening of the dangerous Strait of Magellan, which is in divers places five or six leagues wide, and in two several places more narrow. Under this cape we anchored and lost an anchor, for it was a great storm of foul weather, and lasted three days very dangerous. On the 6th day we put in for the Straits. On the 7th day, between the mouth of the Straits and the narrowest place thereof, we took a Spaniard whose name was Hernando, who was there with twenty-three Spaniards more, which were all that remained of four hundred which were left there three years before in these Straits of Magellan, all the rest being dead with famine. And the same day we passed through the narrowest of the Straits, where the aforesaid Spaniard shewed us the hull of a small barque, which we judged to be a barque called the John Thomas. It is from the mouth of the Straits unto the narrowest of the Straits fourteen leagues, and the course lieth west and by north. The mouth of the Straits standeth in 52 degrees. From the narrowest of the Straits unto Penguin Island is ten leagues, and lieth west-south-west somewhat to the southward, where we anchored on the eighth day, and killed and salted great store of penguins for victuals.

On the 9th day we departed from Penguin Island, and ran south-south-west to King Philip's City, which the Spaniards had built; which town or city had four forts, and every fort had in it one cast piece, which pieces were buried in the ground, the carriages were standing in their places unburied: we digged for them and had them all. They had contrived their city very well, and seated it in the best place of the Straits for wood and water: they had built up their churches by themselves: they had laws very severe among themselves, for they had erected a gibbet, whereon they had done execution upon some of their company. It seemed unto us that the whole living for a great space was altogether upon muscles and limpets, for there was not anything else to be had, except some deer which came out of the mountains down to the fresh rivers to drink. These Spaniards which were there, were only come to fortify the Straits, to the end that no other nation should have passage through into the South Sea, saving only their own; but as it appeared, it was not God's will so to have it. For during the time that they were there, which was two years at the least, they could never have anything to grow or in anywise prosper. And on the other side the Indians oftentimes preyed upon them, until their victuals grew so short (their store being spent which they had brought with them out of Spain, and having no means to renew the same), that they died like dogs in their houses, and in their clothes, wherein we found them still at our coming, until that in the end the town being wonderfully tainted with the smell and the savour of the dead people, the rest which remained alive were driven to bury such things as they had there in their town either for provision or for furniture, and so to forsake the town, and to go along the sea-side, and seek their victuals to preserve them from starving, taking nothing with them, but every man his arquebuse and his furniture that was able to carry it (for some were not able to carry them for weakness) and so lived for the space of a year and more with roots, leaves, and sometimes a fowl which they might kill with their piece. To conclude, they were determined to have travelled towards the River of Plate, only being left alive twenty-three persons, whereof two were women, which were the remainder of four hundred. In this place we watered and wooded well and quietly. Our General named this town Port Famine: it standeth in 53 degrees by observation to the southward.

On the 14th day we departed from this place, and ran south-south-west, and from thence south-west unto Cape Froward, 5 leagues west-south-west, which cape is the southermost part of all the straits, and standeth in the latitude of 54 degrees. From which cape we ran west and by north five leagues, and put into a bay or cove on the south side, which we called Muscle Cove, because there were great store of them: we rode therein six days, the wind being still westerly.

On the 21st of January we departed from Muscle Cove, and went north-west and by west ten leagues to a very fair sandy bay on the north-side, which our General called Elizabeth Bay, and as we rode there that night, one of our men died which went in the Hugh Gallant, whose name was Grey, a carpenter by his occupation, and was buried there in that bay.

On the 22nd day we departed from Elizabeth Bay in the afternoon, and went about two leagues from that place, where there was a fresh water river, where our General went up with the ship-boat about three miles, which river hath very good and pleasant ground about it, and it is low and champaign soil, and so we saw none other ground else in all the straits but that was craggy rocks and monstrous high hills and mountains. In this river are great store of savages, which we saw and had conference with them. They were men-eaters, and fed altogether upon raw flesh and other filthy food; which people had preyed upon some of the Spaniards before spoken of. For they had got knives and pieces of rapiers to make darts of. They used all the means they could possibly to have allured us up farther into the river, of purpose to have betrayed us, which being espied by our General, he caused us to shoot at them with our arquebuses, whereby we killed many of them. So we sailed from this river to the Channel of St. Jerome, which is two leagues off.

From the river of Saint Jerome about three or four leagues we ran west unto a cape which is on the north side; and from that cape into the mouth of the Straits the course lieth north-west and by west and north-east. Between which place and the mouth of the Straits to the southward we lay in harbour until the 23rd of February, by reason of contrary winds and most vile and filthy foul weather, with such rain and vehement stormy winds, which came down from the mountains and high hills, that they hazarded the best cables and anchors that we had for to hold, which if they had failed we had been in great danger to have been cast away, or at the least famished. For during this time, which was a full month, we fed almost altogether upon muscles, and limpets, and birds, or such as we could get on shore, seeking every day for them, as the fowls of the air do, where they can find food, in continual rainy weather. There is at every mile or two miles' end a harbour on both sides of the land. And there are, between the river of Saint Jerome and the mouth of the Straits going into the South Sea about thirty-four leagues by estimation: so that the length of the whole Straits is about ninety leagues. And the said mouth of the Straits standeth in the same height that the entrance standeth in when we pass out of the North Sea, which is about fifty-two degrees and two-thirds to the southward of the line.

On the 24th of February we entered into the South Sea; and on the south side of the going out of the Straits is a fair high cape with a low point adjoining unto it; and on the north side are four or five islands which lie six leagues off the main, and much broken and sunken ground about them. By noon the same day we had brought these islands east of us five leagues off, the wind being southerly. On the 1st of March a storm took us at north, which night the ships lost the company of the Hugh Gallant, being in forty-nine and a-half, and forty-five leagues from the land. This storm continued three or four days, and for that time we in the Hugh Gallant, being separated from the other two ships, looked every hour to sink, our barque was so leak and ourselves so dilvered and weakened with freeing it of water, that we slept not in three days and three nights.

On the 15th of March, in the morning, the Hugh Gallant came in between the Island of St. Mary and the main, where she met with the Admiral and the Content, which had rid at the island called La Mocha two days, which standeth in the southerly latitude of 38 degrees; at which place some of our men went on shore with the Vice-Admiral's boat, where the Indians fought with them with their bows and arrows, and were marvellous wary of their calivers. These Indians were enemies to the Spaniards, and belonged to a great place called Arauco, and took us for Spaniards, as afterward we learned. This place which is called Arauco is wonderful rich and full of gold-mines, and yet could it not be subdued at any time by the Spaniards, but they always returned with the greatest loss of men. For these Indians are marvellous desperate and careless of their lives to live at their own liberty and freedom.

On the 15th day aforesaid, in the afternoon, we weighed anchor and ran under the west side of St. Mary Island, where we rid very well in six fathoms water and very fair ground all that night. On the 16th day our General went on shore himself with seventy or eighty men, everyone with his furniture. There came down to us certain Indians with two which were the principals of the island to welcome us on shore, thinking we had been Spaniards, for it is subdued by them, who brought us up to a place where the Spaniards had erected a church with crosses and altars in it. And there were about this church two or three storehouses, which were full of wheat and barley ready threshed and made up in cades of straw to the quantity of a bushel of corn in every cade. The wheat and barley was as fair, as clean, and everyway as good as any we have in England. There were also the like cades full of potato roots, which were very good to eat, ready made up in the storehouses for the Spaniards against they should come for their tribute. This island also yieldeth many sorts of fruits, hogs, and hens. These Indians are held in such slavery by them that they dare not eat a hen or a hog themselves. But the Spaniards have made them all in that island Christians. Thus we fitted ourselves here with corn as much as we would have, and as many hogs as we had salt to powder them withal, and great store of hens, with a number of bags of potato roots, and about 500 dried dog-fishes, and Guinea wheat, which is called maize. And, having taken as much as we would have, yet we left marvellous great store behind us. Our General had the two principals of the island aboard our ship, and provided great cheer for them, and made them merry with wine; and they in the end perceiving us to be no Spaniards, made signs, as near as our General could perceive, that if we would go over unto the mainland unto Arauco, that there was much gold, making us signs that we should have great store of riches. But because we could not understand them our General made some haste, and within two or three days we furnished ourselves.

On the 18th day, in the morning, we departed from this place, and ran all that day north-north-east about ten leagues, and at night lay with a short sail off and on the coast. On the 19th we ran in east-north-east with the land, and bare in with a place called The Conception, where we anchored under an island, and departed the next morning without going on land. On the 20th we departed from The Conception, and went into a little bay which was sandy, where we saw fresh water and cattle, but we stayed not there.

On the 30th day we came into the Bay of Quintero, which standeth in 33 degrees and 50 minutes. On the said day, presently after we were come to an anchor in the bay, there was a neatherd, or one that kept cattle, which lay upon the point of the hill asleep, which, when he awaked and had espied three ships which were come into the bay, before we could get on shore, he had caught a horse which was feeding by and rode his way as fast as ever he might; and our General, with thirty shot with him, went on shore. He had not been on land one hour but there came three horsemen with bright swords towards us so hard as they might ride, until they came within some twenty or thirty score of us, and so stayed, and would come no nearer unto us. So our General sent unto them a couple of our men with their shot, and one Fernando, which was the Spaniard that we had taken up at the mouth of the Straits, which was one of the 400 that were starved there. But the Spaniards would not suffer our men to come near with their shot, but made signs that one of our men should come alone unto them; so the said Fernando, the Spaniard, went unto them, and our two men stood not far from them. They had great conference, and in the end Fernando came back from them and told our General that he had parleyed with them for some victuals, who had promised as much as we would have. Our General sent him back again with another message and another shot with him; and, being come near unto them, they would not suffer any more than one to approach them; whereupon our men let the Spaniard go unto them alone himself, who, being some good distance from them, they stayed but a small time together but that the said Fernando leaped up behind one of them and rid away with them, for all his deep and damnable oaths which he had made continually to our General and all his company never to forsake him, but to die on his side before he would be false. Our General, seeing how he was dealt withal, filled water all that day with good watch and carried it aboard; and, night being come, he determined the next day to send into the country to find their town, and to have taken the spoil of it, and to have fired it if they could have found it.

On the last of March Captain Havers went up into the country with fifty or sixty men with their shot and furniture with them, and we travelled seven or eight miles into the land; and as we were marching along we espied a number of herds of cattle, of kine and bullocks, which were wonderful wild. We saw, also, great store of horses, mares, and colts, which were very wild and unhandled. There is also great store of hares and coneys, and plenty of partridges and other wild fowls. The country is very fruitful, with fair, fresh rivers all along full of wild fowl of all sorts. Having travelled so far that we could go no further for the monstrous high mountains, we rested ourselves at a very fair, fresh river running in and along fair low meadows at the foot of the mountains, where every man drunk of the river and refreshed themselves. Having so done, we returned to our ships the likest way that we thought their town should be. So we travelled all the day long, not seeing any man, but we met with many wild dogs. Yet there were two hundred horsemen abroad that same day by means of the Spaniard which they had taken the day before from us, who had told them that our force was but small, and that we were wonderfully weak;

who, though they did espy us that day, yet durst they not give the on-set upon us. For we marched along in array, and observed good order, whereby we seemed a great number more than we were, until we came unto our ships that night again.

The next day, being the 1st of April, 1587, our men went on shore to fill water at a pit which was a quarter of a mile from the water's side; and being early hard at their business were in no readiness. In which meanwhile there came pouring down from the hills almost 200 horsemen, and before our people could return to the rocks from the watering-place, twelve of them were cut off, part killed and part taken prisoners, the rest were rescued by our soldiers, which came from the rocks to meet with them, who being but fifteen of us that had any weapons on shore, yet we made the enemy retire in the end with loss of some twenty-four of their men, after we had skirmished with them an hour.

The names of our men that were slain were these :—Thomas Lucas, of London, soldier; Richard Wheeler, of London; Robert Pitcher, of Norfolk, soldier; John Langston, of Gloucestershire; William Kingman, of Dorsetshire, soldier; William Hilles, of Cornwall, out of the Admiral. William Byet of Weymouth; Laurence Gamesby, of Newcastle, killed out of the Vice-Admiral. Henry Blackenals, of Weymouth; William Stevens, of Plymouth, gunner; William Pitte, of Sherborne, in Dorsetshire; Humphrey Derricke, of London, killed out of the Hugh Gallant. After the loss of these men we rid in the road, and watered in despite of them with good watch and ward, until the fifth of the said month. On the fifth day we departed out of this bay of Quintero, and off from the bay there lieth a little island about a league distant, whereon there are great store of penguins and other fowls; whereof we took to serve our turns, and sailed away north, and north and by west : for so lieth the coast along in this place.

On the 15th we came thwart of a place which is called Moro Moreno, which standeth in twenty-three degrees and a-half, and is an excellent good harbour; and there is an island which maketh it an harbour, and a ship may go in at either end of the island. Here we went with our General on shore to the number of thirty men; and at our going on shore upon our landing, the Indians of the place came down from the rocks to meet with us, with fresh water and wood on their backs. They are in mar-
•vellous awe of the Spaniards, and very simple people, and live marvellous savagely; for they brought us to their bidings about

two miles from the harbour, where we saw their women and lodging, which is nothing but the skin of some beast laid upon the ground; and over them instead of houses, is nothing but five or six sticks laid across, which stand upon two forks with sticks on the ground, and a few boughs laid on it. Their diet is raw fish, which stinketh most vilely; and when any of them die, they bury their bows and arrows with them, with their canoe and all that they have; for we opened one of their graves, and saw the order of them. Their canoes or boats are marvellous artificially made of two skins like unto bladders, and are blown full at one end with quills. They have two of these bladders blown full, which are sewn together and made fast with a sinew of some wild beast, which when they are in the water swell, so that they are as tight as may be. They go to sea in these boats, and catch very much fish with them, and pay much of it for tribute unto the Spaniards; but they use it marvellous beastly.

On the 23rd in the morning we took a small barque which came out of Arica road, which we kept and called the George; the men forsook it, and went away with their boat. Our Admiral's pinnace followed the boat, and the Hugh Gallant's boat took the barque. Our Admiral's pinnace could not recover the boat before it got on shore, but went along into the road of Arica, and laid aboard a great ship of a hundred tons, riding in the road right afore the town, but all the men and goods were gone out of it, only the bare ship was left alone. They made three or four very fair shots at the pinnace as she was coming in, but missed her very narrowly with a minion shot which they had in the fort. Whereupon we came into the road with the Admiral and the Hugh Gallant; but the Content, which was Vice-Admiral, was behind out of sight, by means whereof, and for want of her boat to land men withal, we landed not; otherwise if we had been together our General with the company would resolutely have landed to take the town, whatsoever had come of it. The cause why the Content stayed behind was, that she had found about fourteen leagues to the southward of Arica, in a place where the Spaniards had landed, a whole ship's lading of botijas of wine of Castile, whereof the said Content took into her as many as she could conveniently carry, and came after us into the road of Arica the same day. By this time we perceived that the town had gathered all their power together, and also had conveyed all their treasure away, and buried it before we were come near the town, for they had heard of us.

Now because it was very populous with the aid of one or two places up in the land, our General saw there was no landing without the loss of many men, wherefore he gave over that enterprise. While we rid in the road they shot at us, and our ships shot at them again for every shot two. Moreover our pinnace went in hard almost to the shore, and fetched out another barque which rid there in despite of all their forts though they shot still at the pinnace, which they could never hit. After these things our General sent a boat on shore with a flag of truce to know if they would redeem their great ship or no; but they would not, for they had received special commandment from the Viceroy from Lima, not to buy any ship, nor to ransom any man upon pain of death. Our General did this in hope to have redeemed some of our men, which were taken prisoners on shore by the horsemen at Quintero, otherwise he would have made them no offer of parley.

On the 25th, riding still in the said road, we espied a sail coming from the southward, and our General sent out his pinnace to meet her, with all our boats; but the town made such signs from the hill with fires and tokens out of the watch-house, that before our pinnace could get to them, they ran the barque on shore two miles to the southward of the town; but they had small leisure to carry anything with them, but all the men escaped; among whom were certain friars, for we saw them in their friar's weeds as they ran on shore; many horsemen came from the town to rescue them, and to carry them away, otherwise we had landed and taken or killed them. So we went aboard the barque as she lay sunk, and fetched out the pillage; but there was nothing in it of any value, and came aboard our ships again the same night, and the next morning we set the great ship on fire in the road, and sunk one of the barques, and carried the other along with us, and so departed from thence and went away north-west.

On the 27th day we took a small barque, which came from Santiago, near unto Quintero, where we lost our men first. In this barque was one George, a Greek, a reasonable pilot for all the coast of Chili. They were sent to the city of Lima with letters of advice of us, and of the loss of our men. There were also in the said barque one Fleming and three Spaniards, and they were all sworn and received the sacrament before they came to sea by three or four friars, that if we should chance to meet them, they should throw those letters overboard, which (as we were giving them chase with our pinnace) before we could fetch them up, they had accordingly thrown away. Yet our General wrought so with them that they did confess it; but he was fain to cause them to be tormented with their thumbs in a wrench, and to continue them at several times with extreme pain. Also he made the old Fleming believe that he would hang him, and the rope being about his neck he was pulled up a little from the hatches, and yet he would not confess, choosing rather to die, than he would be perjured. In the end it was confessed by one of the Spaniards, whereupon we burnt the barque, and carried the men with us.

On the 3rd of May we came into a bay where are three little towns, which are called Paracca, Chincha, and Pisca, where some of us landed and took certain houses, wherein was bread, wine, figs, and hens; but the sea went so high, that we could not land at the best of the towns without sinking of our boats, and great hazard of us all. This place standeth in thirteen degrees and two-thirds to the southward of the line. On the 5th of May we departed from this harbour, leaving the Content, our Vice-Admiral, within at an island of seals, by which means at that time we lost her company. On the 9th we gave chase to a sail, namely, our Admiral, the Hugh Gallant, and the George, which we had taken before coming out of the road of Arica: the Content, which was our Vice-Admiral, being still lost; but we could not fetch it. The George made after it, but lost it that night. On the 10th day the Hugh Gallant (in which barque I Francis Pretty was) left company of our Admiral.

On the 11th we which were in the Hugh Gallant put into a bay which standeth in twelve degrees and two-thirds, in which bay we found a river of fresh water about eight o'clock at night, and though we were but of small force, and no more but one barque and eighteen men in it, yet we went on shore to fill water; where, having filled one boat's lading, while our boat was in going aboard, two or three of our company which were on shore, as they were going a little from the watering-place with their furniture about them, espied where there were 400 or 500 bags of meal on a heap covered with a few reeds. So that night we filled water and took as much meal as we thought good; which fell out well for us that were then lost and stood in need of victuals, and by break of day in the morning we came aboard, and there stayed and rode until the afternoon. In which

T

mean time the town seeing us ride there still, brought down much cattle to the sea-side to have enticed us to come on shore, but we saw their intent, and weighed anchor and departed the 12th day.

On the 13th day at night we put into a bay which standeth in nine degrees and a third, where we saw horsemen; and that night we landed, namely, Mr. Brewer, captain, myself Francis Pretty, Arthur Warford, John Way, Preacher, John Newman, Andrew White, William Gargefield, and Henry Hilliard. And we eight only, having every man his arquebuse and his furniture about him, marched three-quarters of a mile along the sea-side, where we found a boat of five or six tons haled up dry on the shore about a cable's length from the water; and with extreme labour we launched the barque: when it was on float, Captain Brewer and I went in, while the rest of our company were fetching their things; but suddenly it was ready to sink. And the captain and I stood up to the knees lading out water with our targets: but it sunk down faster than we were able to free it, insomuch as in the end we had much ado to save ourselves from drowning. When we were out, we stood in great fear that our own boat wherein we came on shore was sunk; for we could nowhere see it. Howbeit the captain commanded them to keep it off, for fear of the great surge that went by the shore. Yet in the end we spied it, and went aboard by two and two, and were driven to wade up to the arm-holes sixty paces into the sea before we could get into the boat, by reason of the shoalness; and then departed the 14th day in the morning.

On the 16th we took with the Hugh Gallant, being but sixteen men of us in it, a great ship which came from Guaiaquil, which was called The Lewis, and was of the burthen of three hundred tons, having four-and-twenty men in it, wherein was. pilot one Gonsalvo de Ribas, whom we carried along with us, and a negro called Emmanuel. The ship was laden with nothing but timber and victuals; wherefore we left her seven leagues from the land very leak and ready to sink in seven degrees to the southward of the line; we sunk her boat and took away her foresail and certain victuals.

On the 17th of May we met with our admiral again, and all the rest of our fleet. They had taken two ships, the one laden with sugar, molasses, maize, cordovan-skins, montego de Porco, many packs of pintados, many Indian coats, and some marmalade, and one thousand hens; and the other ship was laden with wheat-meal and boxes of marmalade. One of these ships which had the chief merchandise in it, was worth twenty thousand pounds, if it had been in England or in any other place of Christendom where we might have sold it. We filled all our ships with as much as we could bestow of these goods; the rest we burnt and the ships also; and set the men and women that were not killed on shore.

On the 20th day in the morning we came into the road of Paita, and being at an anchor, our General landed with sixty or seventy men, skirmished with them of the town, and drove them all to flight to the top of the hill which is over the town, except a few slaves and some other which were of the meaner sort, who were commanded by the governors to stay below in the town, at a place which is in building for a fort, having with them a bloody ensign, being in number about one hundred men. Now as we were rowing between the ships and the shore, our gunner shot off a great piece out of one of the barques, and the shot fell among them, and drove them to fly from the fort as fast as they might run, who got them up upon a hill, and from thence shot among us with their small shot. After we were landed and had taken the town, we ran upon them, and chased them so fiercely up the hills for the space of an hour, that we drove them in the end away perforce, and being got up the hills, we found where they had laid all their stuff which they had brought out of the town, and had hidden it there upon the mountains. We also found the quantity of twenty-five pounds weight in silver in pieces of eight reals, and abundance of household stuff and storehouses full of all kinds of wares; but our General would not suffer any man to carry much cloth or apparel away, because they should not cloy themselves with burdens; for he knew not whether our enemies were provided with furniture according to the number of their men; for they were five men to one of us; and we had an English mile and a-half to our ships. Thus we came down in safety to the town, which was very well builded, and marvellous clean kept in every street, with a town-house or Guildhall in the midst, and had to the number of two hundred houses at the least in it. We set it on fire to the ground, and goods to the value of five or six thousand pounds; there was also a barque riding in the road which we set on fire, and departed, directing our course to the Island of Puna.

On the 25th of May we arrived at the Island of Puna, where

is a very good harbour, where we found a great ship of the burden of 250 tons riding at an anchor with all her furniture, which was ready to be hauled on ground; for there is a special good place for that purpose. We sunk it, and went on shore where the lord of the island dwelt, which was by the waterside, who had a sumptuous house, marvellous well contrived, with very many singular good rooms and chambers in it; and out of every chamber was framed a gallery with a stately prospect into the sea on the one side, and into the island on the other side, with a marvellous great hall below, and a very great storehouse at the other end of the hall, which was filled with botijas of pitch and bash, to make cables withal; for the most part of the cables of the South Sea are made upon that island. This great Cacique doth make all the Indians upon the island to work and to drudge for him; and he himself is an Indian born, but is married to a marvellous fair woman which is a Spaniard, by reason of his pleasant habitation and of his great wealth.

This Spanish woman his wife is honoured as a Queen in the Island, and never goeth on the ground upon her feet; but holdeth it too base a thing for her. But when her pleasure is to take the air, or to go abroad, she is always carried in a shadow like unto a horse-litter upon four men's shoulders, with a veil or canopy over her for the sun or the wind, having her gentlewomen still attending about her, with a great troop of the best men of the island with her. But both she and the lord of the island with all the Indians in the town were newly fled out of the island before we could get to an anchor, by reason we were becalmed before we could get in, and were gone over unto the mainland, having carried away with them to the sum of 100,000 crowns, which we knew by a captain of the island, an Indian, which was left there with some other upon the island under him, whom we had taken at sea as we were coming into the road, being in a balsa or canoe for a spy to see what we were.

On the 27th our General himself with certain shot and some targeteers went over into the main into the place where this aforesaid Indian captain which we had taken had told us that the Cacique, which was the lord of the island, was gone unto, and had carried all his treasure with him; but at our coming to the place which we went to land at, we found newly arrived there four or five great balsas, which were laden with plantains, bags of meal, and many other kinds of victuals. Our General marvelled what they were and what they meant, asking the Indian guide and commanding him to speak the truth upon his life; being then bound fast, he answered being very much abashed, as well as our company were, that he neither knew from whence they should come, nor who they should be; for there was never a man in any one of the balsas; and because he had told our General before, that it was an easy matter to take the said Cacique and all his treasure, and that there were but three or four houses standing in a desert place and no resistance, and that if he found it not so he should hang him. Again, being demanded to speak upon his life what he thought these balsas should be, he answered that he could not say from whence they should come, except it were to bring sixty soldiers, which he did hear were to go to a place called Guaiaquil, which was about six leagues from the said island, where two or three of the king's ships were on the stocks in building, where are continually an hundred soldiers in garrisons who had heard of us, and had sent for sixty more for fear of burning of the ships and town. Our General not any whit discouraged either at the sight of the balsas unlooked for, or for hearing of the threescore soldiers not until then spoken of, with a brave courage animating his company in the exploit, went presently forward, being in the night in a most desert path in the woods, until such time as he came to the place; where, as it seemed, they had kept watch either at the waterside, or at the houses, or else at both, and were newly gone out of the houses, having so short warning, that they left their meat both boiling and roasting at the fire and were fled with their treasure with them, or else buried it where it could not be found, being also in the night. Our company took hens and such things as we thought good, and came away.

On the 29th day of May our General went in the ship's-boat into a little island thereby, whereas the said Cacique which was the lord of Puna had caused all the hangings of his chambers, which were of cordovan leather all gilded over, and painted very fair and rich, with all his household stuff, and all the ship's tackling which was riding in the road at our coming in, with great store of nails, spikes of iron, and very many other things to be conveyed; all of which we found, and brought away what our General thought requisite for the ship's business.

This island is very pleasant for all things requisite, and fruitful; but there are no mines of gold nor silver in it. There are at the least two hundred houses in the town about the Cacique's palace, and as many in one or two towns more upon the island, which is almost as big as the Isle of Wight, in England. There is planted on the one side of the Cacique's house a fair garden, with all herbs growing in it, and at the lower end a well of fresh water, and round about it are trees set, whereon bombasin cotton groweth after this manner. The tops of the trees grow full of cods, out of which the cotton groweth, and in the cotton is a seed of the bigness of a pea, and in every cod there are seven or eight of these seeds; and if the cotton be not gathered when it is ripe, then these seeds fall from it, and spring again. There are also in this garden fig-trees which bear continually, also pompions, melons, cucumbers, radishes, rosemary, and thyme, with many other herbs and fruits. At the other end of the house there is also another orchard, where grow oranges sweet and sour, lemons, pomegranates and limes, with divers other fruits.

There is very good pasture ground in this island; and withal many horses, oxen, bullocks, sheep very fat and fair, great store of goats, which be very tame, and are used continually to be milked. They have moreover abundance of pigeons, turkeys, and ducks of a marvellous bigness. There was also a very large and great church hard by the Cacique's house, whither he caused all the Indians in the island to come and hear mass; for he himself was made a Christian when he was married to the Spanish woman before spoken of, and upon his conversion he caused the rest of his subjects to be christened. In this church was an high altar with a crucifix, and five bells hanging in the nether end thereof. We burnt the church and brought the bells away. By this time we had hauled on ground our Admiral, and had made her clean, burnt her keel, pitched and tarred her, and had hauled her on float again; and in the meanwhile continually kept watch and ward in the great house both night and day.

On the 2nd day of June in the morning, by-and-by after break of day, every one of the watch being gone abroad to seek to fetch in victuals, some one way, some another, some for hens, some for sheep, some for goats, upon the sudden there came down upon us a hundred Spanish soldiers with muskets and an ensign, which were landed on the other side of the island that night, and all the Indians of the island with them, everyone with weapons and their baggage after them; which was by means of a negro, whose name was Emmanuel, which fled from us at our first landing there.

Thus being taken at advantage we had the worst; for our company was not past sixteen or twenty; whereof they had slain one or two before they were come to the houses; yet we skirmished with them an hour and a-half; at the last being sore overcharged with multitudes, we were driven down from the hill to the water-side, and there kept them play awhile, until in the end Zacharie Saxie, who with his halberd had kept the way of the hill, and slain a couple of them, as he breathed himself, being somewhat tired, had an honourable death and a short; for a shot struck him to the heart; who feeling himself mortally wounded, cried to God for mercy, and fell down presently dead. But soon after the enemy was driven somewhat to retire from the bank-side to the green; and in the end our boat came and carried as many of our men away as could go in her, which was in hazard of sinking while they hastened into it. And one of our men whose name was Robert Maddocke, was shot through the head with his own piece, being a snap-hance, as he was hastening into the boat. But four of us were left behind, which the boat could not carry; to wit, myself Francis Pretty, Thomas Andrewes, Steven Gunner, and Richard Rose; which had our shot ready and retired ourselves unto a cliff, until the boat came again, which was presently after they had carried the rest aboard. There were forty-six of the enemy slain by us, whereof they had dragged some into bushes, and some into old houses, which we found afterwards. We lost twelve men in manner following:—Zacharie Saxie, Neales Johnson, William Gargefield, Nicholas Hendy, Henry Cooper, slain by the enemy; Robert Maddock, killed with his piece; Henry Mawdley, burnt; Edward, the gunner's-man, Ambrose, the musician, drowned; Walter Tilliard, Edward Smith, Henry Aselye, taken prisoners.

The self-same day, being the 2nd of June, we went on shore again with seventy men, and had a fresh skirmish with the enemies, and drove them to retire, being a hundred Spaniards serving with muskets, and two hundred Indians with bows, arrows, and darts. This done, we set fire on the town and burnt it to the ground, having in it to the number of three hundred houses; and shortly after made havoc of their fields, orchards, and gardens, and burnt four great ships more which were in building on the stocks. On the 3rd of June, the Content, which was our Vice-Admiral, was hauled on ground to grave at the same place in despite of the Spaniards, and also our pinnace, which the Spaniards had burnt, was new trimmed. On the 5th of June we departed out of the road of Puna, where we had remained eleven days, and turned up for a place which is called Rio Dolce, where we watered; at which place also we sunk our Rear-Admiral called the Hugh Gallant, for want of men, being a barque of 40 tons. On the 10th day of the same month we set the Indians on shore, which we had taken before in Abalsa, as we were coming into the road of Puna. On the 11th day we departed with the said Rio Dolce. On the 12th of June we doubled the equinoctial line, and continued our course northward all that month.

On the 1st of July we had sight of the coast of Nueva España, being four leagues distant from land in the latitude of 10 degrees to the northward of the line. On the 9th of July we took a new ship of the burden of 120 tons, wherein was one Michael Sancius, whom our General took to serve his turn to water along the coast; for he was one of the best coasters in the South sea. This Michael Sancius was a Provençal, born in Marseilles, and was the first man that told us news of the great ship called the Santa Anna, which we afterwards took coming from the Philippines. There were six men more in this new ship; we took her sails, her ropes, and fire-wood, to serve our turn, set her on fire, and kept the men. On the 10th day we took another barque which was going with advice of us and our ships all along the coast, as Michael Sancius told us; but all the company that were in the barque were fled on shore. None of both these ships had any goods in them. For they came both from Sonsonate, in the province of Guatimala; the new ship, for fear we should have taken her in the road, and the barque, to carry news of us along the coast; which barque also we set on fire.

On the 26th of July we came to an anchor at 10 fathoms in the river of Copalita, where we made account to water. And the same night we departed with thirty men in the pinnace, and rowed to Aguatulco, which is but two leagues from the aforesaid river; and standeth in 15 degrees 40 minutes to the northward of the equinoctial line.

On the 27th, in the morning by the break of day, we came into the road of Aguatulco, where we found a barque of 50 tons, which was come from Sonsonate laden with cocoas and anile, which they had there landed; and the men were all fled on shore. We landed there and burnt their town, with the church and custom-house, which was very fair and large; in which house were 600 bags of anile to dye cloth, every bag whereof was worth forty crowns; and

400 bags of cocoas, every bag whereof is worth ten crowns. These cocoas go among them for meat and money; for 150 of them are in value one real of plate in ready payment. They are very like unto an almond, but are nothing so pleasant in taste; they eat them and make drink of them. This the owner of the ship told us. I found in this town before we burnt it, a flasket full of boxes of balm. After we had spoilt and burnt the town, wherein there were some hundred houses, the owner of the ship came down out of the hills with a flag of truce unto us, which before with the rest of all the townsmen was run away at our first coming, and at length came aboard our pinnace upon Captain Haver's word of safe return. We carried him to the river of Copalita where our ships rode; and when he came to our General he caused him to be set on shore in safety the same night, because he came upon the captain's word. On the 28th day we set sail from Copalita, because the sea was so great there that we could not fill water, and ran the same night into the road of Aguatulco. On the 29th our General landed and went on shore with thirty men two miles into the woods, where we took a Mestizo, whose name was Michael de Truxillo, who was customer of that town, and we found with him two chambers full of his stuff; we brought him and his stuff aboard. And whereas I say he was a Mestizo, it is to be understood that a Mestizo is one which hath a Spaniard to his father and an Indian to his mother.

On the 2nd of August we had watered and examined the said Mestizo, and set him on shore again, and departed from the port of Aguatulco the same night, which standeth, as I said before, in 15 degrees and 40 minutes to the northward of the line.

Here we overslipped the haven of Acapulco, from whence the ships are set forth for the Philippines. On the 24th of August our General, with thirty of us, went with the pinnace unto an haven called Puerto de Natividad, where we had intelligence by Michael Sancius that there should be a pinnace; but before we could get thither the said pinnace was gone to fish for pearls twelve leagues further, as we were informed by certain Indians which we found there. We took a mulatto in this place in his bed, which was sent with letters of advice concerning us along the coast of Nueva Galicia, whose horse we killed, took his letters, left him behind, set fire on the houses, and burnt two new ships of 200 tons the piece which were in building there on the stocks, and came aboard of our ships again. On the 26th of August we came into the bay of Santiago, where we watered at a fresh river, along which river many plantains are growing. Here is great abundance of fresh fish. Here, also, certain of our company dragged for pearls and caught some quantity.

On the 2nd of September we departed from Santiago at four o'clock in the evening. This bay of Santiago standeth in 19 degrees and 18 minutes to the northward of the line. On the 3rd of September we arrived in a little bay, a league to the westward off Port de Navidad, called Malacca, which is a very good place to ride in. And the same day, about twelve o'clock, our General landed with thirty men or thereabout, and went up to a town of Indians which was two leagues from the road, which town is called Acatlan. There were in it about twenty or thirty houses and a church, which we defaced, and came aboard again the same night. All the people were fled out of the town at the sight of us. On the 4th of September we departed from the road of Malacca and sailed along the coast.

On the 8th we came to the road of Chaccalla, in which bay there are two little houses by the water's side. This bay is eighteen leagues from the Cape de los Corrientes. On the 9th, in the morning, our General sent up Captain Havers with forty men of us before day, and, Michael Sancius being our guide, we went unto a place about two leagues up into the country in a most villainous desert path through the woods and wilderness, and in the end we came to a place where we took three householders with their wives and children and some Indians, one carpenter, which was a Spaniard, and a Portugal; we bound them all and made them to come to the seaside with us. Our General made their wives to fetch us plantains, lemons, and oranges, pineapples, and other fruits, whereof they had abundance, and so let their husbands depart, except Sembrano, the Spanish carpenter, and Diego, the Portugal; and the tenth day we departed the road. On the 12th day we arrived at a little island called the Island of Saint Andrew, on which there is great store of fowl and wood, where we dried and salted as many of the fowls as we thought good. We also killed there abundance of seals and iguanos, which are a kind of serpents, with four feet, and a long, sharp tail, strange to them which have not seen them; but they are very good meat. We rode here until the 17th day, at which time we departed.

On the 24th day we arrived in the road of Massatlan, which

standeth in 23½ degrees, just under the tropic of Cancer. It is a very great river within, but is barred at the mouth; and upon the north side of the bar without is good fresh water; but there is very evil filling of it, because at a low water it is shoaled half a mile off the shore. There is great store of fresh fish in that bay, and good fruits up into the country, whereof we had some, though not without danger.

On the 27th of September we departed from the road of Massatlan, and ran to an island which is a league to the northward the said Massatlan, where we trimmed our ships and new built our pinnace; and there is a little island a quarter of a league from it, on which are seals, where a Spanish prisoner, whose name was Domingo, being sent to wash shirts with one of our men to keep him, made a scape and swam to the main, which was an English mile distant, at which place we had seen thirty or forty Spaniards and Indians, which were horsemen and kept watch there, which came from a town called Chiametla, which was eleven leagues up into the country, as Michael Sancius told us. We found upon the island where we trimmed our pinnace fresh water by the assistance of God in that our great need by digging two or three foot deep in the sand, where no water nor sign of water was before to be perceived. Otherwise we had gone back twenty or thirty leagues to water, which might have been occasion that we might have missed our prey we had long waited for. But God raised one Flores, a Spaniard, which was also a prisoner with us, to make a motion to dig in the sands. Now our General, having had experience once before of the like, commanded to put his motion in practice, and in digging three foot deep we found very good and fresh water. So we watered our ships, and might have filled a thousand tuns more if we had would. We stayed in this island until the 9th of October, at which time we departed at night for the Cape of St. Lucar, which is on the west side of the point of California.

On the 14th of October we fell with the Cape of St. Lucar, which cape is very like the Needles at the Isle of Wight; and within the said cape is a great bay, called by the Spaniards Aguada Segura, into which bay falleth a fair fresh river, about which many Indians use to keep. We watered in the river, and lay off and on from the said Cape of St. Lucar until the 4th of November, and had the winds hanging still westerly.

On the 4th of November the Desire and the Content, wherein

were the number of   Englishmen only living, beating up and down upon the headland of California, which standeth in 23⅔ degrees to the northward ; between seven and eight o'clock in the morning one of the company of our admiral, which was the trumpeter of the ship, going up into the top, espied a sail bearing in from the sea with the cape; whereupon he cried out, with no small joy to himself and the whole company, "A sail! a sail!" with which cheerful word the master of the ship and divers others of the company went also up into the maintop; who, perceiving the speech to be very true, gave information unto our General of these happy news, who was no less glad than the cause required; whereupon he gave in charge presently unto the whole company to put all things in readiness, which being performed, he gave them chase some three or four hours, standing with our best advantage and working for the wind. In the afternoon we gat up unto them, giving them the broadside with our great ordnance and a volley of small shot, and presently laid the ship aboard, whereof the King of Spain was owner, which was Admiral of the South Sea, called the Santa Anna, and thought to be 700 tons in burthen. Now, as we were ready on their ship's side to enter her, being not past fifty or sixty men at the uttermost in our ship, we perceived that the Captain of the said ship had made fights fore and aft, and laid their sails close on their poop, their midship, with their forecastle, and having not one man to be seen, stood close under their fights, with lances, javelins, rapiers, and targets, and an innumerable sort of great stones, which they threw overboard upon our heads and into our ship so fast, and being so many of them, that they put us off the ship again with the loss of two of our men, which were slain, and with the hurting of four or five. But for all this we new trimmed our sails, and fitted every man his furniture, and gave them a fresh encounter with our great ordnance and also with our small shot, raking them through and through, to the killing and maiming of many of their men. Their Captain still, like a valiant man, with his company, stood very stoutly unto his close fights, not yielding as yet. Our General, encouraging his men afresh with the whole noise of trumpets, gave them the third encounter with our great ordnance and all our small shot, to the great discomforting of our enemies, raking them through in divers places, killing and spoiling many of their men. They being thus discomforted and spoiled, and their ship being in hazard of sinking by reason of the great shot which were made, whereof some were under water, within five or six hours' fight set out a flag of truce and parleyed for mercy, desiring our General to save their lives and to take their goods, and they would presently yield. Our General, of his goodness, promised them mercy, and willed them to strike their sails, and to hoise out their boat and to come aboard, which news they were full glad to hear of, and presently struck their sails, hoised their boat out, and one of their chief merchants came aboard unto our General, and, falling down upon his knees, offered to have kissed our General's feet, and craved mercy. Our General most graciously pardoned both him and the rest upon promise of their true dealing with him and his company concerning such riches as were in the ship; and sent for the Captain and their pilot, who, at their coming, used the like duty and reverence as the former did. The General, of his great mercy and humanity, promised their lives and good usage. The said Captain and pilot presently certified the General what goods they had within board—to wit, an hundred and twenty-two thousand pesos of gold; and the rest of the riches that the ship was laden with was in silks, satins, damasks, with musk and divers other merchandise, and great store of all manner of victuals, with the choice of many conserves of all sorts for to eat, and sundry sorts of very good wines. These things being made known to the General by the aforesaid captain and pilot, they were commanded to stay aboard the Desire, and on the 6th of November following we went into a harbour which is called by the Spaniards Aguada Segura or Puerto Seguro.

Here the whole company of the Spaniards, both of men and women to the number of 190 persons, were set on shore, where they had a fair river of fresh water, with great store of fresh fish, fowl, and wood, and also many hares and coneys upon the main land. Our general also gave them great store of victuals, of garvansas, peason, and some wine. Also they had all the sails of their ship to make them tents on shore, with licence to take such store of planks as should be sufficient to make them a barque. Then we fell to hoising in of our goods, sharing of the treasure, and allotting to every man his portion. In division whereof, the eighth of this money, many of the company fell into a mutiny against our General, especially those which were in the Content, which nevertheless were after a sort pacified for the time.

On the 17th day of November, which is the day of the happy Coronation of Her Majesty, our General commanded all his ordnance to be shot off, with the small shot both in his own ship where himself went, and also in the Content, which was our Vice-Admiral. This being done, the same night we had many fireworks and more ordnance discharged, to the great admiration of all the Spaniards which were there; for the most part of them had never seen the like before.

This ended, our General discharged the Captain, gave him a royal reward, with provision for his defence against the Indians, and his company, both of swords, targets, pieces, shot, and powder to his great contentment; but before his departure, he took out of this great ship two young lads born in Japan, which could both write and read their own language, the eldest being about twenty years old was named Christopher, the other was called Cosmus, about seventeen years of age, both of very good capacity. He took also with him out of their ship, three boys born in the islands of Manilla, the one about fifteen, the other about thirteen, and the youngest about nine years old. The name of the eldest was Alphonso, the second Anthony de Dasi, the third remaineth with the Right Honourable the Countess of Essex. He also took from them one Nicholas Roderigo, a Portugal, who hath not only been in Canton and other parts of China, but also in the islands of Japan, being a country most rich in silver mines, and hath also been in the Philippines.

He took also from them a Spaniard, whose name was Thomas de Ersola, which was a very good pilot from Acapulco and the coast of New Spain unto the islands of Ladrones, where the Spaniards do put into water, sailing between Acapulco and the Philippines; in which islands of Ladrones, they find fresh water, plantains, and potato roots; howbeit the people be very rude and heathens. On the 19th day of November aforesaid, about three o'clock in the afternoon, our General caused the king's ship to be set on fire, which having to the quantity of 500 tons of goods in her, we saw burnt unto the water, and then gave them a piece of ordnance and set sail joyfully homewards towards England with a fair wind, which by this time was come about to east-north-east, and night growing near we left the Content astern of us, which was not as yet come out of the road. And here, thinking she would have overtaken us, we lost her company and never saw her after. We were sailing from this haven of Aguada Segura, in California, unto the islands of Ladrones, the rest of November and all December, and so forth until the 3rd of January, 1588, with a fair wind for the space of forty-five days; and we esteemed it to be between 1700 and 1800 leagues. On the 3rd day of January by six o'clock in the morning we had sight of one of the islands of Ladrones called the island of Guana, standing in thirteen degrees and two-thirds towards the north, and sailing with a gentle gale before the wind, by one or two o'clock in the afternoon we were come up within two leagues of the island, where we met with sixty or seventy sail of canoes full of savages, who came off to sea unto us, and brought with them in their boats plantains, cocoas, potato-roots, and fresh fish, which they had caught at sea, and held them up unto us for to truck or exchange with us; which when we perceived we made fast little pieces of old iron upon small cords and fishing-lines, and so veered the iron into their canoes, and they caught hold of them and took off the iron, and in exchange of it they would make fast unto the same line either a potato root or a bundle of plantains, which we hauled in, and thus our company exchanged with them until they had satisfied themselves with as much as did content them; yet we could not be rid of them. For afterward they were so thick about the ship that it stemmed and brake one or two of their canoes; but the men saved themselves, being in every canoe four, six, or eight persons all naked and excellent swimmers and divers. They are of a tawny colour and marvellous fat, and bigger ordinarily of stature than the most part of our men in England, wearing their hair marvellous long; yet some of them have it made up and tied with a knot on the crown, and some with two knots, much like unto their images which we saw them have carved in wood, and standing in the head of their boats like unto the images of the devil. Their canoes were as artificially made as any that ever we had seen, considering they were made and contrived without any edge-tool. They are not above half-a-yard in breadth, and in length some seven or eight yards, and their heads and sterns are both alike; they are made out with rafts of canes and reeds on the starboard side, with mast and sail. Their sail is made of mats of sedges, square or triangle-wise, and they sail as well right against the wind as before the wind. These savages followed us so long, that we could not be rid of them, until in the end our General commanded some half-a-dozen arquebuses to be made ready, and himself struck one of them and the rest shot at them; but they were so yare and nimble, that we could not discern whether they were killed or no, because they could fall backward into the sea, and prevent us by diving.

On the 14th day of January lying at hull with our ship all the middle watch, from twelve at night until four in the morning, by the break of day we fell with an headland of the islands of the Philippines, which is called Cabo del Spirito Santo, which is of very great bigness and length, high land in the midst of it, and very low land as the Cape lieth east and west, trending far into the sea to the westward. This cape or island is distant from the island of Guana, one of the Ladrones, 310 leagues. We were in sailing of this course eleven days with scant winds and some foul weather, bearing no sail two or three nights. This island standeth in thirteen degrees, and is a place much peopled with heathen people, and all woody through the whole land; and it is short of the chiefest island of the Philippines, called Manilla, about sixty leagues. Manilla is well planted and inhabited with Spaniards to the number of 600 or 700 persons; which dwell in a town unwalled, which hath three or four small block-houses, part made of wood and part of stone, being indeed of no great strength; they have one or two small galleys belonging to the town. It is a very rich place of gold and many other commodities; and they have yearly traffic from Acapulco in Nueva España, and also twenty or thirty ships from China and from the Sanguelos, which bring them many sorts of merchandise. The merchants of China and the Sanguelos are part Moors and part heathen people. They bring great store of gold with them, which they traffic and exchange for silver, and give weight for weight. These Sanguelos are men of marvellous capacity in devising and making all manner of things, especially in all handicrafts and sciences, and every one is so expert, perfect, and skilful in his faculty, as few or no Christians are able to go beyond them in that which they take in hand. For drawing and embroidering upon satin, silk, or lawn, either beast, fowl, fish, or worm, for liveliness and perfectness, both in silk, silver, gold and pearl, they excel. Also the 14th day at night we entered the straits between the island of Luçon and the island of Camlaia.

On the 15th of January we fell with an island called Capul, and had betwixt the said island and another island but a narrow passage, and a marvellous rippling of a very great tide with a ledge of rocks lying off the point of the island of Capul; and no danger, but water enough a fair breadth off, and within the point a fair bay and a very good harbour in four fathoms water hard aboard the shore within a cable's length. About ten o'clock in the morning we came to an anchor.

Our ship was no sooner come to an anchor, but presently there came a canoe rowing aboard us, wherein was one of the chief Caciques of the island, whereof there be seven, who, supposing that we were Spaniards, brought us potato roots, which they call camotas, and green cocoas, in exchange whereof we gave his company pieces of linen, to the quantity of a yard, for four cocoas, and as much linen for a basket of potato-roots of a quart in quantity, which roots are very good meat, and excellent sweet either roasted or boiled.

This Cacique's skin was carved and cut with sundry and many streaks and devices all over his body. We kept him still aboard, and caused him to send those men which brought him aboard back to the island to cause the rest of the principals to come aboard; who were no sooner gone on shore, but presently the people of the island came down with their cocoas and potato-roots, and the rest of the principals likewise came aboard and brought with them hens and hogs, and they used the same order with us which they do with the Spaniards. For they took for every hog (which they call Balboye), eight reals of plate, and for every hen or cock one real of plate. Thus we rode at anchor all that day, doing nothing but buying roots, cocoas, hens, hogs, and such things as they brought, refreshing ourselves marvellously well.

The same day at night, being the 15th of January, 1588, Nicolas Roderigo, the Portugal, whom we took out of the great Santa Anna, at the Cape of California, desired to speak with our General in secret; which when our General understood he sent for him, and asked him what he had to say unto him. The Portugal made him this answer, that although he had offended his worship heretofore, yet now he had vowed his faith and true service unto him, and in respect thereof he neither could nor would conceal such treason as was in working against him and his company, and that was this:—That the Spaniard which was taken out of the great Santa Anna for a pilot, whose name was Thomas de Ersola, had written a letter, and secretly sealed it and locked it up in his chest, meaning to convey it by the inhabitants of this island to Manilla, the contents whereof were: That there had been two English ships along the coast of Chili, Peru, Nueva

España, and Nueva Galicia, and that they had taken many ships and merchandise in them, and burnt divers towns, and spoiled all that ever they could come unto, and that they had taken the king's ship which came from Manilla and all his treasure, with all the merchandise that was therein, and had set all the people on shore, taking himself away perforce. Therefore he willed them that they should make strong their bulwarks with their two galleys, and all such provision as they could possibly make. He further signified, that we were riding at an island called Capul, which was at the end of the island of Manilla, being one ship with small force in it, and that the other ship, as he supposed, was gone for the North-west Passage, standing in fifty-five degrees; and that if they could use any means to surprise us, being there at an anchor, they should despatch it; for our force was but small, and our men but weak, and that the place where we rode was but fifty leagues from them. Otherwise if they let us escape, within few years they must make account to have their town besieged and sacked with an army of English. This information being given, our General called for him, and charged him with these things, which at the first he utterly denied; but in the end, the matter being made manifest, and known of certainty by especial trial and proofs, the next morning our General willed that he should be hanged; which was accordingly performed on the 16th of January. We rode for the space of nine days about this Island of Capul, where we had divers kinds of fresh victuals, with excellent fresh water in every bay, and great store of wood. The people of this island go almost all naked, and are tawny of colour. The men wear only a strap about their waists, of some kind of linen of their own weaving, which is made of plantain leaves. These people wholly worship the devil, and often times have conference with him, which appeareth unto them in most ugly and monstrous shape.

On the 23rd day of January, our General, Mr. Thomas Candish, caused all the principals of this island, and of an hundred islands more which he had made to pay tribute unto him (which tribute was in hogs, hens, potatoes, and cocoas) to appear before him, and made himself and his company known unto them, that they were Englishmen, and enemies to the Spaniards; and thereupon spread his ensign and sounded up the drums, which they much marvelled at; to conclude, they promised both themselves and all the islands thereabout to aid him, whensoever he should come again to overcome the Spaniards. Also our General gave them, in token that we were enemies to the Spaniards, money back again for all their tribute which they had paid; which they took marvellous friendly, and rowed about our ships to show us pleasure marvellous swiftly; at the last our General caused a saker to be shot off, whereat they wondered, and with great contentment took their leave of us.

The next day being the 24th of January, we set sail about six of the clock in the morning, and ran along the coast of the Island of Manilla, shaping our course northwest between the Isle of Manilla, and the Isle of Masbat.

On the 28th day in the morning about seven of the clock, riding at an anchor betwixt two islands, we spied a frigate under her two courses, running out between two other islands, which as we imagined came from Manilla, sailing close aboard the shore along the mainland of Panama; we chased this frigate along the shore, and got very fast upon it, until in the end we came so near that it stood into the shore close by a wind, until she was becalmed and was driven to strike her sail, and banked up with her oars; whereupon we came unto an anchor with our ship, a league and a half from the place where the frigate rowed in; and manned our boat with half-a-dozen shot and as many men with swords, which did row the boat; thus we made after the frigate which had hoisted sail and ran into a river, which we could not find. But as we rowed along the shore, our boat came into very shallow water, where many weirs and sticks were set up in divers places in the sea, from whence two or three canoes came forth, whereof one made somewhat near unto us, with three or four Indians in it: we called unto them; but they would not come nearer unto us, but rowed from us; whom we durst not follow too far for fear of bringing ourselves too much to the leeward of our ship. Here, as we looked about us, we espied another balsa or canoe of a great bigness, which they which were in her did set along as we do usually set a barge with long staves or poles, which was builded up with great canes, and below hard by the water made to row with oars; wherein were about five or six Indians and one Spaniard; now as we were come almost at the balsa, we ran aground with our boat; but one or two of our men leaped overboard and freed it again presently, and keeping thwart her head, we laid her aboard and took into us the Spaniard, but the Indians leaped into the sea and dived and rose far off again from us. Presently upon the taking of this canoe, there showed upon the sand a band of soldiers marching with an ensign having a Red Cross like the flag of England, which were about fifty or sixty Spaniards, which were lately come from Manilla to that town which is called Ragaun in a barque to fetch a new ship of the king's, which was building in a river within the bay, and stayed there but for certain irons that did serve for the rudder of the said ship, which they looked for every day.

This band of men shot at us from the shore with their muskets, but hit none of us, and we shot at them again; they also manned a frigate and sent it out after our boat to have taken us, but we with sail and oars went from them; and when they perceived that they could not fetch us, but that they must come within danger of the ordnance of our ship, they stood in with the shore again and landed their men, and presently sent their frigate about the point, but whether we knew not. So we came aboard with this one Spaniard, which was neither soldier nor sailor, but one that was come among the rest from Manilla, and had been in the hospital there a long time before, and was a very simple soul, and such a one as could answer to very little that he was asked, concerning the state of the country. Here we rode at anchor all that night, and perceived that the Spaniards had dispersed their band into two or three parts, and kept great watch in several steads with fires and shooting off their pieces. This island hath much plain ground in it in many places, and many fair and straight trees do grow upon it, fit for to make excellent good masts for all sorts of ships. There are also mines of very fine gold in it which are in the custody of the Indians. And to the southward of this place there is another very great island, which is not subdued by the Spaniards, nor any other nation. The people which inhabit it are all Negroes; and the island is called the Island of Negroes; and is almost as big as England, standing in nine degrees; the most part of it seemeth to be very low land, and by all likelihood is very fruitful.

On the 29th day of January, about six of the clock in the morning, we set sail, sending our boat before until it was two of the clock in the afternoon, passing all this time as it were through a Strait betwixt the said two Islands of Panama and the Island of Negroes, and about sixteen leagues off we espied a fair opening, tending south-west and by south, at which time our boat came aboard, and our General sent commendations to the Spanish captain which we came from the evening before by the Spaniard which we took, and willed him to provide good store of gold; for he meant for to see him with his company at Manilla within few years, and that he did but want a bigger boat to have landed his men, or else he would have seen him then; and so caused him to be set on shore. On the 8th day of February by eight of the clock in the morning we espied an island near Gilolo, called Batochina, which standeth in one degree from the equinoctial line northward. On the 14th day of February we fell in with eleven or twelve very small islands, lying very low and flat, full of trees, and passed by some islands which be sunk and have the dry sands lying in the main sea. These islands near the Moluccas stand in three degrees and ten minutes to the southward of the line.

On the 17th day, one John Gameford, a cooper, died, which had been sick of an old disease a long time. On the 20th day we fell with certain other islands which had many small islands among them, standing four degrees to the southward of the line. On the 21st day of February, being Ash Wednesday Captain Havers died of a most severe and pestilent ague which held him furiously some seven or eight days, to no small grief of our General and of all the rest of the company, who caused two falchions and one saker to be shot off, with all the small shot in the ship; who, after he was shrouded in a sheet and a prayer said, was heaved overboard with great lamentation of us all. Moreover, presently after his death myself with divers others in the ship fell marvellously sick, and so continued in very great pain for the space of three weeks or a month by reason of the extreme heat and intemperateness of the climate.

On the 1st of March, having passed through the straits of Java Minor and Java Major, we came to an anchor under the southwest parts of Java Major; where we espied certain of the people which were fishing by the sea-side in a bay which was under the island. Then our General taking into the ship's-boat certain of his company, and a negro which could speak the Morisco tongue, which he had taken out of the great St. Anna, made towards those fishers, which having espied our boat ran on shore into the wood for fear of our men; but our General caused his negro to call unto them; who no sooner heard him call, but presently one of them came out to the shore-side and made answer. Our General by the negro enquired of him for fresh water, which they found, and caused the fisher to go to the king and to certify him of a ship that was come to have traffic for victuals, and for diamonds, pearls, or any other rich jewels that he had; for which he should have either gold or other merchandise in exchange. The fisherman answered that we should have all manner of victuals that we would request. Thus the boat came aboard again. Within awhile after we went about to furnish our ship thoroughly with wood and water.

About the 8th of March two or three canoes came from the town unto us with eggs, hens, fresh fish, oranges and limes, and brought word we should have had victuals more plentifully, but that they were so far to be brought to us where we rode. Which when our General heard he weighed anchor and stood in nearer for the town; and as we were under sail we met with one of the king's canoes coming towards us; whereupon we shook the ship in the wind and stayed for the canoe until it came aboard of us, and stood into the bay which was hard by and came to an anchor. In this canoe was the king's secretary, who had on his head a piece of dyed linen cloth folded up like unto a Turk's turban; he was all naked saving about his waist; his breast was carved with the broad arrow upon it; he went barefooted; he had an interpreter with him, which was a Mestizo, that is, half an Indian and half a Portugal, who could speak very good Portuguese. This secretary signified unto our General that he had brought him an hog, hens, eggs, fresh fish, sugar-canes, and wine (which wine was as strong as any aqua vitæ, and as clear as any rock water); he told him further that he would bring victuals so sufficiently for him, as he and his company would request, and that within the space of four days. Our General used him singularly well, banqueted him most royally with the choice of many and sundry conserves, wines both sweet and other, and caused his musicians to make him music. This done our General told him that he and his company were Englishmen, and that we had been at China and had had traffic there with them, and that we were come thither to discover, and purposed to go to Malacca. The people of Java told our General that there were certain Portugals in the island which lay there as factors continually to traffic with them, to buy negroes, cloves, pepper, sugar, and many other commodities. This secretary of the king with his interpreter lay one night aboard our ship. The same night because they lay aboard in the evening at the setting of the watch, our General commanded every man in the ship to provide his arquebuse and his shot, and so with shooting off forty or fifty small shot and one saker, himself set the watch with them. This was no small marvel unto these heathen people, who had not commonly seen any ship so furnished with men and ordnance. The next morning we dismissed the secretary and his interpreter with all humanity.

On the fourth day after, which was the 12th of March, according to their appointment came the king's canoes; but the wind being scmewhat scant they could not get aboard that night, but put into a bay under the island until the next day, and presently after the break of day there came to the number of nine or ten of the king's canoes so deeply laden with victuals as they could swim, with two great live oxen, half a score of wonderful great and fat hogs, a number of hens which were alive, drakes, geese, eggs, plantains, sugar-canes, sugar in plates, cocoa, sweet oranges and sour, limes, great store of wine and aqua vitæ, salt to season victuals withal, and almost all manner of victuals else, with divers of the king's officers which were there. Among all the rest of the people, in one of these canoes came two Portugals, which were of middle stature, and men of marvellous proper personage; they were each of them in a loose jerkin, and hose, which came down from the waist to the ancle, because of the use of the country, and partly because it was Lent, and a time for doing of their penance (for they account it as a thing of great dislike among these heathens to wear either hose or shoes on their feet): they had on each of them a very fair and a white lawn shirt, with falling bands on the same, very decently, only their bare legs excepted. These Portugals were no small joy unto our General and all the rest of our company, for we had not seen any Christian, that was our friend, of a year and a-half before. Our General used and entreated them singularly well, with banquets and music. They told us that they were no less glad to see us than we to see them, and enquired of the state of their country, and what was become of Don Antonio, their king, and whether he were living or no; for that they had not of long time been in Portugal, and that the Spaniards had always brought them word that he was dead. Then our General satisfied them in every demand; assuring them that their king was alive, and in England, and had honourable allowance of our Queen, and that there was war between Spain and England, and that we were come under the King of Portugal into the South Sea, and had warred upon the Spaniards there, and had fired, spoiled, and sunk all the ships along the coast that we could meet withal, to the number of eighteen or twenty sail. With this report they were sufficiently satisfied.

On the other side they declared unto us the state of the island of Java. First the plentifulness and great choice and store of victuals of all sorts, and of all manner of fruits as before is set down. Then the great and rich merchandise which are there to be had. Then they described the properties and nature of the people as followeth:—The name of the king of that part of the island was Raja Bolamboam, who was a man had in great majesty and fear among them. The common people may not bargain, sell, or exchange anything with any other nation, without special licence from their king; and if any so do, it is present death for him. The king himself is a man of great years, and hath a hundred wives; his son hath fifty. The custom of the country is, that whensoever the king doth die they take the body so dead and burn it, and preserve the ashes of him, and within five days next after, the wives of the said king so dead, according to the custom and use of their country, everyone of them go together to a place appointed, and the chief of the women, which was nearest unto him in account, hath a ball in her hand, and throweth it from her, and to the place where the ball resteth thither they go all, and turn their faces to the eastward, and everyone with a dagger in their hand, (which dagger they call a creese, and is as sharp as a razor) stab themselves to the heart, and with their hands all to bebathe themselves in their own blood, and falling grovelling on their faces so end their days. This thing is as true as it seemeth to any hearer to be strange.

The men of themselves be very politic and subtle, and singularly valiant, being naked men, in any action they undertake, and wonderfully at commandment and fear of their king. For example, if their king command them to undertake any exploit, be it never so dangerous or desperate, they dare not nor will not refuse it, though they die every man in the execution of the same. For he will cut off the heads of every one of them which return alive without bringing of their purpose to pass; which is such a thing among them, as it maketh them the most valiant people in all the south-east parts of the world; for they never fear any death. For being in fight with any nation, if any of them feeleth himself hurt with lance or sword, he will willingly run himself upon the weapon quite through his body to procure his death the more speedily, and in this desperate sort end his days, or overcome his enemy. Moreover, although the men be tawny of colour and go continually naked, yet their women be fair of complexion and go more apparelled.

After they had thus described the state of the island, and the orders and fashions of the people, they told us further, that if their King Don Antonio would come unto them they would warrant him to have all the Moluccas at commandment, besides China, Sangles, and the isles of the Philippines, and that he might be assured to have all the Indians on his side that are in the country. After we had fully contented these Portugals, and the people of Java which brought us victuals in their canoes, they took their leave of us with promise of all good entertainment at our returns, and our General gave them three great pieces of ordnance at their departing. Thus the next day, being the 16th of March, we set sail towards the Cape of Good Hope, called by the Portuguese Cabo de Buena Esperança, on the southernmost coast of Africa.

The rest of March and all the month of April, we spent in traversing that mighty and vast sea, between the Isle of Java and the main of Africa, observing the heavens, the Crosiers or Southpole, the other stars, the fowls, which are marks unto the seamen of fair weather, foul weather, approaching of lands or islands, the winds, the tempests, the rains and thunders, with the alteration of tides and currents.

On the 10th of May we had a storm at the west, and it blew so hard that it was as much as the ship could stir close by under the wind; and the storm continued all that day and all that night. The next day, being the 11th of May, in the morning one of the company went into the top, and espied land bearing north and north and by west of us, and about noon we espied land to bear west of us, which, as we did imagine, was the Cape of Buena Esperança, whereof, indeed, we were short some forty or fifty leagues. And by reason of the scantiness of the wind we stood along to the south-east until midnight, at which time the wind came fair, and we haled along westward. On the 12th and 13th days we were becalmed, and the sky was very hazy and thick until the 14th day at three o'clock in the afternoon, at which time the sky cleared, and we espied the land again which was the cape called Cabo Falso, which is short of the Cape de Buena Esperança forty or fifty leagues. This cape is very easy to be known; for there are right over it three very high hills standing but a small way one off another, and the highest standeth in the midst, and the ground is much lower by the seaside. The Cape of Good Hope beareth west and by south from the said Cabo Falso.

On the 16th of May, about four o'clock in the afternoon, the wind came up at east a very stiff gale, which held until it was Saturday, with as much wind as ever the ship could go before, at which time, by six o'clock in the morning, we espied the promontory or headland called the Cape de Buena Esperança, which is a reasonable high land, and at the westermost point, a little off the main, do shew two hammocks, the one upon the other, and three other hammocks lying further off into the sea, yet low land between and adjoining unto the sea. This Cape of Buena Esperança is set down and accounted for two thousand leagues from the island of Java in the Portuguese sea-charts; but it is not so much almost by a hundred and fifty leagues, as we found by the running of our ship. We were in running of these eighteen hundred and fifty leagues just nine weeks.

On the 8th of June, by break of day, we fell in sight of the island of St. Helena, seven or eight leagues short of it, having but a small gale of wind, or almost none at all, insomuch as we could not get into it that day, but stood off and on all that night. The next day, being the 9th of June, having a pretty easy gale of wind, we stood in with the shore, our boat being sent away before to make the harbour; and about one o'clock in the afternoon we came unto an anchor in twelve fathoms water, two or three cables' length from the shore, in a very fair and smooth bay under the north-west side of the island. This island is very high land, and lieth in the main sea, standing as it were in the midst of the sea between the mainland of Africa and the main of Brazil and the coast of Guinea, and is in 15 degrees and 48 minutes to the southward of the equinoctial line, and is distant from the Cape of Buena Esperança between five and six hundred leagues.

On the same day, about two or three o'clock in the afternoon, we went on shore, where we found a marvellous fair and pleasant valley, wherein divers handsome buildings and houses were set up, especially one which was a church, which was tiled and whited on the outside very fair and made with a porch, and within the church at the upper end was set an altar, whereon stood a very large table set in a frame having in it the picture of our Saviour Christ upon the cross and the image of our Lady praying, with divers other histories curiously painted in the same. The sides of the church were all hanged with stained cloths having many devices drawn in them. There are two houses adjoining to the church, on each side one, which serve for kitchens to dress meat in, with necessary rooms and houses of office. The coverings of the said houses are made flat, whereon is planted a very fair vine, and through both the said houses runneth a very good and wholesome stream of fresh water. There is also, right over against the said church, a fair causeway made up with stones reaching unto a valley by the seaside, in which valley is planted a garden wherein grow great store of pompions and melons. And upon the said causeway is a frame erected whereon hang two bells wherewith they ring to Mass; and hard unto it is a cross set up, which is squared, framed, and made very artificially of free stone, whereon is carved in cyphers what time it was builded, which was in the year of our Lord 1571.

This valley is the fairest and largest low plot in all the island, and it is marvellous sweet and pleasant, and planted in every place either with fruit-trees or with herbs. There are fig-trees, which bear fruit continually and marvellous plentifully; for on every tree you shall have blossoms, green figs, and ripe figs all at once; and it is so all the year long. The reason is that the island standeth so near the sun. There be also great store of lemon-trees, orange-trees, pomegranate-trees, pomecitron-trees, date-trees, which bear fruit as the fig-trees do, and are planted carefully and very artificially with very pleasant walks under and between them, and the said walks be overshadowed with the leaves of the trees; and in every void place is planted parsley, sorrel, basil, fennel, anise-seed, mustard-seed, radishes, and many special good herbs; and the fresh water brook runneth through divers places of this orchard, and may with very small pains be made to water any one tree in the valley.

This fresh water stream cometh from the tops of the mountains, and falleth from the cliff into the valley the height of a cable, and hath many arms out of it, which refresh the whole island and almost every tree in it. The island is altogether high mountains and steep valleys, except it be in the tops of some hills and down below in some of the valleys, where marvellous store of all these kinds of fruits before spoken of do grow. There is greater store growing in the tops of the mountains than below in the valleys;

but it is wonderful laboursome and also dangerous travelling up unto them and down again, by reason of the height and steepness of the hills.

There is also upon this island great store of partridges, which are very tame, not making any great haste to fly away though one come very near them, but only to run away and get up into the steep cliffs. We killed some of them with a fowling piece. They differ very much from our partridges which are in England both in bigness and also in colour; for they be within a little as big as a hen, and are of an ash colour, and live in coveys twelve, sixteen, and twenty together. You cannot go ten or twelve score but you shall see or spring one or two coveys at the least.

There are likewise no less store of pheasants in the island, which are also marvellous big and fat, surpassing those which are in our country in bigness and in numbers of a company. They differ not very much in colour from the partridges before spoken of.

We found moreover in this place a great store of Guinea cocks, which we call turkeys, of colour black and white, with red heads, They are much about the same bigness which ours be of in England. Their eggs be white, and as big as a turkey's egg.

There are in this island thousands of goats, which the Spaniards call *cabritos*, which are very wild. You shall see one or two hundred of them together, and sometimes you may behold them going in a flock almost a mile long. Some of them (whether it be the nature of the breed of them or of the country I wot not) are as big as an ass, with a mane like a horse and a beard hanging down to the very ground. They will climb up the cliffs, which are so steep that a man would think it a thing impossible for any living thing to go there. We took and killed many of them, for all their swiftness; for there be thousands of them upon the mountains.

Here are in like manner great store of swine, which be very wild and very fat, and of a marvellous bigness. They keep altogether upon the mountains, and will very seldom abide any man to come near them, except it be by mere chance when they be found asleep; or otherwise, according to their kind, be taken laid in the mire.

We found in the houses at our coming three slaves which were negroes and one which was born in the island of Java, which told us that the East Indian fleet, which were in number five sails, the least whereof were in burden 800 or 900 tons, all laden with spices and Calicut cloth, with store of treasure and very rich stones and pearls, were gone from the said island of St. Helena but twenty days before we came thither.

This island hath been found of long time by the Portugals, and hath been altogether planted by them for their refreshing as they come from the East Indies. And when they come they have all things plentiful for their relief, by reason that they suffer none to inhabit there that might spend up the fruit of the island, except some very few sick persons in their company, which they stand in doubt will not live until they come home, whom they leave there to refresh themselves, and take away the year following with the other fleet if they live so long. They touch here rather in their coming home from the East Indies than at their going thither, because they are thoroughly furnished with corn when they set out of Portugal, but are but meanly victualled at their coming from the Indies, where there groweth little corn.

On the 20th of June, having taken in wood and water, and refreshed ourselves with such things as we found there, and made clean our ship, we set sail about eight o'clock in the night toward England. At our setting sail we had the wind at south-east, and we haled away north-west and by west. The wind is commonly off the shore at this island of St. Helena. On Wednesday, being the 3rd of July, we went away north-west, the wind being still at south-east; at which time we were in 1 degree and 48 minutes to the southward of the equinoctial line. On the 12th of July it was very little wind, and toward night it was calm, and blew no wind at all, and so continued until it was Monday, being the 15th of July. On Wednesday, the 17th day of the abovesaid month, we had the wind scant at west-north-west. We found the wind continually to blow at east, and north-east, and east-north-east after we were in 3 or 4 degrees to the northward; and it altered not until we came between 30 and 40 degrees to the northward of the equinoctial line.

On Wednesday, the 21st of August, the wind came up at southwest a fair gale, by which day at noon we were in 38 degrees of northerly latitude. On Friday, in the morning, being the 23rd of August, at four o'clock, we haled east, and east and by south for the northermost islands of the Azores. On Saturday, the 24th day of the said month, by five o'clock in the morning, we fell in sight of the two islands of Flores and Corvo, standing in 39½ degrees, and sailed away north-east. On the 3rd of September we met with a Flemish hulk, which came from Lisbon, and declared unto us the overthrowing of the Spanish Fleet, to the singular rejoicing and comfort of us all. On the 9th of September, after a terrible tempest, which carried away most part of our sails, by the merciful favour of the Almighty we recovered our long-wished port of Plymouth in England, from whence we set forth at the beginning of our voyage.

CAVENDISH.—LAST VOYAGE.

The last Voyage of the Worshipful MR. THOS. CAVENDISH, ESQUIRE, *intended for the South Sea, the* PHILIPPINES, *and the coast of* CHINA, *with three tall ships and two barques. Written by* MR. JOHN JANE, *a man of good observation, employed in the same and many other voyages.*

ON the 26th of August, 1591, we departed from Plymouth with three tall ships and two barques, The Galeon, wherein Mr. Candish went himself, being Admiral, The Roebuck, Vice-Admiral, whereof Mr. Cocke was Captain, The Desire, Rear-Admiral, whereof was Captain Mr. John Davis (with whom and for whose sake I went this voyage), the Black Pinnace, and a barque of Mr. Adrian Gilbert, whereof Mr. Randolph Cotton was Captain.

On the 29th of November we fell in with the Bay of Salvador, upon the coast of Brazil, 12 leagues on this side Cabo Frio, where we were becalmed until the 2nd of December, at which time we took a small barque bound for the River of Plate with sugar, haberdashery wares, and negroes. The master of this barque brought us unto an isle called Placentia, 30 leagues west from Cabo Frio, where we arrived the 1st of December, and rifled six or seven houses inhabited by Portugals. On the 11th we departed from this place, and the 14th we arrived at the Isle of San Sebastian, from whence Mr. Cocke and Captain Davis presently departed with the Desire and the Black Pinnace, for the taking of the town of Santos. On the 15th at evening we anchored at the bar of Santos, from whence we departed with our boats to the town; and the next morning about nine o'clock we came to Santos, where being discovered, we were enforced to land with twenty-four gentlemen, our long boat being far astern, by which expedition we took all the people of the town at mass, both men and women, whom we kept all that day in the church as prisoners. The cause why Mr. Candish desired to take this town was to supply his great wants; for being in Santos, and having it in quiet possession, we stood in assurance to supply all our needs in great abundance. But such was the negligence of our Governor, Mr. Cocke, that the Indians were suffered to carry out of the town whatsoever they would in open view, and no man did control them; and the next day after we had won the town our prisoners were all set at liberty, only four poor old men were kept as pawns to supply our wants. Thus in three days the town that was able to furnish such another fleet with all kind of necessaries, was left unto us nakedly bare, without people and provision.

Eight or ten days after Mr. Candish himself came thither, where he remained until the 22nd of January, seeking by entreaty to have that whereof we were once possessed. But in conclusion we departed out of the town through extreme want of victuals, not being able any longer to live there, and were glad to receive a few canisters or baskets of cassavi meal; so that in every condition we went worse furnished from the town than when we came unto it. On the 22nd of January we departed from Santos, and burnt St. Vincent to the ground. On the 24th we set sail, shaping our course for the Straits of Magellan.

On the 7th of February we had a very great storm, and on the 8th our fleet was separated by the fury of the tempest. Then our Captain called unto him the Master of our ship, whom he found to be a very honest and sufficient man, and conferring with him he concluded to go for Port Desire, which is in the southerly latitude of 48 degrees; hoping that the General would come thither, because that in his first voyage he had found great relief there. For our Captain could never get any direction what course to take in any such extremities, though many times he had intreated for it, as often I have heard him with grief report. In sailing to this port by good chance we met with the Roebuck, wherein Mr. Cocke had endured great extremities, and had lost his boat, and therefore desired our Captain to keep him company, for he was in very desperate case. Our Captain hoisted out his boat and went aboard him to know his estate, and returning told us the hardness thereof, and desired the Master and all the company to be careful in all their watches not to lose The Roebuck, and so we both arrived at Port Desire on the 6th of March.

On the 16th of March the Black Pinnace came unto us, but

Mr. Gilbert's barque came not, but returned home to England, having their Captain aboard the Roebuck without any provision more than the apparel that he wore, who came from thence aboard our ship to remain with our Captain, by reason of the great friendship between them. On the 18th the Galeon came into the road, and Mr. Candish came into the harbour in a boat which he had made at sea; for his long-boat and light-horseman were lost at sea, as also a pinnace which he had built at Santos; and being aboard The Desire he told our Captain of all his extremities, and spake most hardly of his company, and of divers gentlemen that were with him, purposing no more to go aboard his own ship, but to stay in The Desire. We all sorrowed to hear such hard speeches of our good friends; but having spoken with the gentlemen of the Galeon we found them faithful, honest, and resolute in proceeding, although it pleased our General otherwise to conceive of them.

On the 20th of March we departed from Port Desire, Mr. Candish being in The Desire with us. On the 8th of April, 1592, we fell with the Straits of Magellan, enduring many furious storms between Port Desire and the Straits. On the 14th we passed through the first strait. On the 16th we passed the second strait, being 10 leagues distant from the first. On the 18th we doubled Cape Froward, which cape lieth in 53½ degrees. On the 21st we were enforced by the fury of the weather to put into a small cove with our ships, 4 leagues from the said cape, upon the south shore, where we remained until the 15th of May. In the which time we endured extreme storms, with perpetual snow, where many of our men died with cursed famine and miserable cold, not having wherewith to cover their bodies, nor to fill their bellies, but living by muscles, water, and weeds of the sea, with a small relief of the ship's store in meal sometimes. And all the sick men in the Galeon were most uncharitably put ashore into the woods in the snow, rain, and cold, when men of good health could scarcely endure it, where they ended their lives in the highest degree of misery, Mr. Candish all this while being aboard the Desire. In these great extremities of snow and cold, doubting what the end would be, he asked our Captain's opinion, because he was a man that had good experience of the north-west parts, in his three several discoveries that way, employed by the merchants of London. Our Captain told him that this snow was a matter of no long continuance, and gave him sufficient reason for it, and that thereby he could not much be prejudiced or hindered in his proceeding. Notwithstanding, he called together all the company, and told them that he purposed not to stay in the straits, but to depart upon some other voyage, or else to return again for Brazil. But his resolution was to go for the Cape of Buena Esperança. The company answered that if it pleased him, they did desire to stay God's favour for a wind, and to endure all hardness whatsoever, rather than to give over the voyage, considering they had been here but a small time, and because they were within 40 leagues of the South sea, it grieved them now to return; notwithstanding what he purposed that they would perform. So he concluded to go for the Cape of Buena Esperança, and to give over this voyage. Then our Captain, after Mr. Candish was come aboard The Desire from talking with the company, told him that if it pleased him to consider the great extremity of his estate, the slenderness of his provisions, with the weakness of his men, it was no course for him to proceed in that new enterprise; for if the rest of your ships (said he) be furnished answerable to this, it is impossible to perform your determination; for we have no more sails than masts, no victuals, no ground-tackling, no cordage more than is over head, and among seventy and five persons there is but the Master alone that can order the ship, and but fourteen sailors. The rest are gentlemen, serving-men, and artificers. Therefore it will be a desperate case to take so hard an enterprise in hand. These persuasions did our Captain not only use to Mr. Candish, but also to Mr. Cocke. In fine, upon a petition delivered in writing by the chief of the whole company, the General determined to depart out of the Straits of Magellan, and to return again for Santos, in Brazil.

So on the 15th of May we set sail, the General then being in the Galeon. On the 18th we were free of the Straits, but at Cape Froward it was our hard hap to have our boat sunk at our stern in the night, and to be split and sore spoiled, and to lose all our oars.

On the 20th of May, being thwart of Port Desire, in the night the General altered his course, as we suppose, by which occasion we lost him; for in the evening he stood close by a wind to seaward, having the wind at north-north-east, and we standing the same way, the wind not altering, could not the next day see him; so that we then persuaded ourselves that he was gone for Port Desire to relieve himself, or that he had sustained some mischance at sea, and was gone thither to remedy it. Whereupon our Captain called the General's men unto him, with the rest, and asked their opinion what was to be done. Everyone said that they thought that the General was gone for Port Desire. Then the Master, being the General's man, and careful of his master's service, as also of good judgment in sea matters, told the company how dangerous it was to go for Port Desire, if we should there miss the General; for (said he) we have no boat to land ourselves, nor any cables nor anchors that I dare trust in so quick streams as are there; yet in all likelihood concluding that the General was gone thither, we stayed our course for Port Desire, and by chance met with the Black Pinnace, which had likewise lost the fleet, being in very miserable case; so we both concluded to seek the General at Port Desire.

On the 26th of May we came to Port Desire, where not finding our General as we hoped, being most slenderly victualled, without sails, boat, oars, nails, cordage, and all other necessaries for our relief, we were stricken into a deadly sorrow. But referring all to the providence and fatherly protection of the Almighty, we entered the harbour, and by God's favour found a place of quiet road, which before we knew not. Having moored our ship with the pinnace's boat, we landed upon the south shore, where we found a standing pool of fresh water, which by estimation might hold some ten tuns, whereby we were greatly comforted. From this pool we fetched more than forty tuns of water, and yet we left the pool as full as we found it. And because at our first being in this harbour we were at this place and found no water, we persuaded ourselves that God had sent it for our relief. Also there were such extraordinary low ebbs as we had never seen, whereby we got muscles in great plenty. Likewise God sent about our ships great abundance of smelts, so that with hooks made of pins every man caught as many as he could eat; by which means we preserved our ship's victuals, and spent not any during the time of our abode here.

Our Captain and Master falling into the consideration of our estate and dispatch to go to the General, found our wants so great, as that in a month we could not fit our ship to set sail. For we must needs set up a smith's forge, to make bolts, spikes, and nails, besides the repairing of our other wants. Whereupon they concluded it to be their best course to take the pinnace, and to furnish her with the best of the company, and to go to the General with all expedition, leaving the ship and the rest of the company until the General's return; for he had vowed to our Captain that he would return again for the Straits, as he had told us. The Captain and Master of the pinnace being the General's men were well contented with the motion.

But the General having in our ship two most pestilent fellows, when they heard of this determination they utterly misliked it, and in secret dealt with the company of both ships, vehemently persuading them that our Captain and Master would leave them in the country to be devoured of the cannibals, and that they were merciless and without charity; whereupon the whole company joined in secret with them in a night to murder our Captain and Master, with myself, and all those which they thought were their friends. There were marks taken in his cabin how to kill him with muskets through the ship's side, and bullets made of silver for the execution if their other purposes should fail. All agreed hereunto, except it were the boatswain of our ship, who when he knew the matter and the slender ground thereof, revealed it unto our Master, and so to the Captain. Then the matter being called in question, those two most murderous fellows were found out, whose names were Charles Parker and Edward Smith.

The Captain being thus hardly beset, in peril of famine, and in danger of murdering, was constrained to use lenity, and by courteous means to pacify this fury; shewing, that to do the General service, unto whom he had vowed faith in this action, was the cause why he purposed to go unto him in the pinnace, considering that the pinnace was so necessary a thing for him, as that he could not be without her, because he was fearful of the shore in so great ships. Whereupon all cried out, with cursing and swearing, that the pinnace should not go unless the ship went. Then the Captain desired them to shew themselves Christians, and not so blasphemously to behave themselves, without regard or thanksgiving to God for their great deliverance, and present sustenance bestowed upon them, alleging many examples of God's sharp punishment for such ingratitude; and withal promised to do anything that might stand with their good liking. By which gentle speeches the matter was pacified, and the Captain and Master, at the request of the company, were content to forgive this great treachery of Parker and Smith, who after many admonitions concluded in these words:—" The Lord judge between you and me;" which after came to a most sharp revenge even by the punishment of the Almighty. Thus by a general consent it was concluded not to depart, but there to stay for the General's return. Then our Captain and Master, seeing that they could not do the General that service which they desired, made a motion to the company that they would lay down under their hands the losing of the General, with the extremities wherein we then stood; whereunto they consented, and wrote unto their hands as followeth:—

The Testimonial of the Company of THE DESIRE, *touching their losing of their General, which appeareth to have been utterly against their meanings:—*

On the 26th of August, 1591, we whose names be hereunder written, with divers other departed from Plymouth under Mr. Thomas Candish, our General, with four ships of his, to wit, the Galeon, the Roebuck, the Desire, and the Black Pinnace, for the performance of a voyage into the South Sea. On the 19th of November we fell with the bay of Salvador, in Brazil. On the 16th of December we took the town of Santos, hoping there to revictual ourselves, but it fell not out to our contentment. On the 24th of January we set sail from Santos, shaping our course for the Straits of Magellan. On the 8th of February, by violent storms the said fleet was parted; the Roebuck and the Desire arrived in Port Desire the 6th of March. On the 16th of March the Black Pinnace arrived there also, and on the 18th of the same our Admiral came into the road, with whom we departed the 20th of March in poor and weak estate. On the 8th of April, 1592, we entered the Straits of Magellan. On the 21st of April we anchored beyond Cape Froward, within forty leagues of the South Sea, where we rode until the 15th of May, in which time we had great store of snow, with some gusty weather, the wind continuing still at west-north-west against us. In this time we were enforced, for the preserving of our victuals, to live for the most part upon muscles, our provision was so slender, so that many of our men died in this hard extremity. Then our General returned for Brazil there to winter, and to procure victuals for this voyage against the next year. So we departed the Straits on the 15th of May. On the 21st, being thwart of Port Desire, thirty leagues off the shore, the wind then at north-east and by north, at five o'clock at night, lying north-east, we suddenly cast about lying south-east and by south, and sometimes south-east, the whole fleet following the Admiral, our ship coming under his lee shot ahead him, and so framed sail fit to keep company. This night we were severed, by what occasion we protest we know not, whether we lost them or they us. In the morning we only saw the Black Pinnace; then supposing that the Admiral had overshot us, all this day we stood to the eastwards, hoping to find him, because it was not likely that he would stand to the shore again so suddenly. But missing him towards night, we stood to the shoreward, hoping by that course to find him. On the 22nd of May at night we had a violent storm, with the wind at north-west, and we were in-forced to hull, not being able to bear sail, and this night we perished our main trestletrees, so that we could no more use our main-topsail, lying most dangerously in the sea. The pinnace likewise received a great leak, so that we were forced to seek the next shore for our relief. And because famine was like to be the best end, we desired to go for Port Desire, hoping with seals and penguins to relieve ourselves, and so to make shift to follow the General, or there to stay his coming from Brazil. On the 24th of May we had much wind at north. The 25th was calm, and the sea very lofty, so that our ship had dangerous foul weather. On the 26th our fore-shrouds brake, so that if we had not been near the shore, it had been impossible for us to get out of the sea. And now being here moored in Port Desire, our shrouds are all rotten, not having a running-rope whereto we may trust, and being provided only of one shift of sails all worn; our top-sails not able to abide any stress of weather, neither have we any pitch, tar, or nails, nor any store for the supplying of these wants, and we live only upon seals and muscles, having but five hogsheads of pork within board, and meal three ounces for a man a day, with water for to drink. And forasmuch as it hath pleased God to separate our fleet, and to bring us into such hard extremities, that only now by his mere mercy we expect relief, though otherwise we are hopeless of comfort; yet because the wonderful works of God in his exceeding great favour towards us his creatures are far beyond the scope of man's capacity, therefore by him we hope to have deliverance in this our deep distress. Also forasmuch as those upon whom God will bestow the favour of life, with return home to their country, may not only themselves remain blameless, but also manifest the truth of our actions, we have thought good in Christian charity to lay down under our hands the truth of all our proceedings, even till the time of this our distress.

Given in Port Desire the 2nd of June, 1592. Beseeching the

Almighty God of his mercy to deliver us from this misery, how or when it shall please His Divine Majesty.

John Davis (Captain), Randolph Cotton, John Pery, William Maber (gunner), Charles Parker, Rowland Miller, Edward Smith, Thomas Purpet, Matthew Stubbes, John Jenkinson, Thomas Edwards, Edward Granger, John Lewis, William Hayman, George Straker, Thomas Walbie, William Wyeth, Richard Alard, Stephen Popham, Alexander Cole, Thomas Watkins, George Cunington, John Whiting, James Ling, the Boatswain, Francis Smith, John Layes, the Boatswain's Mate, — Fisher, John Austin, Francis Copstone, Richard Garet, James Eversby, Nicolas Parker, — Leonard, John Pick, — Benjamin, William Maber, James Not, Christopher Hauser.

After they had delivered this relation unto our Captain under their hands, then we began to travail for our lives, and we built up a smith's forge, and made a coal-pit, and burnt coals, and there we made nails, bolts, and spikes, others made ropes of a piece of our cable, and the rest gathered muscles, and took smelts for the whole company. Three leagues from this harbour there is an island with four small islands about it, where there are great abundance of seals, and at the time of the year the penguins come thither in great plenty to breed. We concluded with the pinnace that she should sometimes go thither to fetch seals for us; upon which condition we would share our victuals with her man for man; whereunto the whole company agreed. So we parted our poor store, and she laboured to fetch us seals to eat, wherewith we lived when smelts and muscles failed: for in the neap streams we could get no muscles. Thus in most miserable calamity we remained until the 6th of August, still keeping watch upon the hills to look for our General, and so great was our vexation and anguish of soul, as I think never flesh and blood endured more. Thus our misery daily increasing, time passing, and our hope of the General being very cold, our Captain and Master were fully persuaded that the General might perhaps go directly for the Straits, and not come to this harbour; whereupon they thought no course more convenient than to go presently for the Straits, and there to stay his coming, for in that place he could not pass, but of force we must see him; whereunto the company most willingly consented, as also the Captain and Master of the pinnace; so that upon this determination we made all possible speed to depart.

On the 6th of August we set sail, and went to Penguin Island, and the next day we salted twenty hogsheads of seals, which was as much as our salt could possibly do; and so we departed for the Straits the poorest wretches that ever were created. On the 7th of August toward night we departed from Penguin Island, shaping our course for the Straits, where we had full confidence to meet with our General. On the 9th we had a sore storm, so that we were constrained to hull, for our sails were not to endure any force. On the 14th we were driven in among certain islands never before discovered by any known relation, lying fifty leagues or better from the shore east and northerly from the Straits; in which place, unless it had pleased God of his wonderful mercy to have ceased the wind, we must of necessity have perished. But the wind shifting to the east, we directed our course for the Straits, and on the 18th of August we fell with the Cape in a very thick fog, and the same night we anchored ten leagues within the Cape. On the 19th day we passed the first and the second Straits. On the 21st we doubled Cape Froward. On the 22nd we anchored in Savage Cove, so named because we found many savages there; notwithstanding the extreme cold of this place, yet do all these wild people go naked, and live in the woods like satyrs, painted and disguised, and fly from you like wild deer. They are very strong, and threw stones at us of three or four pounds weight an incredible distance. On the 24th in the morning we departed from this cove, and the same day we came into the north-west reach, which is the last reach of the Straits. On the 25th we anchored in a good cove, within fourteen leagues of the South Sea: in this place we purposed to stay for the General, for the Strait in this place is scarce three miles broad, so that he could not pass but we must see him. After we had stayed here a fortnight in the depth of winter, our victuals consuming, (for our seals stunk most vilely, and our men died pitifully through cold and famine, for the greatest part of them had not clothes to defend the extremity of the winter's cold); being in this heavy distress, our captain and master thought it the best course to depart from the Straits into the South Sea, and to go for the Isle of Santa Maria, which is to the northward of Baldivia, in thirty-seven degrees and a quarter, where we might have relief, and be in a temperate clime, and there stay for the General, for of necessity he must come by that Isle. So we departed on the 13th of September, and came in sight of the South Sea. On the 14th we were forced back again, and recovered a cove three leagues within the Straits from the South Sea. Again we put forth, and being eight or ten leagues free of the land, the wind rising furiously at west-north-west, we were enforced again into the Straits only for want of sails; for we never durst bear sail in any stress of weather, they were so weak; so again we recovered the cove three leagues within the Straits, where we endured most furious weather, so that one of our two cables broke, whereby we were hopeless of life. Yet it pleased God to calm the storm, and we unrived our sheets, tacks, halliers, and other ropes, and moored our ship to the trees close by the rocks. We laboured to recover our anchor again, but could not by any means, it lay so deep in the water, and, as we think, clean covered with ooze. Now had we but one anchor which had but one whole fluke, a cable spliced in two places, and a piece of an old cable. In the midst of these our troubles it pleased God that the wind came fair on the 1st of October; whereupon with all expedition we loosed our moorings, and weighed our anchor, and so towed off into the channel; for we had mended our boat in Port Desire, and had five oars of the pinnace. When we had weighed our anchor, we found our cable broken. Only one strand held: then we praised God; for we saw apparently His mercies in preserving us. Being in the channel, we rived our ropes, and again rigged our ship; no man's hand was idle, but all laboured even for the last gasp of life. Here our company was divided; some desired to go again to Port Desire, and there to be set on shore, where they might travail for their lives, and some stood with the captain and master to proceed. Whereupon the captain said to the master: "Master, you see the wonderful extremity of our estate, and the great doubts among our company of the truth of your reports, as touching relief to be had in the South Sea; some say in secret, as I am informed, that we undertake these desperate attempts through blind affection that we bear to the General. For my own part I plainly make known unto you, that the love which I bear to the General caused me first to enter into this action, whereby I have not only heaped upon my head this bitter calamity now present, but also have in some sort procured the dislike of my best friends in England, as it is not unknown to some in this company. But now being thus entangled by the providence of God for my former offences (no doubt) I desire that it may please his Divine Majesty to show us such merciful favour, that we may rather proceed, than otherwise; or if it be his will, that our mortal being shall now take an end, I rather desire that it may be in proceeding than in returning. And because I see in reason, that the limits of our time are now drawing to an end, I do in Christian charity entreat you all, first to forgive me in whatsoever I have been grievous unto you; secondly, that you will rather pray for our General, than use hard speeches of him; and let us be fully persuaded, that not for his cause or negligence, but for our own offences against the Divine Majesty we are presently punished; lastly, let us forgive one another and be reconciled as children in love and charity, and not think upon the vanities of this life; so shall we in leaving this life live with our glorious Redeemer, or abiding in this life, find favour with God. And now (good master) forasmuch as you have been in this voyage once before with your master the General, satisfy the company of such truths as are to you best known; and you, the rest of the General's men, which likewise have been with him in his first voyage, if you hear anything contrary to the truth, spare not to reprove it, I pray you. And so I beseech the Lord to bestow his mercy upon us." Then the master began in these speeches: "Captain, your request is very reasonable, and I refer to your judgment my honest care, and great pains taken in the General's service, my love towards him, and in what sort I have discharged my duty, from the first day to this hour. I was commanded by the General to follow your directions, which hitherto I have performed. You all know that when I was extremely sick, the General was lost in my mate's watch, as you have well examined; since which time in what anguish and grief of mind I have lived God only knoweth, and you are in some part a witness. And now if you think good to return, I will not gainsay it; but this I assure you, if life may be preserved by any means, it is in proceeding. For at the Isle of Santa Maria I do assure you of wheat, pork, and roots enough. Also I will bring you to an isle where pelicans be in great abundance, and at Santos we shall have meal in great plenty, besides all our possibility of intercepting some ships upon the coast of Chili and Peru. But if we return there is nothing but death to be hoped for; therefore do as you like. I am ready, but my desire is to proceed." These his speeches being confirmed by others that were in the former voyage, there was a general consent of proceeding; and so on the 2nd of October we put into the South Sea, and were free of all land. This night the wind began to blow very much at west-north-west, and still increased in fury, so that we were in great doubt what course to take; to put into the Straits we durst not for lack of ground-tackle; to bear sail we doubted, the tempest was so furious, and our sails so bad. The pinnace came room with us, and told us that she had received many grievous seas, and that her ropes did every hour fail her, so as they could not tell what shift to make; we being unable in any sort to help them, stood under our courses in view of the lee-shore, still expecting our ruinous end.

On the 4th of October the storm growing beyond all reason furious, the pinnace being in the wind of us, struck suddenly ahull, so that we thought she had received some grievous sea, or sprung a leak, or that her sails failed her, because she came not with us; but we durst not hull in that unmerciful storm, but sometimes tried under our main course, sometimes with a haddock of our sail, for our ship was very leeward, and most laboursome in the sea. This night we lost the pinnace, and never saw her again.

On the 5th, our foresail was split, and all to torn; then our master took the mizzen, and brought it to the foremast, to make our ship work, and with our spritsail we mended our foresail, the storm continuing without all reason in fury, with hail, snow, rain, and wind, such and so mighty, as that in nature it could not possibly be more, the seas such and so lofty, with continual breach, that many times we were doubtful whether our ship did sink or swim.

On the 10th of October being by the account of our captain and master very near the shore, the weather dark, the storm furious, and most of our men having given over to travail, we yielded ourselves to death, without further hope of succour. Our captain sitting in the gallery very pensive, I came and brought him some *Rosa solis* to comfort him; for he was so cold that he was scarce able to move a joint. After he had drunk, and was comforted in heart, he began for the ease of his conscience to make a large repetition of his forepassed time, and with many grievous sighs he concluded in these words: "Oh, most glorious God, with whose power the mightiest things among men are matters of no moment, I most humbly beseech Thee, that the intolerable burden of my sins may, through the blood of Jesus Christ, be taken from me; and end our days with speed, or show us some merciful sign of Thy love and our preservation." Having thus ended, he desired me not to make known to any of the company his intolerable grief and anguish of mind, because they should not thereby be dismayed. And so suddenly, before I went from him, the sun shined clear; so that he and the master both observed the true elevation of the Pole, whereby they knew by what course to recover the Straits. Wherewithal our captain and master were so revived, and gave such comfortable speeches to the company, that every man rejoiced, as though we had received a present deliverance. The next day, being the 11th of October, we saw Cabo Deseado, being the Cape on the south shore (the north shore is nothing but a company of dangerous rocks, isles, and shoals). This cape being within two leagues to leeward of us, our master greatly doubted that we could not double the same; whereupon the captain told him: "You see there is no remedy; either we must double it, or before noon we must die; therefore loose your sails, and let us put it to God's mercy." The master, being a man of good spirit, resolutely made quick despatch and set sail. Our sails had not been half an hour aboard, but the footrope of our foresail broke, so that nothing held but the eyelet holes. The seas continually broke over the ship's poop, and flew into the sails with such violence, that we still expected the tearing of our sails, or oversetting of the ship, and withal to our utter discomfort, we perceived that we fell still more and more to leeward, so that we could not double the cape; we were now come within half a mile of the cape, and so near the shore, that the counter-surf of the sea would rebound against the ship's side, so that we were much dismayed with the horror of our present end. Being thus at the very pinch of death, the wind and seas raging beyond measure, our master veered some of the main sheet; and whither it was by that occasion, or by some current, or by the wonderful power of God, as we verily think it was, the ship quickened her way, and shot past that rock, where we thought she would have shored. Then between the cape and the point there was a little bay; so that we were somewhat farther from the shore; and when we were come so far as the cape, we yielded to death; yet our good God, the Father of all mercies, delivered us, and we doubled the cape about the length of our ship, or very little more. Being shot past the cape, we presently took in our sails, which only God had preserved unto us; and when we were shot in between the highlands, the wind blowing trade, without any inch of sail, we spooned before the sea, three men being not able to guide the helm, and in six hours we were put five-and-twenty leagues within the Straits, where we found a sea answerable to the ocean.

In this time we freed our ship from water, and after we had rested a little our men were not able to move; their sinews were stiff and their flesh dead, and many of them (which is most lamentable to be reported) were so eaten with lice as that in their flesh did lie clusters of lice as big as peas, yea, and some as big as beans. Being in this misery, we were constrained to put into a cove for the refreshing our men. Our Master, knowing the shore and every cove very perfectly, put in with the shore and moored to the trees as beforetime we had done, laying our anchor to the seaward. Here we continued until the 20th of October; but not being able any longer to stay through extremity of famine, on the 21st we put off into the channel, the weather being reasonable calm; but before night it blew most extremely at west-north-west. The storm growing outrageous, our men could scarcely stand by their labour; and, the Straits being full of turning reaches, we were constrained by discretion of the Captain and Master in their accounts to guide the ship in the hell-dark night, when we could not see any shore, the channel being in some places scarce three miles broad. But our Captain, as we first passed through the Straits, drew such an exquisite plot of the same as I am assured it cannot in any sort be bettered, which plot he and the Master so often perused, and so carefully regarded, as that in memory they had every turning and creek; and in the deep dark night, without any doubting, they conveyed the ship through that crooked channel. So that I conclude the world hath not any so skilful pilots for that place as they are; for otherwise we could never have passed in such sort as we did.

On the 25th we came to an island in the Straits named Penguin Isle, whither we sent our boat to seek relief; for there were great abundance of birds, and the weather was very calm. So we came to an anchor by the island in seven fathoms. While our boat was at shore, and we had great store of penguins, there arose a sudden storm, so that our ship did drive over a breach, and our boat sank at the shore. Captain Cotton and the Lieutenant, being on shore, leapt into the boat and freed the same, and threw away all the birds, and with great difficulty recovered the ship. Myself also was in the boat the same time, where for my life I laboured to the best of my power. The ship all this while driving upon the lee-shore, when we came aboard we helped to set sail and weighed the anchor; for before our coming they could scarce hoist up their yards, yet with much ado they set their fore-course. Thus, in a mighty fret of weather, on the 27th of October, we were free of the Straits, and on the 30th of October we came to Penguin Isle, being three leagues from Port Desire, the place which we purposed to seek for our relief.

When we came to this isle we sent our boat on shore, which returned laden with birds and eggs; and our men said that the penguins were so thick upon the isle that ships might be laden with them; for they could not go without treading upon the birds, whereat we greatly rejoiced. Then the Captain appointed Charles Parker and Edward Smith, with twenty others, to go on shore and to stay upon the isle for the killing and drying of those penguins, and promised after the ship was in harbour to send the rest, not only for expedition, but also to save the small store of victuals in the ship. But Parker, Smith, and the rest of their faction suspected that this was a device of the Captain to leave his men on shore, that by these means there might be victuals for the rest to recover their country. And when they remembered that this was the place where they would have slain their Captain and Master, surely (thought they) for revenge hereof will they leave us on shore. Which, when our Captain understood, he used these speeches unto them:—"I understand that you are doubtful of your security through the perverseness of your own guilty consciences. It is an extreme grief unto me that you should judge me bloodthirsty, in whom you have seen nothing but kind conversation. If you have found otherwise, speak boldly, and accuse me of the wrongs that I have done; if not, why do you then measure me by your own uncharitable consciences? All the company knoweth, indeed, that in this place you practised to the utmost of your powers to murder me and the master causeless, as God knoweth, which evil in this place we did remit you. And now I may conceive, without doing you wrong, that you again purpose some evil in bringing these matters to repetition. But God hath so shortened your confederacy as that I nothing doubt you. It is for your Master's sake that I have forborne you in your unchristian practices. And here I protest before God that for his sake alone I will yet endure this injury, and you shall in no sort be prejudiced, or in anything be by me commanded. But when we come into England (if God so favour us) your Master shall know your honesties. In the mean space be void of your suspicions, for, God I call to witness, revenge is no part of my thought." They gave him thanks, desiring to go into the harbour with the ship, which he granted. So there were ten left upon the isle, and on the last of October we entered the harbour. Our Master at our last being here, having taken careful notice of every creek in the river, in a very convenient place, upon sandy ooze, ran the ship on ground, laying our anchor to seaward, and with our running ropes moored her to stakes upon the shore which he had fastened for that purpose, where the ship remained till our departure.

On the 3rd of November our boat, with water, wood, and as many as she could carry, went for the Isle of Penguins; but, being deep, she durst not proceed, but returned again the same night. Then Parker, Smith, Townesend, Purpet, with five others, desired that they might go by land, and that the boat might fetch them when they were against the isle, it being scarce a mile from the shore. The Captain bade them do what they thought best, advising them to take weapons with them; "For," said he, "although we have not at any time seen people in this place, yet in the country there may be savages." They answered that here were great store of deer and ostriches; but if there were savages they would devour them. Notwithstanding, the Captain caused them to carry weapons, calivers, swords, and targets. So on the 6th of November they departed by land, and the boat by sea; but from that day to this day we never heard of our men. On the 11th, while most of our men were at the isle, only the Captain and Master with six others being left in the ship, there came a great multitude of savages to the ship, throwing dust in the air, leaping and running like brute beasts, having vizards on their faces like dog's faces, or else their faces are dog's faces indeed. We greatly feared lest they would set our ship on fire, for they would suddenly make fire, whereat we much marvelled. They came to windward of our ship and set the bushes on fire, so that we were in a very stinking smoke. But as soon as they came within our shot, we shot at them, and, striking one of them in the thigh, they all presently fled, so that we never heard nor saw more of them. Hereby we judged that these cannibals had slain our nine men. When we considered what they were that thus were slain, and found that they were the principal men that would have murdered our Captain and Master, with the rest of their friends, we saw the just judgment of God, and made supplication to His Divine Majesty to be merciful unto us. While we were in this harbour our Captain and Master went with the boat to discover how far this river did run, that, if need should enforce us to leave our ship, we might know how far we might go by water. So they found that farther than twenty miles they could not go with the boat. At their return they sent the boat to the Isle of Penguins, whereby we understood that the penguins dried to our heart's content, and that the multitude of them was infinite. This penguin hath the shape of a bird, but hath no wings, only two stumps in the place of wings, by which he swimmeth under water with as great swiftness as any fish. They live upon smelts, whereof there is great abundance upon this coast. In eating they be neither fish nor flesh. They lay great eggs, and the bird is of a reasonable bigness, very near twice so big as a duck. All the time that we were in this place we fared passing well with eggs, penguins, young seals, young gulls, besides other birds such as I know not; of all which we had great abundance. In this place we found a herb called scurvy-grass, which we fried with eggs, using train oil instead of butter. This herb did so purge the blood, that it took away all kind of swellings, of which many died, and restored us to perfect health of body, so that we were in as good case as when we came first out of England. We stayed in this harbour until the 22nd of December, in which time we had dried 20,000 penguins; and the Captain, the Master, and myself had made some salt by laying salt water upon the rocks in holes, which in six days would be kerned. Thus God did feed us even as it were with manna from heaven.

On the 22nd of December we departed with our ship for the isle, where with great difficulty, by the skilful industry of our Master, we got 14,000 of our birds, and had almost lost our Captain in labouring to bring our birds aboard; and had not our Master been very expert in the set of those wicked tides, which run after many fashions, we had also lost our ship in the same place. But God of His goodness hath in all our extremities been our protector. So on the 22nd, at night, we departed with 14,000 dried penguins, not being able to fetch the rest, and shaped our course for Brazil. Now our Captain rated our victuals, and brought us to such allowance as that our victuals might last six months; for our hope was that within six months we might recover our country, though our sails were very bad. So the allowance was two ounces and a-half of meal for a man a-day, and to have so twice a week, so that five ounces did serve for a week. Three days a week we had oil, three spoonfuls for a man a day; and two days in a week peas, a pint between four men a day, and every day five penguins for four men, and six quarts of water for four men a day. This was our allowance, wherewith (we praise God) we lived, though weakly and very feeble. On the 30th of January we arrived at the island of Placentia, in Brazil, the first place that outward bound we were at; and having made the shoal, our ship lying off at sea, the Captain with twenty-four of the company went with the boat on shore, being a whole night before they could recover it. On the last of January at sun-rising they suddenly landed, hoping to take the Portugals in their houses, and by that means to recover some cassavi-meal, or other victuals for our relief; but when they came to the houses they were all razed and burnt to the ground, so that we thought no man had remained on the island. Then the Captain went to the gardens, and brought from thence fruits and roots for the company, and came aboard the ship, and brought her into a fine creek which he had found out, where we might moor her by the trees, and where there was water and hoops to trim our casks. Our case being very desperate, we presently laboured for despatch away; some cut hoops, which the coopers made, others laboured upon the sails and ship, every man travailing for his life, and still a guard was kept on shore to defend those that laboured, every man having his weapon likewise by him. On the 3rd of February our men with twenty-three shot went again to the gardens, being three miles from us upon the north shore, and fetched cassavi-roots out of the ground, to relieve our company instead of bread, for we spent not of our meal whilst we staid here. On the 5th of February, being Monday, our Captain and Master hasted the company to their labour; so some went with the coopers to gather hoops, and the rest laboured aboard. This night many of our men in the ship dreamed of murder and slaughter. In the morning they reported their dreams, one saying to another, this night I dreamt that thou wert slain; another answered, and I dreamed that thou wert slain; and this was general through the ship. The Captain hearing this, who likewise had dreamed very strangely himself, gave very strict charge that those which went on shore should take weapons with them, and saw them himself delivered into the boat, and sent some of purpose to guard the labourers. All the forenoon they laboured in quietness, and when it was ten o'clock, the heat being extreme, they came to a rock near the wood's side (for all this country is nothing but thick woods), and there they boiled cassavi-roots, and dined; after dinner some slept, some washed themselves in the sea, all being stripped to their shirts, and no man keeping watch, no match lighted, not a piece charged. Suddenly as they were thus sleeping and sporting, having gotten themselves into a corner out of sight of the ship, there came a multitude of Indians and Portugals upon them, and slew them sleeping; only two escaped, one very sore hurt, the other not touched, by whom we understood of this miserable massacre; with all speed we manned our boat, and landed to succour our men, but we found them slain, and laid naked on a rank one by another, with their faces upward, and a cross set by them; and withal we saw two very great pinnaces come from the river Janeiro very full of men; whom we mistrusted came from thence to take us, because there came from Janeiro soldiers to Santos, when the General had taken the town, and was strong in it. Of seventy-six persons which departed in our ship out of England, we were now left but twenty-seven, having lost thirteen in this place, with their chief furniture, as muskets, calivers, powder, and shot. Our cask was all in decay, so that we could not take in more water than was in our ship for want of cask, and that which we had was marvellous ill-conditioned; and being there moored by trees, for want of cables and anchors, we still expected the cutting of our moorings, to be beaten from our decks with our own furniture, and to be assailed by them of Janeiro; what distress we were now driven into I am not able to express. To depart with eight tons of water in such bad cask was to starve at sea, and in staying our case was ruinous. These were hard choices; but being thus perplexed, we made choice rather to fall into the hands of the Lord than into the hands of men; for his exceeding mercies we had tasted, and of the others' cruelty we were not ignorant. So concluding to depart, on the 6th of February we were off in the channel, with our ordnance and small shot in a readiness for any affair that should come, and having a small gale of wind, we recovered the sea in most deep distress. Then bemoaning our estate one to another, and recounting over all our extremities, nothing grieved us more than the loss of our men twice, first by the slaughter of the cannibals at Port Desire, and at this isle of Placentia by the Indians and Portugals. And considering what they were that were lost, we found that all those that conspired the murdering of our Captain and Master were now slain by the savages, the gunner only excepted. Being thus at sea, when we came to Cape Frio the wind was contrary; so that for three weeks we were grievously vexed with cross winds, and our water consuming, our hope of life was very small. Some desired to go to Bahia, and to submit themselves to the Portugals, rather than to die for thirst; but the Captain with fair persuasions altered their purpose of yielding to the Portugals. In this distress it pleased God to send us rain in such plenty as that we were well watered, and in good comfort to return. But after we came near unto the sun, our dried penguins began to corrupt, and there bred in them a most loathsome and ugly worm of an inch long. This worm did so mightily increase, and devour our victuals, that there was in reason no hope how we should avoid famine, but be devoured of these wicked creatures; there was nothing that they did not devour, only iron excepted. Our clothes, boots, shoes, hats, shirts, stockings; and for the ship they did so eat the timbers, as that we greatly feared they would undo us, by gnawing through the ship's side. Great was the care and diligence of our Captain, Master, and company to consume these vermin, but the more we laboured to kill them the more they increased, so that at the last we could not sleep for them, but they would eat our flesh, and bite like mosquitos. In this woeful case, after we had passed the equinoctial toward the north, our men began to fall sick of such a monstrous disease, as I think the like was never heard of; for in their ankles it began to swell, from thence in two days it would be in their breasts, so that they could not draw their breath. Whereupon our men grew mad with grief. Our Captain with extreme anguish of his soul was in such woeful case, that he desired only a speedy end, and though he were scarce able to speak for sorrow, yet he persuaded them to patience, and to give God thanks, and like dutiful children to accept of his chastisement. For all this divers grew raging mad, and some died in most loathsome and furious pain. It were incredible to write our misery as it was; there was no man in perfect health, but the Captain and one boy. The Master being a man of good spirit, with extreme labour bore out his grief, so that it grew not upon him. To be short, all our men died except sixteen, of which there were but five able to move. The Captain was in good health, the Master indifferent, Captain Cotton and myself swollen and short-winded, yet better than the rest that were sick, and one boy in health; upon us five only the labour of the ship did stand. The Captain and Master, as occasion served, would take in and heave out the top-sails, the master only attended on the sprit-sail, and all of us at the capstan without sheets and tacks. In fine, our misery and weakness was so great, that we could not take in nor heave out a sail; so our top-sail and sprit-sails were torn all in pieces by the weather. The Master and Captain taking their turns at the helm, were mightily distressed and monstrously grieved with the most woeful lamentation of our sick men. Thus, as lost wanderers upon the sea, the 11th of June, 1593, it pleased God that we arrived at Berehaven, in Ireland, and there ran the ship on shore; where the Irish men helped us to take in our sails, and to moor our ship for floating; which slender pains of theirs cost the Captain some ten pounds before he could have the ship in safety. Thus without victuals, sails, men, or any furniture, God only guided us into Ireland, where the Captain left the Master and three or four of the company to keep the ship, and within five days after he and certain others had passage in an English fisher-boat to Padstow, in Cornwall. In this manner our small remnant by God's only mercy were preserved, and restored to our country, to whom be all honour and glory, world without end.

RALEIGH.

THE connection of Sir Walter Raleigh with American history has been more than once illustrated in these pages. We have already found him taking part in the enterprise of his half-brother, Gilbert (p. 185), and "setting forth" the barque Raleigh, at his own expense, in the first colonizing expedition which left the shores of England. After Gilbert's failure, we have found Raleigh himself taking in hand the task of colonization, and despatching Amadas and Barlow to survey, with a view to settlement, that part of the American shore which lay to the north of Florida (p. 211). The colony, which Raleigh afterwards sent, proved a failure, and the emigrants were brought back by Drake (p. 252). When the events recorded in the present narrative happened, it was above eight years since Drake had reconducted the first Virginian colonists to England. During those eight years the ultimate fortunes of the New World had been slowly unfolding. The attempt to colonize the shores of "Virginia" had been repeated, and had again ended in failure. But this failure had been outbalanced by the continued success which had attended the English navigators in their naval contests with the Spaniards. Raleigh had himself equipped more than one great buccaneering expedition, and had been as successful as Drake and Cavendish when fortune had most favoured them. These successes had included one which was signally great and decisive. The chief event of these eight years had been the failure of the great naval expedition sent by Philip against England in 1588. This great catastrophe seemed to prove abundantly, and once for all, that Spaniards were no match for Englishmen at sea, even in numerical disproportion which seemed overwhelming, and that wherever Spain had not already secured her American possessions by fortification and settlement, those possessions lay at the mercy of England. The way was thus prepared for the English settlements in the West Indian islands, in Chesapeake Bay, and on the coast of New England.

But before the history of America, as affected by English enterprise, thus took its definitive shape, a singular historical illusion had to be dissipated. Among the ignorant Spanish adventurers who dwelt in America it was believed that there existed yet a third great native empire, called Guiana, equal in size and wealth to those two famous empires which had been discovered and conquered in the days of their grandfathers.

While Raleigh was enjoying the fruits of his enterprise and good fortune in the retirement of Sherborne, he seems to have been laying his plans for the conquest of this rich empire, which was intended to do for England what the conquest of Mexico and Peru had done for Aragon and Castile two generations before. Had the reports in question been founded in fact, the career of Raleigh might have had a different end. They were, in truth, mere fables: and a career of fame and success thenceforth became one of disaster and disgrace.

The belief in this fabulous empire dates back to the conquest of Peru by Pizarro, above half a century before the expedition of Raleigh. When the Spanish conquerors inquired for other populous districts, and more fenced cities, stored with gold and silver, like Cuzco, they were generally directed to the east, and to the region between the great rivers Marañon and Orinoco. Ordaz, a Knight of the Order of Saint James of

Compostella, undertook, by the direction of Gonzalez Pizarro, to explore in this direction: and one Juan Martinez, who is described by Raleigh as "Master of the Munition" to Ordaz, was apparently the first of the series of lying travellers who declared that they had seen the great city of Manoa, or Eldorado, the capital of a descendant of the ancient Incas of Peru, who ruled the vast and populous empire of Guiana. The account attributed to Martinez, as Raleigh heard it from his prisoner Berreo, the Governor of Trinidad, will be found at p. 340 of the present narrative. More information was contributed by Peter de Urra, a Spanish military adventurer, who claimed to have visited Manoa in 1541. He declared that, after a journey of many days, he had beheld this vast city from the top of a mountain; that he saw afar off the palace of a governor, and a temple, in which he was told there were golden idols representing a woman and children; that its population was apparently vast, and its order and polity worthy of all admiration. Urra, according to his own account, was only prevented from pushing on and entering the city by an overwhelming force of armed Indians, which the news of his advance had assembled to resist him. Humboldt inclines to think that Urra's story may possibly be but an exaggeration. Southey, with more judgment, pronounces it to be a gross fabrication. Another lying traveller, called Santos, praised the neatness and beauty of the streets, and added that the roofs of the houses were covered with gold and silver, and that the high priest who officiated in the great temple was anointed with turtle-fat and covered with gold-dust, like the Inca himself.

Such were the tales which had induced Spanish adventurers, even down to the time of Raleigh's own "Discovery," to explore the wooded shores of the Orinoco in fruitless search of

"Guiana, the magazine of rich metals" (p. 332). The English heard of these expeditions though the piratical voyages of Drake and his followers. Men who had taken part in them were among the prisoners made by the English buccaneer captains on the South American coast (p. 344); and their captors eagerly questioned them as to the exact locality in which the city of Eldorado was to be sought. It was generally agreed that this city was situated on a great salt-water lake two hundred leagues long, which might be likened to the Caspian Sea (p. 338); and this lake was said to be reached from one of the tributaries of either the Amazon or the Orinoco. The famous city of Mexico had been found on a lake similarly situated, and this fact lent probability to the current description. No such lake did in fact exist; but it will appear that one of the tributaries of the Orinoco presented physical conditions which in some degree accounted for this current description.

The search for Guiana passed on from one generation of Spanish emigrants to another. Gonzalez Ximenes, one of the conquerors of New Granada, had engaged in it, and Raleigh found among his prisoners one who had been with him. From Ximenes the enterprise was inherited by his son-in-law, Antonio de Berreo, who, in Raleigh's time, was Governor of Trinidad. Some sought the unknown land from the Pacific side, by way of Peru; others, as Raleigh did, from the Atlantic side, by ascending the Orinoco; others, from the side of the Caribbean sea, by way of New Granada. Berreo chose the latter route. Taking with him seven hundred Spanish horsemen, besides Indians and slaves, he crossed the mountains and reached the head waters of the Orinoco; but he neither found this great and populous city, nor could obtain tidings of it until he reached the district of Amapaia, which was said to be eight hundred miles from the mouth of the river. The Amapaians informed him that to the south of their land there was a country very rich in gold; and this, again, Berreo concluded to be Guiana. It was separated from the valley of the Orinoco by one of the great ridges of the Andes. Berreo found no pass over this ridge. Even if he had found a pass, he had no means of transport: the natives were openly hostile, and he suspected them of having given warning of his approach to the inhabitants of the rich and powerful empire which he was purposing to invade; and, lastly, his invading force had been reduced by sickness to only 120 men. In these circumstances he abandoned his attempt, and descended the Orinoco, passing the mouths of a hundred of its tributaries. On his way he again gathered tidings of Guiana from a cacique named Carapana (p. 350). But it was now too late to return. Berreo reached the mouth of the Orinoco, and returned to his home in New Granada by way of Trinidad and the sea-coast.

The Spaniards afterwards partially occupied the territory of Carapana. They never succeeded in reaching the city of Manoa, and the search of it was practically abandoned: but those who resided there collected large quantities of gold, which served to keep alive the traditions of Eldorado. Such was the condition of things when, in 1594, Raleigh directed Jacob Whiddon, an English pirate captain, to procure information as to the great empire of which so much had been heard.

In the next year, following Whiddon's directions, Raleigh sailed for Guiana with five vessels and a hundred men.

The incidents of his exploration of the Orinoco are minutely described in the present narrative. Confined as it was to those parts of the Orinoco basin which were already well known to the Spaniards, it added little or nothing to previous information, and, in the strict sense of the word, was no

"Discovery" at all. But the present narrative widely popularised the information, true and false, which already existed. In an age of adventure, a new and attractive field appeared to be opened: and contemporary literature clearly indicates in many places how profoundly the idea of rich Guiana had sunk into the English mind. Bishop Hall thus satirizes the adventurers who sought it :—

> "Vent'rous Fortunio his farm hath sold,
> And gads to Guian land to fish for gold:
> Meeting, perhaps, if Orenoque deny,
> Some straggling pinnace of Polonian rye:
> Then comes home, floating with a silken sail,
> That Severn shaketh with his cannon peal."
>
> BOOK IV., Sat. 3.

Among the wonders vouched for by Raleigh, none so much took the English fancy as his account of the Ewaipanoma race, who had their eyes in their shoulders, and their mouths in the middle of their breasts. Shakspere clearly alludes to Raleigh's account in the person of Othello, whose "travel's history" told of—

> ". . . Antres vast, and deserts idle,
> "Rough quarries, rocks, and hills whose heads touch heaven,
> And of the Cannibals, that each other eat,
> (The Anthropophagi,) and men whose heads
> Do grow beneath their shoulders. . . ."

Donne compares "Guiana's rarities" with the fabled monsters of Africa. In estimating the credulity of Raleigh with regard to the former, it should not be forgotten that Bacon did not disbelieve in the latter.

The belief in Guiana did not cease after the failures of Raleigh. Drayton speaks of "Manoa's mighty seat:" and Milton classes the great city, the riches of which still awaited the European spoiler, with those which had already met their fate :—

> "Rich Mexico, the seat of Montezume,
> And Cuzco in Peru, the richer seat
> Of Atabalipa, and yet unspoil'd
> Guiana, whose great city Geryon's sons
> Call El Dorado."
>
> PARADISE LOST, Book xi.

Even while Milton was writing his poem, the French Jesuits were pursuing the fruitless search. But by this time, a discovery had been made which tended to dissipate this illusion. The Jesuits had reached the Salt-lake on the shore of which Manoa was said to stand. The valley at the head of the Parima river is inundated to a vast extent during the rainy season. The saltness of the soil is communicated to the water: and the story of the great Salt-Lake was now explained. No wealthy city had been found: but the Parima river became henceforth the centre of exploration. The search in its neighbourhood soon came to an end, and the rich empire of Guiana passed into the region of fable. Dutch and Spanish adventurers, however, were seeking for it as late as the middle of the last century.

RALEIGH.

The Discovery of GUIANA.

On Thursday, the 6th of February, in the year 1595, we departed England, and the Sunday following had sight of the North Cape of Spain, the wind for the most part continuing prosperous; we passed in sight of the Burlings, and the Rock, and so onwards for the Canaries, and fell with Fuerteventura on the 17th of the same month, where we spent two or three days, and relieved our companies with some fresh meat. From thence we coasted by the Grand Canary, and so to Teneriffe, and stayed there for the Lion's Whelp, your Lordship's ship, and for Captain Amyas Preston and the rest. But when after seven or eight days we found them not, we departed and directed our course for Trinidad, with mine own ship, and a small barque of Captain Cross's only (for we had before lost sight of a small Galego on the coast of Spain, which came with us from Plymouth). We arrived at Trinidad on the 22nd of March, casting anchor at Point Curiapan, which the Spaniards call Punta de Gallo, which is situate in eight degrees or thereabouts. We abode there four or five days, and in all that time we came not to the speech of any Indian or Spaniard. On the coast we saw a fire, as we sailed from the Point Carao towards Curiapan, but for fear of the Spaniards none durst come to speak with us. I myself coasted it in my barge close aboard the shore and landed in every cove, the better to know the island, whilst the ships kept the channel. From Curiapan after a few days we turned up northeast to recover that place which the Spaniards call Puerto de los Españoles, and the inhabitants Conquerabia, and as before (revictualling my barge) I left the ships and kept by the shore, the better to come to speech with some of the inhabitants, and also to understand the rivers, watering-places, and ports of the island, which (as it is rudely done) my purpose is to send your Lordship after a few days. From Curiapan I came to a port and seat of Indians called Parico, where we found a fresh water river, but saw no people. From thence I rowed to another port, called by the naturals Piche, and by the Spaniards Tierra de Brea. In the way between both were divers little brooks of fresh water and one salt river that had store of oysters upon the branches of the trees, and were very salt and well tasted. All their oysters grow upon those boughs and sprays, and not on the ground; the like is commonly seen in other places of the West Indies, and elsewhere. This tree is described by Andrew Thevet, in his France Antarctique, and the form figured in the book as a plant very strange, and by Pliny in his twelfth book of his Natural History. But in this island, as also in Guiana, there are very many of them.

At this point, called Tierra de Brea or Piche, there is that abundance of stone pitch that all the ships of the world may be therewith laden from thence; and we made trial of it in trimming our ships to be most excellent good, and melteth not with the sun as the pitch of Norway, and therefore for ships trading the south parts very profitable. From thence we went to the mountain foot called Annaperima, and so passing the river Carone on which the Spanish city was seated, we met with our ships at Puerto de los Españoles or Conquerabia.

This island of Trinidad hath the form of a sheephook, and is but narrow; the north part is very mountainous, the soil is very excellent and will bear sugar, ginger, or any other commodity that the Indies yield. It hath store of deer, wild porks, fruit, fish, and fowl; it hath also for bread sufficient maize, cassavi, and of those roots and fruits which are common everywhere in the West Indies. It hath divers beasts which the Indies have not; the Spaniards confessed that they found grains of gold in some of the rivers; but they having a purpose to enter Guiana (the magazine of all rich metals) cared not to spend time in the search thereof any further. This island is called by the people thereof Cairi, and in it are divers nations; those about Parico are called Jajo, those at Punta de Carao are of the Arwacas, and between Carao and Curiapan they are called Salvajos, between Carao and Punta de Galera are the Nepojos, and those about the Spanish city term themselves Carinepagotes. Of the rest of the nations, and of other ports and rivers I leave to speak here, being impertinent to my purpose, and mean to describe them as they are situate in the particular plot and description of the island, three parts whereof I coasted with my barge, that I might the better describe it.

Meeting with the ships at Puerto de los Españoles, we found at the landing-place a company of Spaniards who kept a guard at the descent; and they offering a sign of peace, I sent Captain Whiddon to speak with them, whom afterwards to my great grief I left buried in the said island after my return from Guiana, being a man most honest and valiant. The Spaniards seemed to be desirous to trade with us, and to enter into terms of peace, more for doubt of their own strength than for aught else, and in the end, upon pledge, some of them came aboard; the same evening there stole also aboard us in a small canoe two Indians, the one of them being a cacique or lord of the people called Cantyman, who had the year before been with Captain Whiddon, and was of his acquaintance. By this Cantyman we understood what strength the Spaniards had, how far it was to their city, and of Don Antonio de Berreo, the governor, who was said to be slain in his second attempt of Guiana, but was not.

While we remained at Puerto de los Españoles some Spaniards came aboard us to buy linen of the company, and such other things as they wanted, and also to view our ships and company, all which I entertained kindly and feasted after our manner; by means whereof I learned of one and another as much of the estate of Guiana as I could, or as they knew, for those poor soldiers having been many years without wine, a few draughts made them merry, in which mood they vaunted of Guiana and the riches thereof, and all what they knew of the ways and passages, myself seeming to purpose nothing less than the entrance or discovery thereof, but bred in them an opinion that I was bound only for the relief of those English which I had planted in Virginia, whereof the bruit was come among them; which I had performed in my return, if extremity of weather had not forced me from the said coast.

I found occasions of staying in this place for two causes. The one was to be revenged of Berreo, who the year before, 1594, had betrayed eight of Captain Whiddon's men, and took them while he departed from them to seek the Edward Bonaventure, which arrived at Trinidad the day before from the East Indies: in whose absence Berreo sent a canoe aboard the pinnace only with Indians and dogs inviting the company to go with them into the woods to kill a deer. Who, like wise men, in the absence of their captain followed the Indians, but were no sooner one arquebuse shot from the shore, but Berreo's soldiers lying in ambush had them all notwithstanding that he had given his word to Captain Whiddon that they should take water and wood safely. The other cause of my stay was, for that by discourse with the Spaniards I daily learned more and more of Guiana, of the rivers and passages, and of the enterprise of Berreo, by what means or fault he failed, and how he meant to prosecute the same.

While we thus spent the time I was assured by another cacique of the north side of the island, that Berreo had sent to Margarita and Cumana for soldiers, meaning to have given me a *cassado* at parting, if it had been possible. For although he had given order through all the island that no Indian should come aboard to trade with me upon pain of hanging and quartering, (having executed two of them for the same, which I afterwards found) yet every night there came some with most lamentable complaints of his cruelty: how he had divided the island and given to every soldier a part; that he made the ancient caciques, which were lords of the country, to be their slaves; that he kept them in chains, and dropped their naked bodies with burning bacon; and such other torments, which I found afterwards to be true. For in the city, after I entered the same, there were five of the lords or little kings (which they call caciques in the West Indies) in one chain almost dead of famine, and wasted with torments. These are called in their own language Acarewana, and now of late since English, French, and Spanish, are come among them, they call themselves Captains, because they perceive that the chiefest of every ship is called by that name. Those five Captains in the chain were called Wannawanare, Carroaori, Maquarima, Tarroopanama, and Aterima. So as both to be revenged of the former wrong, as also considering that to enter Guiana by small boats, to depart 400 or 500 miles from my ships, and to leave a garrison in my back interested in the same enterprise, who also daily expected supplies out of Spain, I should have savoured very much of the ass; and therefore taking a time of most advantage, I set upon the *Corps du garde* in the evening, and having put them to the sword, sent Captain Calfield onwards with sixty soldiers, and myself followed with forty more, and so took their new city, which they called St. Joseph, by break of day.

They abode not any fight after a few shot, and all being dismissed, but only Berreo and his companion, I brought them with me aboard, and at the instance of the Indians I set their new city of St. Joseph on fire.

The same day arrived Captain George Gifford with your lordship's ship, and Captain Keymis, whom I lost on the coast of Spain, with the Galego, and in them divers gentlemen and others, which to our little army was a great comfort and supply.

We then hasted away towards our purposed discovery, and first I called all the captains of the island together that were enemies to the Spaniards; for there were some which Berreo had brought out of other countries, and planted there to eat out and waste those that were natural of the place, and by my Indian interpreter, which I carried out of England, I made them understand that I was the servant of a Queen, who was the great cacique of the north, and a virgin, and had more caciqui under her than there were trees in that island; that she was an enemy to the *Castellani* in respect of their tyranny and oppression, and that she delivered all such nations about her, as were by them oppressed, and having freed all the coast of the northern world from their servitude, had sent me to free them also, and withal to defend the country of Guiana from their invasion and conquest. I shewed them Her Majesty's picture, which they so admired and honoured, as it had been easy to have brought them idolatrous thereof.

The like and a more large discourse I made to the rest of the nations, both in my passing to Guiana and to those of the borders, so as in that part of the world Her Majesty is very famous and admirable, whom they now call Ezrabeta Cassipuna Aquerewana, which is as much as "Elizabeth, the great princess or greatest commander." This done, we left Puerto de los Españoles, and returned to Curiapan, and having Berreo my prisoner, I gathered from him as much of Guiana as he knew.

This Berreo is a gentleman well descended, and had long served the Spanish king in Milan, Naples, the Low Countries, and elsewhere, very valiant and liberal, and a gentleman of great assuredness, and of a great heart. I used him according to his estate and worth in all things I could, according to the small means I had.

I sent Captain Whiddon the year before to get what knowledge he could of Guiana: and the end of my journey at this time was to discover and enter the same. But my intelligence was far from truth, for the country is situate about six hundred English miles further from the sea than I was made believe it had been. Which afterwards understanding to be true by Berreo, I kept it from the knowledge of my company, who else would never have been brought to attempt the same. Of which six hundred miles I passed four hundred, leaving my ship so far from me at anchor in the sea, which was more of desire to perform that discovery than of reason, especially having such poor and weak vessels to transport ourselves in. For in the bottom of an old galego which I caused to be fashioned like a galley, and in one barge, two wherries, and a ship-boat of the Lion's Whelp, we carried one hundred persons and their victuals for a month in the same, being all driven to lie in the rain and weather in the open air, in the burning sun, and upon the hard boards, and to dress our meat, and to carry all manner of furniture in them. Wherewith they were so pestered and unsavory, that what with victuals being most fish, with the wet clothes of so many men thrust together, and the heat of the sun, I will undertake there was never any prison in England that could be found more unsavoury and loathsome, especially to myself, who had for many years before been dieted and cared for in a sort far more differing.

If Captain Preston had not been persuaded that he should have come too late to Trinidad to have found us there (for the month was expired which I promised to tarry for him there ere he could recover the coast of Spain) but that it had pleased God he might have joined with us, and that we had entered the country but some ten days sooner ere the rivers were overflown, we had adventured either to have gone to the great city of Manoa, or at least taken so many of the other cities and towns nearer at hand, as would have made a royal return. But it pleased not God so much to favour me at this time; if it shall be my lot to prosecute the same, I shall willingly spend my life therein, and if any else shall be enabled thereunto, and conquer the same, I assure him thus much, he shall perform more than ever was done in Mexico by Cortez, or in Peru by Pizarro, whereof the one conquered the Empire of Mutezuma, the other of Guascar, and Atabalipa. And whatsoever prince shall possess it, that prince shall be lord of more gold, and of a more beautiful Empire, and of more cities and people, than either the King of Spain or the Great Turk.

But because there may arise many doubts how this Empire of Guiana is become so populous, and adorned with so many great cities, towns, temples, and treasures, I thought good to make it known, that the Emperor now reigning is descended from those magnificent princes of Peru, of whose large territories, of whose policies, conquests, edifices, and riches, Pedro de Cieza, Francisco Lopez, and others have written large discourses; for when Francisco Pizarro, Diego Almagro and others conquered the said Empire of Peru, and had put to death Atabalipa, son to Guaynacapa, which Atabalipa had formerly caused his eldest brother Guascar to be slain, one of the younger sons of Guaynacapa fled out of Peru, and took with him many thousands of those soldiers of the Empire called Orejones, and with those and many others that followed him, he vanquished all that tract and valley of America which is situate between the great river of Amazons and Baraquan, otherwise called Orenoque and Marannon.

The Empire of Guiana is directly east from Peru towards the sea, and lieth under the equinoctial line, and it hath more abundance of gold than any part of Peru, and as many or more great cities than ever Peru had when it flourished most; it is governed by the same laws, and the Emperor and people observe the same religion, and the same form and policies in government as were used in Peru, not differing in any part; and I have been assured by such of the Spaniards as have seen Manoa, the Imperial city of Guiana, which the Spaniards call El Dorado, that for the greatness, for the riches, and for the excellent seat, it far exceedeth any of the world, at least of so much of the world as is known to the Spanish nation: it is founded upon a lake of salt water of 200 leagues long, like unto *Mare Caspium*. And if we compare it to that of Peru, and but read the report of Francisco Lopez and others, it will seem more than credible; and because we may judge of the one by the other, I thought good to insert part of the 120th chapter of Lopez in his general history of the Indies, wherein he describeth the Court and magnificence of Guaynacapa, ancestor to the Emperor of Guiana, whose very words are these:—
"Todo el servicio de su casa, mesa y cocina era de oro y de plata, y cuando menos de plata y cobre, por mas recio. Tenia en su recamara estatuas huecas de oro, que parescian gigantes, y las figuras al propio, y tamaño de cuantos animales, aves, arboles, y yerbas produce la tierra, y de cuantos peces cria la mar y agua de sus reynos. Tenia asimesmo sogas, costales, cestas, y troxes de oro y plata; rimeros de palos de oro, que pareciesen leña rajada para quemar. En fin no avia cosa en su tierra, que no la tuviese de oro contrahecha; y aun dizen, que tenian los Ingas un verjel

en una isla cerca de la Puna, donde se iban a holgar, quando querian mar, que tenia la hortaliza, las flores, y arboles de oro y plata, invencion y grandeza hasta entonces nunca vista. Allende de todo esto tenia infinitisima cantidad de plata y oro por labrar en el Cuzco, que se perdio por la muerte de Guascar; ca los Indios lo escondieron, viendo que los Españoles se lo tomavan, y embiavan a España." That is, "All the vessels of his house, table, and kitchen, were of gold and silver, and the meanest of silver and copper for strength and hardness of metal. He had in his wardrobe hollow statues of gold which seemed giants, and the figures in proportion and bigness of all the beasts, birds, trees, and herbs, that the earth bringeth forth; and of all the fishes that the sea or waters of his kingdom breedeth. He had also ropes, budgets, chests, and troughs of gold and silver, heaps of billets of gold, that seemed wood marked out to burn. Finally, there was nothing in his country whereof he had not the counterfeit in gold. Yea, and they say, the Ingas had a garden of pleasure in an island near Puna, where they went to recreate themselves, when they would take the air of the sea, which had all kinds of garden-herbs, flowers, and trees of gold and silver, an invention and magnificence till then never seen. Besides all this, he had an infinite quantity of silver and gold unwrought in Cuzco, which was lost by the death of Guascar, for the Indians hid it, seeing that the Spaniards took it, and sent it into Spain."

And in the 117th chapter, Francisco Pizarro caused the gold and silver of Atabalipa to be weighed after he had taken it, which Lopez setteth down in these words following:—"Hallaron cincuenta y dos mil marcos de buena plata, y un millon y trecientos y veinte y seis mil y quinientos pesos de oro." Which is, "They found fifty and two thousand marks of good silver, and one million and three hundred and twenty and six thousand and five hundred pezos of gold."

Now, although these reports may seem strange, yet, if we consider the many millions which are daily brought out of Peru into Spain, we may easily believe the same. For we find that by the abundant treasure of that country the Spanish King vexes all the princes of Europe, and is become, in a few years, from a poor King of Castile, the greatest monarch of this part of the world, and likely every day to increase if other princes forslow the good occasions offered, and suffer him to add this empire to the rest, which by far exceedeth all the rest. If his gold now endanger us, he will then be unresistible. Such of the Spaniards as afterwards endeavoured the conquest thereof (whereof there have been many, as shall be declared hereafter) thought that this Inga (of whom this Emperor now living is descended) took his way by the river of Amazons, by that branch which is called Papamene; for by that way followed Orellana (by the commandment of Gonzalo Pizarro, in the year 1542), whose name the river also beareth this day, which is also by others called Marañon, although Andrew Thevet doth affirm that between Marañon and Amazons there are 120 leagues; but sure it is that those rivers have one head and beginning, and the Marañon, which Thevet describeth, is but a branch of Amazons or Orellana, of which I will speak more in another place. It was attempted by Ordas; but it is now little less than seventy years since that Diego Ordas, a Knight of the Order of Santiago, attempted the same; and it was in the year 1542 that Orellana discovered the river of Amazons; but the first that ever saw Manoa was Juan Martinez, master of the munition to Ordas. At a port called Morequito, in Guiana, there lieth at this day a great anchor of Ordas's ship. And this port is some 300 miles within the land, upon the great river of Orenoque.

I rested at this port four days: twenty days after I left the ships at Curiapan. The relation of this Martinez (who was the first that discovered Manoa), his success, and end, are to be seen in the Chancery of Saint Juan de Puerto Rico, whereof Berreo had a copy, which appeared to be the greatest encouragement as well to Berreo as to others that formerly attempted the discovery and conquest. Orellana, after he failed of the discovery of Guiana by the said river of Amazons, passed into Spain, and there obtained a patent of the King for the invasion and conquest, but died by sea about the islands, and his fleet severed by tempest, the action for that time proceeded not. Diego Ordas followed the enterprise, and departed Spain with 600 soldiers and thirty horse. Who, arriving on the coast of Guiana, was slain in a mutiny, with the most part of such as favoured him, as also of the rebellious part, insomuch as his ships perished and few or none returned; neither was it certainly known what became of the said Ordas until Berreo found the anchor of his ship in the river of Orenoque; but it was supposed, and so it is written by Lopez, that he perished on the seas, and of other writers diversely conceived and reported. And hereof it came that Martinez entered so far within the land, and arrived at that city of Inga the Emperor; for it chanced that while Ordas

with his army rested at the port of Morequito (who was either the
first or second that attempted Guiana), by some negligence the
whole store of powder provided for the service was set on fire, and
Martinez, having the chief charge, was condemned by the General
Ordas to be executed forthwith. Martinez, being much favoured by
the soldiers, had all the means possible procured for his life; but it
could not be obtained in other sort than this:—That he should be
set into a canoe alone, without any victual, only with his arms, and
so turned loose into the great river. But it pleased God that the
canoe was carried down the stream, and certain of the Guianians
met it the same evening, and, having not at any time seen any
Christian nor any man of that colour, they carried Martinez into
the land to be wondered at, and so from town to town, until he
came to the great city of Manoa, the seat and residence of Inga
the Emperor. The Emperor, after he had beheld him, knew him
to be a Christian (for it was not long before that his brethren
Guascar and Atabalipa were vanquished by the Spaniards in Peru)
and caused him to be lodged in his palace and well entertained.
He lived seven months in Manoa, but was not suffered to wander
into the country anywhere. He was also brought thither all the
way blindfold, led by the Indians, until he came to the entrance of
Manoa itself, and was fourteen or fifteen days in the passage. He
avowed at his death that he entered the city at noon, and then
they uncovered his face, and that he travelled all that day till night
through the city, and the next day from sun rising to sun setting
ere he came to the palace of Inga. After that Martinez had lived
seven months in Manoa, and began to understand the language of
the country, Inga asked him whether he desired to return into his
own country, or would willingly abide with him. But Martinez, not
desirous to stay, obtained the favour of Inga to depart, with whom
he sent divers Guianians to conduct him to the river of Orenoque,
all laden with as much gold as they could carry, which he gave to
Martinez at his departure. But when he was arrived near the
river's side, the borderers, which are called the Orenoqueponi,
robbed him and his Guianians of all the treasure (the borderers
being at that time at wars, which Inga had not conquered) save
only of two great bottles of gourds, which were filled with beads of
gold curiously wrought, which those Orenoqueponi thought had
been no other thing than his drink or meat, or grain for food, with
which Martinez had liberty to pass. And so in canoes he fell
down from the river of Orenoque to Trinidad and from thence to

Margarita, and also to Saint Juan de Puerto Rico, where, remaining a long time for passage into Spain, he died. In the time of his extreme sickness, and when he was without hope of life, receiving the sacrament at the hands of his confessor, he delivered these things, with the relation of his travels, and also called for his *calabazas* or gourds of the gold beads, which he gave to the church and friars to be prayed for. This Martinez was he that christened the city of Manoa by the name of El Dorado, and, as Berreo informed me, upon this occasion, " Those Guianians, and also the borderers, and all other in that tract which I have seen, are marvellous great drunkards; in which vice I think no nation can compare with them. And at the times of their solemn feasts, when the Emperor carouseth with his captains, tributaries, and governors, the manner is thus. All those that pledge him are first stripped naked and their bodies anointed all over with a kind of white balsam (by them called *curca*), of which there is great plenty, and yet very dear amongst them, and it is of all other the most precious, whereof we have had good experience. When they are anointed all over, certain servants of the Emperor, having prepared gold made into fine powder, blow it through hollow canes upon their naked bodies, until they be all shining from the foot to the head; and in this sort they sit drinking by twenties and hundreds, and continue in drunkenness sometimes six or seven days together." The same is also confirmed by a letter written into Spain which was intercepted, which Mr. Robert Dudley told me he had seen. Upon this sight, and for the abundance of gold which he saw in the city, the images of gold in their temples, the plates, armours, and shields of gold which they use in the wars, he called it El Dorado. After the death of Ordas and Martinez, and after Orellana, who was employed by Gonzalo Pizarro, one Pedro de Osua, a knight of Navarre, attempted Guiana, taking his way into Peru, and built his brigantines upon a river called Oia, which rises to the southward of Quito, and is very great. This river falleth into Amazons, by which Osua with his companies descended, and came out of that province which is called Mutylonez; and it seemeth to me that this empire is reserved for Her Majesty and the English nation, by reason of the hard success which all these and other Spaniards found in attempting the same, whereof I will speak briefly, though impertinent in some sort to my purpose. This Pedro de Osua had among his troops a Biscayan called Agiri, a man meanly born, who bare no other office than a sergeant or *alferez:*

but after certain months, when the soldiers were grieved with travels and consumed with famine, and that no entrance could be found by the branches or body of Amazons, this Agiri raised a mutiny, of which he made himself the head, and so prevailed as he put Osua to the sword and all his followers, taking on him the whole charge and commandment, with a purpose not only to make himself Emperor of Guiana but also of Peru and of all that side of the West Indies. He had of his party seven hundred soldiers, and of those many promised to draw in other captains and companies, to deliver up towns and forts in Peru; but neither finding by the said river any passage into Guiana, nor any possibility to return towards Peru by the same Amazons, by reason that the descent of the river made so great a current, he was enforced to disembogue at the mouth of the said Amazons, which cannot be less than a thousand leagues from the place where they embarked. From thence he coasted the land till he arrived at Margarita to the north of Mompatar, which is at this day called Puerto de Tyranno for that he there slew Don Juan de Villa Andreda, Governor of Margarita, who was father to Don Juan Sarmiento, Governor of Margarita when Sir John Burgh landed there and attempted the island. Agiri put to the sword all other in the island that refused to be of his party, and took with him certain Simerones and other desperate companions. From thence he went to Cumana and there slew the Governor, and dealt in all as at Margarita. He spoiled all the coast of Caracas and the province of Venezuela and of Rio de la Hacha; and, as I remember, it was the same year that Sir John Hawkins sailed to Saint Juan de Ullua in the Jesus of Lubeck; for himself told me that he met with such a one upon the coast that rebelled, and had sailed down all the river of Amazons. Agiri from thence landed about Santa Marta and sacked it also, putting to death so many as refused to be his followers, purposing to invade Nuevo Reyno de Granada and to sack Pamplon, Merida, Lagrita, Tunxa, and the rest of the cities of Nuevo Reyno, and from thence again to enter Peru; but in a fight in the said Nuevo Reyno he was overthrown, and, finding no way to escape, he first put to the sword his own children, foretelling them that they should not live to be defamed or upbraided by the Spaniards after his death, who would have termed them the children of a traitor or a tyrant; and that, since he could not make them princes, he would yet deliver them from shame and reproach. These were the ends and tragedies of Ordas, Martinez, Orellana, Osua, and Agiri.

Also soon after Ordas followed Jeronimo Ortal de Saragosa with one hundred and fifty soldiers, who failing his entrance by sea, was cast with the current on the coast of Paria, and peopled about S. Miguel de Neveri. It was then attempted by Don Pedro de Silva, a Portuguese of the family of Ruy Gomes de Silva, and by the favour which Ruy Gomes had with the king he was set out; but he also shot wide of the mark; for being departed from Spain with his fleet, he entered by Marañon and Amazons, where by the nations of the river, and by the Amazons, he was utterly overthrown, and himself and all his army defeated; only seven escaped, and of those but two returned.

After him came Pedro Hernandez de Serpa, and landed at Cumana, in the West Indies, taking his journey by land towards Orenoque, which may be some 120 leagues; but ere he came to the borders of the said river, he was set upon by a nation of the the Indians, called Wikiri, and overthrown in such sort, that of 300 soldiers, horsemen, many Indians, and negroes, there returned but eighteen. Others affirm that he was defeated in the very entrance of Guiana, at the first civil town of the empire called Macureguarai. Captain Preston, in taking Santiago de Leon (which was by him and his companies very resolutely performed, being a great town, and far within the land) held a gentleman prisoner, who died in his ship, that was one of the company of Hernandez de Serpa, and saved among those that escaped, who witnessed what opinion is held among the Spaniards thereabouts of the great riches of Guiana, and El Dorado, the city of Inga. Another Spaniard was brought aboard me by Captain Preston, who told me in the hearing of himself and divers other gentlemen, that he met with Berreo's camp-master at Caraccas, when he came from the borders of Guiana, and that he saw with him forty most pure plates of gold, curiously wrought, and swords of Guiana, decked and inlaid with gold, feathers garnished with gold, and divers rarities which he carried to the Spanish king.

After Hernandez de Serpa, it was undertaken by the Adelantado, Don Gonzales Ximenes de Casada, who was one of the chiefest in the conquest of Nuevo Reino, whose daughter and heir Don Antonio de Berreo married. Gonzales sought the passage also by the river called Papamene, which riseth by

Quito, in Peru, and runneth south-east one hundred leagues, and then falleth into Amazons, but he also failing the entrance, returned with the loss of much labour and cost. I took one Captain George, a Spaniard, that followed Gonzales in this enterprise. Gonzales gave his daughter to Berreo, taking his oath and honour to follow the enterprise to the last of his substance and life; who since, as he hath sworn to me, hath spent 300,000 ducats in the same, and yet never could enter so far into the land as myself with that poor troop, or rather a handful of men, being in all about one hundred gentlemen, soldiers, rowers, boat-keepers, boys, and of all sorts; neither could any of the forepassed undertakers, nor Berreo himself, discover the country, till now lately by conference with an ancient king, called Carapana, he got the true light thereof; for Berreo came about 1,500 miles ere he understood aught, or could find any passage or entrance into any part thereof, yet he had experience of all these forenamed, and divers others, and was persuaded of their errors and mistakings. Borreo sought it by the river Cassamar, which falleth into a great river called Pato: Pato falleth into Meta, and Meta into Baraquan, which is also called Orenoque.

He took his journey from Nuevo Reyno de Granada, where he dwelt, having the inheritance of Gonzales Ximenes in those parts; he was followed with 700 horse, he drove with him 1000 head of cattle, he had also many women, Indians, and slaves. How all these rivers cross and encounter; how the country lieth and is bordered, the passage of Ximenes and Berreo, mine own discovery, and the way that I entered, with all the rest of the nations and rivers, your lordship shall receive in a large chart or map, which I have not yet finished, and which I shall most humbly pray your lordship to secrete, and not to suffer it to pass your own hands; for by a draught thereof all may be prevented by other nations; for I know it is this very year sought by the French, although by the way that they now take, I fear it not much. It was also told me ere I departed England, that Villiers, the Admiral, was in preparation for the planting of Amazons, to which river the French have made divers voyages, and returned with much gold and other rarities. I spake with a captain of a French ship that came from thence, his ship riding in Falmouth the same year that my ships came first from Virginia.

There was another this year in Helford, that also came from thence, and had been fourteen months at an anchor in Amazons, which were both very rich. Although, as I am persuaded, Guiana cannot be entered that way, yet no doubt the trade of gold from thence passeth by branches of rivers into the river of Amazons, and so it doth on every hand far from the country itself; for those Indians of Trinidad have plates of gold from Guiana, and those cannibals of Dominica which dwell in the islands by which our ships pass yearly to the West Indies, also the Indians of Paria, those Indians called Tucaris, Chochi, Apotomios, Cumanagotos, and all those other nations inhabiting near about the mountains that run from Paria through the province of Venezuela, and in Maracapana, and the cannibals of Guanipa, the Indians called Assawa, Coaca, Ajai, and the rest (all which shall be described in my description as they are situate) have plates of gold of Guiana. And upon the river of Amazons, Thevet writeth that the people wear croissants of gold, for of that form the Guianians most commonly make them; so as from Dominica to Amazons, which is above 250 leagues, all the chief Indians in all parts wear of those plates of Guiana. Undoubtedly those that trade Amazons return much gold, which (as is aforesaid) cometh by trade from Guiana, by some branch of a river that falleth from the country into Amazons, and either it is by the river which passeth by the nations called Tinados, or by Caripuna. I made enquiry amongst the most ancient and best travelled of the Orenoqueponi, and I had knowledge of all the rivers between Orenoque and Amazons, and was very desirous to understand the truth of those warlike women, because of some it is believed, of others not. And though I digress from my purpose, yet I will set down that which hath been delivered me for truth of those women, and I spake with a cacique, or lord of people, that told me he had been in the river, and beyond it also. The nations of these women are on the south side of the river in the provinces of Topago, and their chiefest strength and retreats are in the islands situate on the south side of the entrance some sixty leagues within the mouth of the said river. The memories of the like women are very ancient as well in Africa as in Asia. In Africa those that had Medusa for Queen; others in Scythia, near the rivers of Tanais and Thermodon. We find, also, that Lampedo and Marthesia were Queens of the Amazons. In many histories they are verified to have been, and in divers ages and provinces; but they which are not from Guiana do assemble but once in a year, and for the time of one month, which I gather by their relation, to be in April; and that time all kings of the borders assemble, and queens of the Amazons; and after the queens have chosen, the rest cast lots for their valentines. This one month they feast, dance, and drink of their wines in abundance; and the moon being done they all depart to their own provinces.

*   *   *   *   *   *

They are said to be very cruel and bloodthirsty, especially to such as offer to invade their territories. These Amazons have likewise great store of these plates of gold, which they recover by exchange chiefly for a kind of green stones, which the Spaniards call *Piedras hijadas*, and we use for spleen stones; and for the disease of the stone we also esteem them. Of these I saw divers in Guiana, and commonly every king or cacique hath one, which their wives for the most part wear, and they esteem them as great jewels.

But to return to the enterprise of Berreo, who (as I have said) departed from Nuevo Reyno with 700 horse. Besides the provisions above rehearsed, he descended by the river called Cassanar, which riseth in Nuevo Reyno out of the mountains by the city of Tuvia; from which mountain also springeth Pato; both which fall into the great river of Meta ; and Meta riseth from a mountain joining to Pamplon, in the same Nuevo Reyno de Granada. These, as also Guaiare, which issueth out of the mountains by Timana, fall all into Baraquan, and are but of his heads ; for at their coming together they lose their names, and Baraquan farther down is also rebaptized by the name of Orenoque. On the other side of the city and hills of Timana riseth Rio Grande, which falleth into the sea by Santa Marta. By Cassonar first, and so into Meta, Berreo passed, keeping his horsemen on the banks, where the country served them for to march ; and where otherwise, he was driven to embark them in boats which he builded for the purpose, and so come with the current down the river of Meta, and so into Baraquan. After he entered that great and mighty river, he began daily to lose of his companies both men and horse; for it is in many places violently swift, and hath forcible eddies, many sands, and divers islands sharp pointed with rocks ; but after one whole year, journeying for the most part by river, and the rest by land, he grew daily to fewer numbers; for both by sickness, and by encountering with the people of those regions through which he travelled, his companies were much wasted, especially by divers encounters with the Amapaians; and in all this time he never could learn of any passage into Guiana, nor any news or fame thereof, until he came to a further border of the said Amapaia, eight days' journey from the river Caroli, which was the furthest river that he entered. Among those of Amapaia, Guiana was famous, but few of these people accosted Berreo, or would trade with him the first three months of the six which he sojourned there. This Amapaia is also marvellous rich in gold (as both Berreo confessed and those of Guiana, with whom I had most conference) and is situate upon Orenoque also. In this country Berreo lost sixty of his best soldiers, and most of all his horse that remained in his former year's travel; but in the end, after divers encounters with those nations, they grew to peace, and they presented Berreo with ten images of fine gold among divers other plates and croissants, which, as he sware to me, and divers other gentlemen, were so curiously wrought, as he had not seen the like either in Italy, Spain, or the Low Countries; and he was resolved, that when they came to the hands of the Spanish king, to whom he had sent them by his campmaster, they would appear very admirable, especially being wrought by such a nation as had no iron instruments at all, nor any of those helps which our goldsmiths have to work withal. The particular name of the people in Amapaia which gave him these pieces, are called Anebas, and the river of Orenoque at that place is about twelve English miles broad, which may be from his outfall into the sea 700 or 800 miles.

This province of Amapaia is a very low and a marish ground near the river; and by reason of the red water which issueth out in small branches through the fenny and boggy ground, there breed divers poisonful worms and serpents; and the Spaniards not suspecting, nor in any sort foreknowing the danger, were infected with a grievous kind of flux by drinking thereof; and even the very horses poisoned therewith, insomuch as at the end of the six months that they abode there, of all their troops there were not left above 120 soldiers, and neither horse nor cattle; for Berreo hoped to have found Guiana by 1,000 miles nearer than it fell out to be in the end; by means whereof they sustained much want, and much hunger, oppressed with grievous diseases, and all the miseries that could be imagined. I demanded of those in Guiana that had travelled Amapaia, how they lived with that tawny or red water when they travelled thither; and they told me that after the sun was near the middle of the sky, they used to fill their pots and pitchers with that water, but either before that time or towards the setting of the sun it was dangerous to drink of, and in the night strong poison. I learned also of divers other rivers of that nature among them, which were also (while the sun was in the meridian) very safe to drink, and in the morning, evening, and night, wonderful dangerous and infective. From this province Berreo hasted away as soon as the spring and beginning of summer appeared, and sought his entrance on the borders of Orenoque on the south-side; but there ran a ledge of so high and impassable mountains, as he was not able by any means to march over them, continuing from the east sea into which Orenoque falleth, even to Quito in Peru; neither had he means to carry victual or munition over those craggy, high, and fast hills, being all woody, and those so thick and spiny, and so full of prickles, thorns, and briars, as it is impossible to creep through them; he had also neither friendship among the people, nor any interpreter to persuade or treat with them; and more, to his disadvantage, the caciques and kings of Amapaia had given knowledge of his purpose to the Guianians, and that he sought to sack and conquer the Empire, for the hope of their so great abundance and quantities of gold. He passed by the mouths of many great rivers which fell into Orenoque both from the north and south, which I forbear to name, for tediousness, and because they are more pleasing in describing than reading.

Berreo affirmed that there fell an hundred rivers into Orenoque from the north and south, whereof the least was as big as Rio Grande, that passed between Popayan and Nuevo Reyno de Granada (Rio Grande being esteemed one of the renowned rivers in all the West Indies, and numbered among the great rivers of the world); but he knew not the names of any of these, but Caroli only; neither from what nations they descended, neither to what provinces they led; for he had no means to discourse with the inhabitants at any time; neither was he curious in these things, being utterly unlearned, and not knowing the east from the west. But of all these I got some knowledge, and of many more, partly by my own travel, and the rest by conference; of some one I learned one, of others the rest, having with me an Indian that

spake many languages, and that of Guiana naturally. I sought
out all the aged men, and such as were greatest travellers, and by
the one and the other I came to understand the situations, the
rivers, the kingdoms from the east sea to the borders of Peru, and
from Orenoque southward as far as Amazons or Marannon, and
the religions of Maria Tamball, and of all the kings of provinces,
and captains of towns and villages, how they stood in terms of
peace or war, and which were friends or enemies the one with the
other, without which there can be neither entrance nor conquest in
those parts, nor elsewhere; for by the dissension between Guascar
and Atabalipa, Pizarro conquered Peru, and by the hatred that the
Tlaxcallians bare to Mutezuma, Cortez was victorious over Mexico;
without which both the one and the other had failed of their enterprise, and of the great honour and riches which they attained
unto.

Now Berreo began to grow into despair, and looked for no other
success than his predecessor in this enterprise, until such time as
he arrived at the province of Emeria towards the east sea and
mouth of the river, where he found a nation of people very
favourable, and the country full of all manner of victuals. The
king of this land is called Carapana, a man very wise, subtle, and
of great experience, being little less than an hundred years old. In
his youth he was sent by his father into the island of Trinidad, by
reason of civil war among themselves, and was bred at a village in
that island, called Parico. At that place in his youth he had seen
many Christians, both French and Spanish, and went divers times
with the Indians of Trinidad to Margarita and Cumaná, in the
West Indies (for both those places have ever been relieved with
victuals from Trinidad) by reason whereof he grew of more understanding, and noted the difference of the nations, comparing the
strength and arms of his country with those of the Christians, and
ever after temporised so as whosoever else did amiss, or was
wasted by contention, Carapana kept himself and his country in
quiet and plenty; he also held peace with the Caribs or cannibals,
his neighbours, and had free trade with all nations, whosoever else
had war.

Berreo sojourned and rested his weak troop in the town of
Carapana six weeks, and from him learned the way and passage
to Guiana, and the riches and magnificence thereof; but being
then utterly unable to proceed, he determined to try his fortune
another year, when he had renewed his provisions, and regathered

more force, which he hoped for as well out of Spain as from Nuevo Reyno, where he had left his son Don Antonio Ximenes to second him upon the first notice given of his entrance, and so for the present embarked himself in canoes, and by the branches of Orenoque arrived at Trinidad, having from Carapana sufficient pilots to conduct him. From Trinidad he coasted Paria, and so recovered Margarita; and having made relation to Don Juan Sarmiento, the Governor, of his proceeding, and persuaded him of the riches of Guiana, he obtained from thence fifty soldiers, promising presently to return to Carapana, and so into Guiana. But Berreo meant nothing less at that time; for he wanted many provisions necessary for such an enterprise, and therefore departed from Margarita, seated himself in Trinidad, and from thence sent his camp-master and his sergeant-major back to the borders to discover the nearest passage into the Empire, as also to treat with the borderers, and to draw them to his party and love; without which, he knew he could neither pass safely, nor in any sort be relieved with victuals or aught else. Carapana directed his company to a king called Morequito, assuring them that no man could deliver so much of Guiana as Morequito could, and that his dwelling was but five days journey from Macureguarai, the first civil town of Guiana.

Now your lordship shall understand that this Morequito, one of the greatest lords or kings of the borders of Guiana, had two or three years before been at Cumaná and at Margarita, in the West Indies, with great store of plates of gold, which he carried to exchange for such other things as he wanted in his own country, and was daily feasted, and presented by the governors of those places, and held amongst them some two months, in which time one Vides, Governor of Cumaná, won him to be his conductor into Guiana, being allured by those croissants and images of gold which he brought with him to trade, as also by the ancient fame and magnificence of El Dorado; whereupon Vides sent into Spain for a patent to discover and conquer Guiana, not knowing of the precedence of Berreo's patent, which, as Berreo affirmeth, was signed before that of Vides; so as when Vides understood of Berreo, and that he had made entrance into that territory, and foregone his desire and hope, it was verily thought that Vides practised with Morequito to hinder and disturb Berreo in all he could, and not to suffer him to enter through his seignory, nor any of his companies; neither to victual, nor guide them in any sort; for Vides, Governor of Cumaná, and Berreo, were become mortal enemies, as well for that Berreo had gotten Trinidad into his patent with Guiana, as also in that he was by Berreo prevented in the journey of Guiana itself; howsoever it was, I know not, but Morequito for a time dissembled his disposition, suffered Spaniards and a friar (which Berreo had sent to discover Manoa) to travel through his country, gave them a guide for Macureguarai, the first town of civil and appareled people, from whence they had other guides to bring them to Manoa, the great city of Inga; and being furnished with those things which they had learned of Carapana, were of most price in Guiana, went onward, and in eleven days arrived at Manoa, as Berreo affirmeth for certain; although I could not be assured thereof by the lord which now governeth the province of Morequito, for he told me that they got all the gold they had in other towns on this side Manoa, there being many very great and rich, and (as he said) built like the towns of Christians, with many rooms.

When these ten Spaniards were returned, and ready to put out of the border of Aromaia, the people of Morequito set upon them, and slew them all but one that swam the river, and took from them to the value of forty thousand pezos of gold; and one of them only lived to bring the news to Berreo, that both his nine soldiers and holy father were benighted in the said province. I myself spake with the captains of Morequito that slew them, and was at the place where it was executed. Berreo enraged here withal, sent all the strength he could make into Aromaia, to be revenged of him, his people, and country. But Morequito suspecting the same, fled over Orenoque, and through the territories of the Siama, and Wikiri, recovered Cumaná, where he thought himself very safe, with Vides the governor. But Berreo sending for him in the king's name, and his messengers finding him in the house of one Fashardo, on the sudden, ere he was suspected, so as he could not then be conveyed away, Vides durst not deny him, as well to avoid the suspicion of the practice, as also for that an holy father was slain by him and his people. Morequito offered Fashardo the weight of three quintals of gold, to let him escape; but the poor Guianian, betrayed on all sides, was delivered to the camp-master of Berreo, and was presently executed.

After the death of this Morequito, the soldiers of Berreo spoiled his territory and took divers prisoners; among others they took the uncle of Morequito, called Topiawari, who is now king of Aromaia (whose son I brought with me into England) and is a man of great understanding and policy; he is above a hundred years old, and yet is of a very able body. The Spaniards led him in a chain seventeen days, and made him their guide from place to place between his country and Emeria, the province of Carapana aforesaid, and he was at last redeemed for an hundred plates of gold, and divers stones called Piedras Hijadas, or spleen-stones. Now Berreo for executing of Morequito, and other cruelties, spoils, and slaughters done in Aromaia, hath lost the love of the Orenoqueponi, and of all the borderers, and dare not send any of his soldiers any further into the land than to Carapana, which he called the port of Guiana; but from thence by the help of Carapana he had trade further into the country, and always appointed ten Spaniards to reside in Carapana town, by whose favour, and by being conducted by his people, those ten searched the country thereabouts, as well for mines as for other trades and commodities.

They also have gotten a nephew of Morequito, whom they have christened and named Don Juan, of whom they have great hope, endeavouring by all means to establish him in the said province. Among many other trades, those Spaniards used canoes to pass to the rivers of Barema, Pawroma, and Dissequebe, which are on the south side of the mouth of Orenoque, and there buy women and children from the cannibals, which are of that barbarous nature, as they will for three or four hatchets sell the sons and daughters of their own brethren and sisters, and for somewhat more, even their own daughters. Hereof the Spaniards make great profit; for buying a maid of twelve or thirteen years for three or four hatchets, they sell them again at Margarita in the West Indies for fifty and a hundred pezos, which is so many crowns.

The master of my ship, John Douglas, took one of the canoes which came laden from thence with people to be sold, and the most of them escaped; yet of those he brought, there was one as well favoured and as well shaped as ever I saw any in England; and afterwards I saw many of them, which but for their tawny colour may be compared to any in Europe. They also trade in those rivers for bread of cassavi, of which they buy an hundred pound weight for a knife, and sell it at Margarita for ten pezos. They also recover great store of cotton, Brazil wood, and those beds which they call Hamacas or Brazil beds, wherein in hot countries all the Spaniards use to lie commonly, and in no other, neither did we ourselves while we were there. By means of which trades, for ransom of divers of the Guianians, and for exchange of hatchets and knives, Berreo recovered some store of gold plates, eagles of gold, and images of men and divers birds, and dispatched his camp-master for Spain, with all that he had gathered, therewith to levy soldiers, and by the show thereof to draw others to the love of the enterprise. And having sent divers images as well of men as beasts, birds, and fishes, so curiously wrought in gold, he doubted not but to persuade the king to yield to him some further help, especially for that this land hath never been sacked, the mines never wrought, and in the Indies their works were well spent, and the gold drawn out with great labour and charge. He also despatched messengers to his son in Nuevo Reyno to levy all the forces he could, and to come down the river Orenoque to Emeria, the province of Carapana, to meet him; he had also sent to Santiago de Leon on the coast of the Caracas, to buy horses and mules.

After I had thus learned of his proceedings past and purposed, I told him that I had resolved to see Guiana, and that it was the end of my journey, and the cause of my coming to Trinidad, as it was indeed, and for that purpose I sent Jacob Whiddon the year before to get intelligence: with whom Berreo himself had speech at that time, and remembered how inquisitive Jacob Whiddon was of his proceedings, and of the country of Guiana. Berreo was stricken into a great melancholy and sadness, and used all the arguments he could to dissuade me, and also assured the gentlemen of my company that it would be labour lost, and that they should suffer many miseries if they proceeded. And first he delivered that I could not enter any of the rivers with any barque or pinnace, or hardly with any ship's boat, it was so low, sandy, and full of flats, and that his companies were daily grounded in their canoes, which drew but twelve inches water. He further said, that none of the country would come to speak with us, but would all fly; and if we followed them to their dwellings, they would burn their own towns: and besides that, the way was long, the winter at hand, and that the rivers beginning once to swell, it was impossible to stem the current, and that we could not in those small boats by any means carry victuals for half the time, and that (which indeed most discouraged my company) the kings and lords of all the borders of Guiana had decreed that none of them should trade with any Christians for gold, because the same would be their own overthrow, and that for the love of gold the Christians meant to conquer and dispossess them of all together.

Many and the most of these I found to be true, but yet I resolving to make trial of whatsoever happened, directed Captain George Gifford, my Vice-Admiral, to take the Lion's Whelp, and Captain Caulfield his barque, to turn to the eastward, against the mouth of a river called Capuri, whose entrance I had before sent Captain Whiddon and John Douglas the master to discover, who found some nine feet of water or better upon the flood, and five at low water, to whom I had given instructions that they should anchor at the edge of the shoal, and upon the best of the flood to thrust over, which shoal John Douglas buoyed and beckoned for them before; but they laboured in vain; for neither could they turn it up altogether so far to the east, neither did the flood continue so long, but the water fell ere they could have passed the sands; as we after found by a second experience: so as now we must either give over our enterprise, or leaving our ships at adventure four hundred miles behind us, must run up in our ship's boats, one barge, and two wherries. But being doubtful how to carry victuals for so long a time in such baubles, or any strength of men, especially for that Berreo assured us that his son must be by that time come down with many soldiers, I sent away one King, master of the Lion's Whelp, with his ship's boat, to try another branch of the river in the bottom of the Bay of Guanipa, which was called Amana, to prove if there were water to be found for either of the small ships to enter. But when he came to the mouth of Amana, he found it as the rest, but stayed not to discover it thoroughly, because he was assured by an Indian, his guide, that the cannibals of Guanipa would assail them with many canoes, and that they shot poisoned arrows; so as if he hasted not back, they should all be lost.

In the meantime, fearing the worst, I caused all the carpenters we had to cut down a galego boat, which we meant to cast off, and to fit her with banks to row on, and in all things to prepare her the best they could, so as she might be brought to draw but five feet: for so much we had on the bar of Capuri at low water. And doubting of King's return, I sent John Douglas again in my long barge, as well to relieve him, as also to make a perfect search in the bottom of the bay; for it hath been held for infallible, that whatsoever ship or boat shall fall therein can never disembogue again, by reason of the violent current which setteth into the said bay, as also for that the breeze and easterly wind bloweth directly into the same. Of which opinion I have heard John Hampton, of Plymouth, one of the greatest experience of England, and divers other besides that have traded to Trinidad.

I sent with John Douglas an old Cacique of Trinidad for a pilot, who told us that we could not return again by the bay or gulf, but that he knew a by-branch which ran within the land to the eastward, and he thought by it we might fall into Capuri, and so return in four days. John Douglas searched those rivers, and found four goodly entrances, whereof the least was as big as the Thames at Woolwich; but in the bay thitherward it was shoal and but six feet water; so as we were now without hope of any ship or barque to pass over, and therefore resolved to go on with the boats, and the bottom of the galego, in which we thrust sixty men. In the Lion's Whelp's boat and wherry we carried twenty, Captain Caulfield in his wherry carried ten more, and in my barge other ten, which made up a hundred; we had no other means but to carry victuals for a month in the same, and also to lodge therein as we could, and to boil and dress our meat. Captain Gifford had with him Mr. Edward Porter, Captain Eynos, and eight more in his wherry, with all their victual, weapons, and provisions. Captain Caulfield had with him my cousin Butshead Gorges, and eight more. In the galley, of gentlemen and officers myself had Captain Thyn, my cousin John Greenvile, my nephew John Gilbert, Captain Whiddon, Captain Keymis, Edward Hancock, Captain Clarke, Lieutenant Hughes, Thomas Upton, Captain Facy, Jerome Ferrar, Anthony Welles, William Connock, and above fifty more. We could not learn of Berreo any other way to enter but in branches, so far to windward, as it was impossible for us to recover; for we had as much sea to cross over in our wherries, as between Dover and Calais, and in a great billow, the wind and current being both very strong, so as we were driven to go in those small boats directly before the wind into the bottom of the Bay of Guanipa, and from thence to enter the mouth of some one of those rivers which John Douglas had last discovered. We had with us for pilot an Indian of Barema, a river to the south of Orenoque, between that and Amazons, whose canoes we had formerly taken as he was going from the said Barema, laden with cassavi bread to sell at Margarita. This Arwacan promised to bring me into the great river of Orenoque; but indeed of that which he entered he was utterly ignorant, for he had not seen it in twelve years before; at which time he was very young, and of no judgment: and if God had not sent us another help, we might have wandered a whole year in that labyrinth of rivers, ere we had found any way, either out or in, especially after we were past ebbing and flowing which was in four days. For I know all the earth doth not yield the like confluence of streams and branches, the one crossing the other so many times, and all so fair and large, and so like one to another, as no man can tell which to take: and if we went by the sun or compass, hoping thereby to go directly one way or other yet that way we were also carried in a circle amongst multitudes of islands, and every island so bordered with high trees as no man could see any further than the breadth of the river, or length of the breach. But this it chanced, that entering into a river (which because it had no name, we called the river of the Red Cross, ourselves being the first Christians that ever came therein) on the 22nd of May, as we were rowing up the same, we espied a small canoe with three Indians, which (by the swiftness of my barge, rowing with eight oars) I overtook ere they could cross the river. The rest of the people on the banks, shadowed under the thick wood, gazed on with a doubtful conceit what might befall those three which we had taken. But when they perceived that we offered them no violence, neither entered their canoe with any of ours, nor took out of the canoe any of theirs, they then began to show themselves on the bank's side, and offered to traffic with us for such things as they had. And as we drew near, they all stayed, and we came with our barge to the mouth of a little creek which came from their town into the great river.

As we abode here awhile, our Indian pilot, called Ferdinando, would needs go ashore to their village to fetch some fruits and to drink of their artificial wines, and also to see the place and know the lord of it against another time, and took with him a brother of his which he had with him in the journey. When they came to the village of these people the lord of the island offered to lay hands on them, purposing to have slain them both, yielding for reason that this Indian of ours had brought a strange nation into their territory to spoil and destroy them. But the pilot being quick and of a disposed body, slipt their fingers and ran into the woods, and his brother, being the better footman of the two, recovered the creek's mouth, where we stayed in our barge, crying out that his brother was slain. With that we set hands on one of them that was next us, a very old man, and brought him into the barge, assuring him that if we had not our pilot again we would presently cut off his head. This old man, being resolved that he should pay the loss of the other, cried out to those in the woods to save Ferdinando, our pilot; but they followed him notwithstanding, and hunted after him upon foot with the deer-dogs, and with so many a cry that all the woods echoed with the shout they made, But at the last this poor, chased Indian recovered the river side and got upon a tree, and, as we were coasting, leaped down and swam to the barge half dead with fear. But our good hap was that we kept the other old Indian, which we handfasted, to redeem our pilot withal; for, being natural of those rivers, we assured ourselves that he knew the way better than any stranger could. And, indeed, but for this chance, I think we had never found the way either to Guiana or back to our ships; for Ferdinando after a few days knew nothing at all, nor which way to turn; yea, and many times the old man himself was in great doubt which river to take. Those people which dwell in these broken islands and drowned lands are generally called Tivitivas. There are of them two sorts—the one called Ciawani, and the other Waraweete.

The great river of Orenoque or Baraquan hath nine branches which fall out on the north side of his own main mouth. On the south side it hath seven other fallings into the sea, so it disembogueth by sixteen arms in all between islands and broken ground; but the islands are very great, many of them as big as the Isle of Wight, and bigger, and many less. From the first branch on the north to the last of the south it is at least 100 leagues, so as the river's mouth is 300 miles wide at his entrance into the sea, which I take to be far bigger than that of Amazons. All those that inhabit in the mouth of this river upon the several north branches are these Tivitivas, of which there are two chief lords which have continual wars one with the other. The islands which lie on the right hand are called Pallamos; and the land on the left, Horotomaka; and the river by which John Douglas returned within the land from Amana to Capuri they call Macuri.

These Tivitivas are a very goodly people and very valiant, and have the most manly speech and most deliberate that I ever heard of what nation soever. In the summer they have houses on the ground as in other places; in the winter they dwell upon the trees, where they build very artificial towns and villages, as it is written in the Spanish story of the West Indies that those people do in the low lands near the gulf of Uraba; for between May and September the river of Orenoque riseth thirty foot upright, and then are those islands overflowed twenty foot high above the level of the ground, saving some few raised grounds in the middle of them. And for this cause they are enforced to live in this manner. They never eat of anything that is set or sown; and as at home they use neither planting nor other manurance, so when they come abroard they refuse to feed of aught but of that which nature without labour bringeth forth. They use the tops of palmitos for bread, and kill deer, fish, and porks for the rest of their sustenance. They have also many sorts of fruits that grow in the woods, and great variety of birds and fowls.

And if to speak of them were not tedious and vulgar, surely we saw in those passages fowls of very rare colours and forms not elsewhere to be found, for as much as I have either seen or read. Of these people those that dwell upon the branches of Orenoque, called Capuri and Macureo, are for the most part carpenters of canoes, for they make the most and fairest canoes, and sell them into Guiana for gold and into Trinidad for tobacco, in the excessive taking whereof they exceed all nations. And notwithstanding the moistness of the air in which they live, the hardness of their diet, and the great labours they suffer to hunt fish and fowl for their in living, all my life, either in the Indies or in Europe, did I never behold a more goodly or better-favoured people or a more manly. They were wont to make war upon all nations, and especially on the cannibals, so as none durst without a good strength trade by those rivers; but of late they are at peace with their neighbours, all holding the Spaniards for a common enemy. When their commanders die they use great lamentation, and when they think the flesh of their bodies is putrified and fallen from their bones, then they take up the carcase again and hang it in the Cacique's house that died, and deck his skull with feathers of all colours, and hang all his gold plates about his arms, thighs, and legs. Those nations which are called Arwacas, which dwell on the south of Orenoque (of which place and nation our Indian pilot was), are dispersed in many other places, and do use to beat the bones of their lords into powder, and their wives and friends drink it all in their several sorts of drinks.

After we departed from the port of these Ciawani we passed up the river with the flood and anchored the ebb, and in this sort we went onward. The third day that we entered the river our galley came on ground, and stuck so fast as we thought that even there our discovery had ended, and that we must have left fourscore and ten of our men to have inhabited like rooks upon trees with those nations; but the next morning, after we had cast out all her ballast, with tugging and hauling to and fro we got her afloat and went on. At four days' end we fell into as goodly a river as ever I beheld, which was called The Great Amana, which ran more directly without windings and turnings than the other; but soon after the flood of the sea left us, and, being enforced either by main strength to row against a violent current, or to return as wise as we went out, we had then no shift but to persuade the companies that it was but two or three days' work, and therefore desired them to take pains, every gentleman and others taking their turns to row and to spell one the other at the hour's end. Every day we passed by goodly branches of rivers, some falling from the west, others from the east, into Amana; but those I leave to the description in the chart of discovery, where every one shall be named with his rising and descent. When three days more were overgone, our companies began to despair, the weather being extreme hot, the river bordered with very high trees that kept away the air, and the current against us every day stronger than other; but we evermore commanded our pilots to promise an end the next day, and used it so long as we were driven to assure them from four reaches of the river to three, and so to two, and so to the next reach. But so long we laboured that many days were spent and we driven to draw ourselves to harder allowance, our bread even at the last, and no drink at all, and our men and ourselves so wearied and scorched, and doubtful withal whether we should ever perform it or no, the heat increasing as we drew towards the line; for we were now in five degrees.

The further we went on (our victuals decreasing and the air breeding great faintness) we grew weaker and weaker, when we had most need of strength and ability; for hourly the river ran more violently than other against us, and the barge, wherries, and ship's-boat of Captain Gifford and Captain Caulfield, had spent all their provisions; so as we were brought into despair and discomfort, had we not persuaded all the company that it was but only one day's work more to attain the land where we should be relieved of all we wanted, and if we returned, that we were sure to starve by the way, and that the world would also laugh us to scorn. On the banks of these rivers were divers sorts of fruits good to eat, flowers and trees of such variety as were sufficient to make ten volumes of herbals; we relieved ourselves many times with the fruits of the country, and sometimes with fowl and fish. We saw birds of all colours, some carnation, some crimson, orange-tawny, purple, watchet, and of all other sorts, both simple and mixed, and it was unto us a great good passing of the time to behold them, besides the relief we found by killing some store of them with our fowling pieces; without which, having little or no bread, and less drink, but only the thick and troubled water of the river, we had been in a very hard case.

Our old pilot of the Ciawani (whom, as I said before, we took to redeem Ferdinando) told us, that if we would enter a branch of a river on the right hand with our barge and wherries, and leave the galley at anchor the while in the great river, he would bring us to a town of the Arwacas, where we should find store of bread, hens, fish, and of the country wine; and persuaded us, that departing from the galley at noon we might return ere night. I was very glad to hear this speech, and presently took my barque, with eight musketeers, Captain Gifford's wherry, with himself and four musketeers, and Captain Caulfield with his wherry, and as many; and so we entered the mouth of this river; and because we were persuaded that it was so near, we took no victuals with us at all. When we had rowed three hours, we marvelled we saw no sign of any dwelling, and asked the pilot where the town was; he told us a little further. After three hours more, the sun being almost set, we began to suspect that he led us that way to betray us; for he confessed that those Spaniards which fled from Trinidad, and also those that remained with Carapana in Emeria, were joined together in some village upon that river. But when it grew towards night, and we demanded where the place was, he told us but four reaches more. When we had rowed four and four, we saw no sign; and our poor watermen, even heart-broken and tired, were ready to give up the ghost; for we had now come from the galley near forty miles.

At the last we determined to hang the pilot; and if we had well known the way back again by night, he had surely gone; but our own necessities pleaded sufficiently for his safety; for it was as dark as pitch, and the river began so to narrow itself, and the trees to hang over from side to side, as we were driven with arming swords to cut a passage through those branches that covered the water. We were very desirous to find this town, hoping of a feast, because we made but a short breakfast aboard the galley in the morning, and it was now eight o'clock at night, and our stomachs began to gnaw apace; but whether it was best to return or go on, we began to doubt, suspecting treason in the pilot more and more; but the poor old Indian ever assured us that it was but a little further, but this one turning and that turning; and at the last about one o'clock after midnight we saw a light, and rowing towards it we heard the dogs of the village. When we landed we found few people; for the lord of that place was gone with divers canoes above four hundred miles off, upon a journey towards the head of Orenoque, to trade for gold, and to buy women of the cannibals, who afterwards unfortunately passed by us as we rode at an anchor in the port of Morequito in the dark of the night, and yet came so near us as his canoes grated against our barges; he left one of his company at the port of Morequito, by whom we understood that he had brought thirty young women, divers plates of gold, and had great store of fine pieces of cotton cloth, and cotton beds. In his house we had good store of bread, fish, hens, and Indian drink, and so rested that night, and in the morning, after we had traded with such of his people as came down, we returned towards our galley, and brought with us some quantity of bread, fish, and hens.

On both sides of this river we passed the most beautiful country that ever mine eyes beheld; and whereas all that we had seen before was nothing but woods, prickles, bushes, and thorns, here we beheld plains of twenty miles in length, the grass short and green, and in divers parts groves of trees by themselves, as if they had been by all the art and labour in the world so made of purpose; and still as we rowed, the deer came down feeding by the water's side as if they had been used to a keeper's call. Upon this river there were great store of fowl, and of many sorts; we saw in it divers sorts of strange fishes, and of marvellous bigness; but for lagartos it exceeded, for there were thousands of those ugly serpents; and the people call it, for the abundance of them, the river of Lagartos in their language. I had a negro, a very proper young fellow, who leaping out of the galley to swim in the mouth of this river, was in all our sights taken and devoured with one of those lagartos. In the meanwhile our companies in the galley thought we had been all lost, (for we promised to return before night) and sent the Lion's Whelp's ship's-boat with Captain Whiddon to follow us up the river; but the next day, after we had rowed up and down some fourscore miles, we returned, and went on our way up the river; and when we were even at the last cast for want of victuals, Captain Gifford being before the galley and the rest of the boats, seeking out some place to land upon the banks to make fire, espied four canoes coming down the river; and with no small joy caused his men to try the uttermost of their strengths, and after a while two of the four gave over and ran themselves ashore, every man betaking himself to the fastness of the woods, the two other lesser got away, while he landed to lay hold on these; and so turned into some by-creek, we knew not whither. Those canoes that were taken were loaded with bread, and were bound for Margarita in the West Indies, which those Indians (called Arwacas) proposed to carry thither for exchange; but in the lesser there were three Spaniards, who having heard of the defeat of their Governor in Trinidad, and that we purposed to enter Guiana, came away in those canoes; one of them was a cavallero, as the captain of the Arwacas after told us, another a soldier, and the third a refiner.

In the meantime, nothing on the earth could have been more welcome to us, next unto gold, than the great store of very excellent bread which we found in these canoes; for now our men cried, "Let us go on, we care not how far." After that Captain Gifford had brought the two canoes to the galley, I took my barge and went to the bank-side with a dozen shot, where the canoes first ran themselves ashore, and landed there, sending out Captain Gifford and Captain Thyn on one hand, and Captain Caulfield on the other, to follow those that were fled into the woods. And as I was creeping through the bushes, I saw an Indian basket hidden, which was the refiner's basket; for I found in it his quicksilver, saltpetre, and divers things for the trial of metals, and also the dust of such ore as he had refined, but in those canoes which escaped there was a good quantity of ore and gold. I then landed more men, and offered five hundred pound to what soldier soever could take one of those three Spaniards that we thought were landed. But our labours were in vain in that behalf; for they put themselves into one of the small canoes, and so while the greater canoes were in taking, they escaped. But seeking after the Spaniards we found the Arwacas hidden in the woods, which were pilots for the Spaniards, and rowed their canoes; of which I kept the chiefest for a pilot, and carried him with me to Guiana, by whom I understood where and in what countries the Spaniards had laboured for gold, though I made not the same known to all; for when the springs began to break, and the rivers to raise themselves so suddenly as by no means we could abide the digging of any mine, especially for that the richest are defended with rocks of hard stones, which we call the white spar, and that it required both time, men, and instruments fit for such a work, I thought it best not to hover thereabouts, lest if the same had been perceived by the company, there would have been by this time many barques and ships set out, and perchance other nations would also have gotten of ours for pilots; so as both ourselves might have been prevented, and all our care taken for good usage of the people been utterly lost, by those that only respect present profit, and such violence or insolence offered as the nations which are borderers would have changed the desire of our love and defence into hatred and violence. And for any longer stay to have brought a more quantity (which I heard had been often objected) whosoever had seen or proved the fury of that river after it began to arise, and had been a month and odd days, as we were, from hearing aught from our ships, leaving them meanly manned 400 miles off, would perchance have turned somewhat sooner than we did, if all the mountains had been gold, or rich stones. And to say the truth, all the branches and small rivers which fell into Orenoque were raised with such speed, as if we waded them over the shoes in the morning outward, we were covered to the shoulders homeward the very same day; and to stay to dig our gold with our nails, had been *Opus laboris* but not *Ingenii;* such a quantity as would have served our turns we could not have had, but a discovery of the mines to our infinite disadvantage we had made, and that could have been the best profit of farther search or stay; for those mines are not easily broken, nor opened in haste, and I could have returned a good quantity of gold ready cast if I had not shot at another mark than present profit.

This Arwacan pilot with the rest, feared that we would have eaten them, or otherwise have put them to some cruel death: for the Spaniards, to the end that none of the people in the passage towards Guiana, or in Guiana itself, might come to speech with us, persuaded all the nations that we were men-eaters and cannibals. But when the poor men and women had seen us, and that we gave them meat, and to every one something or other, which was rare and strange to them, they began to conceive the deceit and purpose of the Spaniards, who indeed (as they confessed) took from them both their wives and daughters daily, and especially such as they took in this manner by strength.

But I protest before the Majesty of the living God, that I neither know nor believe, that any of our company one or other, did offer insult to any of their women, and yet we saw many hundreds, and had many in our power, and of those very young and excellently favoured, which came among us without deceit, stark naked. Nothing got us more love amongst them than this usage; for I suffered not any man to take from any of the nations so much as a pine or a potato root without giving them contentment, nor any man so much as to offer to touch any of their wives or daughters; which course, so contrary to the Spaniards (who tyrannize over them in all things), drew them to admire Her Majesty, whose commandment I told them it was, and also wonderfully to honour our nation.

But I confess it was a very impatient work to keep the meaner sort from spoil and stealing when we came to their houses; which, because in all I could not prevent, I caused my Indian interpreter at every place when we departed, to know of the loss or wrong done, and if aught were stolen or taken by violence, either the same restored, and the party punished in their sight, or else was paid for to their uttermost demand.

They also much wondered at us, after they heard that we had slain the Spaniards at Trinidad, for they were before resolved that no nation of Christians durst abide their presence, and they wondered more when I had made them know of the great overthrow that Her Majesty's army and fleet had given them of late years in their own countries.

After we had taken in this supply of bread, with divers baskets of roots, which were excellent meat, I gave one of the canoes to the Arwacas, which belonged to the Spaniards that were escaped, and when I had dismissed all but the Captain (who by the Spaniards was christened Martin) I sent back in the same canoe the old Ciawani, and Ferdinando, my first pilot, and gave them both such things as they desired, with sufficient victual to carry them back, and by them wrote a letter to the ships, which they promised to deliver, and performed it, and then I went on, with my new hired pilot, Martin the Arwacan. But the next or second day after, we came aground again with our galley, and were like to cast her away, with all our victuals and provisions, and so lay on the sand one whole night, and were far more in despair at this time to free her than before, because we had no tide of flood to help us, and therefore feared that all our hopes would have ended in mishaps. But we fastened an anchor upon the land, and with main strength drew her off; and so the fifteenth day we discovered afar off the mountains of Guiana, to our great joy, and towards the evening had a slent of a northerly wind that blew very strong, which brought us in sight of the great river Orenoque; out of which this river descended wherein we were. We descried afar off three other canoes as far as we could discern them, after whom we hastened with our barge and wherries, but two of them passed out of sight, and the third entered up the great river, on the right hand to the westward, and there stayed out of sight, thinking that we meant to take the way eastward towards the province of Carapana, for that way the Spaniards keep, not daring to go upwards to Guiana, the people in those parts being all their enemies, and those in the canoes thought us to have been those Spaniards that were fled from Trinidad, and escaped killing; and when we came so far down as the opening of that branch into which they slipped, being near them with our barge and wherries, we made after them, and ere they could land came within call, and by our interpreter told them what we were, wherewith they came back willingly aboard us; and of such fish and tortoise eggs as they had gathered they gave us, and promised in the morning to bring the Lord of that part with them, and to do us all other services they could.

That night we came to an anchor at the parting of the three goodly rivers (the one was the river of Amana, by which we came from the north, and ran athwart towards the south, the other two were of Orenoque, which crossed from the west and ran to the sea towards the east) and landed upon a fair sand, where we found thousands of tortoise eggs, which are very wholesome meat, and greatly restoring, so as our men were now well filled and highly contented both with the fare, and nearness of the land of Guiana, which appeared in sight.

In the morning there came down, according to promise, the Lord of that border, called Toparimaca, with some thirty or forty followers, and brought us divers sorts of fruits, and of his wine, bread, fish, and flesh, whom we also feasted as we could; at least we drank good Spanish wine (whereof we had a small quantity in bottles), which above all things they love. I conferred with this Toparimaca of the next way to Guiana, who conducted our galley and boats to his own port, and carried us from thence some mile and a-half to his town, where some of our captains caroused of his wine till they were reasonable pleasant, for it is very strong with pepper, and the juice of divers herbs and fruits digested and purged. They keep it in great earthen pots of ten or twelve gallons, very clean and sweet, and are themselves at their meetings and feasts the greatest carousers and drunkards of the world. When we came to his town we found two Caciques, whereof one was a stranger that had been up the river in trade, and his boats, people, and wife encamped at the port where we anchored, and the other was of that country, a follower of Toparimaca. They lay each of them in a cotton hamaca, which we call Brazil beds, and two women attending them with six cups, and a little ladle to fill them out of an earthen pitcher of wine; and so they drank each of them three of those cups at a time one to the other, and in this sort they drink drunk at their feasts and meetings.

That Cacique that was a stranger had his wife staying at the port where we anchored, and in all my life I have seldom seen a better favoured woman. She was of good stature, with black eyes, fat of body, of an excellent countenance, her hair almost as long as herself, tied up again in pretty knots, and it seemed she stood not in that awe of her husband as the rest, for she spake and discoursed, and drank among the gentlemen and captains, and was very pleasant, knowing her own comeliness, and taking great pride therein. I have seen a lady in England so like to her, as but for the difference of colour, I would have sworn might have been the same.

The seat of this town of Toparimaca was very pleasant, standing on a little hill, in excellent prospect, with goodly gardens a mile compass round about it, and two very fair and large ponds of excellent fish adjoining. This town is called Arowocai; the people are of the nation called Nepoios, and are followers of Carapana. In that place I saw very aged people, that we might perceive all their sinews and veins without any flesh, and but even as a case covered only with skin. The Lord of this place gave me an old man for pilot, who was of great experience and travel, and knew the river most perfectly both by day and night; and it shall be requisite for any man that passeth it to have such a pilot, for it is four, five, and six miles over in many places, and twenty miles in other places, with wonderful eddies and strong currents, many great islands, and divers shoals, and many dangerous rocks, and besides upon any increase of wind so great a billow, as we were sometimes in great peril of drowning in the galley, for the small boats durst not come from the shore but when it was very fair.

The next day we hasted thence, and having an easterly wind to help us, we spared our arms from rowing; for after we entered Orenoque, the river lieth for the most part east and west, even from the sea unto Quito, in Peru. This river is navigable with barques, little less than a thousand miles, and from the place where we entered it may be sailed up in small pinnaces to many of the best parts of Nuevo Reyna de Granada and of Popayan; and from no place may the cities of these parts of the Indies be so easily taken and invaded as from hence. All that day we sailed up a branch of that river, having on the left hand a great island, which they call Assapana, which may contain some five-and-twenty miles in length, and six miles in breadth, the great body of the river running on the other side of this island. Beyond that middle branch there is also another island, in the river called Iwana, which is twice as big as the Isle of Wight, and beyond it, and between it and the main of Guiana, runneth a third branch of Orenoque, called Arraroopana; all three are goodly branches, and all navigable for great ships. I judge the river in this place to be at least thirty miles broad, reckoning the islands which divide the branches in it, for afterwards I sought also both the other branches.

After we reached to the head of the island called Assapana, a little to the westward on the right hand there opened a river which came from the north, called Europa, and fell into the great river, and beyond it on the same side we anchored for that night by another island, six miles long and two miles broad, which they call Ocaywita. From hence, in the morning, we landed two Guianians, which we found in the town of Toparimaca, that came with us, who went to give notice of our coming to the Lord of that country called Putyma, a follower of Topiawari, chief Lord of Aromaia, who succeeded Morequito, whom (as you have heard before) Berreo put to death; but his town being far within the land, he came not unto us that day, so as we anchored again that night near the banks of another land of bigness much like the other, which they call Putapayma, over against which island, on the main land, was a very high mountain called Oecope. We coveted to anchor rather by these islands in the river than by the main, because of the tortugas' eggs, which our people found on them in great abundance, and also because the ground served better for us to cast our nets for fish, the main banks being for the most part stony and high and the rocks of a blue, metalline colour, like unto the best steel-ore, which I assuredly take it to be. Of the same blue stone are also divers great mountains which border this river in many places.

The next morning, towards nine o'clock, we weighed anchor, and the breeze increasing, we sailed always west up the river, and, after a while, opening the land on the right side, the country appeared to be champaign and the banks shewed very perfect red. I therefore sent two of the little barges with Captain Gifford, and with him Captain Thyn, Captain Caulfield, my cousin Greenvile, my nephew John Gilbert, Captain Eynos, Mr. Edward Porter, and my cousin Butshead Gorges, with some few soldiers, to march over the banks of that red land and to discover what manner of country it was on the other side; who at their return found it all a plain level as far as they went or could discern from the highest tree they could get upon. And my old pilot, a man of great travel, brother to the Cacique Toparimaca, told me that those were called the Plains of the Sayma, and that the same level reached to Cumaná and Caracas, in the West Indies, which are a hundred and twenty leagues to the north, and that there inhabited four principal nations. The first were the Sayma, the next Assawai, the third and greatest the Wikiri, by whom Pedro Hernandez de Serpa, before mentioned, was overthrown as he passed with three hundred horse from Cumaná towards Orenoque in his enterprise of Guiana; the fourth are called Aroras, and are as black as negroes, but have smooth hair, and these are very valiant (or rather desperate) people, and have the most strong poison on their arrows, and most dangerous of all nations, of which I will speak somewhat, being a digression not unnecessary.

There was nothing whereof I was more curious than to find out the true remedies of these poisoned arrows; for besides the mortality of the wound they make, the party shot endureth the most insufferable torment in the world, and abideth a most ugly and lamentable death, sometimes dying stark mad, sometimes their bowels breaking out of their bellies, which are presently discoloured as black as pitch, and so unsavory as no man can endure to cure or to attend them. And it is more strange to know that in all this time there was never Spaniard, either by gift or torment, that could attain to the true knowledge of the cure, although they have martyred and put to invented torture I know not how many of them. But everyone of these Indians knew it not, no, not one among thousands, but their soothsayers and priests, who do conceal it, and only teach it but from the father to the son.

Those medicines which are vulgar and serve for the ordinary poison are made of the juice of a root called tupara; the same also quencheth marvellously the heat of burning fevers, and healeth inward wounds and broken veins that bleed within the body. But I was more beholding to the Guianians than any other; for Antonio de Berreo told me that he could never attain to the knowledge thereof, and yet they taught me the best way of healing as well thereof as of all other poisons. Some of the Spaniards have been cured in ordinary wounds of common poisoned arrows with the juice of garlic. But this is a general rule for all men that shall hereafter travel the Indies where poisoned arrows are used, that they must abstain from drink; for if they take any liquor into their body, as they shall be marvellously provoked thereunto by drought, I say, if they drink before the wound be dressed, or soon upon it, there is no way with them but present death.

And so I will return again to our journey, which for this third day we finished, and cast anchor again near the continent or the left hand between two mountains, the one called Aroami and the other Aio. I made no stay here but till midnight; for I feared hourly lest any rain should fall, and then it had been impossible to have gone any further up, notwithstanding that there is every day a very strong breeze and easterly wind. I deferred the search of the country on Guiana side till my return down the river.

The next day we sailed by a great island in the middle of the river, called Manoripono, and, as we walked awhile on the island, while the galley got ahead of us, there came for us from the main a small canoe with seven or eight Guianians, to invite us to anchor in their port, but I deferred till my return. It was that Cacique to whom those Nepoios went, which came with us from the town of Toparimaca. And so the fifth day we reached as high up as the province of Aromaia, the country of Morequito, whom Berreo executed, and anchored to the west of an island called Murrecotima, ten miles long and five broad. And that night the Cacique Aramiary (to whose town we made our long and hungry voyage out of the river of Amana) passed by us.

The next day we arrived at the port of Morequito, and anchored there, sending away one of our pilots to seek the King of Aromaia, uncle to Morequito, slain by Berreo as aforesaid. The next day following, before noon, he came to us on foot from his house, which was fourteen English miles (himself being a hundred and ten years old), and returned on foot the same day, and with him many of the borderers, with many women and children, that came to wonder at our nation and to bring us down victual, which they did in great plenty, as venison, pork, hens, chickens, fowl, fish, with divers sorts of excellent fruits and roots, and great abundance of pines, the princes of fruits that grow under the sun, especially those of Guiana. They brought us, also, store of bread and of their wine, and a sort of paraquitos no bigger than wrens, and of all other sorts both small and great. One of them gave me a beast called by the Spaniards armadillo, which they call cassacam, which seemeth to be all barred over with small plates somewhat like to a rhinoceros, with a white horn growing in his hinder parts as big as a great hunting-horn, which they use to wind instead of a trumpet. Monardus writeth that a little of the powder of that horn put into the ear cureth deafness.

After this old King had rested awhile in a little tent that I caused to be set up, I began by my interpreter to discourse with him of the death of Morequito, his predecessor, and afterward of the Spaniards; and ere I went any farther I made him know the cause of my coming thither, whose servant I was, and that the Queen's pleasure was I should undertake the voyage for their defence and to deliver them from the tyranny of the Spaniards, dilating at large (as I had done before to those of Trinidad) Her Majesty's greatness, her justice, her charity to all oppressed nations, with as many of the rest of her beauties and virtues as either I could express or they conceive. All which being with great admiration attentively heard and marvellously admired, I began to sound the old man as touching Guiana and the state thereof, what sort of commonwealth it was, how governed, of what strength and policy, how far it extended, and what nations were friends or enemies adjoining, and finally of the distance and way to enter the same. He told me that himself and his people, with all those down the river towards the sea, as far as Emeria, the province of Carapana, were of Guiana, but that they called themselves Orenoqueponi, and that all the nations between the river and those mountains in sight, called Wacarima, were of the same cast and appellation; and that on the other side of those mountains of Wacarima there was a large plain (which after I discovered in my return) called the Valley of Amariocapana. In all that valley the people were also of the ancient Guianians.

I asked what nations those were which inhabited on the further side of those mountains, beyond the Valley of Amariocapana. He answered with a great sigh (as a man which had inward feeling of the loss of his country and liberty, especially for that his eldest son was slain in a battle on that side of the mountains, whom he most entirely loved) that he remembered in his father's lifetime, when he was very old and himself a young man, that there came down into that large valley of Guiana a nation from so far off as the sun slept (for such were his own words), with so great a multitude as they could not be numbered nor resisted, and that they wore large coats, and hats of crimson colour, which colour he expressed by shewing a piece of red wood wherewith my tent was supported, and that they were called Orejones and Epuremei, those that had slain and rooted out so many of the ancient people as there were leaves in the wood upon all the trees, and had now made themselves lords of all, even to that mountain foot called Curaa, saving only of two nations, the one called Iwarawaqueri and the other Cassipagotos, and that in the last battle fought between the Epuremei and the Iwarawaqueri his eldest son was chosen to carry to the aid of the Iwarawaqueri a great troop of the Orenoqueponi, and was there slain with all his people and friends, and that he had now remaining but one son; and farther told me that those Epuremei had built a great town called Macureguarai at the said mountain foot, at the beginning of the great plains of Guiana, which have no end; and that their houses have many rooms, one over the other, and that therein the great King of the Orejones and Epuremei kept three thousand men to defend the borders against them, and withal daily to invade and slay them; but that of late years, since the Christians offered to invade his territories and those frontiers, they were all at peace, and traded one with another, saving only the Iwarawaqueri and those other nations upon the head of the river of Caroli called Cassipagotos, which we afterwards discovered, each one holding the Spaniard for a common enemy.

After he had answered thus far, he desired leave to depart, saying that he had far to go, that he was old and weak, and was every day called for by death, which was also his own phrase. I desired him to rest with us that night, but I could not entreat him, but he told me that at my return from the country above he would again come to us, and in the meantime provide for us the best he could, of all that his country yielded; the same night he returned to Orocotona, his own town; so as he went that day eight-and-twenty miles, the weather being very hot, the country being situate between four and five degrees of the equinoctial.

This Topiawari is held for the proudest and wisest of all the Orenoqueponi, and so he behaved himself towards me in all his answers at my return, as I marvelled to find a man of that gravity and judgment, and of so good discourse, that had no help of learning nor breed.

The next morning we also left the port, and sailed westward up to the river, to view the famous river called Caroli, as well because it was marvellous of itself, as also for that I understood it led to the strongest nations of all the frontiers, that were enemies to the Epuremei, which are subjects to Inga, Emperor of Guiana and Manoa, and that night we anchored at another island called Caiama, of some five or six miles in length, and the next day arrived at the mouth of Caroli. When we were short of it as low or further down as the port of Morequito, we heard the great roar and fall of the river: but when we came to enter with our barge and wherries, thinking to have gone up some forty miles to the nations of the Cassipagotos, we were not able with a barge of eight oars to row one stone's cast in an hour, and yet the river is as broad as the Thames at Woolwich, and we tried both sides, and the middle, and every part of the river, so as we encamped upon the banks adjoining, and sent off our Orenoquepone (which came with us from Morequito) to give knowledge to the nations upon the river of our being there, and that we desired to see the Lords of Canuri, which dwelt within the province upon that river, making them know that we were enemies to the Spaniards (for it was on this river side that Morequito slew the friar, and those nine Spaniards which came from Manoa, the city of Inga, and took from them 14,000 pezos of gold) so as the next day there came down a Lord or Cacique, called Wanuretona, with many people with him, and brought all store of provisions to entertain us, as the rest had done. And as I had before made my coming known to Topiawari, so did I acquaint this Cacique therewith, and how I was sent by Her Majesty for the purpose aforesaid, and gathered also what I could of him touching the estate of Guiana, and I found that those also of Caroli were not only enemies to the Spaniards, but most of all to the Epuremei, which abound in gold, and by this Wanuretona I had knowledge that on the head of this river were three mighty nations, which were seated on a great lake, from whence this river descended, and were called Cassipagotos, Eparegotos, and Arawagotos, and that all those either against the Spaniards or the Epuremei would join with us, and that if we entered the land over the mountains of Curaa we should satisfy ourselves with gold and all other good things. He told us farther of a nation called Iwarawaqueri, before spoken of, that held daily war with the Epuremei that inhabited Macureguarai, the first civil town of Guiana, of the subjects of Inga, the Emperor.

Upon this river one Captain George, that I took with Berreo, told me that there was a great silver mine, and that it was near the banks of the said river. But by this time as well Orenoque, Caroli, as all the rest of the rivers were risen four or five feet in height, so as it was not possible by the strength of any men, or with any boat whatsoever, to row into the river against the stream. I therefore sent Captain Thyn, Captain Greenvile, my nephew John Gilbert, my cousin Butshead Gorges, Captain Clarke, and some thirty shot more to coast the river by land, and to go to a town some twenty miles over the valley called Amnatapoi, and they found guides there to go farther towards the mountain foot to another great town called Capurepana, belonging to a Cacique called Haharacoa (that was a nephew to old Topiawari, king of Aromaia, our chiefest friend), because this town and province of Capurepana adjoined to Macureguarai, which was a frontier town of the empire ; and the meanwhile myself with Captain Gifford, Captain Caulfield, Edward Hancock, and some half-a-dozen shot marched overland to view the strange overfalls of the river of Caroli, which roared so far off, and also to see the plains adjoining, and the rest of the province of Canuri. I sent also Captain Whiddon, William Connock, and some eight shot with them, to see if they could find any mineral stone alongst the river side. When we were come to the tops of the first hills of the plains adjoining to the river, we beheld that wonderful breach of waters, which ran down Caroli ; and might from that mountain see the river how it ran in three parts, above twenty miles off, and there appeared some ten or twelve overfalls in sight, every one as high over the other as a church-tower, which fell with that fury, that the rebound of water made it seem as if it had been all covered over with a great shower of rain, and in some places we took it at the first for a smoke that had risen over some great town. For my own part I was well persuaded from thence to have returned, being a very ill footman, but the rest were all so desirous to go near the said strange thunder of waters, as they drew me on by little and little, till we came into the next valley, where we might better discern the same. I never saw a more beautiful country, nor more lively prospects, hills so raised here and there over the valleys, the river winding into divers branches, the plains adjoining without bush or stubble, all fair green grass, the ground of hard sand, easy to march on, either for horse or foot, the deer crossing in every path, the birds towards the evening singing on every tree with a thousand several tunes, cranes and herons of white, crimson, and carnation, perching in the river's side, the air fresh with a gentle easterly wind, and every stone that we stooped to take up promised either gold or silver by his complexion. Your Lordship shall see of many sorts, and I hope some of them cannot be bettered under the sun; and yet we had no means but with our daggers and fingers to tear them out here and there, the rocks being most hard of that mineral spar aforesaid, which is like a flint, and is altogether as hard or harder, and besides the veins lie a fathom or two deep in the rocks. But we wanted all things requisite save only our desire and good will to have performed more if it had pleased God. To be short, when both our companies returned, each of them brought also several sorts of stones that appeared very fair, but were such as they found loose on the ground, and were for the most part but coloured, and had not any gold fixed in them; yet such as had no judgment or experience kept all that glittered, and would not be persuaded but it was rich because of the lustre, and brought of those, and of marquesite withal, from Trinidad, and have delivered of those stones to be tried in many places, and have thereby bred an opinion that all the rest is of the same; yet some of these stones I shewed afterwards to a Spaniard of the Caracas, who told me that it was *El Madre del Oro*, that is the mother of gold, and that the mine was farther in the ground.

But it shall be found a weak policy in me, either to betray myself or my country with imaginations, neither am I so far in love with that lodging, watching, care, peril, diseases, ill-favours, bad fare, and many other mischiefs that accompany these voyages, as to woo myself again into any of them, were I not assured that the sun covereth not so much riches in any part of the earth. Captain Whiddon, and our surgeon, Nicholas Millechamp, brought me a kind of stones like sapphires; what they may prove I know not. I showed them to some of the Orenoqueponi, and they promised to bring me to a mountain that had of them very large pieces growing diamond-wise; whether it be crystal of the mountain, Bristol diamond, or sapphire I do not yet know, but I hope the best; sure I am that the place is as likely as those from whence all the rich stones are brought, and in the same height or very near.

On the left hand of this river Caroli are seated those nations which I called Iwarawaqueri before remembered, which are enemies to the Epuremei; and on the head of it, adjoining to the great lake Cassipa, are situate those other nations which also resist Inga, and the Epuremei, called Cassipagotos, Eparegotos, and Arawagotos. I farther understood that this lake of Cassipa is so large, as it is above one day's journey for one of their canoes to cross, which may be some forty miles, and that thereinto fall divers rivers, and that great store of grains of gold are found in the summer time when the lake falleth by the banks, in those branches.

There is also another goodly river beyond Caroli which is called Arui, which also runneth through the lake Cassipa, and falleth into Orenoque farther west, making all that land between Caroli and Arui an island, which is likewise a most beautiful country. Next unto Arui there are two rivers Atoica and Caora, and on that branch which is called Caora, are a nation of people whose heads appear not above their shoulders, which though it may be thought a mere fable, yet for mine own part I am resolved it is true, because every child in the provinces of Aromaia and Canuri affirm the same. They are called Ewaipanoma. They are reported to have their eyes in their shoulders, and their mouths in the middle of their breasts, and that a long train of hair groweth backward between their shoulders. The son of Topiawari, which I brought with me into England, told me that they were the most mighty men of all the land, and use bows, arrows, and clubs, thrice as big as any of Guiana or of the Orenoqueponi, and that one of the Iwarawaqueri took a prisoner of them the year before our arrival there, and brought him into the borders of Aromaia, his father's country. And, farther, when I seemed to doubt of it, he told me that it was no wonder among them, but that they were as great a nation and as common as any other in all the provinces, and had of late years slain many hundreds of his father's people, and of other nations their neighbours, but it was not my chance to hear of them till I was come away, and if I had but spoken one word of it while I was there I might have brought one of them with me to put the matter out of doubt. Such a nation was written of by Mandevile, whose reports were holden for fables many years, and yet since the East Indies were discovered, we find his relations true of such things as heretofore were held incredible. Whether it be true or no, the matter is not great, neither can there be any profit in the imagination; for mine own part I saw them not, but I am resolved that so many people did not all combine, or forethink to make the report.

When I came to Cumana in the West Indies afterwards by chance I spake with a Spaniard dwelling not far from thence, a man of great travel, and after he knew that I had been in Guiana, and so far directly west as Caroli, the first question he asked me was, whether I had seen any of the Ewaipanoma, which are those without heads; who being esteemed a most honest man of his word, and in all things else, told me that he had seen many of them; I may not name him, because it may be for his disadvantage, but he is well known to Monsieur Mucheron's son of London, and to Peter Mucheron, merchant, of the Flemish ship that was there in trade, who also heard what he avowed to be true of those people.

The fourth river to the west of Caroli is Casnero : which falleth into the Orenoque on this side of Amapaia. And that river is greater than Danubius, or any of Europe: it riseth on the south of Guiana from the mountains which divide Guiana from Amazons, and I think it to be navigable many hundred miles. But we had no time, means, nor season of the year, to search those rivers, for the causes aforesaid, the winter being come upon us, although the winter and summer as touching cold and heat differ not, neither do the trees ever sensibly lose their leaves, but have always fruit either ripe or green, and most of them doth blossom, leaves, ripe fruit, and green at one time: but their winter only consisteth of terrible rains, and overflowing of the rivers, with many great storms and gusts, thunder and lightnings, of which we had our fill ere we returned.

On the north side, the first river that falleth into the Orenoque is Cari. Beyond it on the same side is the river of Limo. Between these two is a great nation of cannibals, and their chief town beareth the name of the river, and is called Acamacari; at this town is a continual market of women for three or four hatchets apiece; they are bought by the Arwacas, and by them sold into the West Indies. To the west of Limo is the river Pao, beyond it Caturi, beyond that, Voari, and Capuai, which falleth out of the great river of Meta, by which Berreo descended from Nuevo Reyno de Granada. To the westward of Capuri is the province of Amapaia, where Berreo wintered, and had so many of his people poisoned with the tawny water of the marshes of the Anebas. Above Amapaia, towards Nuevo Reyno, fall in Meta, Pato and Cassanar. To the west of those, towards the provinces of the Ashaguas and Catetios, are the rivers of Beta, Dawney, and Ubarro, and toward the frontier of Peru are the provinces of Thomebamba, and Caxamalca. Adjoining to Quito in the north side of Peru are the rivers of Guiacar and Goavar; and on the other side of the said mountains the river of Papamene which descendeth into Marannon or Amazons, passing through the province Mutylones, where Don Pedro de Osua, who was slain by the traitor Agiri before rehearsed, built his brigantines, when he sought Guiana by the way of Amazons.

Between Dawney and Beta lieth a famous island in Orenoque now called Baraquan (for above Meta is not known by the name of Orenoque) which is called Athule, beyond which ships of burden cannot pass by reason of a most forcible overfall, and current of waters; but in the eddy all smaller vessels may be drawn even to Peru itself. But to speak of more of these rivers without the description were but tedious, and therefore I will leave the rest to the description. This river of Orenoque is navigable for ships little less than 1,000 miles, and for lesser vessels near 2,000. By it (as aforesaid) Peru, Nuevo Reyno, and Popayan, may be invaded: it also leadeth to the great empire of Inga, and to the provinces of Amapaia and Anebas, which abound in gold; his branches of Casnero, Manta, Caora descended from the middle land and valley, which lieth between the eastern province of Peru and Guiana; and it falls into the sea between Marannon and Trinidad in two degrees and a half: all of which your honours shall better perceive in the general description of Guiana, Peru, Nuevo Reyno, the kingdom of Popayan, and Roidas, with the province of Venezuela, to the Bay of Uraba, behind Cartagena westward; and to Amazons southward. While we lay at anchor on the coast of Canuri, and had taken knowledge of all the nations upon the head and branches of this river, and had found out so many several people, which were enemies to the Epuremei and the new conquerors, I thought it time lost to linger any longer in that place, especially for that the fury of Orenoque began daily to threaten us with dangers in our return: for no half day passed but the river began to rage and overflow very fearfully, and the rains came down in terrible showers, and gusts in great abundance; and withal our men began to cry out for want of shift, for no man had place to bestow any other apparel than that which he wore on his back, and that was thoroughly washed on his body for the most part ten times in one day; and we had now been well near a month, every day passing to the westward farther and farther from our ships. We therefore turned towards the east, and spent the rest of the time in discovering the river towards the sea, which we had not viewed, and which was most material.

The next day following we left the mouth of Caroli, and arrived again at the port of Morequito where we were before; for passing down the stream we went without labour, and against the wind, little less than a hundred miles a day. As soon as I came to anchor, I sent away one for old Topiawari, with whom I much desired to have further conference, and also to deal with him for some one of his country, to bring with us into England, as well to learn the language, as to confer withal by the way, the time being now spent of any longer stay there. Within three hours after my messenger came to him, he arrived also, and with him such a rabble of all sorts of people, and everyone laden with somewhat, as if it had been a great market or fair in England; and our hungry companies clustered thick and threefold among their baskets, every one laying hand on what he liked. After he had rested awhile in my tent, I shut out all but ourselves and my interpreter, and told him that I knew that both the Epuremei and the Spaniards were enemies to him, his country and nations: that the one had conquered Guiana already, and the other sought to regain the same from them both; and therefore I desired him to instruct me what he could, both of the passage into the golden parts of Guiana, and to the civil towns and appareled people of Inga. He gave me an answer to this effect: first, that he could not perceive that I meant to go onward towards the city of Manoa, for neither the time of the year served neither could he perceive any sufficent numbers for such an enterprise: and if I did, I was sure with all my company to be buried there, for the Emperor was of that strength, as that many times so many men more were too few; besides he gave me this good council and advised me to hold it in mind (as for himself he knew he could not live till my return) that I should not offer by any means hereafter to invade the strong parts of Guiana without the help of all those nations which were also their enemies; or that it was impossible without those, either to be conducted, to be victualled, or to have aught carried with us, our people not being able to endure the march in so great heat, and travel, unless the borderers gave them help, to cart with them both their meat and furniture. For he remembered that in the plains of Macureguarai three hundred Spaniards were overthrown, who were tired out, and had none of the borderers to their friends; but meeting their enemies as they passed the frontier, were environed on all sides, and the people setting the long dry grass on fire, smothered them, so as they had no breath to fight, nor could discern their enemies for the great smoke. He told me further that four days' journey from his town was Macureguarai, and that those were the next and nearest of the subjects of Inga, and of the Epuremei, and the first town of appareled and rich people, and that all those plates of gold which were scattered among the borderers and carried to other nations far and near, came from the said Macureguarai and were there made, but that those of the land within were far finer, and were fashioned after the images of men, beasts, birds, and fishes. I asked him whether he thought that those companies that I had there with me were sufficient to take that town or no. He told me that he thought they were. I then asked him whether he would assist me with guides, and some companies of his people to join with us. He answered that he would go himself with all the borderers, if the rivers did remain fordable, upon this condition, that I would leave with him till my return again fifty soldiers, which he undertook to victual. I answered that I had not above fifty good men in all there; the rest were labourers and rowers, and that I had no provision to leave with them of powder, shot, apparel, or aught else, and that without those things necessary for their defence, they should be in danger of the Spaniards in my absence, who I knew would use the same measures towards mine that I offered them at Trinidad. And although upon the motion Captain Caulfield, Captain Greenvile, my nephew John Gilbert and divers others were desirous to stay, yet I was resolved that they must needs have perished, for Berreo expected daily a supply out of Spain, and looked also hourly for his son to come down from Nuevo Reyno de Granada, with many horse and foot, and had also in Valencia in the Caracas, two hundred horse ready to march, and I could not have spared above forty, and had not any store at all of powder, lead, or match to have left with them, nor any other provision, either spade, pickaxe, or aught else to have fortified withal.

When I had given him reason that I could not at this time leave him such a company, he then desired me to forbear him and his country for that time; for he assured me that I should be no sooner three days from the coast but those Epuremei would invade him and destroy all the remain of his people and friends, if he should any way either guide us or assist us against them.

He further alleged that the Spaniards sought his death, and as they had already murdered his nephew Morequito, lord of that province, so they had him seventeen days in a chain before he was King of the country, and led him like a dog from place to place until he had paid a hundred plates of gold and divers chains of spleen-stones for his ransom; and now, since he became owner of that province, that they had many times laid wait to take him, and that they would be now more vehement when they should understand of his conference with the English; "And because," said he, "they would the better displant me, if they cannot lay hands on me, they have gotten a nephew of mine called Eparacano, whom they have christened Don Juan, and his son Don Pedro, whom they have also appareled and armed, by whom they seek to make a party against me in mine own country. He also had taken to wife one Loviana, of a strong family, which are borderers and neighbours, and myself now being old and in the hands of death am not able to travel nor to shift as when I was of younger years." He therefore prayed us to defer it till the next year, when he would undertake to draw in all the borderers to serve us, and then, also, it would be more seasonable to travel; for at this time of the year we should not be able to pass any river, the waters were and would be so grown ere our return.

He further told me that I could not desire so much to invade Macureguarai and the rest of Guiana but that the borderers would be more vehement than I; for he yielded for a chief cause that in the wars with the Epuremei they were spoiled of their women, and that their wives and daughters were taken from them, so as for their own parts they desired nothing of the gold or treasure for their labours, but only to recover women from the Epuremei; for he farther complained very sadly (as it had been a matter of great consequence) that whereas they were wont to have ten or twelve wives, they were now enforced to content themselves with three or four, and that the lords of the Epuremei had fifty or a hundred. And in truth they war more for women than either for gold or dominion. For the lords of countries desire many children of their own bodies to increase their races and kindreds, for in those consist their greatest trust and strength. Divers of his followers afterwards desired me to make haste again, that they might sack the Epuremei, and I asked them of what. They answered, "Of their women for us, and their gold for you." For the hope of those many of women they more desire the war than either for gold or for the recovery of their ancient territories. For what between the subjects of Inga and the Spaniards, those frontiers are grown thin of people, and also great numbers are fled to other nations farther off for fear of the Spaniards.

After I received this answer of the old man we fell into consideration whether it had been of better advice to have entered Macureguarai and to have begun a war upon Inga at this time, yea or no, if the time of the year and all things had sorted. For mine own part (as we were not able to march it for the rivers, neither had any such strength as was requisite, and durst not abide the coming of the winter, or to tarry any longer from our ships (I thought it were evil counsel to have attempted it at that time, although the desire for gold will answer many objections; but it would have been, in mine opinion, an utter overthrow to the enterprise, if the same should be hereafter by Her Majesty attempted; for then (whereas now they have heard we were enemies to the Spaniards and were sent by Her Majesty to relieve them) they would as good cheap have joined with the Spaniards at our return as to have yielded unto us when they had proved that we came both for one errand, and that both sought but to sack and spoil them. But as yet our desire of gold, or our purpose of invasion, is not known to them of the empire. And it is likely that if Her Majesty undertake the enterprise they will rather submit themselves to her obedience than to the Spaniards, of whose cruelty both themselves and the borderers have already tasted; and therefore, till I had known Her Majesty's pleasure, I would rather have lost the sack of one or two towns (although they might have been very profitable) than to have defaced or endangered the future hope of so many millions, and the great good and rich trade which England may be possessed of thereby. I am assured now that they will all die, even to the last man, against the Spaniards in hope of our succour and return. Whereas, otherwise, if I had either laid hands on the borderers or ransomed the lords, as Berreo did, or invaded the subjects of Inga, I know all had been lost for hereafter.

After that I had resolved Topiawari, Lord of Aromaia, that I could not at this time leave with him the companies he desired, and that I was contented to forbear the enterprise against the Epuremei till the next year, he freely gave me his only son to take with me into England, and hoped that though he himself had but a short time to live, yet that by our means his son should be established after his death. And I left with him one Francis Sparrow, a servant of Captain Gifford (who was desirous to tarry, and could describe a country with his pen) and a boy of mine called Hugh Goodwin to learn the language. I after asked the manner how the Epuremei wrought those plates of gold, and how they could melt it out of the stone. He told me that the most of the gold which they made in plates and images was not severed from the stone, but that on the lake of Manoa, and in a multitude of other rivers, they gathered it in grains of perfect gold and in pieces as big as small stones, and that they put it to a part of copper, otherwise they could not work it; and that they used a great earthen pot with holes round about it, and when they had mingled the gold and copper together they fastened canes to the holes, and so with the breath of men they increased the fire till the metal ran, and then they cast it into moulds of stone and clay, and so make those plates and images. I have sent your honours of two sorts such as I could by chance recover, more to shew the manner of them than for the value. For I did not in any sort make my desire of gold known, because I had neither time nor power to have a great quantity. I gave among them many more pieces of gold than I received, of the new money of twenty shillings with Her Majesty's picture to wear, with promise that they would become her servants thenceforth.

I have also sent your honours of the ore, whereof I know some is as rich as the earth yieldeth any, of which I know there is sufficient, if nothing else were to be hoped for. But besides that we were not able to tarry and search the hills, so we had neither pioneers, bars, sledges, nor wedges of iron to break the ground, without which there is no working in mines. But we saw all the hills with stones of the colour of gold and silver, and we tried them to be no marquesite, and therefore such as the Spaniards call *El madre del Oro* or The mother of gold, which is an undoubted assurance of the general abundance; and myself saw the outside of many mines of the spar, which I know to be the same that all covet in this world, and of those more than I will speak of.

Having learned what I could in Canuri and Aromaia, and received a faithful promise of the principallest of those provinces to become servants to Her Majesty, and to resist the Spaniards if they made any attempt in our absence, and that they would draw in the nations about the Lake of Cassipa and those of Iwarawaqueri, I then parted from old Topiawari, and received his son for a pledge between us, and left with him two of ours as aforesaid. To Francis Sparrow I gave instructions to travel to Marcureguarai with such merchandises as I left with them, thereby to learn the place, and if it were possible, to go on to the great city of Manoa, which being done, we weighed anchor and coasted the river on Guiana side, because we came upon the north side, by the lawns of the Saima and Wikiri.

There came with us from Aromaia a Cacique called Putijma, that commanded the province of Warapana (which Putijma slew the nine Spaniards from Caroli before spoken of), who desired us to rest in the port of his country, promising to bring us unto a mountain adjoining to his town that had stones of the colour of gold, which he performed. And after we had rested there one night I went myself in the morning with most of the gentlemen of my company overland towards the said mountain, marching by a river's side called Mana,-leaving on the right hand a town called Tuteritona, standing in the province of Tarracoa, of which Wariaaremagoto is principal. Beyond it lieth another town towards the south, in the valley of Amariocapana, which beareth the name of the said valley, whose plains stretch themselves some sixty miles in length, east and west, as fair ground and as beautiful fields as any man hath ever seen, with divers copses scattered here and there by the river's side, and all as full of deer as any forest or park in England, and in every lake and river the like abundance of fish and fowl, of which Irraparragota is lord.

From the river of Mana we crossed another river in the said beautiful valley called Oiana, and rested ourselves by a clear lake which lay in the middle of the said Oiana, and one of our guides kindling us fire with two sticks, we stayed awhile to dry our shirts, which with the heat hung very wet and heavy on our shoulders. Afterwards we sought the ford to pass over towards the mountain called Iconuri, where Putijma foretold us of the mine. In this lake we saw one of the great fishes, as big as a wine pipe, which they call manati, being most excellent and wholesome meat. But after I perceived that to pass the said river would require half-a-day's march more, I was not able myself to endure it, and therefore I sent Captain Keymis with six shot to go on, and gave him order not to return to the port of Putijma, which is called Chiparepare, but to take leisure, and to march down the said valley as far as a river called Cumaca, where I promised to meet him again, Putijma himself promising also to be his guide; and as they marched, they left the towns of Emperapana and Capurepana, on the right hand, and marched from Putijma's house, down the said valley of Amariocapana; and we returning the same day to the river's side, saw by the way many rocks like unto gold ore, and on the left hand a round mountain which consisted of mineral stone.

From hence we rowed down the stream, coasting the province of Parino. As for the branches of rivers which I overpass in this discourse, those shall be better expressed in the description with the mountains of Aio, Ara, and the rest, which are situate in the provinces of Parino and Carricurrina. When we were come as far down as the land called Ariacoa (where Orenoque divideth itself into three great branches, each of them being most goodly rivers), I sent away Captain Henry Thyn, and Captain Greenvile with the galley, the nearest way, and took with me Captain Gifford, Captain Caulfield, Edward Porter, and Captain Eynos with mine own barge and the two wherries, and went down that branch of Orenoque, which is called Cararoopana, which leadeth towards Emeria, the province of Carapana, and towards the east sea, as well to find out Captain Keymis, whom I had sent overland, as also to acquaint myself with Carapana, who is one of the greatest of all the Lords of the Orenoqueponi; and when I came to the river of Cumaca (to which

Putijma promised to conduct Captain Keymis), I left Captain Eynos and Master Porter in the said river to expect his coming, and the rest of us rowed down the stream towards Emeria.

In this branch called Cararoopana were also many goodly islands, some of six miles long, some of ten, some of twenty. When it grew towards sunset, we entered a branch of a river that fell into Orenoque, called Winicapora, where I was informed of the mountain of crystal, to which in truth for the length of the way, and the evil season of the year, I was not able to march, nor abide any longer upon the journey; we saw it afar off, and it appeared like a white church-tower of an exceeding height. There falleth over it a mighty river which toucheth no part of the side of the mountain, but rusheth over the top of it, and falleth to the ground with so terrible a noise and clamour, as if a thousand great bells were knocked one against another. I think there is not in the world so strange an overfall, nor so wonderful to behold. Berreo told me that there were diamonds and other precious stones on it, and that they shined very far off; but what it hath I know not, neither durst he or any of his men ascend to the top of the said mountain, those people adjoining being his enemies (as they were) and the way to it so impassable.

Upon this river of Winicapora we rested a while, and from thence marched into the country to a town called after the name of the river, whereof the captain was one Timitwara, who also offered to conduct me to the top of the said mountain called Wacarima. But when we came in first to the house of the said Timitwara, being upon one of their said feast days, we found them all as drunk as beggars, and the pots walking from one to another without rest. We that were weary and hot with marching were glad of the plenty, though a small quantity satisfied us, their drink being very strong and heady, and so rested ourselves awhile. After we had fed, we drew ourselves back to our boats upon the river, and there came to us all the Lords of the country, with all such kind of victuals as the place yielded, and with their delicate wine of Pinas, and with abundance of hens and other provisions, and of those stones which we call spleen-stones.

We understood by the chieftains of Winicapora, that their Lord, Carapana, was departed from Emeria, which was now in sight, and that he was fled to Cairamo, adjoining to the mountains of Guiana, over the valley called Amariocapana, being persuaded by those ten Spaniards which lay at his house that we would destroy him and his country.

But after these Caciques of Winicapora and Saporatona his followers perceived our purpose, and saw that we came as enemies to the Spaniards only, and had not so much as harmed any of those nations, no, though we found them to be of the Spaniards' own servants, they assured us that Carapana would be as ready to serve us as any of the Lords of the provinces which we had passed; and that he durst do no other till this day but entertain the Spaniards, his country lying so directly in their way, and next of all other to any entrance that should be made in Guiana on that side.

And they further assured us, that it was not for fear of our coming that he was removed, but to be acquitted of the Spaniards or any other that should come hereafter. For the province of Cairoma is situate at the mountain foot, which divideth the plains of Guiana from the countries of the Orenoqueponi; by means whereof if any should come in our absence into his towns, he would slip over the mountains into the plains of Guiana among the Epuremei, where the Spaniards durst not follow him without great force.

But in mine opinion, or rather I assure myself, that Carapana (being a notable wise and subtle fellow, a man of one hundred years of age and therefore of great experience), is removed to look on, and if he find that we return strong he will be ours; if not, he will excuse his departure to the Spaniards, and say it was for fear of our coming.

We therefore thought it bootless to row so far down the stream, or to seek any further of this old fox; and therefore from the river of Waricapana (which lieth at the entrance of Emeria), we returned again, and left to the eastward those four rivers which fall from the mountains of Emeria into Orenoque, which are Waracayari, Coirama, Akaniri, and Iparoma. Below those four are also these branches and mouths of Orenoque, which fall into the east sea, whereof the first is Araturi, the next Amacura, the third Barima, the fourth Wana, the fifth Morooca, the sixth Paroma, the last Wijmi. Beyond them there fall out of the land between Orenoque and Amazons fourteen rivers, which I forbear to name, inhabited by the Arwacas and cannibals.

It is now time to return towards the north, and we found it a wearisome way back from the borders of Emeria, to recover up again to the head of the river Carerupana, by which we descended, and where we parted from the galley, which I directed to take the next way to the port of Toparimaca, by which we entered first.

All the night it was stormy and dark, and full of thunder and great showers, so as we were driven to keep close by the banks in our small boats, being all heartily afraid both of the billow and terrible current of the river. By the next morning we recovered the mouth of the river of Cumaca, where we left Captain Eynos and Edward Porter to attend the coming of Captain Keymis overland; but when we entered the same, they had heard no news of his arrival, which bred in us a great doubt what might become of him. I rowed up a league or two further into the river, shooting off pieces all the way, that he might know of our being there ; and the next morning we heard them answer us also with a piece. We took them aboard us, and took our leave of Putijma, their guide, who of all others most lamented our departure, and offered to send his son with us into England, if we could have stayed till he had sent back to his town. But our hearts were cold to behold the great rage and increase of Orenoque, and therefore departed, and turned towards the west, till we had recovered the parting of the three branches aforesaid, that we might put down the stream after the galley.

The next day we landed on the island of Assapano (which divideth the river from that branch by which we sent down to Emeria), and there feasted ourselves with that beast which is called armadillo, presented unto us before at Winicapora, and the day following we recovered the galley at anchor at the port of Toparimaca, and the same evening departed with very foul weather, and terrible thunder and showers, for the winter was come on very far; the best was, we went no less than one hundred miles a day down the river ; but by the way we entered it was impossible to return, for that the river of Amana, being in the bottom of the bay of Guanipa, cannot be sailed back by any means, both the breeze and currents of the sea were so forcible, and therefore we followed a branch of Orenoque called Capuri, which entered into the sea eastward of our ships, to the end we might bear with them before the wind ; and it was not without need, for we had by that way as much to cross of the main sea after we came to the river's mouth as between Gravelin and Dover, in such boats as your honour hath heard.

To speak of what passed homeward were tedious, either to describe or name any of the rivers, islands, or villages of the Tivitivas, which dwell on trees ; we will leave all those to the general map. And to be short, when we were arrived at the sea-side, then grew our greatest doubt, and the bitterest of all our journey forepassed, for I protest before God, that we were in a most desperate estate: for the same night which we anchored in the mouth of the river of Capuri, where it falleth into the sea, there arose a mighty storm, and the river's mouth was at least a league broad, so as we ran before night close under the land with our small boats, and brought the galley as near as we could ; but she had as much ado to live as could be, and there wanted little of her sinking, and all those in her ; for mine own part, I confess I was very doubtful which way to take, either to go over in the pestered galley, there being but six foot water over the sands for two leagues together, and that also in the channel, and she drew five ; or to adventure in so great a billow, and in so doubtful weather, to cross the seas in my barge. The longer we tarried the worse it was, and therefore I took Captain Gifford, Captain Caulfield, and my cousin Greenvile into my barge ; and after it cleared up about midnight we put ourselves to God's keeping, and thrust out into the sea, leaving the galley at anchor, who durst not adventure but by daylight ; and so being all very sober and melancholy, one faintly cheering another to shew courage, it pleased God that the next day about nine o'clock, we descried the island of Trinidad, and steering for the nearest part of it, we kept the shore till we came to Curiapan, where we found our ships at anchor, than which there was never to us a more joyful sight.

Now that it hath pleased God to send us safe to our ships, it is time to leave Guiana to the sun, whom they worship, and steer away towards the north. I will, therefore, in a few words finish the discovery thereof. Of the several nations which we found upon this discovery I will once again make repetition, and how they are affected. At our first entrance into Amana, which is one of the outlets of Orenoque, we left on the right hand of us in the bottom of the bay, lying directly against Trinidad, a nation of inhuman cannibals, which inhabit the rivers of Guanipa and Berbeese. In the same bay there is also a third river, which is called Areo, which riseth on Paria side towards Cumaná, and that river is inhabited with the Wikiri, whose chief town upon the said river is Sayma. In this bay there are no more rivers but these three before rehearsed and the four branches of Amana, all which in the winter thrust so great an abundance of water into the sea, as the same is taken up fresh two or three leagues from the land. In the passages towards Guiana (that is, in all those lands which the eight branches of Orenoque fashion into islands) there are but one sort of people, called Tivitivas, but of two castes, as they term them, the one called Ciawani, the other Waraweeti, and those war one with another.

On the hithermost part of Orenoque, as at Toparimaca and Winicapora, those are of a nation called Nepoios, and are the followers of Carapana, Lord of Emeria. Between Winicapora and the port of Morequito, which standeth in Aromaia, and all those in the valley of Amariocapana, are called Orenoqueponi, and did obey Morequito and are now followers of Topiawari. Upon the river of Caroli are the Canuri, which are governed by a woman (who is inheritrix of that province) who came far off to see our nation, and asked me divers questions of Her Majesty, being much delighted with the discourse of Her Majesty's greatness, and wondering at such reports as we truly made of Her Highness's many virtues. And upon the head of Caroli and on the lake of Cassipa are the three strong nations of the Cassipagotos. Right south into the land are the Capurepani and Emparepani, and beyond those adjoining to Macureguarai (the first city of Inga) are the Iwarawakeri. All these are professed enemies to the Spaniards, and to the rich Epuremei also. To the west of Caroli are divers nations of cannibals and of those Ewaiponoma without heads. Directly west are the Amapaias and Anebas, which are also marvellous rich in gold. The rest towards Peru we will omit. On the north of Orenoque, between it and the West Indies, are the Wikiri, Saymi, and the rest before spoken of, all mortal enemies to the Spaniards. On the south side of the main mouth of Orenoque are the Arwacas; and beyond them, the cannibals; and to the south of them, the Amazons.

To make mention of the several beasts, birds, fishes, fruits, flowers, gums, sweet woods, and of their several religions and customs, would for the first require as many volumes as those of Gesnerus, and for the next another bundle of Decades. The religion of the Epuremei is the same which the Ingas, Emperors of Peru used, which may be read in Cieza and other Spanish stories, how they believe the immortality of the soul, worship the sun, and bury with them alive their best beloved wives and treasure, as they likewise do in Pegu, in the East Indies, and other places. The Orenoqueponi bury not their wives with them, but their jewels, hoping to enjoy them again. The Arwacas dry the bones of their lords, and their wives and friends drink them in powder. In the graves of the Peruvians the Spaniards found their greatest abundance of treasure. The like, also, is to be found among these people in every province. They have all many wives, and the lords five-fold to the common sort. Their wives never eat with their husbands, nor among the men, but serve their husbands at meals and afterwards feed by themselves. Those that are past their younger years make all their bread and drink, and work their cotton-beds, and do all else of service and labour; for the men do nothing but hunt, fish, play, and drink when they are out of the wars.

I will enter no further into discourse of their manners, laws, and customs. And because I have not myself seen the cities of Inga I cannot avow on my credit what I have heard, although it be very likely that the Emperor Inga hath built and erected as magnificent palaces in Guiana as his ancestors did in Peru, which were for their riches and rareness most marvellous, and exceeding all in Europe, and, I think, of the world, China excepted, which also the Spaniards (which I had) assured me to be true, as also the nations of the borderers, who, being but savages to those of the inland, do cause much treasure to be buried with them. For I was informed of one of the Caciques of the valley of Amariocapana which had buried with him a little before our arrival a chair of gold most curiously wrought, which was made either in Macureguarai adjoining or in Manoa. But if we should have grieved them in their religion at the first, before they had been taught better, and have digged up their graves, we had lost them all. And therefore I held my first resolution, that Her Majesty should either accept or refuse the enterprise ere anything should be done that might in any sort hinder the same. And if Peru had so many heaps of gold, whereof those Ingas were princes, and that they delighted so much therein, no doubt but this which now liveth and reigneth in Manoa hath the same honour, and, I am assured, hath more abundance of gold within his territory than all Peru and the West Indies.

For the rest, which myself have seen, I will promise these things that follow, which I know to be true. Those that are desirous to discover and to see many nations may be satisfied within this river, which bringeth forth so many arms and branches leading to several countries and provinces, above 2,000 miles east and west and 800 miles south and north, and of these the most either rich in gold or in other merchandises. The common soldier shall here fight for gold, and pay himself, instead of pence, with plates of half-a-foot broad, whereas he breaketh his bones in other wars for provant and penury. Those commanders and chieftains that shoot at honour and abundance shall find there more rich and beautiful cities, more temples adorned with golden images, more sepulchres filled with treasure than either Cortez found in Mexico or Pizarro in Peru. And the shining glory of this conquest will eclipse all those so far-extended beams of the Spanish nation. There is no country which yieldeth more pleasure to the inhabitants, either for those common delights of hunting, hawking, fishing, fowling, or the rest, than Guiana doth. It hath so many plains, clear rivers, and abundance of pheasants, partridges, quails, rails, cranes, herons, and all other fowl. Deer of all sorts, porks, hares, lions, tigers, leopards, and divers other sorts of beasts, either for chase or food. It hath a kind of beast called cama or anta, as big as an English beef, and in great plenty.

To speak of the several sorts of every kind I fear would be troublesome to the reader, and therefore I will omit them, and conclude that both for health, good air, pleasure, and riches, I am resolved it cannot be equalled by any region either in the east or west. Moreover the country is so healthful, as of a hundred persons and more (which lay without shift most sluttishly, and were every day almost melted with heat in rowing and marching, and suddenly wet again with great showers, and did eat of all sorts of corrupt fruits, and made meals of fresh fish without seasoning, of tortugas, of lagartos or crocodiles, and of all sorts good and bad, without either order or measure, and besides lodged in the open air every night) we lost not any one, nor had one ill-disposed to my knowledge, nor found any calentura or other of those pestilent diseases which dwell in all hot regions, and so near the equinoctial line.

Where there is store of gold it is in effect needless to remember other commodities for trade; but it hath, towards the south part of the river, great quantities of brazil-wood and divers berries that dye a most perfect crimson and carnation. And for painting, all France, Italy, or the East Indies yield none such. For the more the skin is washed, the fairer the colour appeareth, and with which even those brown and tawny women spot themselves and colour their cheeks. All places yield abundance of cotton, of silk, of balsamum, and of those kinds most excellent and never known in Europe, of all sorts of gums, of Indian pepper; and what else the countries may afford within the land we know not, neither had we time to abide the trial and search. The soil besides is so excellent and so full of rivers, as it will carry sugar, ginger, and all those other commodities which the West Indies have.

The navigation is short, for it may be sailed with an ordinary wind in six weeks, and in the like time back again, and by the way neither lee-shore, enemies' coast, rocks, nor sands, all which in the voyages to the West Indies and all other places we are subject unto; as the channel of Bahama, coming from the West Indies, cannot well be passed in the winter, and when it is at the best, it is a perilous and a fearful place. The rest of the Indies for calms, and diseases very troublesome, and the sea about the Bermudas a hellish sea for thunder, lightning, and storms.

This very year (1595) there were seventeen sail of Spanish ships lost in the channel of Bahama, and the great Philip, like to have sunk at the Bermudas, was put back to St. Juan de Puerto Rico. And so it falleth out in that navigation every year for the most part, which in this voyage are not to be feared; for the time of year to leave England is best in July, and the summer in Guiana is in October, November, December, January, February, and March, and then the ships may depart thence in April, and so return again into England in June, so as they shall never be subject to winter weather, either coming, going, or staying there: which, for my part, I take to be one of the greatest comforts and encouragements that can be thought on, having (as I have done) tasted in this voyage by the West Indies so many calms, so much heat, such outrageous gusts, such weather, and contrary winds.

To conclude, Guiana is a country that hath yet her maidenhead, never sacked, turned, nor wrought; the face of the earth hath not been torn, nor the virtue and salt of the soil spent by manurance; the graves have not been opened for gold, the mines not broken with sledges, nor their images pulled down out of their temples. It hath never been entered by any army of strength, and never conquered or possessed by any Christian prince. It is besides so defensible, that if two forts be built in one of the provinces which I have seen, the flood setteth in so near the bank, where the channel also lieth, that no ship can pass up but within a pike's length of the artillery, first of the one, and afterwards of the other: Which two forts will be a sufficient guard both to the Empire of Inga, and to an hundred other several kingdoms, lying within the said river, even to the city of Quito in Peru.

There is therefore great difference between the easiness of the conquest of Guiana, and the defence of it being conquered, and the West or East Indies; Guiana hath but one entrance by the sea (if it hath that) for any vessels of burden; so as whosoever shall first possess it, it shall be found unaccessible for any enemy, except he come in wherries, barges, or canoes, or else in flat-bottomed boats, and if he do offer to enter it in that manner, the woods are so thick two hundred miles together upon the rivers of such entrance, as a mouse cannot sit in a boat unhit from the bank. By land it is more impossible to approach, for it hath the strongest situation of any region under the sun, and is so environed with impassable mountains on every side, as it is impossible to victual any company in the passage; which hath been well proved by the Spanish nation, who since the conquest of Peru have never left five years free from attempting this empire, or discovering some way into it, and yet of three-and-twenty several gentlemen, knights, and noblemen, there was never any that knew which way to lead an army by land, or to conduct ships by sea, anything near the said country. Orellana, of whom the river of Amazons taketh name, was the first, and Don Antonio de Berreo (whom we displanted) the last: and I doubt much whether he himself or any of his yet know the best way into the said Empire. It can therefore hardly be regained, if any strength be formerly set down, but in one or two places, and but two or three crumsters or galleys built, and furnished upon the river within. The West Indies have many ports, watering places, and landings, and nearer than three hundred miles to Guiana, no man can harbour a ship, except he know one only place, which is not learned in haste, and which I will undertake there is not any one of my companies that knoweth, whosoever hearkened most after it.

Besides, by keeping one good fort, or building one town of strength, the whole Empire is guarded, and whatsoever companies shall be afterwards planted within the land, although in twenty several provinces, those shall be able all to reunite themselves upon any occasion either by the way of one river, or be able to march by land without either wood, bog, or mountain; whereas in the West Indies there are few towns or provinces that can succour or relieve one the other by land or sea. By land the countries are either desert, mountainous, or strong enemies; by sea, if any man evade to the eastward, those to the west cannot in many months turn against the breeze and eastern wind; besides, the Spaniards are therein so dispersed as they are nowhere strong, but in Nueva España only; the sharp mountains, the thorns, and poisoned prickles, the sandy and deep ways in the valleys, the smothering heat and air, and want of water in other places are their only and best defence, which (because those nations that invade them are not victualled or provided to stay, neither have any place to friend adjoining) do secure them instead of good arms and great multitudes.

The West Indies were first offered her Majesty's grandfather by Columbus, a stranger, in whom there might be doubt of deceit; and besides it was then thought incredible that there were such and so many lands and regions never written of before. This Empire is made known to her Majesty by her own vassal, and by him that oweth to her more duty than an ordinary subject, so that it shall ill sort with the many graces and benefits which I have received to abuse her Highness, either with fables or imaginations. The country is already discovered, many nations won to her Majesty's love and obedience, and those Spaniards which have latest and longest laboured about the conquest, beaten out, discouraged, and disgraced, which among these nations were thought invincible. Her Majesty may in this enterprise employ all those soldiers and gentlemen that are younger brethren, and all captains and chieftains that want employment, and the charge will be only the first setting out in victualling and arming them; for after the first or second year I doubt not but to see in London a contractation house of more receipt for Guiana than there is now in Seville for the West Indies.

And I am resolved that if there were but a small army afoot in Guiana, marching towards Manoa, the chief city of Inga, he would yield to her Majesty by composition so many hundred thousand pounds yearly as should both defend all enemies abroad, and defray all expenses at home, and that he would besides pay a garrison of three or four thousand soldiers very royally to defend him against other nations. For he cannot but know how his predecessors, yea, how his own great uncles, Guascar and Atabalipa, sons to Guainacapa, Emperor of Peru, were (while they contended for the Empire) beaten out by the Spaniards, and that both of late years and ever since the said conquest, the Spaniards have sought the passages and entry of his country; and of their cruelties used to the borderers he cannot be ignorant. In which respects no doubt but he will be brought to tribute with great gladness; if not, he hath neither shot nor iron weapon in all his Empire, and therefore may easily be conquered.

And I further remember that Berreo confessed to me and others (which I protest before the Majesty of God to be true) that there was found among the prophesies in Peru (at such time as the Empire was reduced to the Spanish obedience) in their chiefest temples, amongst divers others which foreshowed the loss of the said Empire, that from Inglatierra those Ingas should be again in time to come restored, and delivered from the servitude of the said conquerors. And I hope, as we with these few hands have displanted the first garrison, and driven them out of the said country, so her Majesty will give order for the rest, and either defend it, and hold it as tributary, or conquer and keep it as Empress of the same. For whatsoever Prince shall possess it, shall be greatest, and if the King of Spain enjoy it, he will become unresistible. Her Majesty hereby shall confirm and strengthen the opinions of all nations, as touching her great and princely actions. And where the south border of Guiana reacheth to the Dominion and Empire of the Amazons, those women shall hereby hear the name of a virgin, which is not only able to defend her own territories and her neighbours, but also to invade and conquer so great Empires and so far removed.

To speak more at this time I fear would be but troublesome: I trust in God, this being true, will suffice, and that he which is King of all Kings, and Lord of Lords, will put it into her heart which is Lady of Ladies to possess it; if not, I will judge those men worthy to be kings thereof, that by her grace and leave will undertake it of themselves.

THE END.

THOS. DE LA RUE AND CO., PRINTERS, BUNHILL ROW, LONDON.

ADVERTISEMENTS.

ADVERTISEMENTS.

PUBLISHED BY THOS. DE LA RUE & CO. LONDON,
AND SOLD BY ALL BOOKSELLERS.

NEW PUBLICATIONS.

Crown 8vo. Cloth. With Portrait of the Author. Price 7s. 6d.
CARD ESSAYS, CLAY'S DECISIONS, AND CARD-TABLE TALK.
By "CAVENDISH,"
Author of "THE LAWS AND PRINCIPLES OF WHIST," etc., etc.

Crown 8vo. Cloth. Price 7s.
BOSWELL'S CORRESPONDENCE
WITH
THE HON. ANDREW ERSKINE,
AND HIS
JOURNAL OF A TOUR TO CORSICA
(Reprinted from the original editions).
EDITED, WITH A PREFACE, INTRODUCTION, AND NOTES, BY
GEORGE BIRKBECK HILL, D.C.L.
Author of "DR. JOHNSON: his Friends and his Critics."

Demy 8vo. Cloth. Price 25s. With Map, and Illustrations on Wood.
JUNGLE LIFE IN INDIA,
OR THE
JOURNEYS AND JOURNALS OF AN INDIAN GEOLOGIST.
BY V. BALL, M.A., F.G.S.,
Fellow of the Calcutta University, and Assistant, Geological Survey of India.

A NEW EDITION, REVISED AND CORRECTED BY THE AUTHORESS.
Crown 8vo, 2 vols. Cloth. Price 10s. 6d.
AN ART-STUDENT IN MUNICH.
BY ANNA MARY HOWITT-WATTS.

Crown 8vo, 2 vols. Cloth Price 15s.
STRANGE STORIES FROM A CHINESE STUDIO,
Translated and annotated by HERBERT A. GILES, of H.M.'s Consular Service.

Crown 8vo, 2 vols. Cloth. Price 10s. 6d.
ERNESTINE.
A NOVEL. By the Authoress of the "VULTURE-MAIDEN."
Translated from the German by the REV. S. BARING-GOULD.

Crown 8vo. Cloth. Price 10s.
A SIMPLE STORY, AND NATURE AND ART.
BY MRS. INCHBALD,
With a Portrait and Introductory Memoir by WILLIAM BELL SCOTT.

ADVERTISEMENTS.

PUBLISHED BY THOS. DE LA RUE & CO. LONDON,
AND SOLD BY ALL BOOKSELLERS.

THE LAWS & PRINCIPLES OF WHIST.
By "CAVENDISH." 12th Edition. Greatly Enlarged and Revised. Handsomely printed in red and black. Price 5*s.*

THE LAWS OF PIQUET,
Adopted by the Portland Club, with a Treatise on the Game
By "CAVENDISH." Price 3*s.* 6*d.*

THE LAWS OF ÉCARTÉ,
Adopted by the Turf Club, with a Treatise on the Game
By "CAVENDISH." Price 2*s.* 6*d.*

ROUND GAMES AT CARDS.
By "CAVENDISH." 8vo. Price 1*s.* 6*d.*

THE POCKET SERIES.
By "CAVENDISH." Price 6*d.* each.

POCKET GUIDE TO BÉZIQUE.
POCKET GUIDE TO POLISH BÉZIQUE.
POCKET GUIDE TO CRIBBAGE.
POCKET GUIDE TO WHIST.
POCKET LAWS OF WHIST.
POCKET RULES FOR LEADING AT WHIST.
POCKET GUIDE TO ÉCARTÉ.
POCKET GUIDE TO EUCHRE.

POCKET GUIDE TO SPOIL-FIVE.
POCKET GUIDE TO CALABRASELLA.
POCKET GUIDE TO SIXTY-SIX.
POCKET GUIDE TO GO-BANG.
POCKET GUIDE TO DRAUGHTS AND POLISH DRAUGHTS.
POCKET GUIDE TO CHESS.
POCKET GUIDE TO BACKGAMMON AND RUSSIAN BACKGAMMON.

Elegantly bound in cloth, extra gilt, Price 21*s.* 2*nd Edition.*

BILLIARDS.
By JOSEPH BENNETT, Ex-Champion. Edited by "CAVENDISH."
With upwards of 200 Illustrations.

Price One Shilling.

THE SPOT-STROKE.
By JOSEPH BENNETT, Ex-Champion. Edited by "CAVENDISH."

Price One Shilling.

LAWN TENNIS AND BADMINTON,
With the Authorized Laws. By "CAVENDISH."

ADVERTISEMENTS.

PUBLISHED BY THOS. DE LA RUE & CO. LONDON,
AND SOLD BY ALL BOOKSELLERS.

DE LA RUE'S
INDELIBLE DIARIES
AND
RED-LETTER CALENDARS.

POCKET DIARIES.

DE LA RUE'S IMPROVED INDELIBLE DIARIES AND MEMORANDUM BOOKS, in three sizes, fitted in Velvet, Russia, Calf, Turkey Morocco, Persian, or French Morocco cases; plain or richly gilt, with gilt clasps or elastic bands, in a great variety of styles. All these Diaries are fitted with electro-gilt indelible pencils. Also supplied in enamelled paper covers.

A size .... 3¼ by 1¾ inches.
B „   .... 3¾ by 2½ „   also, same size, F F (oblong)
C „   .... 4½ by 2¾ „   „   „   G G („)

CONDENSED DIARIES & ENGAGEMENT BOOKS,
In three sizes (A, B, & C, as above), and in a great variety of Plain and Ornamental leather cases; they are also published in enamelled paper covers, suitable for the Card Case or Purse.

COMPANION MEMORANDUM BOOKS,
For use with the Condensed Diaries; A, B, & C sizes, as above.

N.B.—All Condensed Diary and Calendar Cases (except the Tuck) are fitted with an extra elastic band for the reception of these books.

DESK DIARY.
DE LA RUE'S IMPROVED DIARY AND MEMORANDUM BOOK; for Library or Counting-house use. E size, 7½ by 4¾ inches.

POCKET CALENDARS.
DE LA RUE'S RED LETTER CALENDARS AND ALMANACS, in three sizes (A, B, & C, as above), in enamelled paper covers, suitable for the Card Case or Pocket Book. Also interleaved; and in Russia, Persian, and French Morocco cases.

"FINGER-SHAPED" DIARIES AND CALENDARS,
In elegant sliding cases, extra gilt. Adapted for the Pocket or Reticule.

MONTHLY TABLET OR EASEL CALENDARS,
Printed in colours, in a variety of shapes and sizes. In Gilt and Nickeled Metal, Leather, and Leatherette cases.

DE LA RUE'S CHRISTMAS CARDS, BIRTHDAY CARDS, VALENTINES, AND EASTER CARDS,
In great variety, prepared from Original Designs, and Illustrated by Original Verses.

www.ingramcontent.com/pod-product-compliance
Lightning Source LLC
Chambersburg PA
CBHW022107290426
44112CB00008B/579